GRANADA

To my parents.

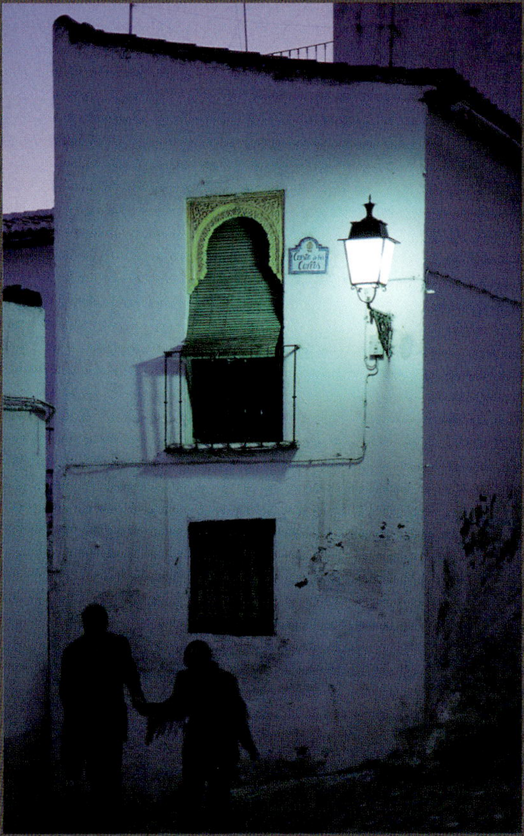

GRANADA

Text and photographies
LUCAS VALLECILLOS

TRIANGLE POSTALS

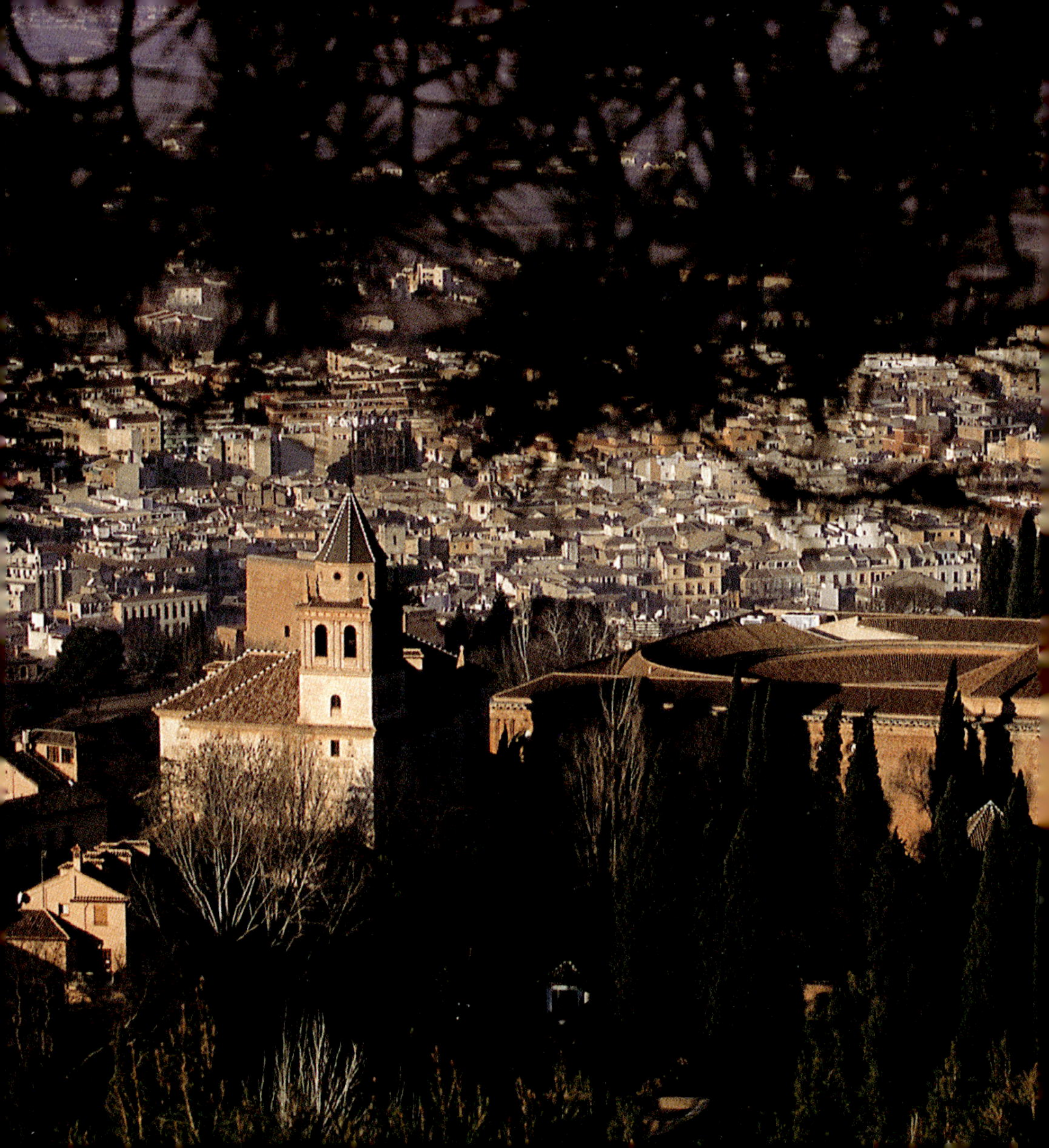

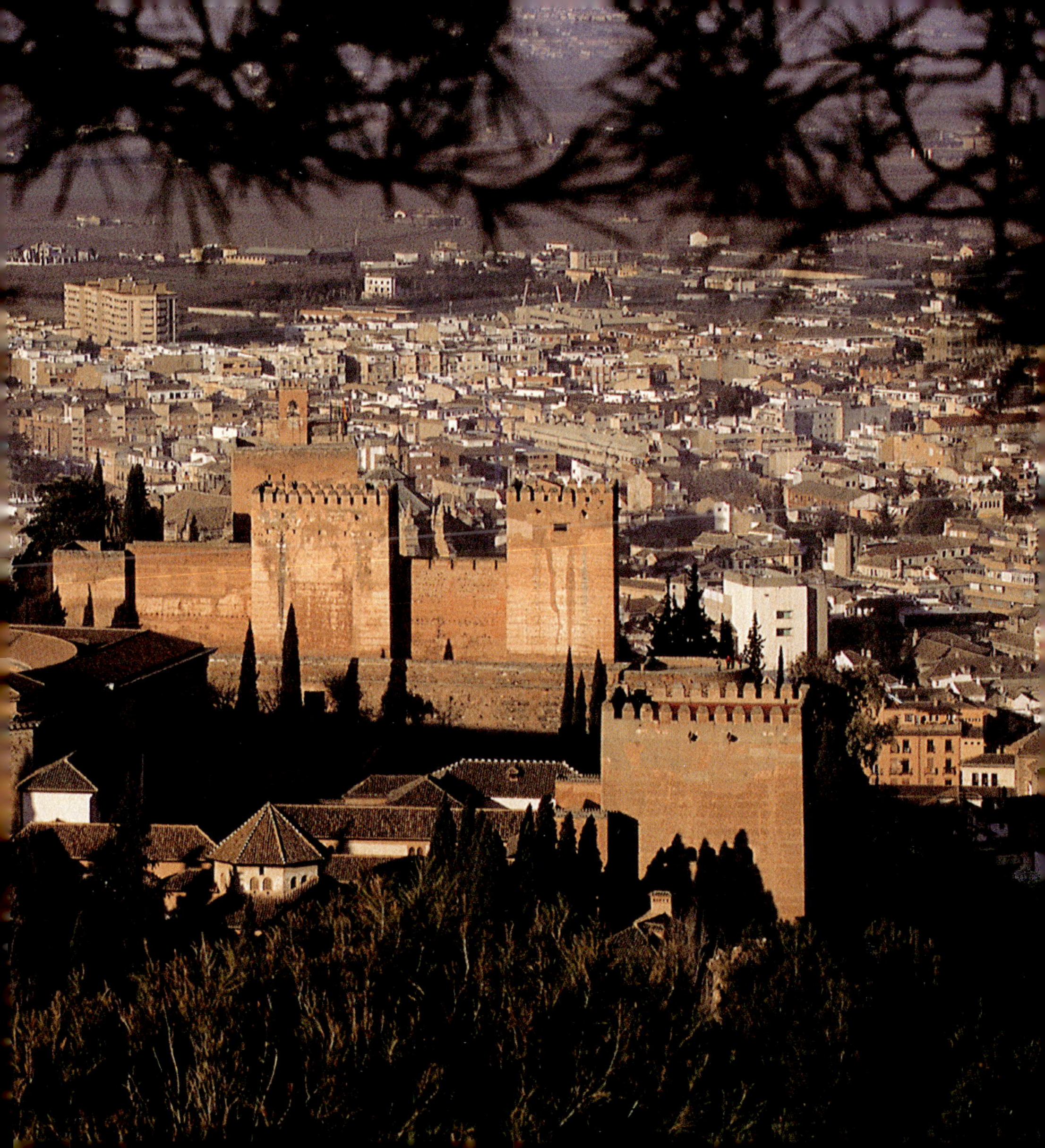

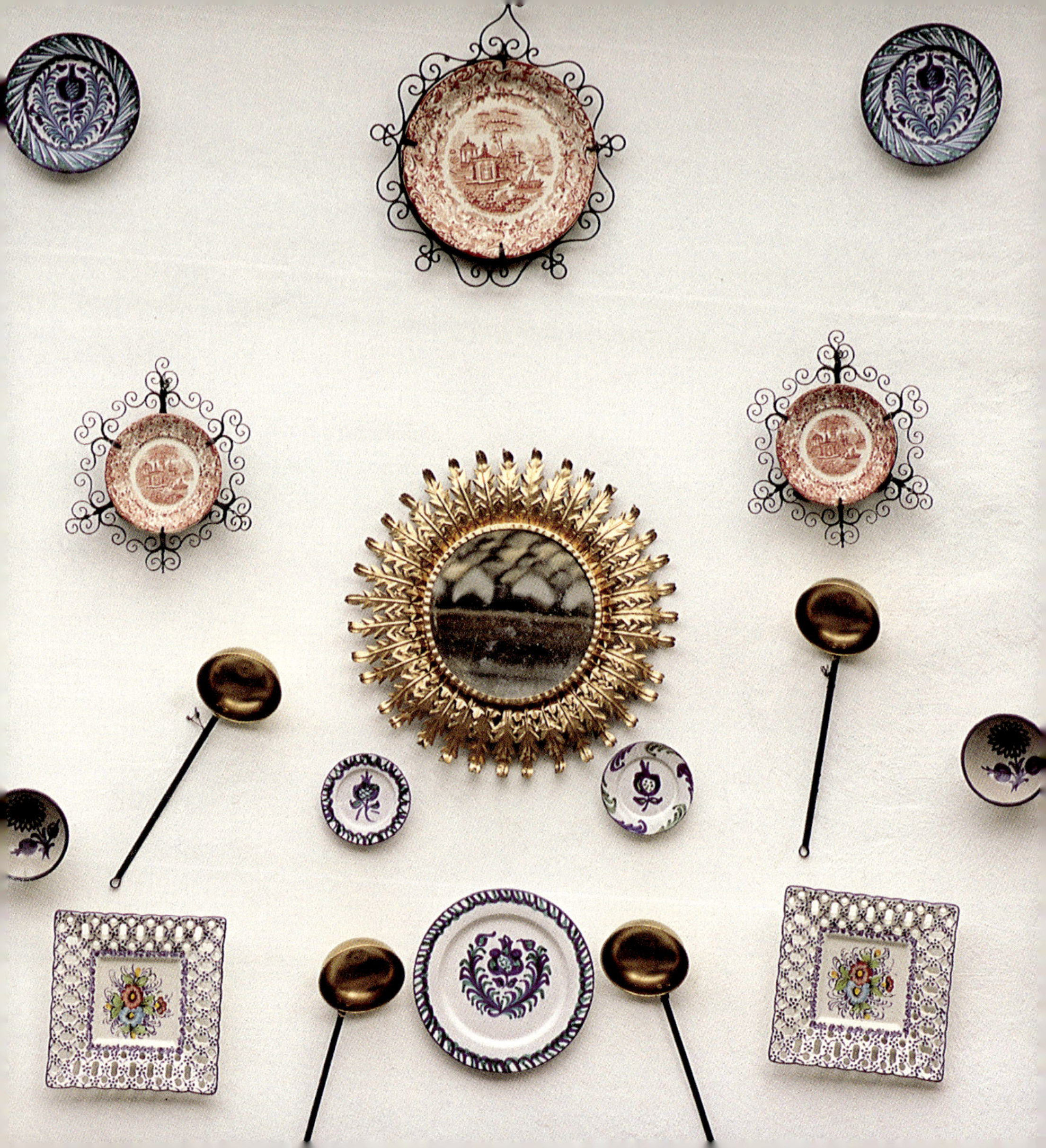

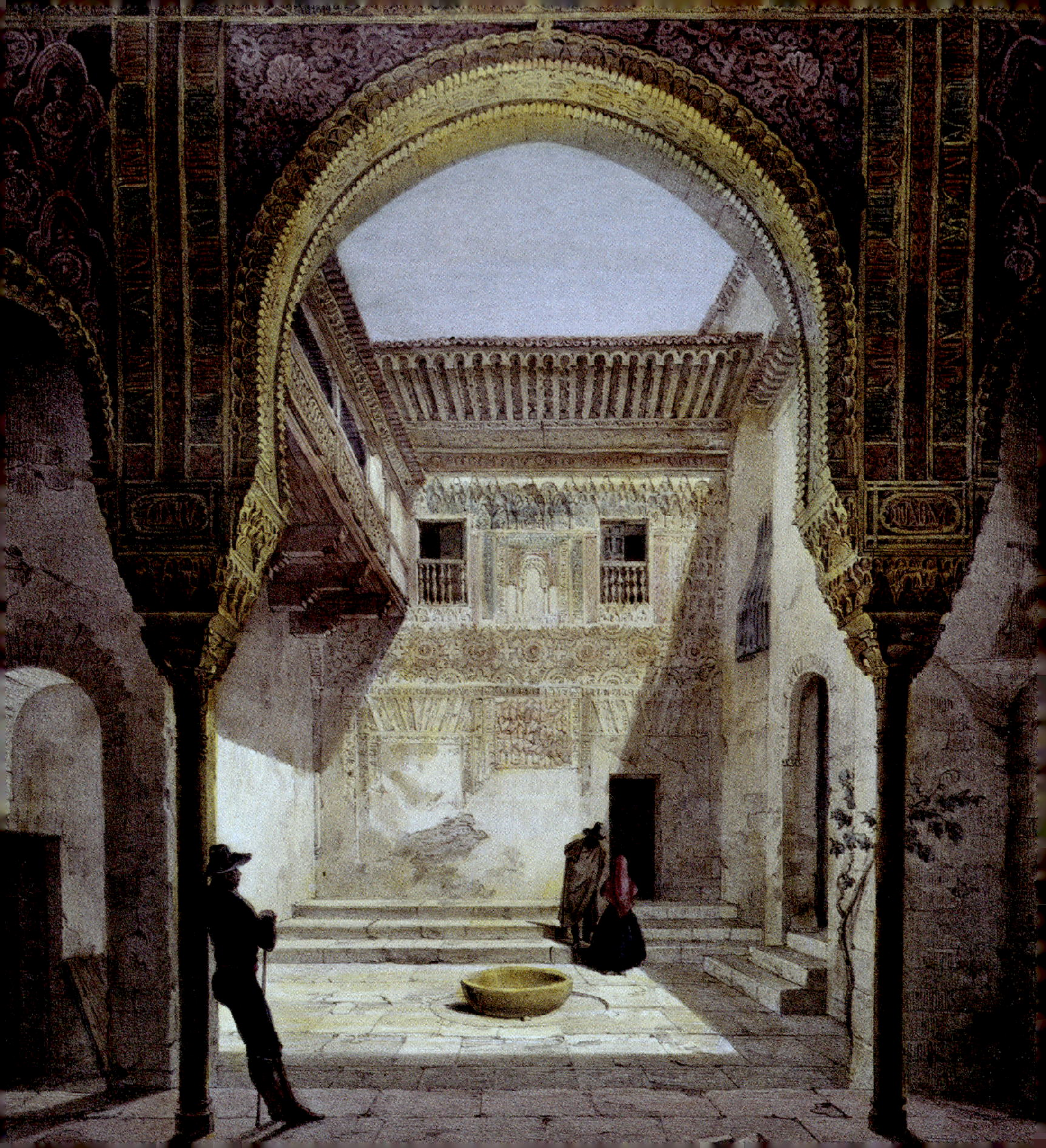

HISTORICAL OVERVIEW

In the southeast of Andalusia, at the foot of the Sierra Nevada range and at the confluence of the rivers Darro and Genil, Granada stretches from the hills that are home to the Sacromonte, the Albayzin and the Alhambra as far as the fertile plain irrigated by the Genil, where it takes on its more urban character.

The capital of the Granada region has its origin in a Turdetan settlement, an Iberian tribe that during the 5th century BC were already minting coins that bore the Iberian name of Ihberir (new city). In the 1st century AD, and after the Roman conquest, the coins bore the inscription *Municipium florentium Iliberitanum*, which means that it enjoyed the status of municipality within the empire. Many archaeological findings reveal that the forum and the basilica of Roman Granada were in what today are the Placeta de las Minas and the Albayzin.

19TH CENTURY ENGRAVING
Work by the Frenchman Léon Auguste Asselineau.

After the fall of the Roman Empire the city passed into the hands of the Visigoths, who maintained the Roman district headed by Iliberis without altering the capital or its borders. During the 6th century they transformed the Roman municipality into a large fortress, as can be seen from the oldest remains of the Alcazaba. Alongside Iliberis, in the space occupied by the city today, Garnata or Granata was built, which was occupied by a large Jewish colony, providing the name for the first Granada kingdom that the Zirid dynasty founded centuries later.

In 711, during the Umayyad dynasty, the Arabs entered the Iberian Peninsula. Aided by the divisions in the Visigoth factions, they did not take long to reach Granada, which was easily conquered due to the complicity of the Jewish population of Garnata, and came to form part of the territories governed by the Emirate of Cordoba, who was in turn subject to the rule of the Caliphate of Damascus. That was until 755, when during the fierce conflicts between the Abbasids and Umayyads for the control of the great Arab empires of the time, just one Umayyad escaped alive who decided to settle in Cordoba and act as an independent caliphate.

With the death of Al-Mansur (978-1002), the territory on the peninsula lost its political unity and disintegrated into several Taifa kingdoms. The Zirids, a North African clan, made Granada an independent kingdom (1013) that flourished greatly throughout the period it was governed by this enthusiastic dynasty; they extended the Alcazaba, built several mosques in the Albayzin, built water deposits, constructed the Puente del Cadí and baths such as the Bañuelo baths. In 1090, Granada lost its independent nature and became part of the territories controlled by the Almoravids and later by the Almohads. For more than a century, the city experienced continual growth in both size and infrastructures, which were boosted by the new governors in order to meet the needs of inhabitants displaced from other cities, fleeing from the Christians.

The crushing defeat suffered by the Almohads in Navas de Tolosa (1212) clearly showed the big push that the Christian kingdoms were making during the Reconquest and showed up the weakness of the Muslim territorial unity, which once again split into new Taifa kingdoms. Granada, with the arrival of the Nasrid dynasty in 1238, became the capital of the richest and most powerful kingdom of all. It must have been Mohammed I Al-Ahmar (1238-1272), the first of the Nasrid lineage, who began the work on the Nasrid Palaces within the protective walls of the old fortress facing the Albayzin and marked out the outlines to be followed by the succeeding kings in what would be the precinct of the Alhambra. Yusuf I (1333-1353) and his son Mohammed V (1354-1391) were the most determined monarchs in making Granada a great city. The city experienced its age of splendour under their reigns: they extended and improved both the Nasrid Palaces and the Alhambra precinct and built the big gateways to the city, the *Alhóndiga Yidida*, the commercial exchange centre, filled the Madraza, the university, with pageantry, designed new gardens and gave the city fine buildings, turning it into a beautiful paradise inhabited by 400,000 people.

Practically from the time he arrived in Granada, with the Christian Reconquest in full flow, Mohammed I Al-Ahmar began a period of treaties, ceasefires and ruptures with Christian kingdoms that show the intelligence of the Nasrid dynasty, which turned its domains into the last Arab kingdom on the peninsula. All efforts were made to prolong the life of a kingdom that had twenty three sultans and lasted two and a half centuries as much as possible, until Boabdil, as the last representative of the lineage, surrendered Granada to the Catholic Monarchs on the 2nd of January 1492.

With the Christians, the city experienced a great metamorphosis, with all the mosques converted into churches and their minarets into bell towers. In the 16th century Granada had a new appearance where the art of the victors and the defeated was fused into a new style called Mudejar, and was the time that saw the construction of churches such as those of San Cristóbal, San José, San Miguel or Santa Ana. Moreover, the early Gothic-Renaissance constructions began to be raised, such as the Cathedral, the Royal Palace or the Hospital Real. The city acquired greater status when Charles V (1500-1558) ordered his court to move there for the summer of 1526 and decided to place one of his residences here, building the monumental palace that bears his name. That same year the monarch also founded the University of Granada.

In 1568, due to the prohibition of the Muslim language and customs, there was an uprising that would mark the architectural evolution of the

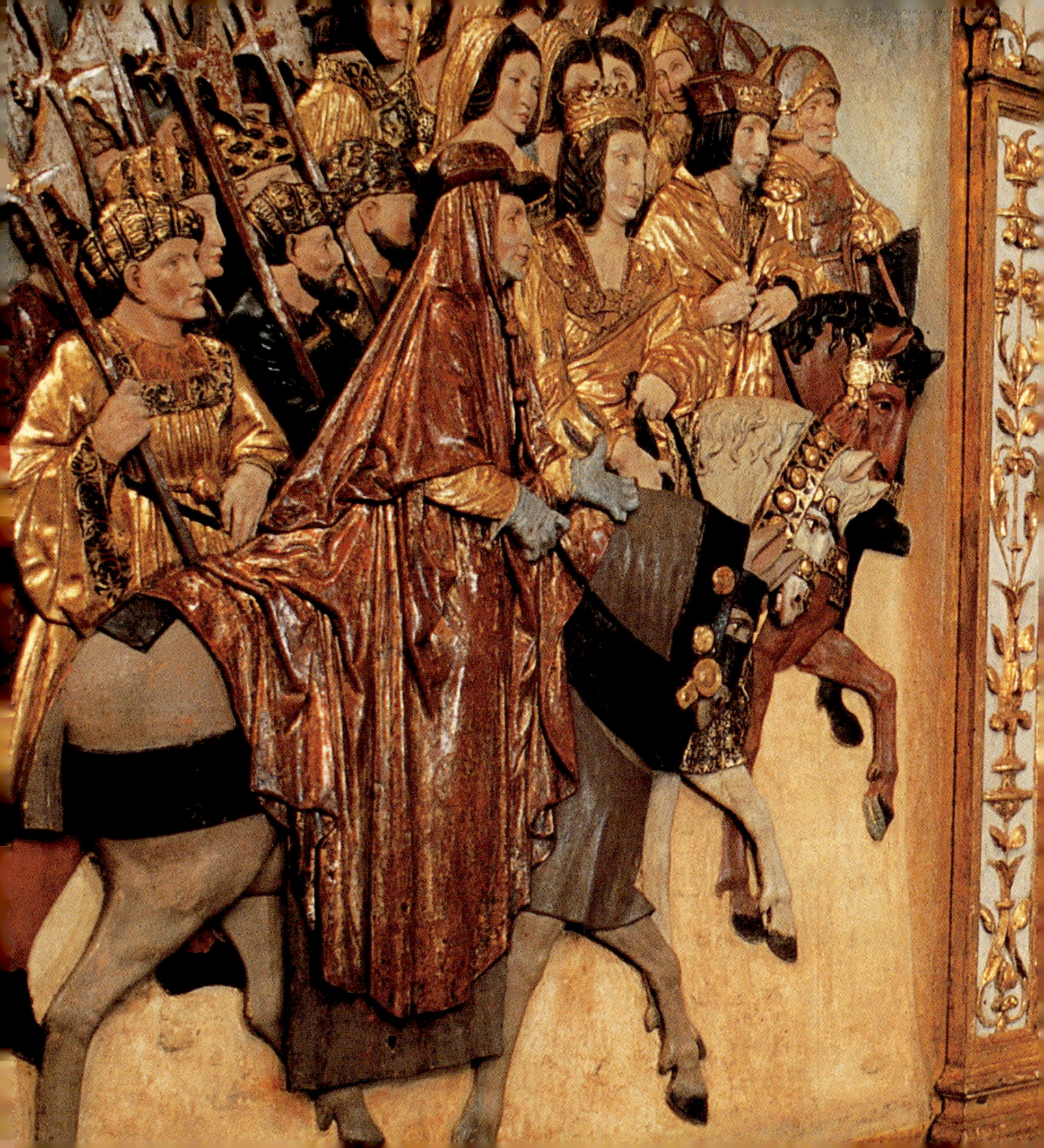

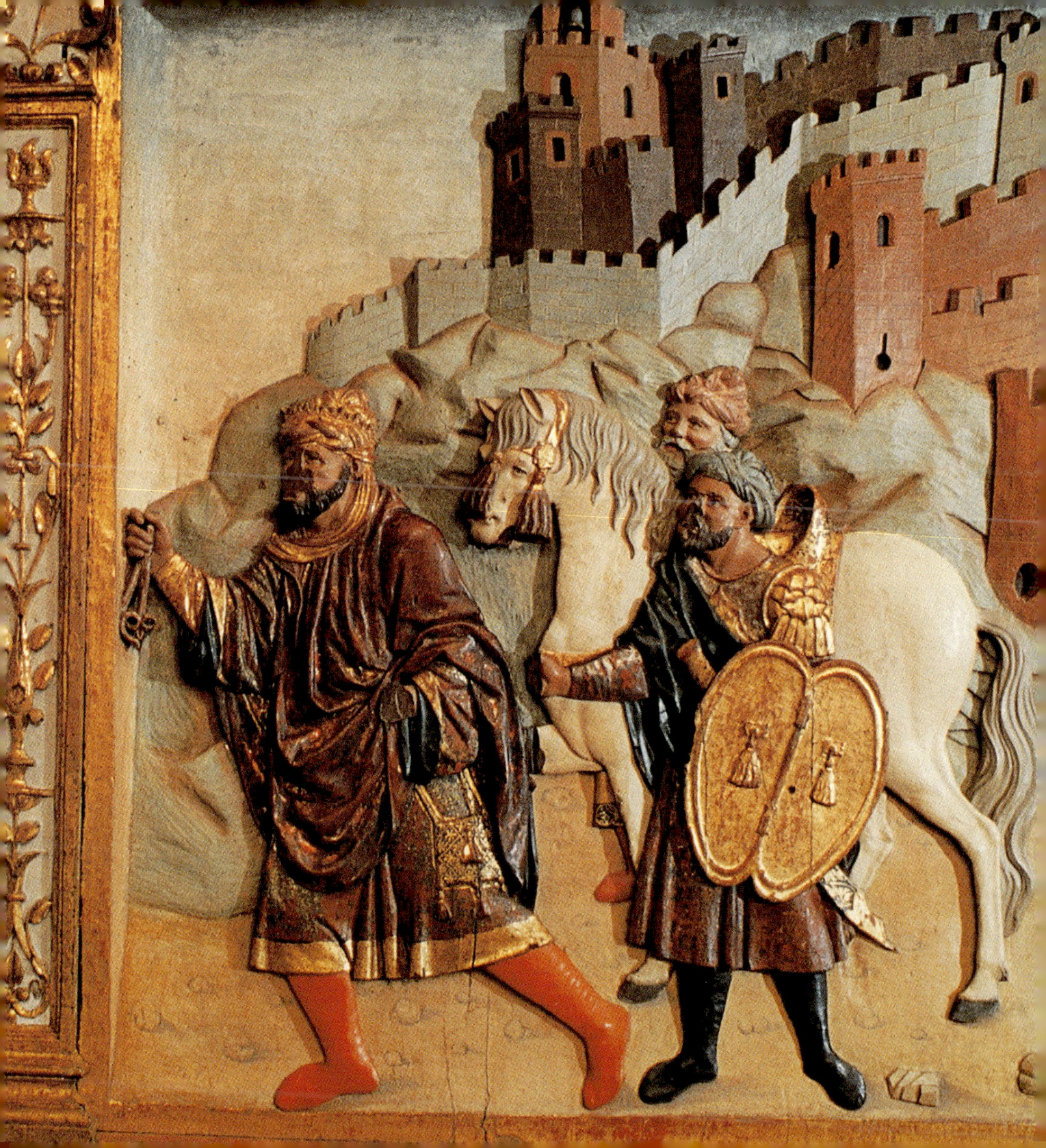

city, since the insurgents were expelled and as result disappeared from the new Moorish-inspired buildings, leaving the field open to the Renaissance and Baroque styles that took over the new urban outline during the 17th and 18th centuries. In the mid-18th century, Baroque had taken off in a big way in works such as the Monastery of the Cartuja or the Hospital and Church of San Juan de Dios. It should be pointed out, however, that in the second half of the 18th century some neo-classical buildings began to give a new air to the silhouette of the city. During the 19th century Granada experienced big changes, new squares, parks and avenues such as the Salón or the Bomba, giving the city a certain French touch.

Throughout the past century, above all in the second half, the population of Granada grew unceasingly as a result of a large influx of people from the country, creating a series of property speculations with large insipid buildings along two new thoroughfares, Camino de Ronda and Calle Pedro Antonio de Alarcón. The city thus developed until current times, equipped with a working Congress Hall and an innovative Science Park, which faces the challenges of the new century with the character that is marked by the bustling past along with the renewed ambition transmitted by the massive university population that Granada plays host to.

HALL OF THE KINGS
Paintings from the Nasrid period that gave the room its name.

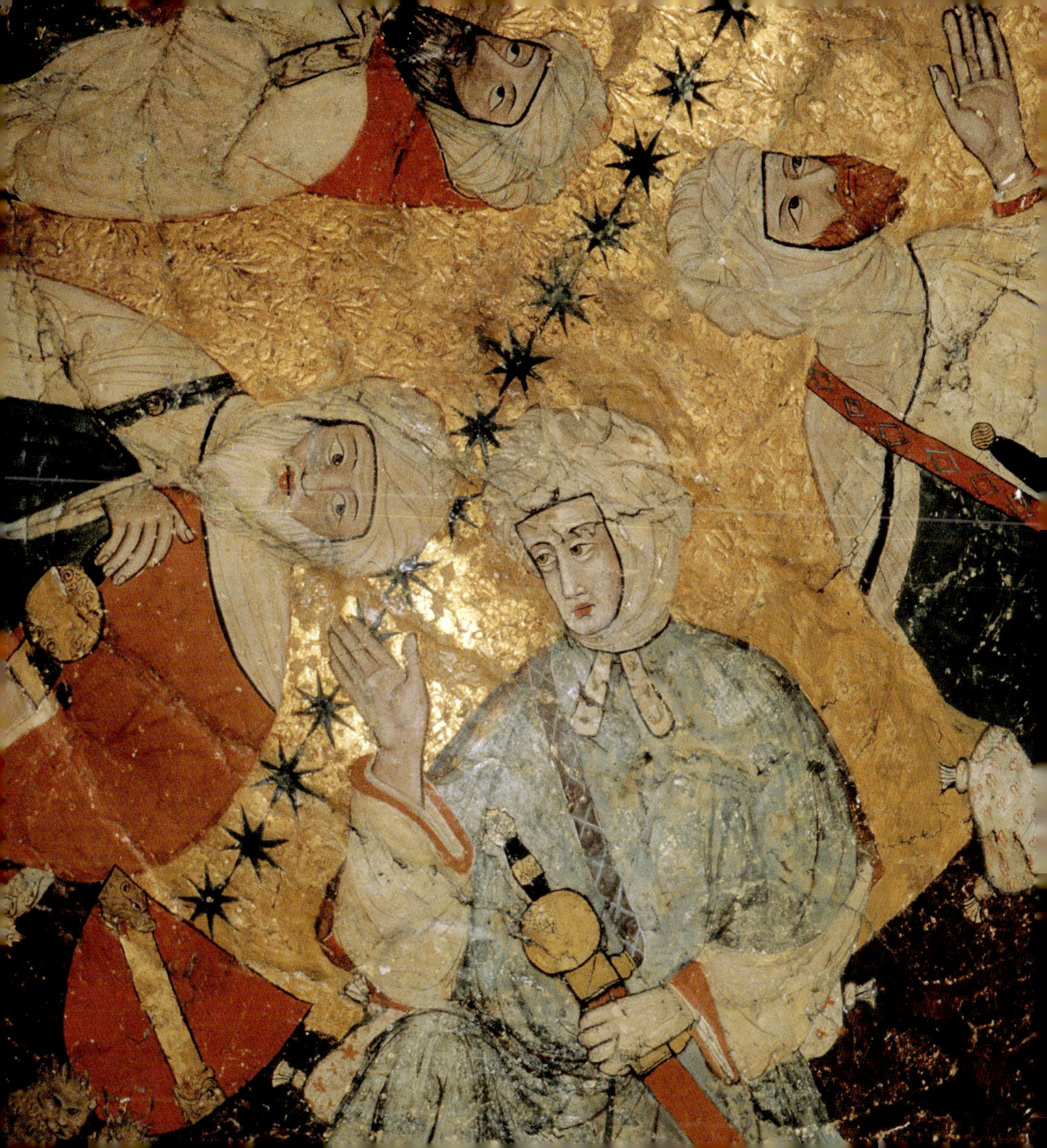

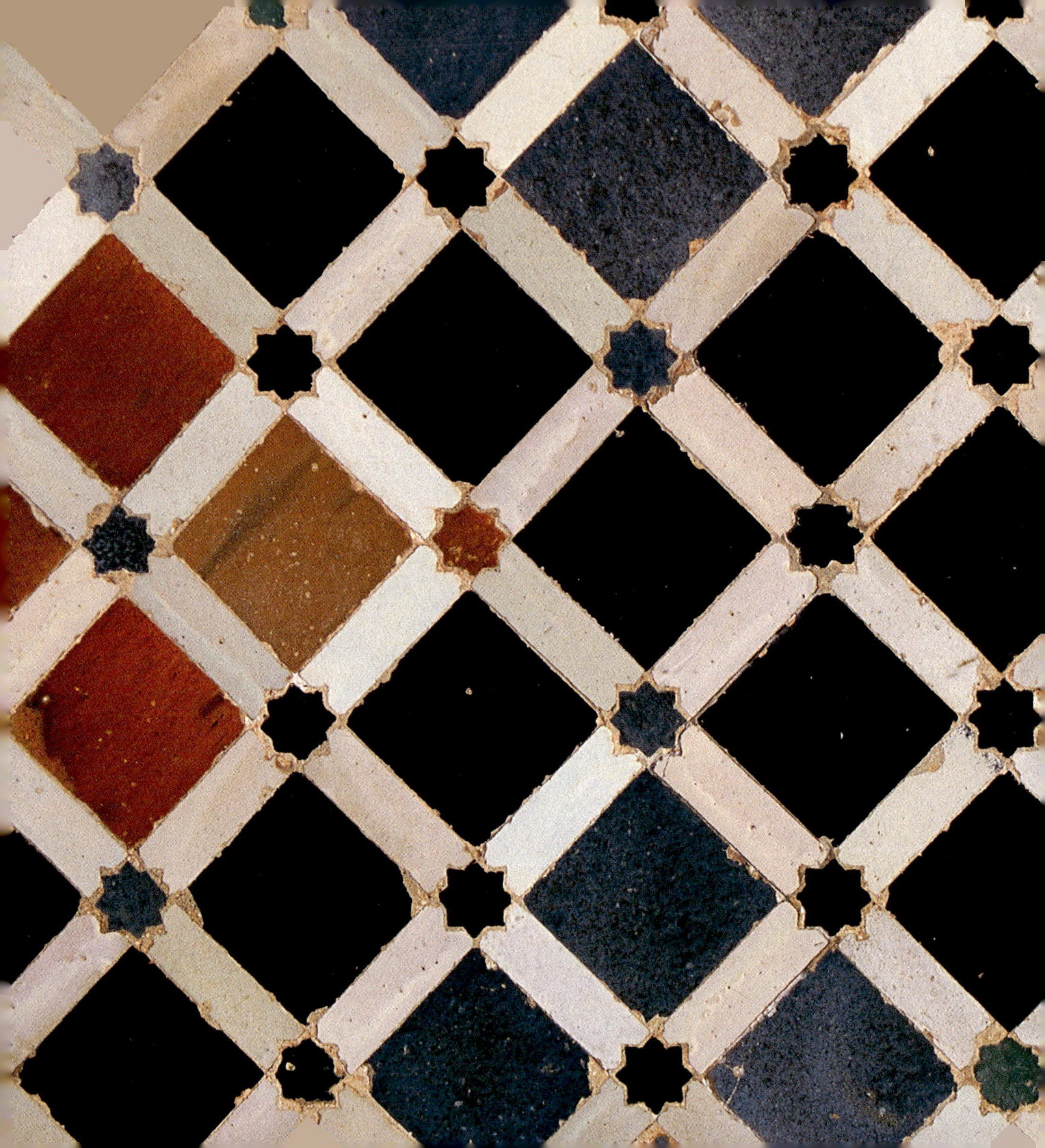

THE ALHAMBRA

Built over the hill that the Muslims called *Al-Sabika*, on a high foothill of the Sierra Nevada facing the Albayzin, the Alhambra overlooks the fertile plain that has produced wealth for the city and its environs for centuries. An emblem and the pride of the people of Granada, the architectural area is the symbol of the last Arab kingdom on the Iberian Peninsula. Its Arab name, *Qal'at al Hamra,* means red fortress and refers to the reddish colour of its walls.

PATIO OF THE MYRTLES
Detail of the tiling.

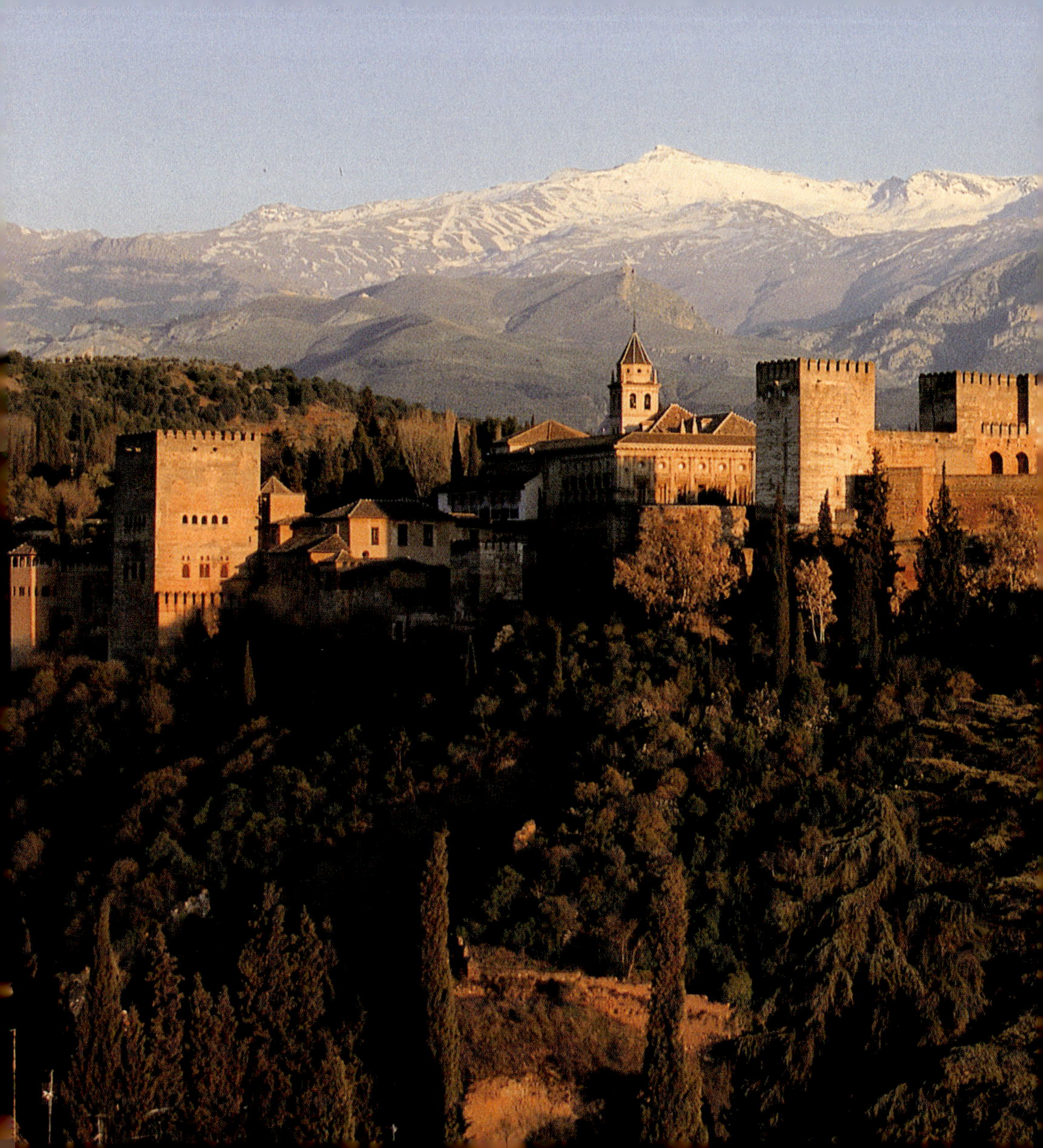

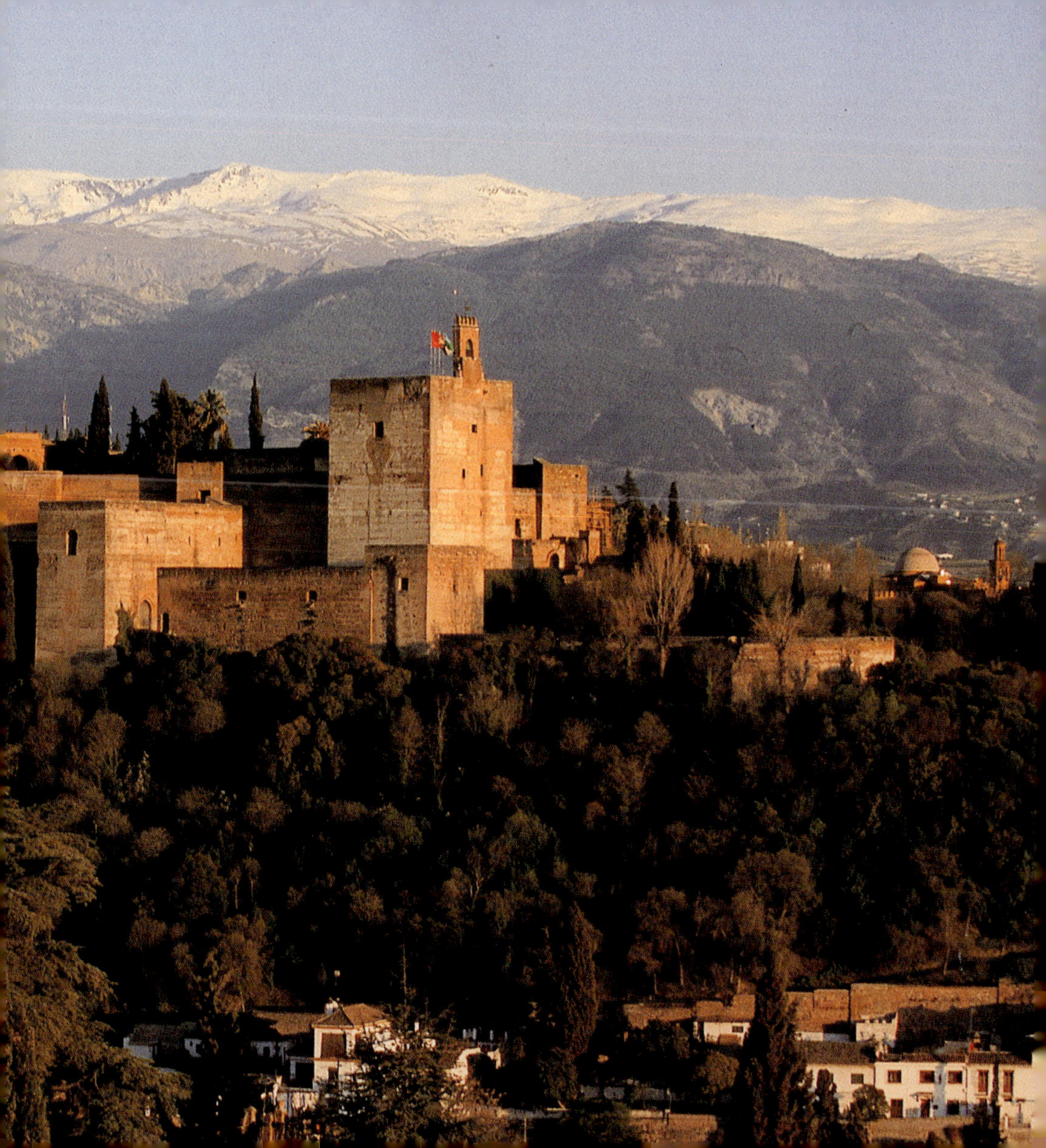

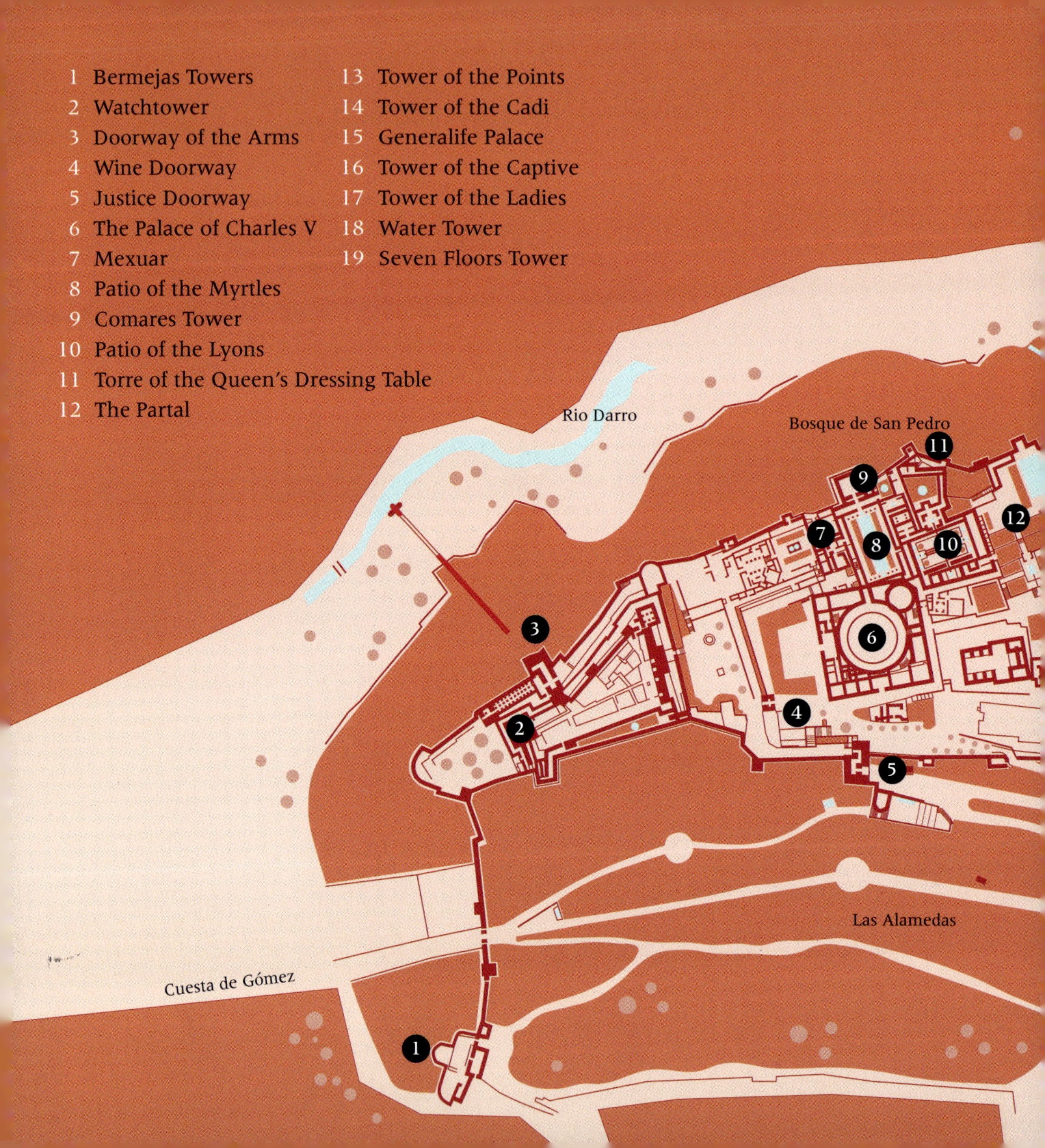
1 Bermejas Towers
2 Watchtower
3 Doorway of the Arms
4 Wine Doorway
5 Justice Doorway
6 The Palace of Charles V
7 Mexuar
8 Patio of the Myrtles
9 Comares Tower
10 Patio of the Lyons
11 Torre of the Queen's Dressing Table
12 The Partal
13 Tower of the Points
14 Tower of the Cadi
15 Generalife Palace
16 Tower of the Captive
17 Tower of the Ladies
18 Water Tower
19 Seven Floors Tower
Rio Darro
Bosque de San Pedro
Las Alamedas
Cuesta de Gómez

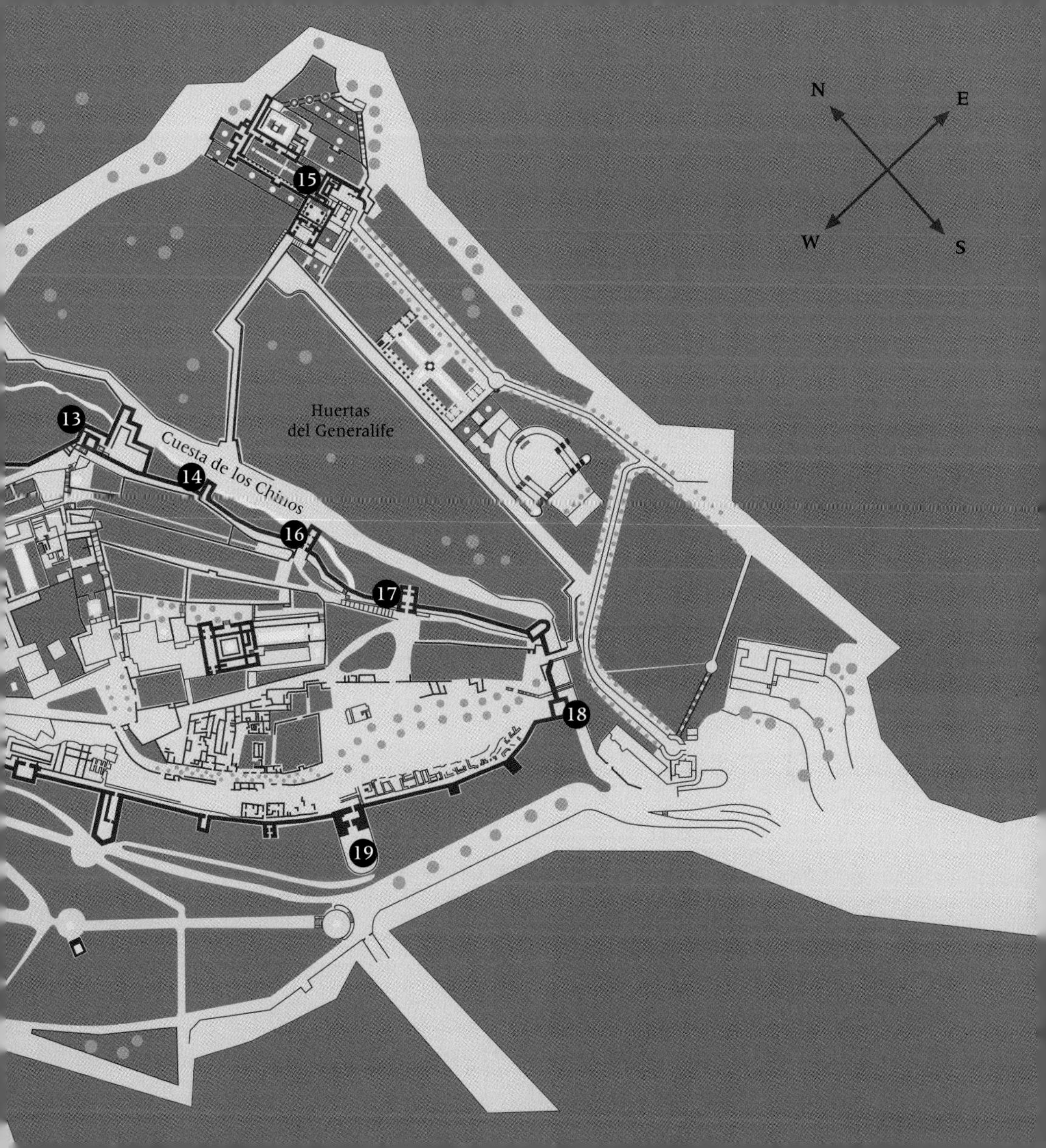

N
E
W
S
Huertas
del Generalife
Cuesta de los Chinos
13
14
15
16
17
18
19

From the time Granada was taken over by the Muslims, it suffered serious civil conflict which greatly concerned the capital of the Cordoba Caliphate. In one of these uprisings, the Arab leader Sawwar ibn Hamdun had to take measures to safeguard his physical wellbeing: in 889, on the site where today the Alcazaba stands, he built a modest castle that formed the origins of the Alhambra. It was most probable, however, as many historians point out, that given the strategic position of the hill, there must have been a fortress there in Roman times that the Visigoths enlarged, some people even arguing that its origin must date back to an Iberian settlement. Nevertheless, when the Zirid dynasty founded the Kingdom of Granada they settled in the district of the Albayzin, and did not move their residence to the top of the *Al-Sabika* hill until they built a wall that surrounded the whole city, in the 11th century. It was then that they saw that the most impregnable spot was on the other bank of the Darro, where they built a small palace and some gardens within the early castle. The city thus became a large fortress that was the setting for the bloodiest disputes between Almoravids and Almohads.

With the arrival of the Nasrids in the 13th century, Granada was once again established as the capital of a Taifa kingdom. Mohammed I Al-Ahmar, the forerunner of the dynasty, decided to build his palace within the fortress on the *Al-Sabika* hill, and this was the period when the Alhambra experienced one of its greatest transformations personally supervised by the monarch, with the rebuilding of the Alcazaba and the construction of the Watchtower and the Keep. Al-Ahmar also apparently began the work on the Nasrid Palaces and the wall surrounding the complex, constructions that were continued and complemented by the lineage with new buildings. During this last Arab kingdom the area experienced diverse alterations that emphasised more its palatial appearance at the expense of the military aspect.

THE ALHAMBRA
From the Cerro del Sol at twilight.

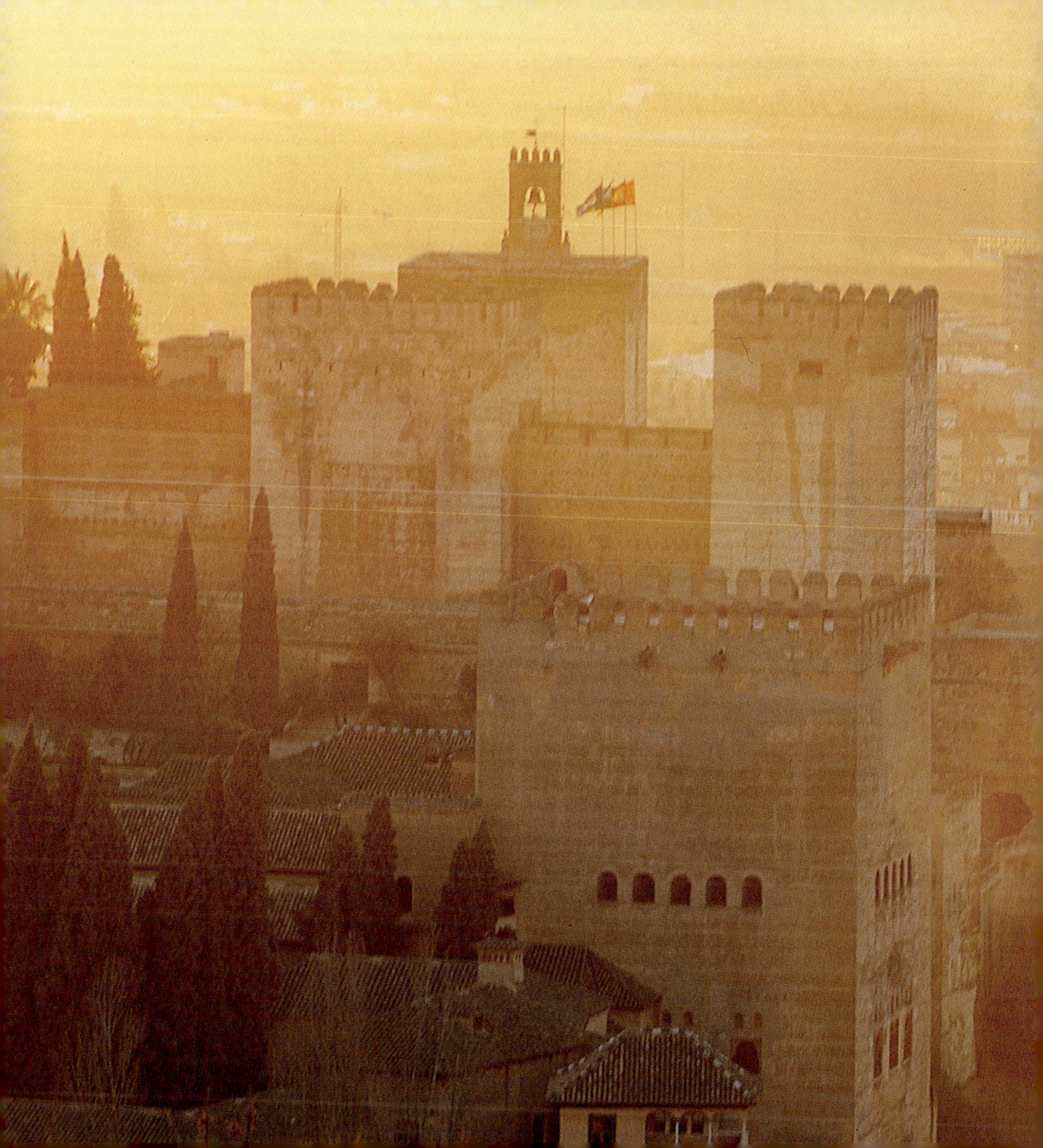

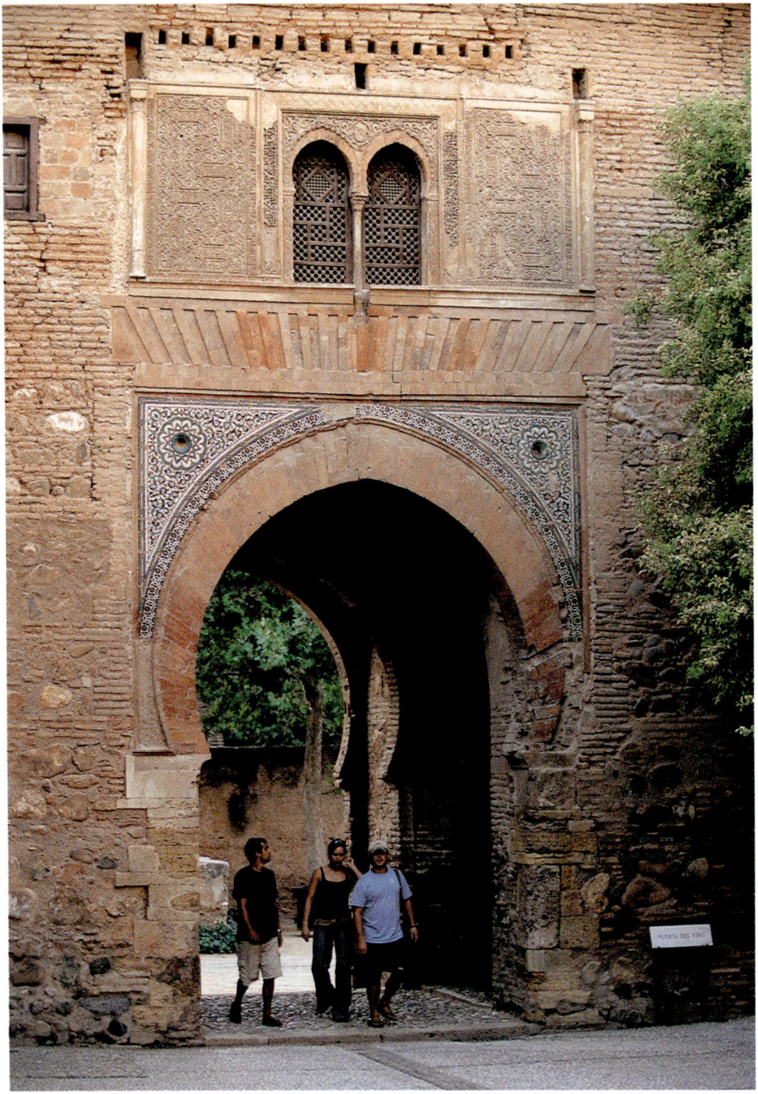

WINE DOORWAY
It links the Plaza de los Aljibes with the Alcazaba.

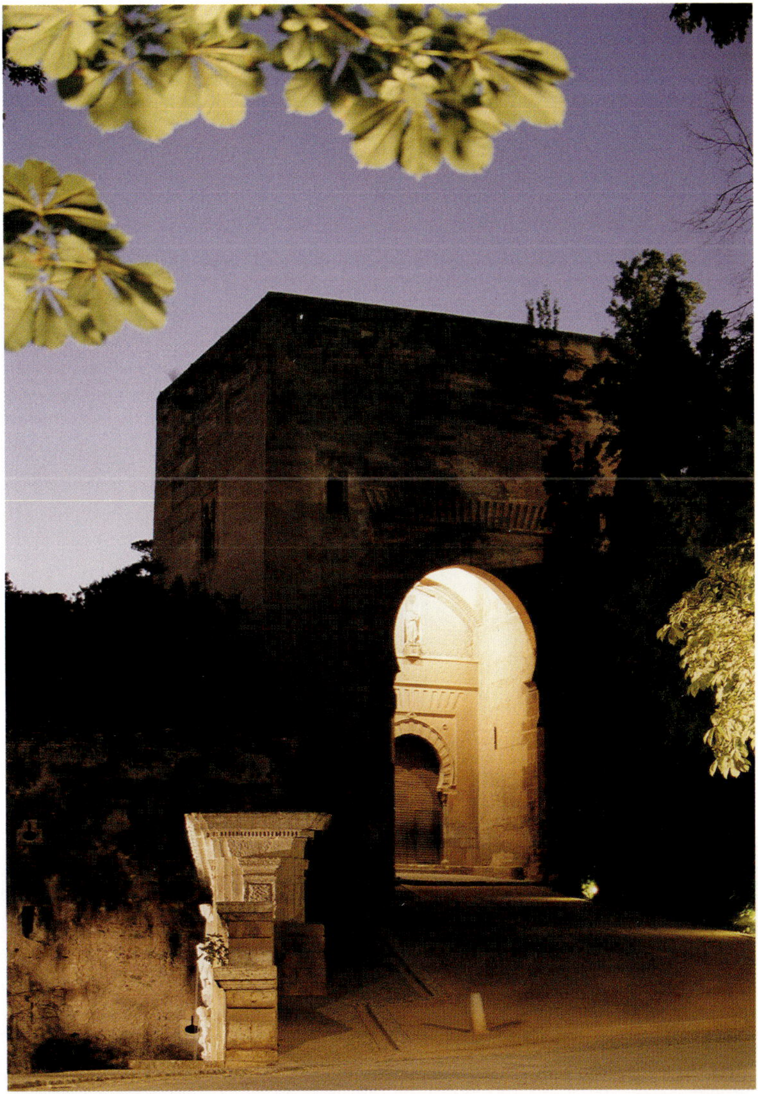

JUSTICE DOORWAY
It was built by Yusuf I.

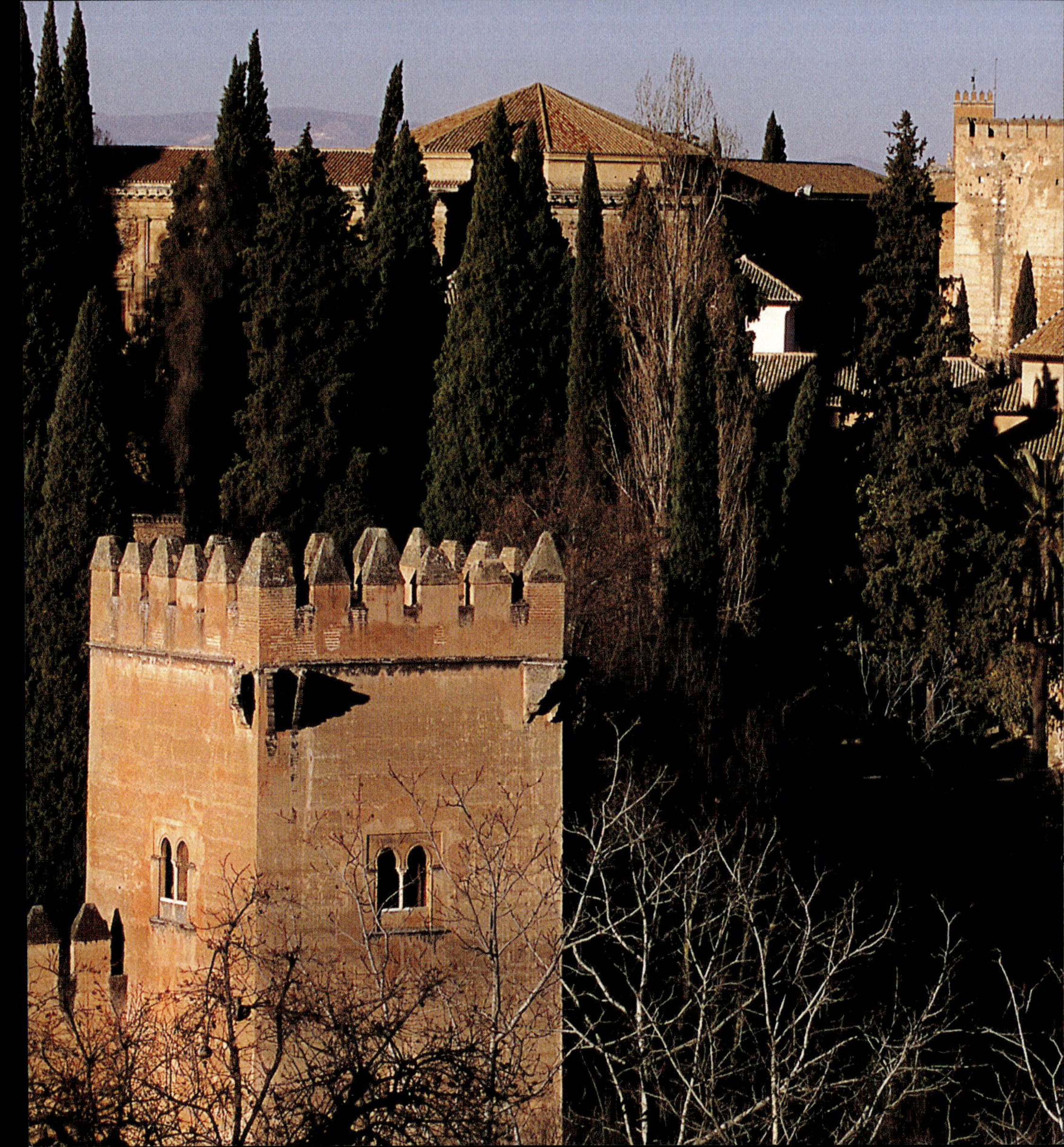

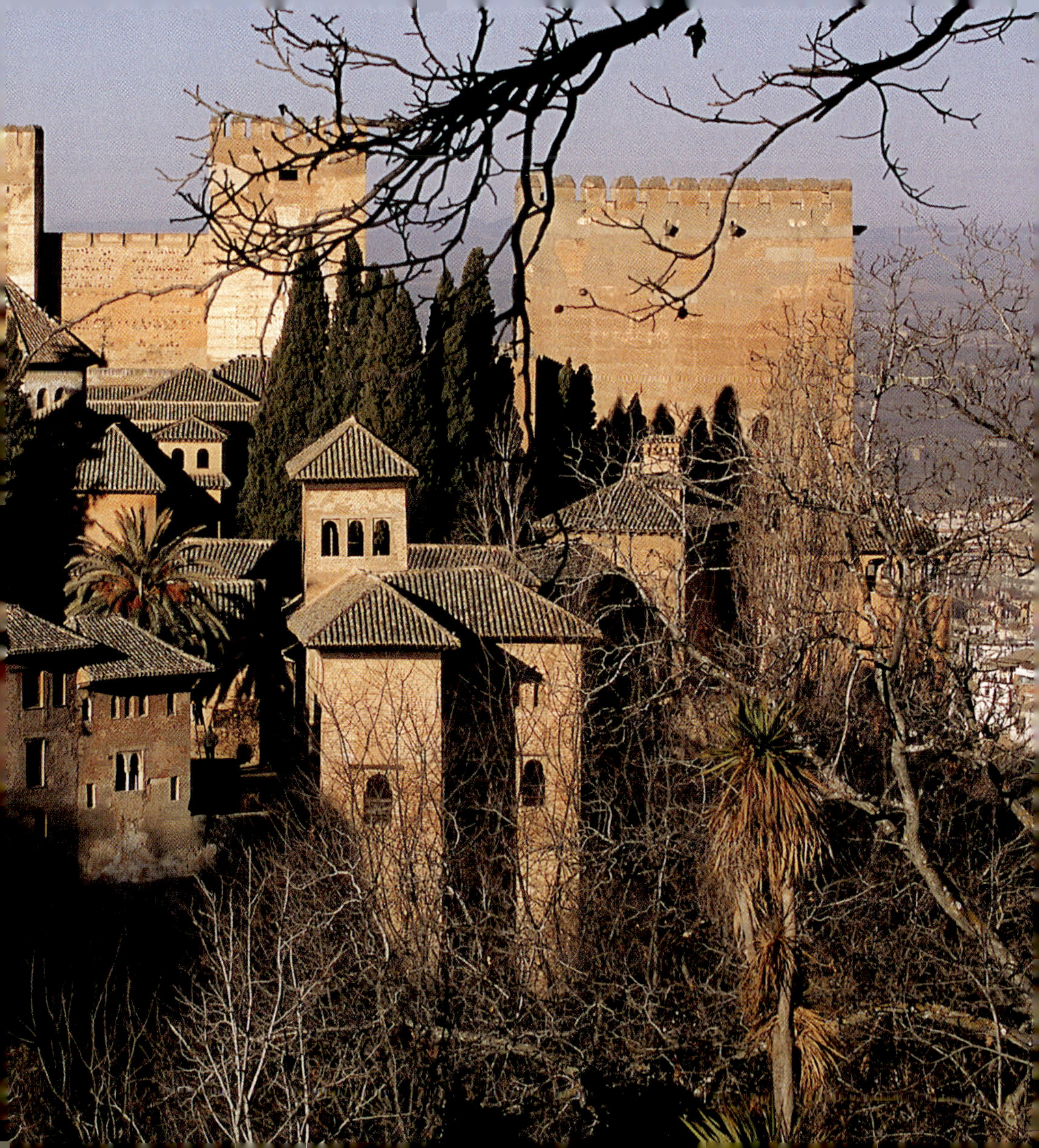

With the seventh Nasrid monarch Yusuf I, and his son Mohammed V who succeeded him, the Alhambra experienced a development that practically left it as it is now seen today. Yusuf I extended the perimeter around the complex, adding towers until there were more than thirty in number: some, like the Cautiva, were small palaces. He also transformed the Alcazaba and the palaces, built the baths and started the Comares Hall that was finished by his son, who was also responsible for the Patio of the Lions and its adjoining rooms and the decoration for the room known as the Barca.

The following sultans, until the disappearance of the Nasrid kingdom, were not as lavish in the remodelling or enlargement of the Alhambra. They were more worried about the advance of the Christians and internal conspiracies than emphasising the grandeur of the Red Fortress.

This is where the evolution of the Nasrid style ended then, an exquisite compendium of all the Hispano-Arab tendencies enriched with the constant arrival of artists from the invaded territories and, impoverished by the tough taxes that the Nasrid monarchs paid as vassalage to the Christians to survive in a dignified form, their eventual disappearance was just a question of time. This produced a curious paradox: the more the kingdom was militarily and economically depleted, the richer was its cultural life.

Once Granada had been taken by the Catholic Monarchs, they repaired the damage the walls had incurred and opened up new entrances to the Alhambra. The palaces and the Alcazaba were handed over to figures that had played an important role in the conquest, the rest being under the command of Iñigo López de Mendoza, Count of Tendilla, who was free of all legal restraint and had his own exclusive garrison. The successive monarchs took great care of the monument, spending huge amounts of money on its preservation. Charles V even built a Renaissance-style palace alongside the others that carries his name, as well as creating the Plaza de los Aljibes, repairing walls and conditioning several rooms of the Nasrid palaces. Under Felipe V, during the 18th century, it suffered total abandonment caused by the dismissal of the incumbents in charge of the monument, the Marquises of Mondéjar who were descendants of and succeeded the Counts of Tendilla, for supporting Archduke Charles during the War of Succession (1701-1714). The Red Fortress was almost left to oblivion, in a state of continual deterioration until the arrival of Charles III, who took care of and organised it. In 1792, continuing his father's work, Charles IV decided to put aside an annual sum from the crown's coffers for the most important repairs. With the French invasion the Alhambra was used as a barracks by the enemy, and although they made some repairs, in 1812 it was partially blown up by the troops when they abandoned it, leaving the Water, Princesses and Seven Floors towers in total ruin, which with the passing of time meant it was in a deplorable state. This represented the monument's worst period of deterioration, until in 1830 Ferdinand VII assigned fifty thousand *reales* for its restoration. In 1868, with the bourgeois revolution, it was confiscated for being an asset of the royal heritage, being declared a national monument two years later, which meant that it received an annual sum from the state budget, thus enabling a policy of conservation and restoration to be undertaken with initiatives that were achieved to a greater or lesser extent. Interest in its recovery grew enormously due to the worldwide fame that the 19th-century romantics gave the Alhambra, such as Washington Irving or Alexandre de Laborde, in their books describing its charms.

During the 20th century it was subject to a great many restorations based on very serious studies, with a highly appropriate focus, and where the committed figure of Leopoldo Torres Balbás stands out at the head of the all the architects who were involved. He was responsible for the recovery of the Alhambra just as we know it today. Today the whole complex is in the hands of the Junta de Andalucía, the regional government, which it runs through the Alhambra Trust. Since 1984 it has enjoyed the privilege bestowed on it by UNESCO of a World Heritage Site for being a unique artistic work and for constituting an extraordinary architectural example that illustrates the period of Arab domination on the Peninsula.

Although the whole complex is known by the general name of Alhambra, we should distinguish what amount to its three parts, all highly differentiated from each other. The first is the Alcazaba, at the extreme west of the *Al-Sabika* hill, which housed the troops that guarded the area. The second part contains the places, separated from the Alcazaba by the Plaza de los Aljibes, where the monarchs lived and administered their domains; and the third part, the Generalife, the royal villa and summer leisure home.

THE ALHAMBRA
With Sierra Nevada in the background.

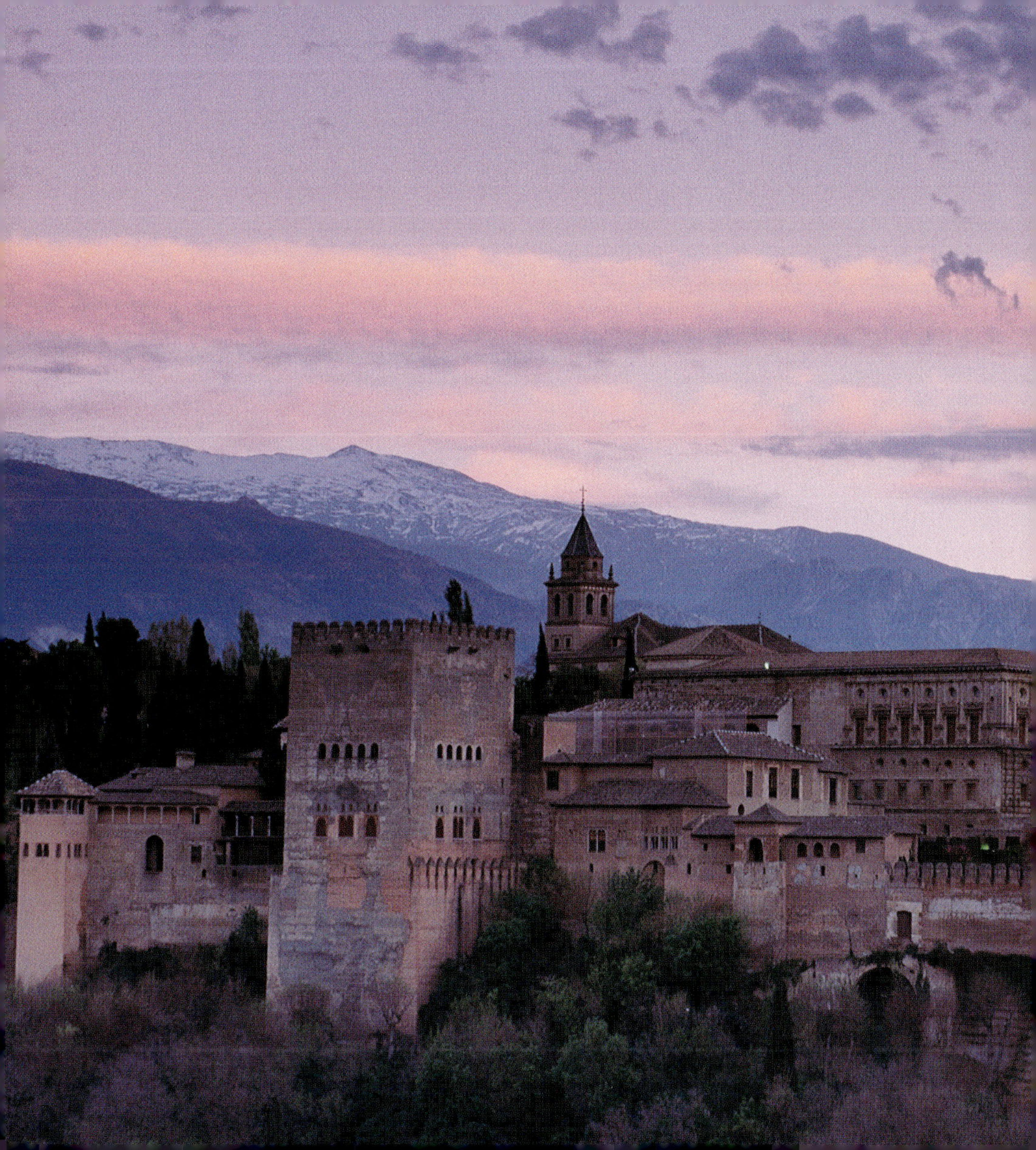

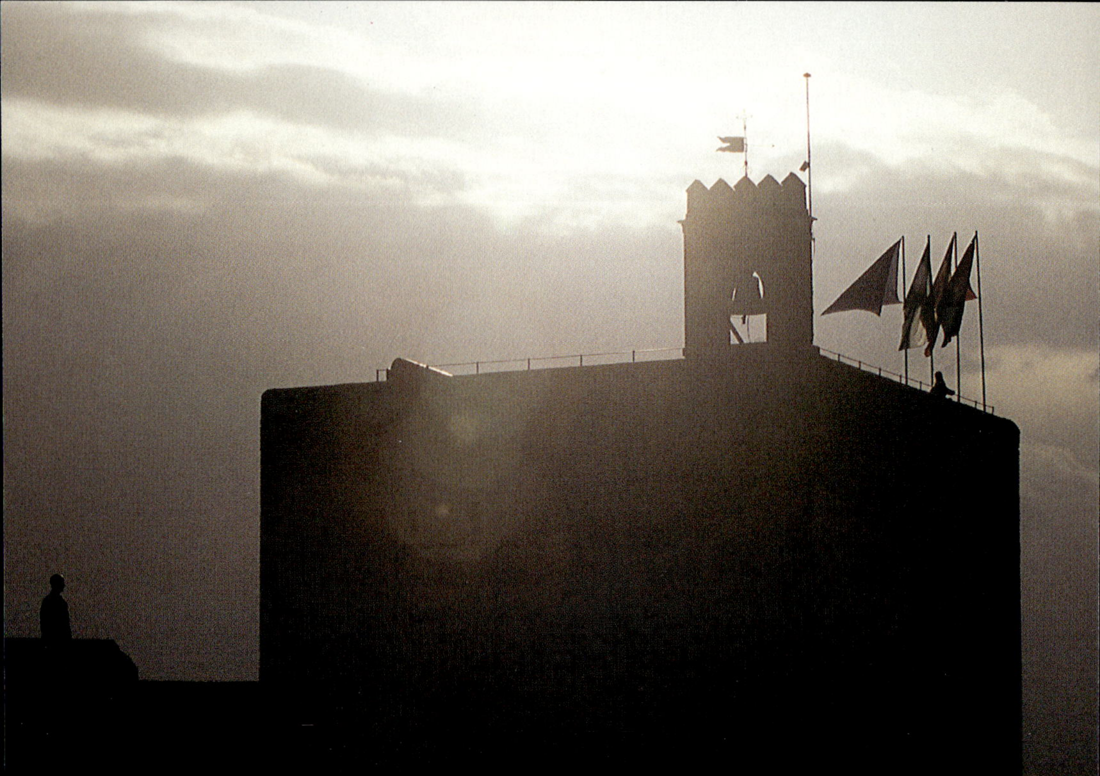

THE ALCAZABA

Alongside the Bermeja Towers, which were one of the first defences of the old Garnata, the Alcazaba is the oldest building in the Alhambra, an heir of fortifications of older cultures in the westernmost part of the *Al-Sabika* hill. The first written record where it is mentioned dates back to the mid-9th century, where Ibn Al-Jatib stated that it was built by the Qaysi Sawwar Ibn Hamdun to protect himself from a series of very tough conflicts with the Granada ruling class. Its current appearance is down to Mohammed I al-Ahmar, who lived here and turned it into the early castle within a large fortress, surrounding it with a walled perimeter with ravelin, raising in the west the Watchtower and to the east the irregular tower alongside the Keep. The royal residence was in the Alcazaba until the fifth Nasrid monarch built the first palace, according to documentary evidence. The fortification was then only used for military purposes. The military city was in the Plaza de Armas with the troops' quarters, arms stores and dungeons.

WATCHTOWER
It was previously known as the Bell Tower, placed by the Christians on its steeple.

Over all the constructions of the Alcazaba, with great clarity, stands the Watchtower with its haughty air: built over a square ground plan the side measures 16 metres, the height almost 27 metres and it is crowned by a belfry that contains a bell, the tolls of which until quite recently controlled the irrigation times of the plain and alerted the city in any emergency situation. On the 2nd of January 1492, perhaps because it was the best spot in the Alhambra for observing the city, the Christians climbed to the top to celebrate the taking of Granada with great ostentation; in the name of the Catholic Monarchs, Cardinal Mendoza climbed up to the very top of the tower raising a cross and waving the royal flags and the standard of Saint James.

PLAZA DE ARMAS
Remains of the barracks that housed the troops. The Ravine Tower to the right and the Keep to the left.

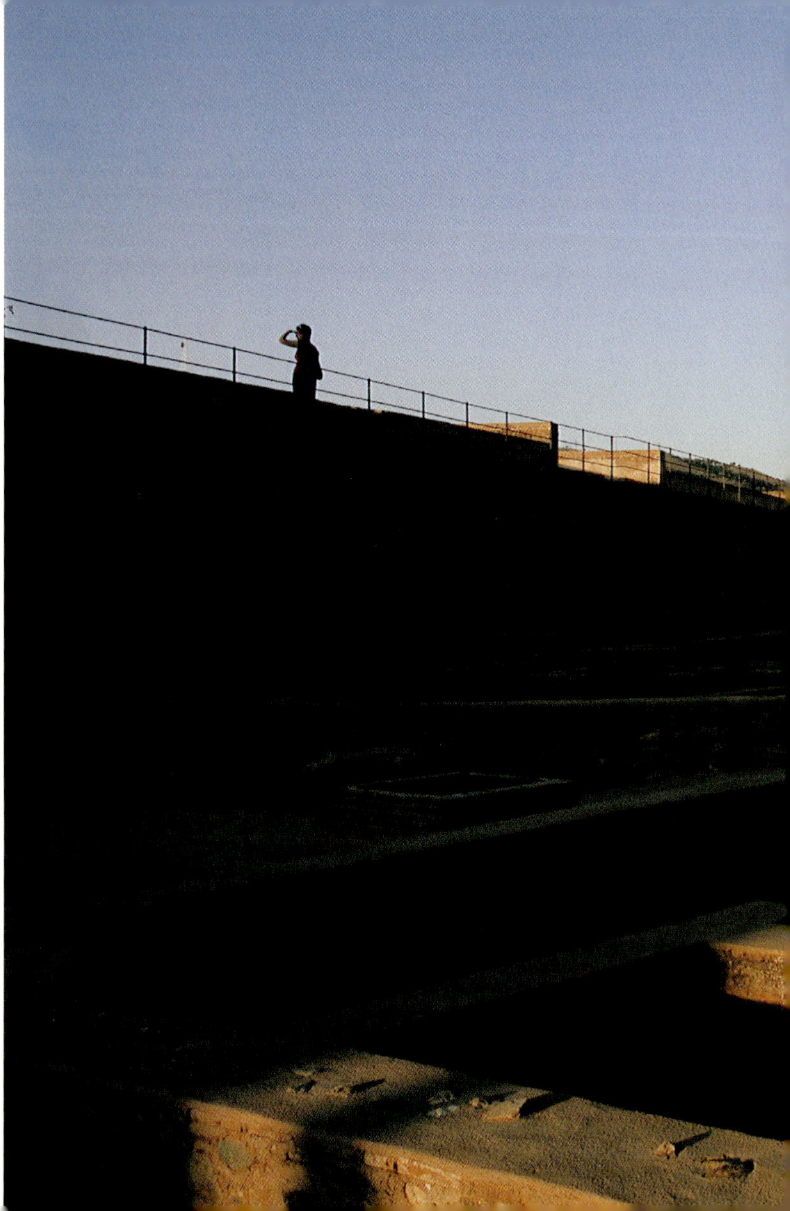

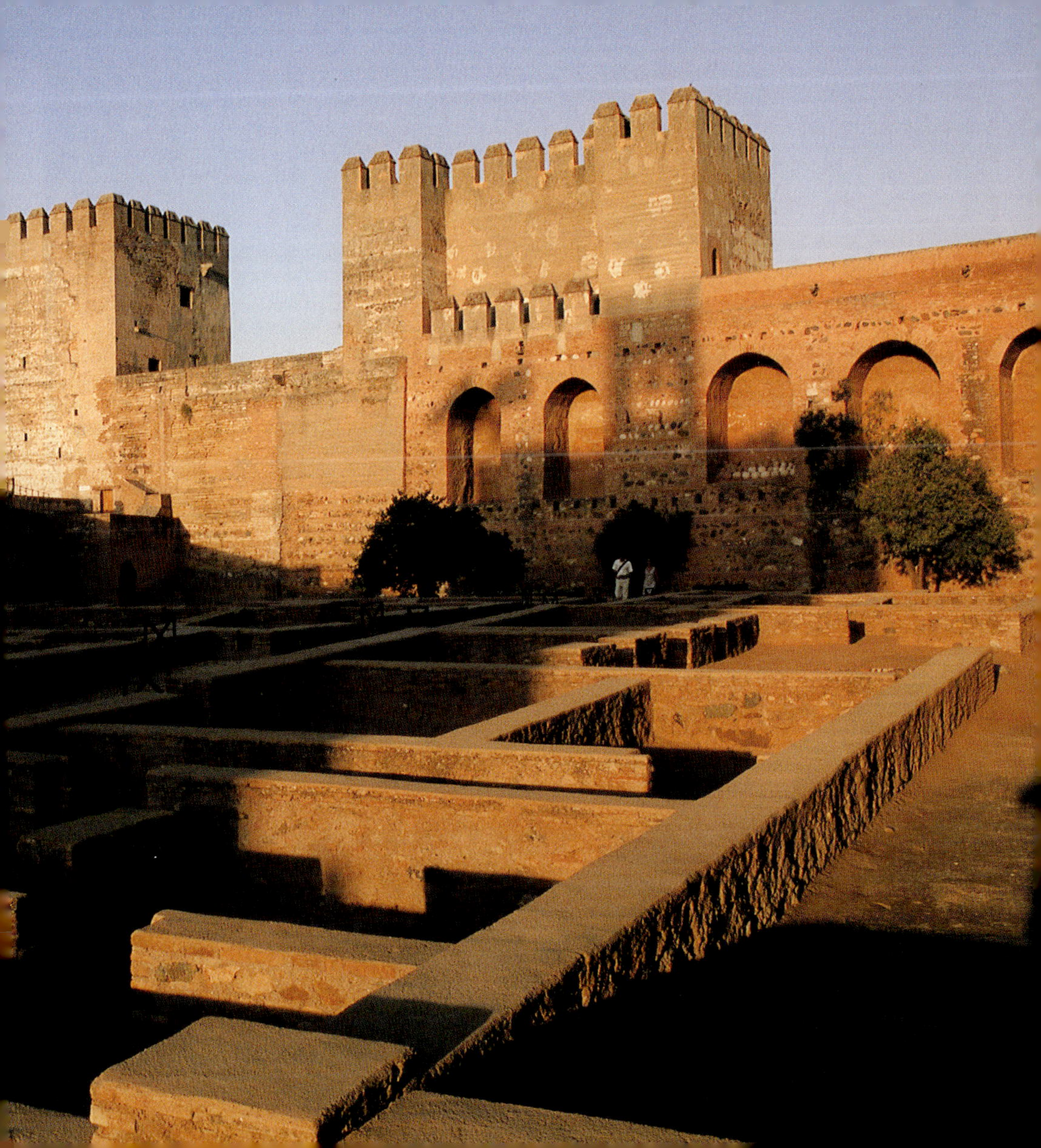

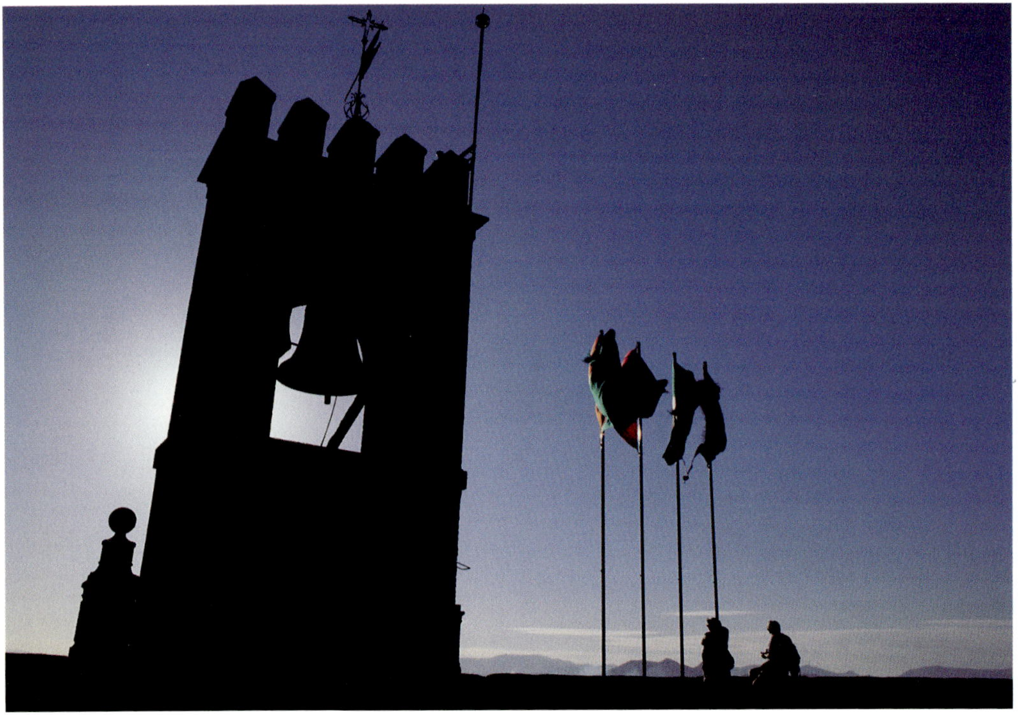

WATCHTOWER
A symbol for the people of Granada, its silhouette forms part of the city's coat of arms.

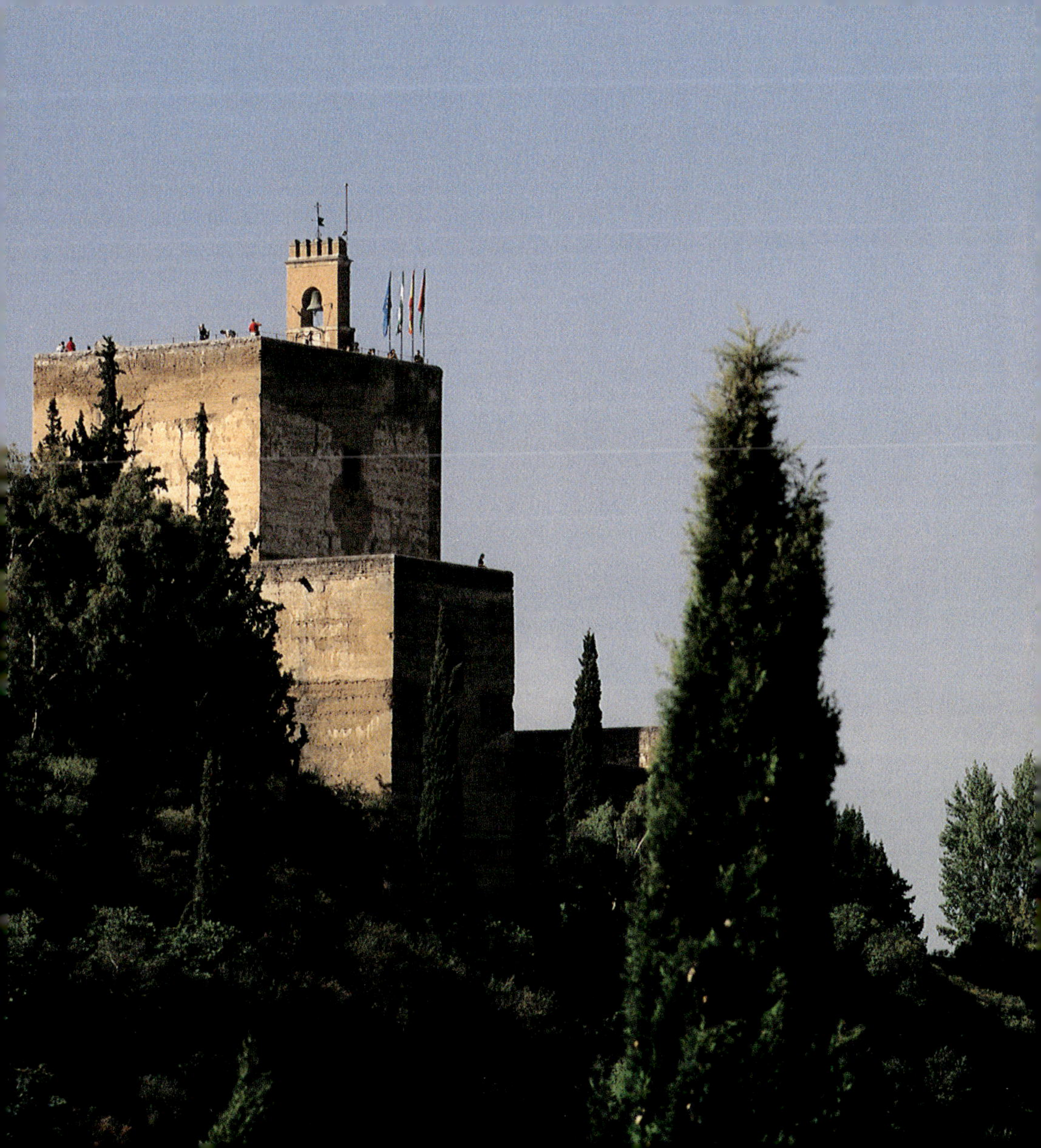

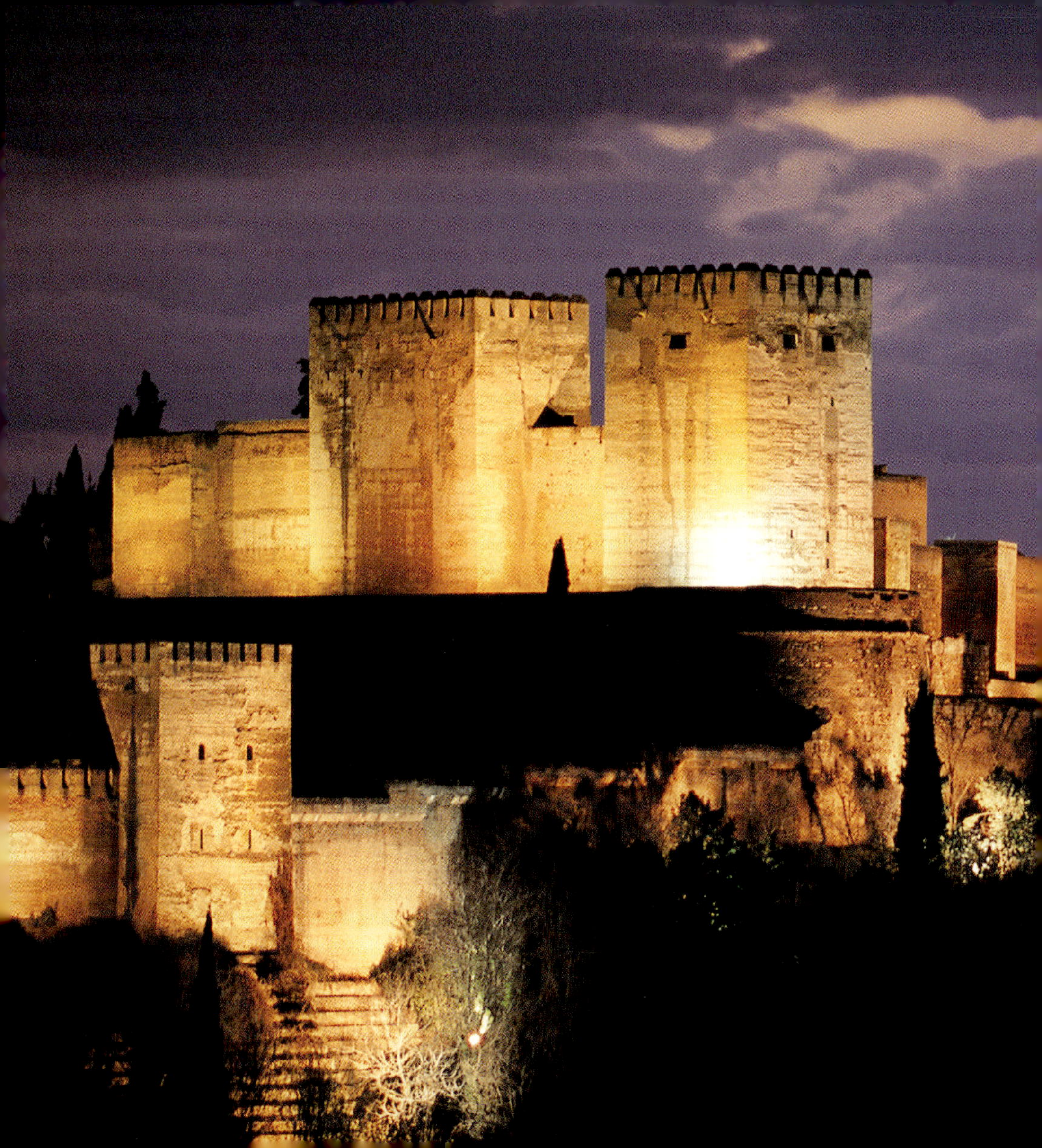

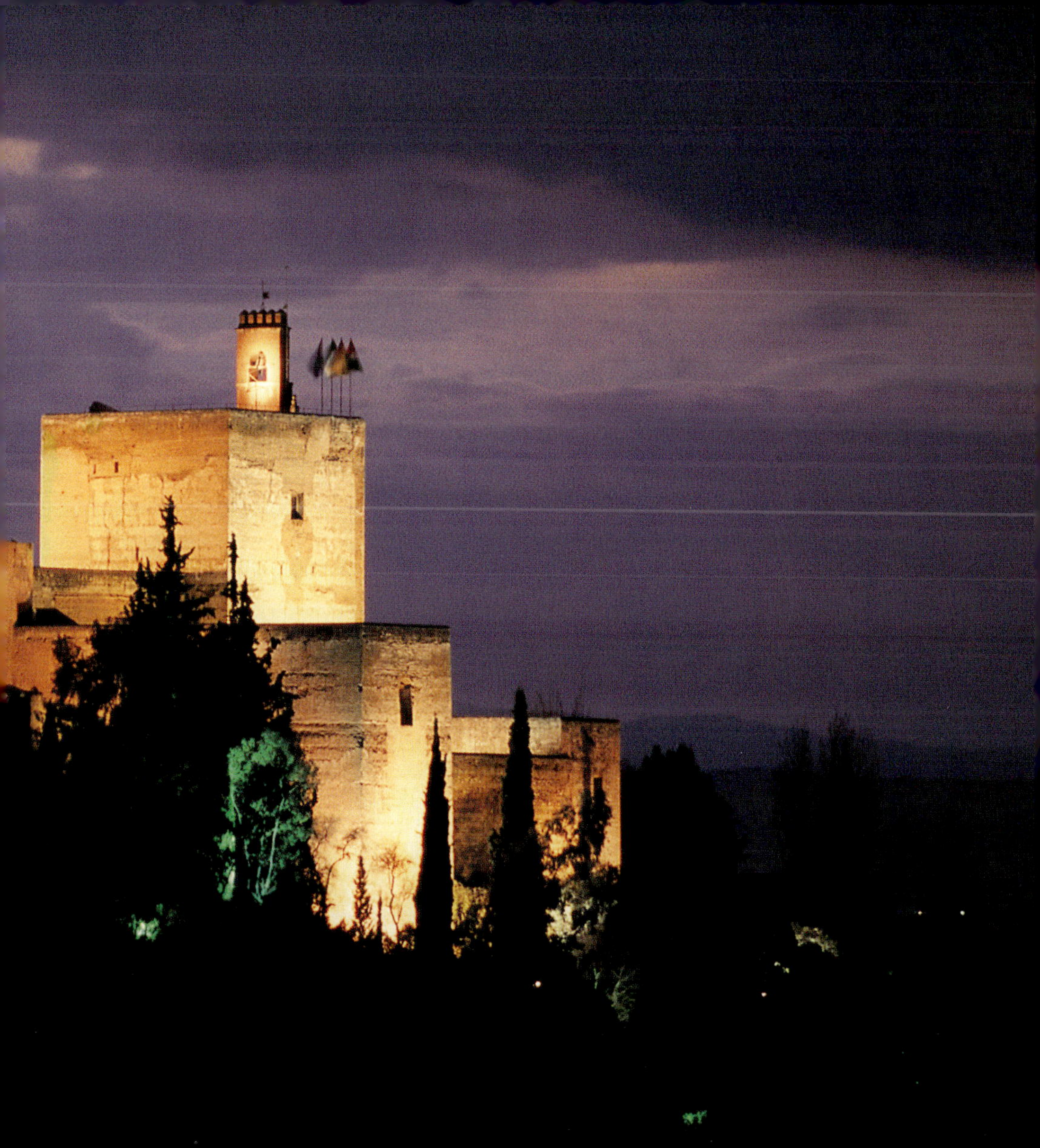

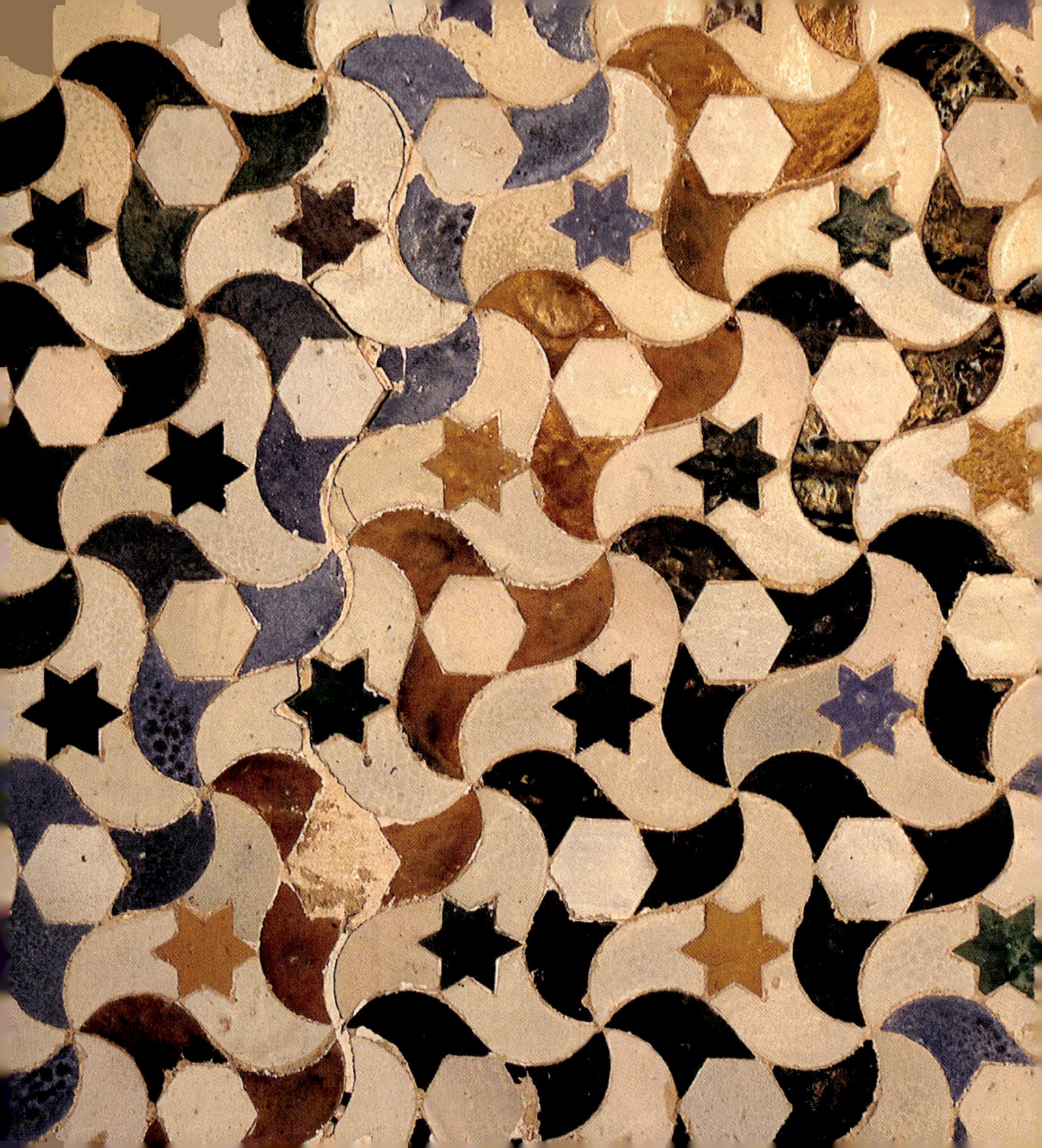

THE NASRID PALACES

It is almost certain that Mohammed I Al-Ahmar began work on the fortress. Nevertheless, until the reign of the fifth Nasrid king, Abu l-Walid Ismail (1314-1325), there is no written evidence regarding the construction of any palace. This monarch built one alongside the Great Mosque and the Rauda Tower, of which only the Mexuar remains. Yusif I demolished it to make room for his own projects: he made the baths and remodelled the Comares area, which was completed during the reign of his son, Mohammed V, who also combined this work with the Mexuar and built the Palace of the Lions. These two kings, father and son, were the most important people in giving the Nasrid Palaces their grandeur and splendour. They are divided into four large spaces: the Mexuar, which was used as the courts of justice and for administrative purposes; the Comares Palace, also known as the Serrallo, which was the official residence; the Palace of the Lions, which housed the private rooms of the sultan; and the Partal, with the small palaces of the nobility who lived alongside the Royal Palace. The heart of this sophisticated complex was the Comares Palace, the perfect type of official Arab residence reserved for the seat of the crown.

COMARES PALACE
Detail of the tiling.

The palatine Nasrid architecture solves any constructive problems by means of cubic volumes, with light roofs supported by thin columns and relatively narrow pillars. On the outside the walls appear strictly sober with small openings and in the inside the rooms and patios possess a lavish ornamentation made from simple materials. The arch always appears as a decorative element, leaving aside its traditional function of transforming the vertical vector of the weight into oblique forces that rest over the imposts. The lower parts of the rooms are often covered with fine tiling, in ceramics and glazed tiles, that give it a great deal of charm.

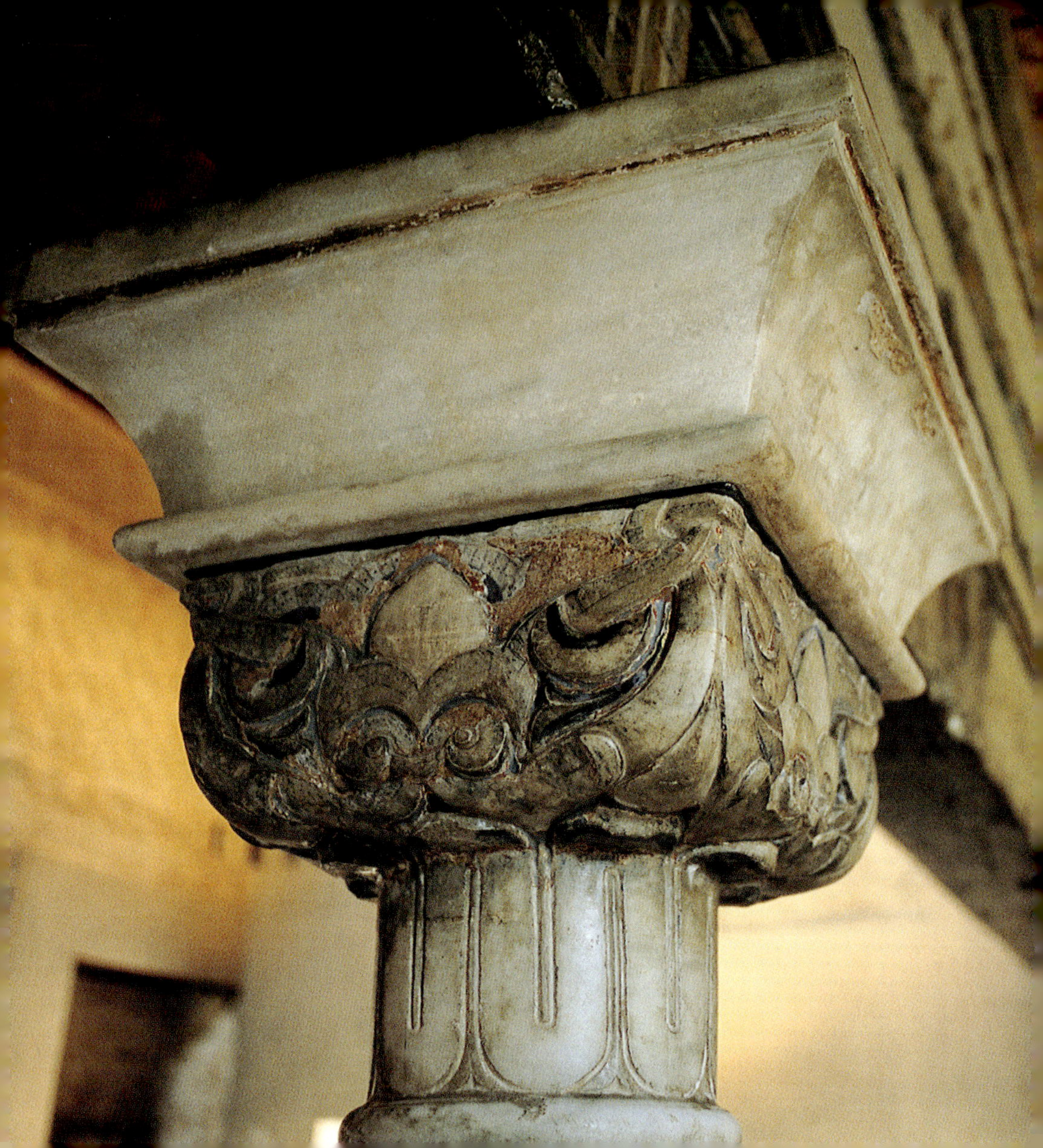

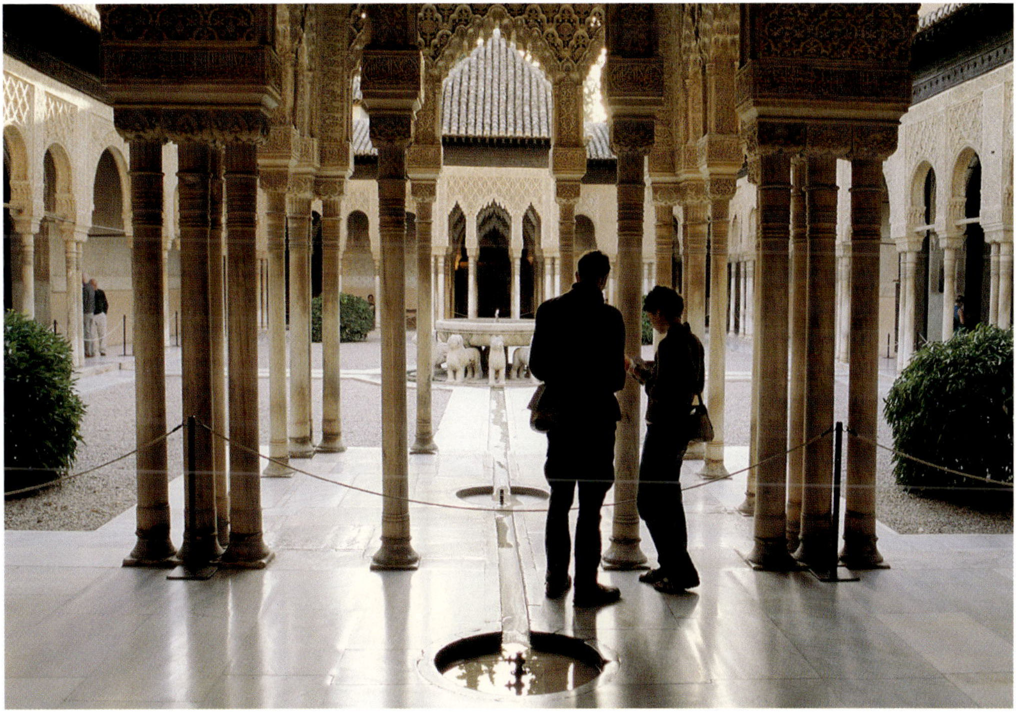

MEXUAR
Detail of a capital of the four columns that the room has.

PATIO OF THE LIONS
Here Nasrid art reaches its zenith.

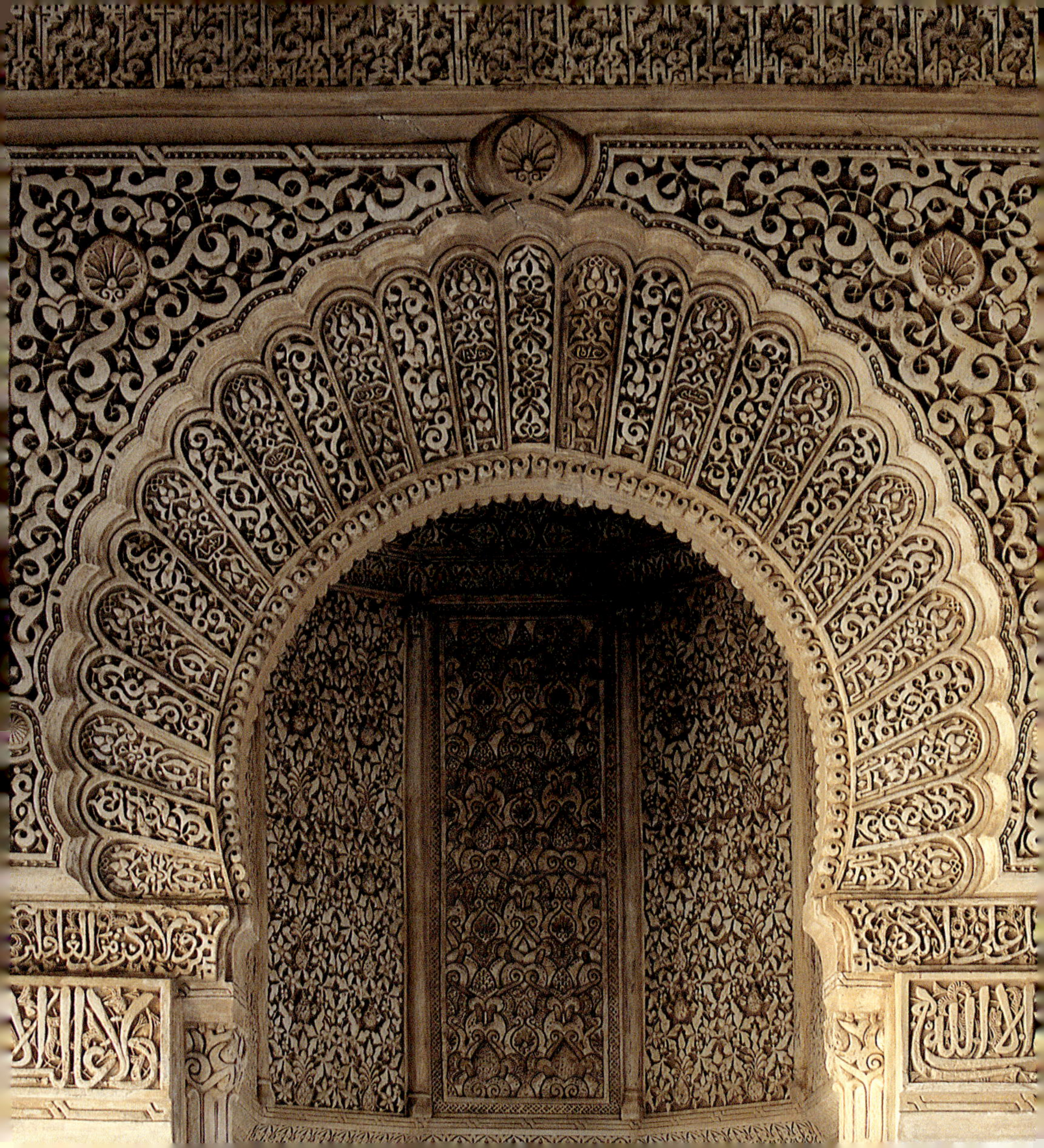

THE MEXUAR AND THE GILDED ROOM

At the entrance to the Nasrid palaces, a small patio leads to the door that in turn leads to the Mexuar. This is where the meetings of the Royal Council were held to deal out justice in the Nasrid territories. It has experienced so many interior and exterior reforms since it was built, particularly so after the arrival of the Christians, that it is very difficult to describe its original appearance. Today it is a rectangular room with four columns where mocárabe corbels are supported and ornamentation that fuses Christian and Arab styles. Above the tiling the coat of arms of Charles V stands out and on the oldest plasterwork the following inscription can be read; "Glory to our lord the Emir of the Muslims Abu l-Walid Ismail", which leads many academics to state that there was a palace of this king here, which must have been the oldest part of the palatial buildings. At the end of the room there is a small viewpoint-oratory, with four windows of twin arches to provide splendid views of the Albayzin, and a mihrab that has a voussoired horseshoe arch with several inscriptions that refer to the precepts of the Koran.

MEXUAR
Mihrab of the small viewpoint-oratory.

Passing the Mexuar after going through a small horseshoe arch, as a delicate aperitif to what is awaiting us further in, appearing before the visitor is the extraordinary patio of the Gilded Room, built by Mohammed IV according to the inscriptions. It is overlooked by a circular fountain in the centre, and to one side the room that provides the name of the space, because of its Mudejar-style painting on its coffered ceiling, and on the other side, the impressive façade of the Comares Palace made up of five openings and an attractive combination of tiling on the door frames and skirting, with extremely fine plasterwork that in its time was polychrome, like all of those to be found in the Alhambra.

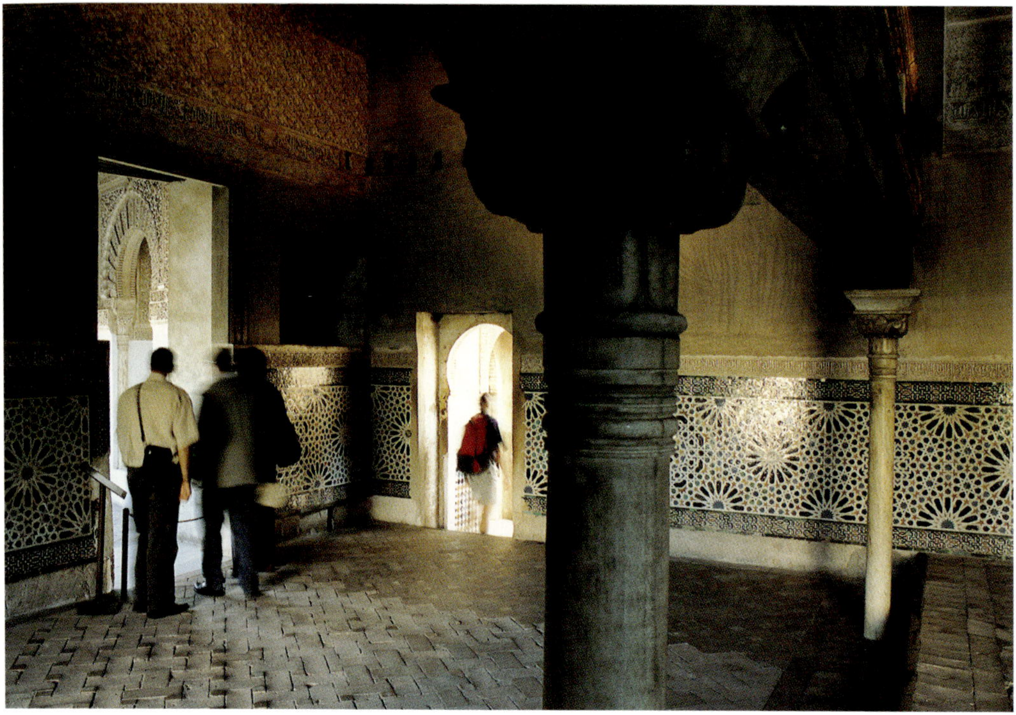

MEXUAR
It is the room where the visit to the Nasrid Palaces begins.

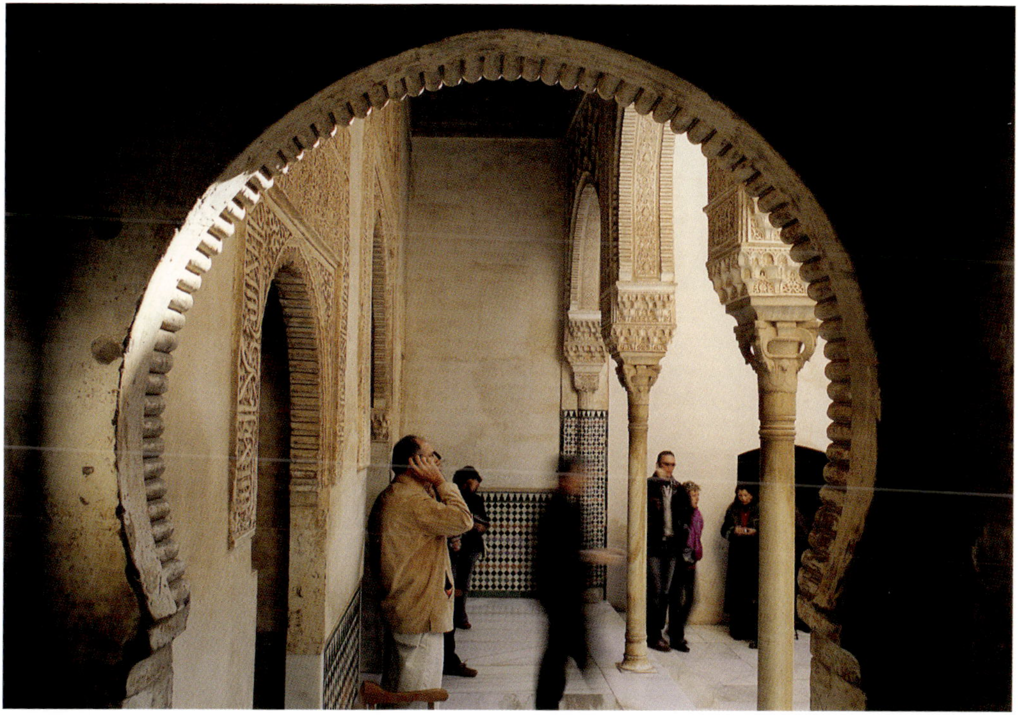

MEXUAR
Horseshoe arch that leads to the Patio of the Gilded Room.

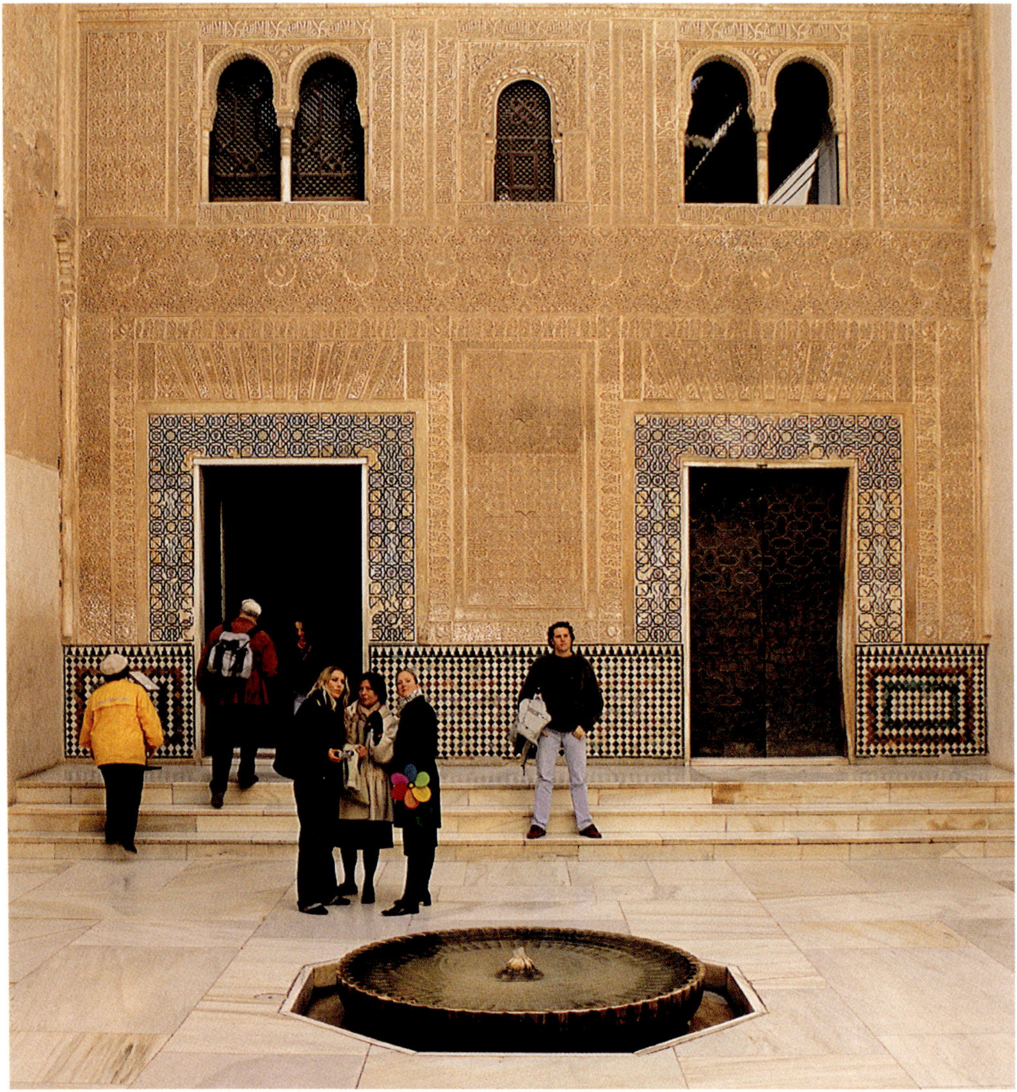

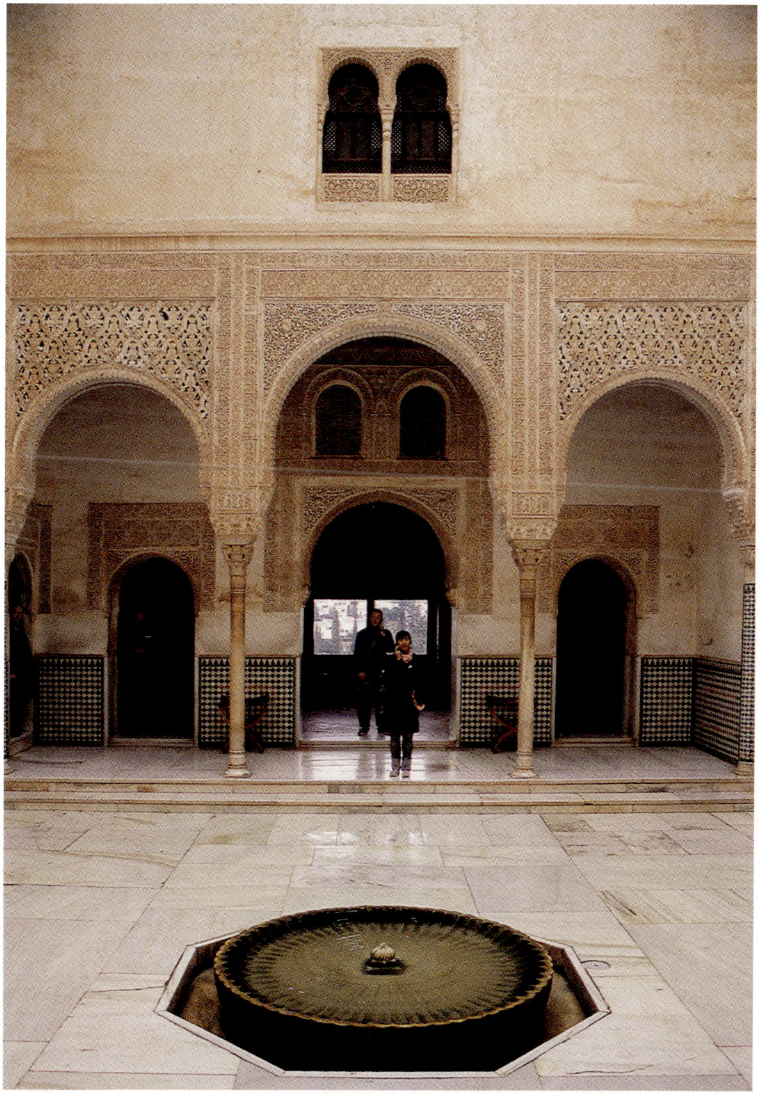

PATIO OF
THE GILDED ROOM
Main façade of the Comares Palace.

Western gateway.

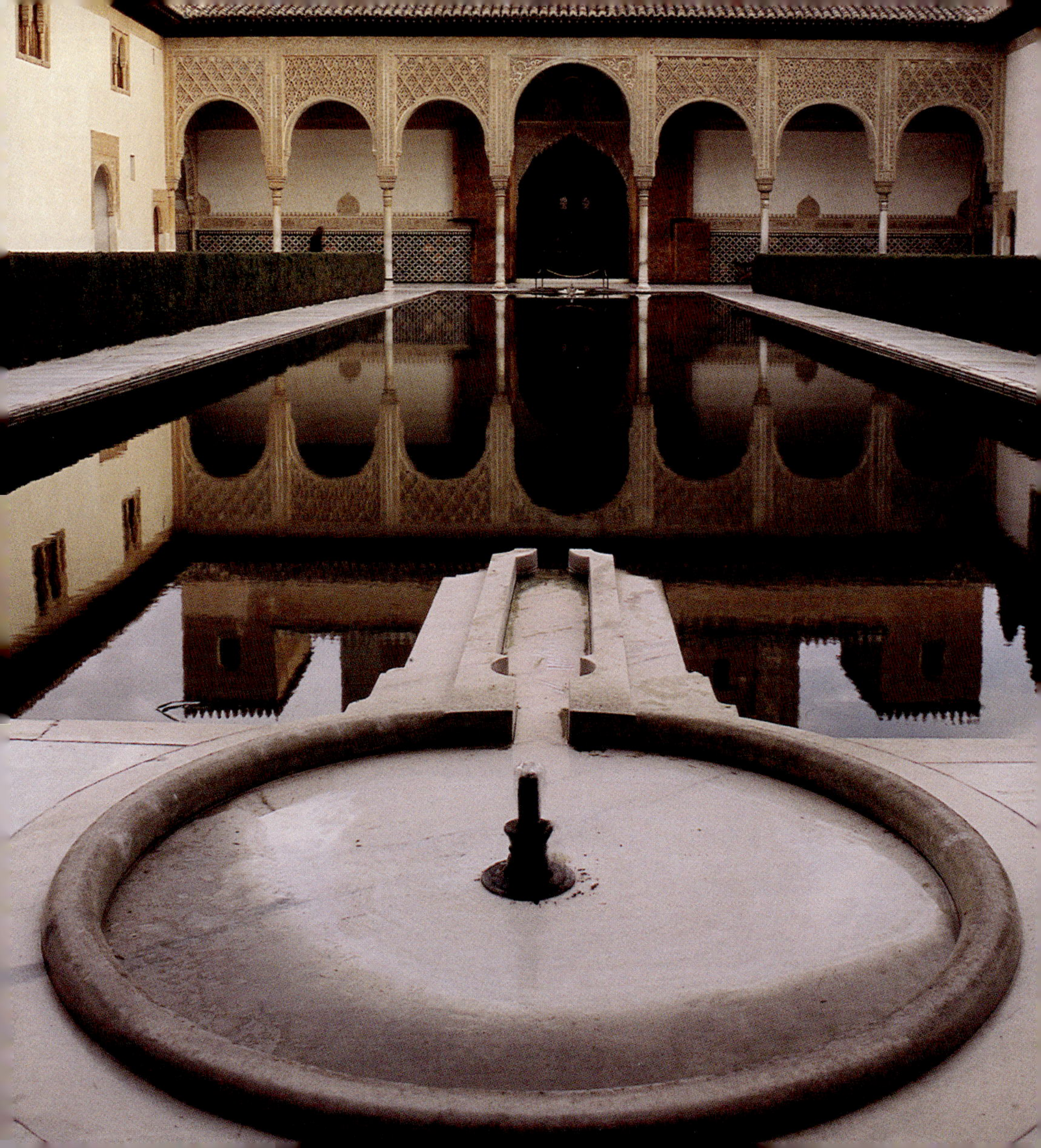

THE COMARES PALACE

The Comares Palace, as the sultan's official residence, is the most important nucleus of the Royal Palace. The rooms are organised around the Patio of the Myrtles, which has a large pool that reflects the arches of the adjoining galleries and the figure of the highest tower of the Alhambra; a paradigm of the Andalusian Arabic patio, it is flanked by seven semicircular arches on the two short sides. The north gallery, over which is built the 45 metres of the solid Comares Tower, leads to the Hall of the Boat via a pointed arch of mocárabes, which in turn leads to the inside of the tower where the Hall of the Ambassadors is situated, named thus for being the space where the throne was placed and used for official visits. This is where the political events of an exceptional nature took place, such as the meeting between the Catholic Monarchs and Columbus to arrange the voyage that took him to the American continent or the Council at which Boabdil decided to surrender Granada. The hall lives up to the importance of its use and is the most solemn of all the palaces. It has a square ground plan measuring almost 12 metres and is 18 metres high with massive walls, extremely delicate plasterwork, crowned by a delightful wooden dome made in sections of cedar covered with bows and knots.

PATIO OF THE MYRTLES
It is overlooked by a pool measuring 34 x 7.10 metres.

The last big room in the Comares Palace is the Royal baths, the arrangement of which is in the classical style of Roman thermal baths. Made during the reign of Yusuf I, the first room is known as the Hall of the Beds, where simple architecture, with simple tiled skirting, smooth horseshoe arches and vaults with starred skylights transmit a magical serenity.

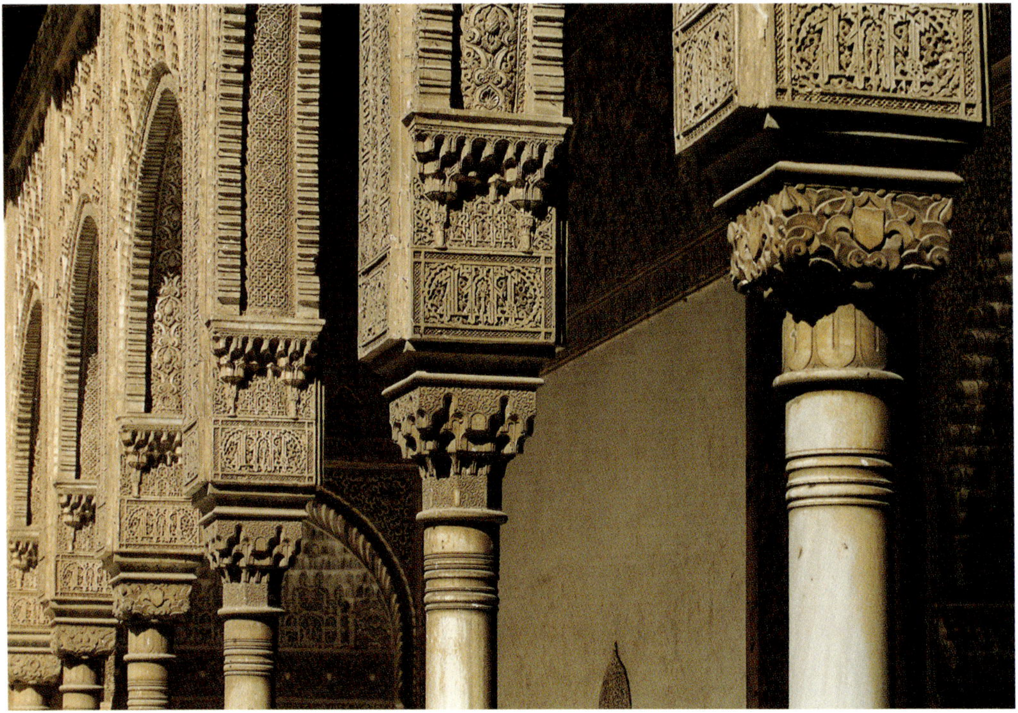

PATIO OF THE MYRTLES
North gallery gateway.
In Islamic ornamentation, *atauriques* (raised works common to Arab art), geometric designs and writing are often combined.

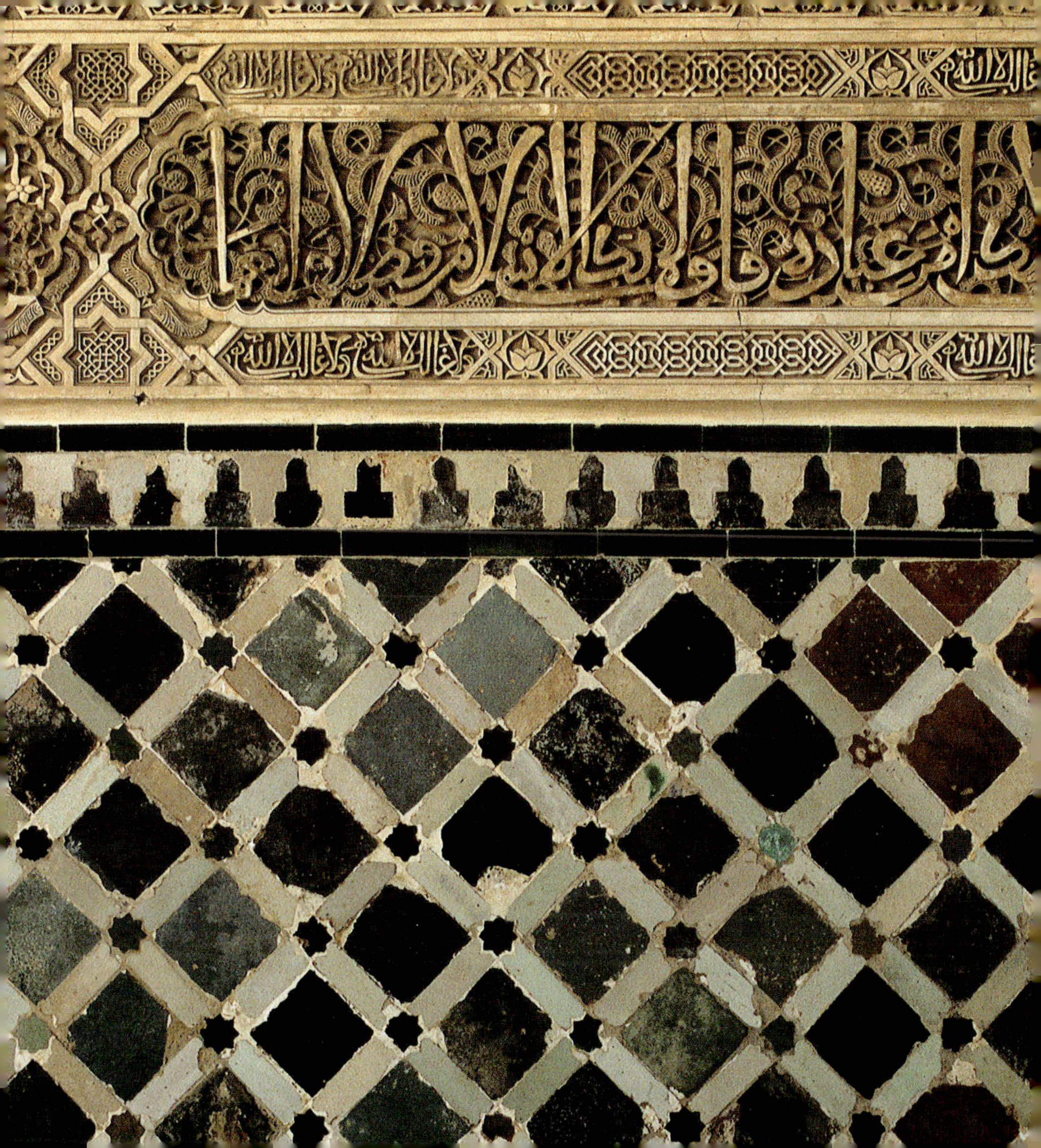

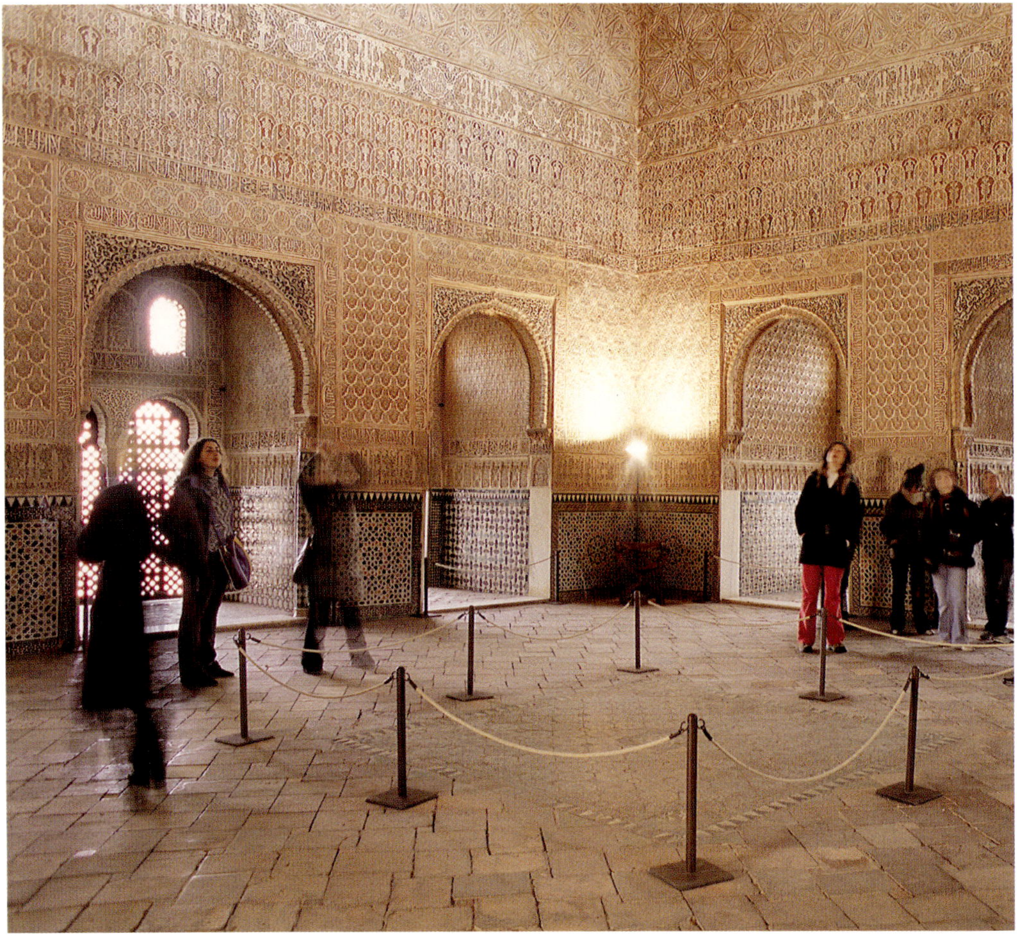

HALL OF THE AMBASSADORS
It was originally paved with marble.

PATIO OF THE MYRTLES
Detail of the tiling and plasterwork.

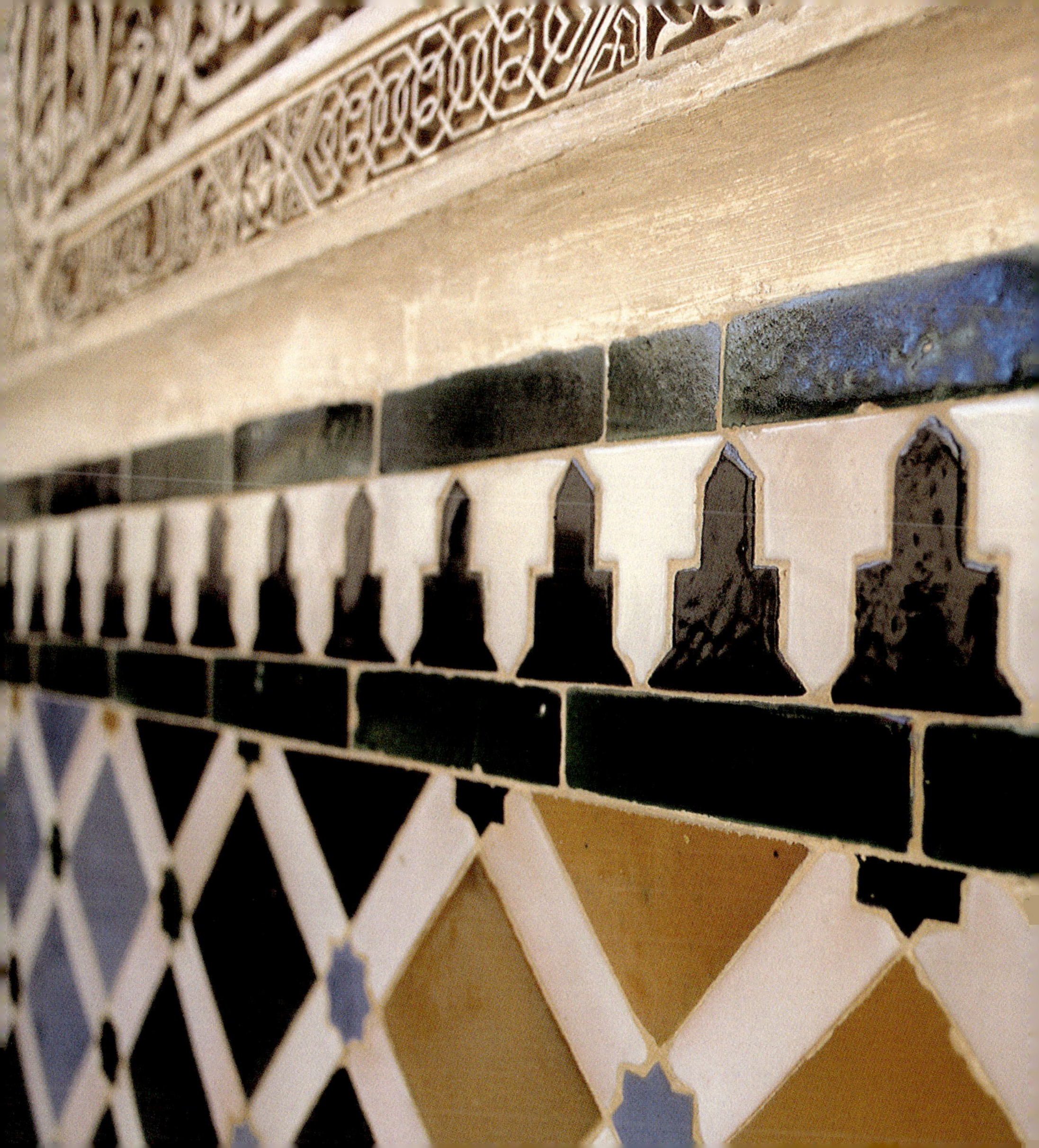

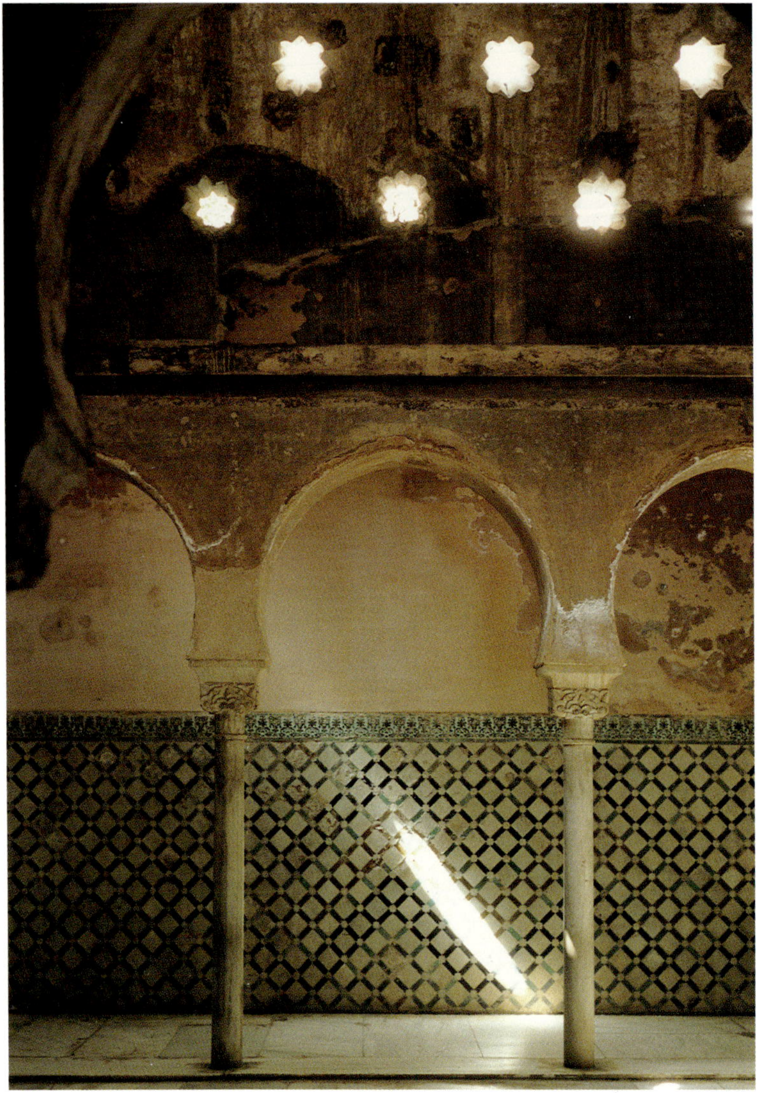

ROYAL BATHS
Main chamber.

The skylights give it a special charm.

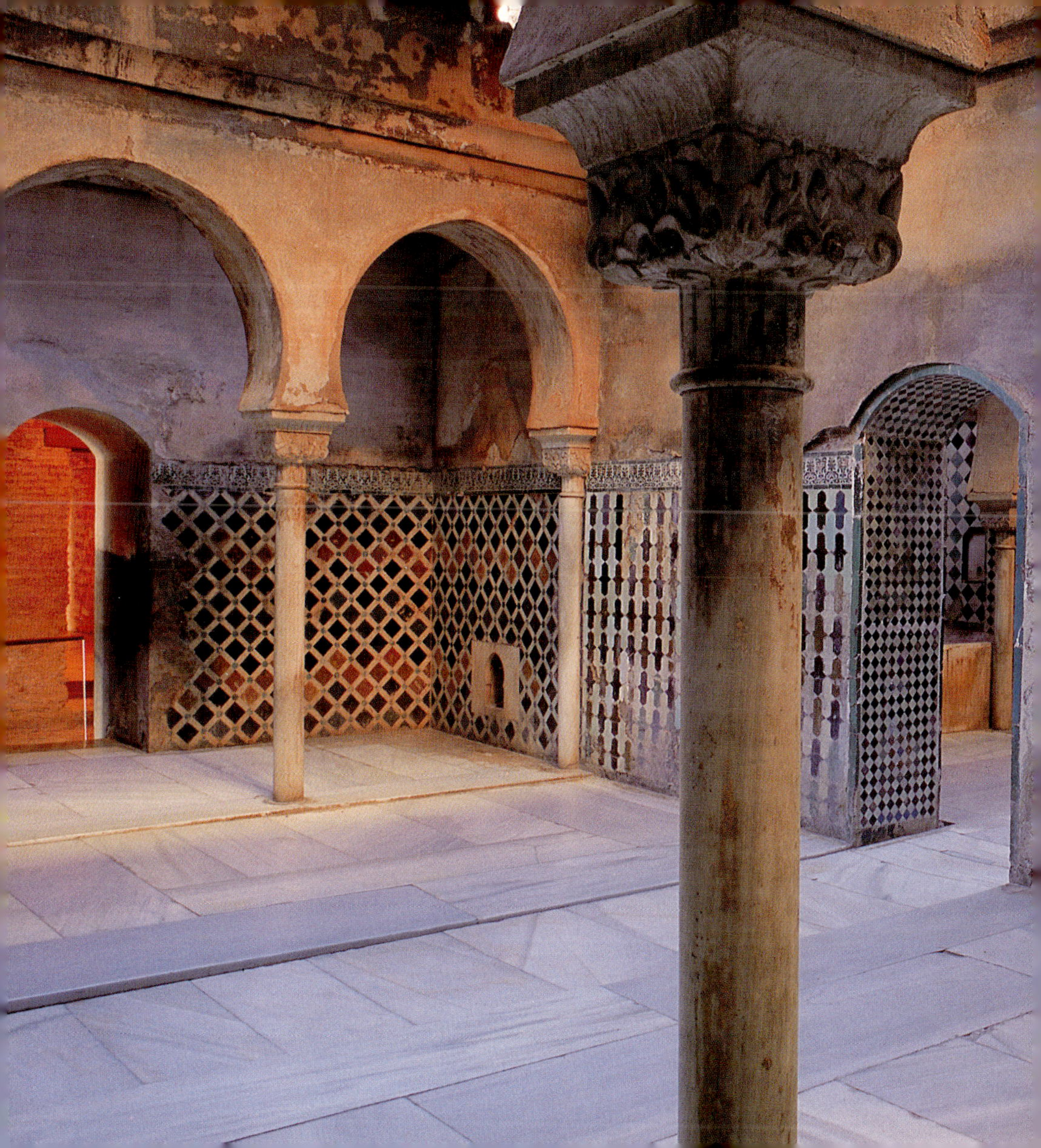

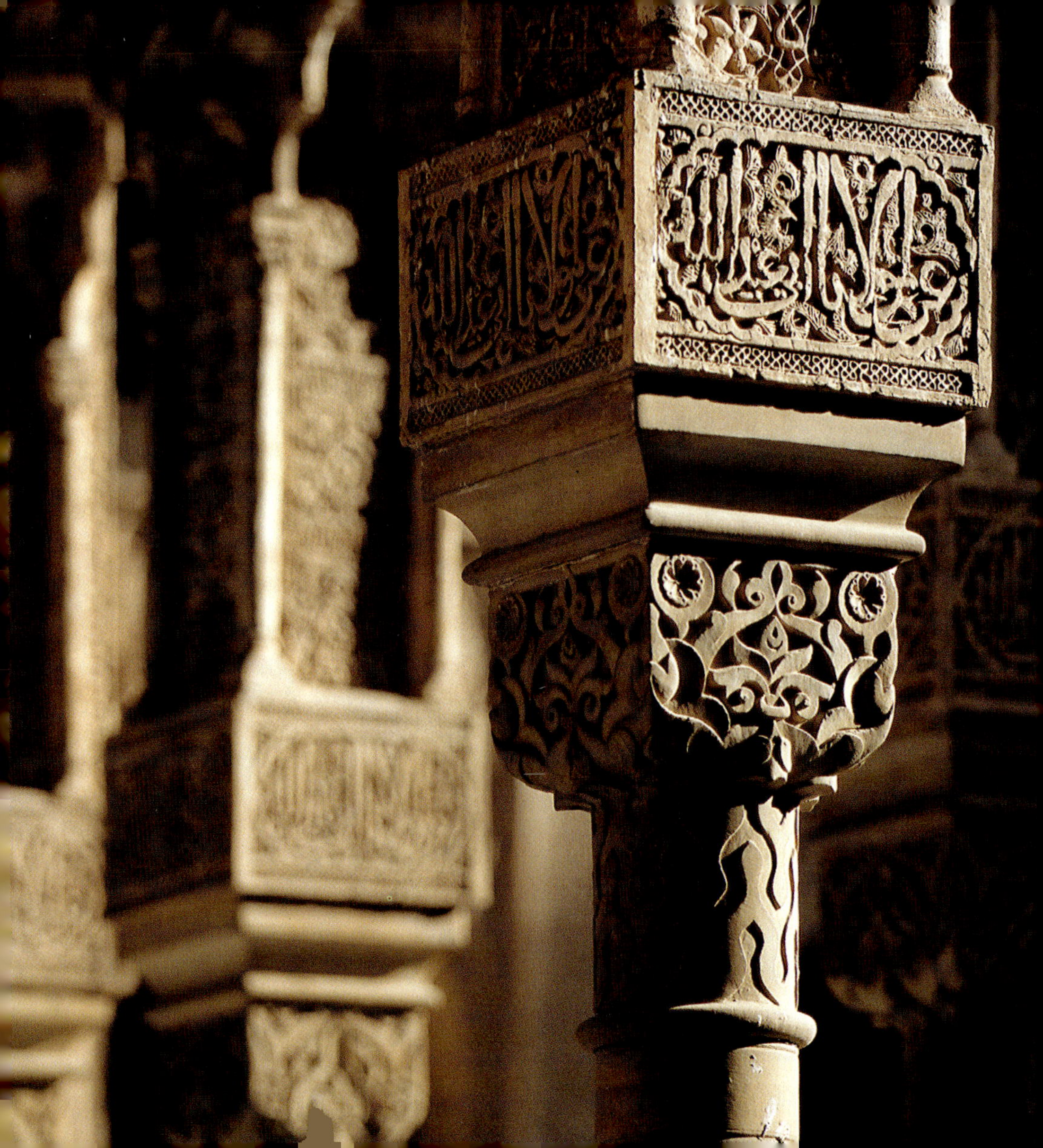

THE PALACE OF THE LIONS

Repeated thousands of times in calendars and postcards, the Palace of the Lions is the most popular of all. Mohammed V built it around a patio surrounded by four porticoed galleries, which enclose the famous fountain that gives the space its name, with 124 marble columns that have cubic capitals and canted arches that lead to the other rooms.

In the western part is the Hall of the Mocárabes, the name of which derives from a large dome that had been there and which was replaced by a Renaissance ceiling after the damage caused by the gunpowder explosion in 1590.

The Hall of the Kings occupies nearly all the eastern end and is reached by three openings with triple mocárabe arches that are supported by slender columns. This area features paintings dating from the late 14th or early 15th centuries, which shows ten Nasrid kings and which gives the space its name; it is attributed to an artist of Italian or French influence, inexpert in Arabic subject matter and fluent in Christian interpretations.

PATIO OF THE LIONS
Detail of one of the 124 columns that form the four arcaded galleries that surround it.

The northern gallery leads to the Hall of the Two Sisters, a square room with a marble floor that has a fountain in the centre. In terms of beauty, the most outstanding piece here is the mocárabe dome on the ceiling. The room is surrounded by a series of interior spaces featuring the Hall of the Ajimeces (mullioned windows) that connects with the wonderful Daraxa's Mirador, by means of a large pointed arch.

Opposite the Hall of the Two Sisters, in the southern part of the Palace is the Hall of the Abencerrajes, whose name derives from the 36 Abencerraje knights who were beheaded after rising up against Mohammed X. The room is crowned by an extraordinary mocárabe dome that extends its hanging prisms as far as the eight squinch arches that support it.

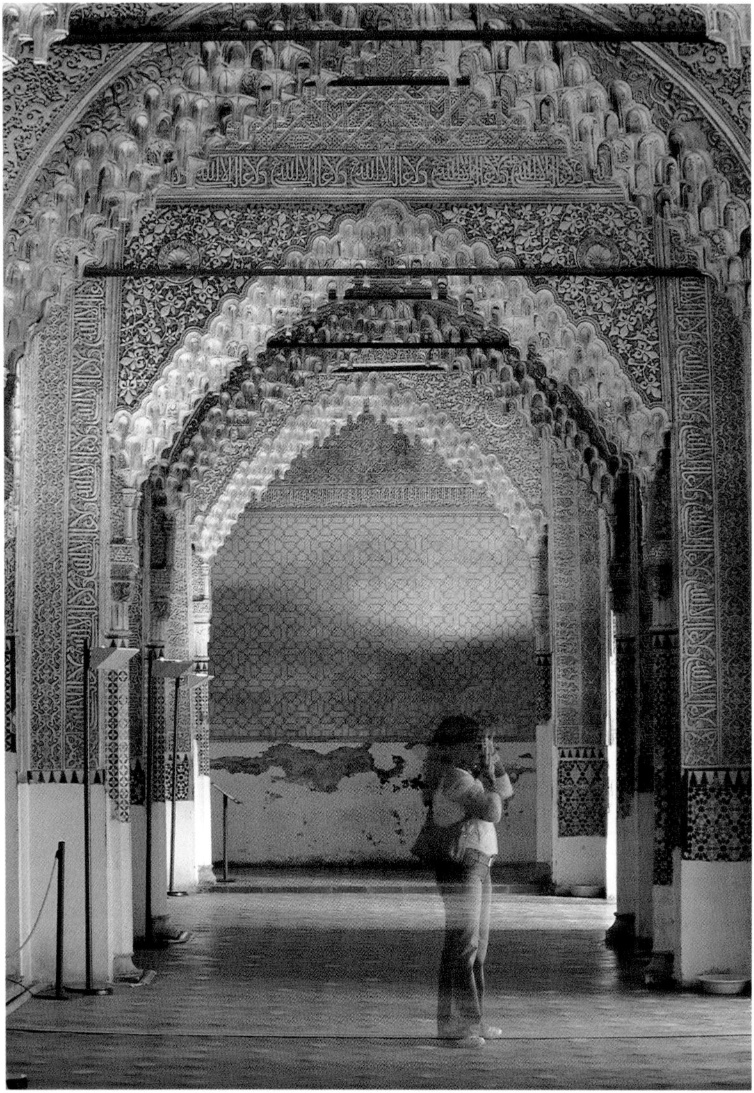

HALL OF THE KINGS
It is said that the monarchs of the Nasrid Kingdom slept here: the king at one end of the room and the queen at the other.

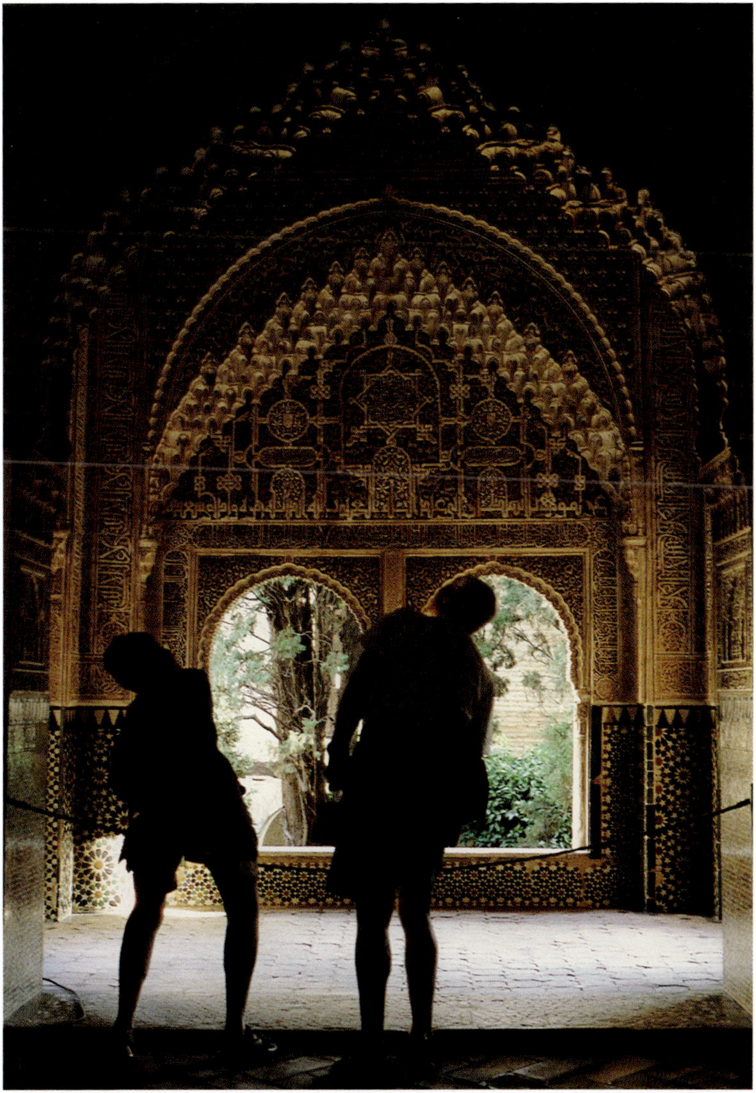

DARAXA'S MIRADOR
A corner of exquisite sculptural art.

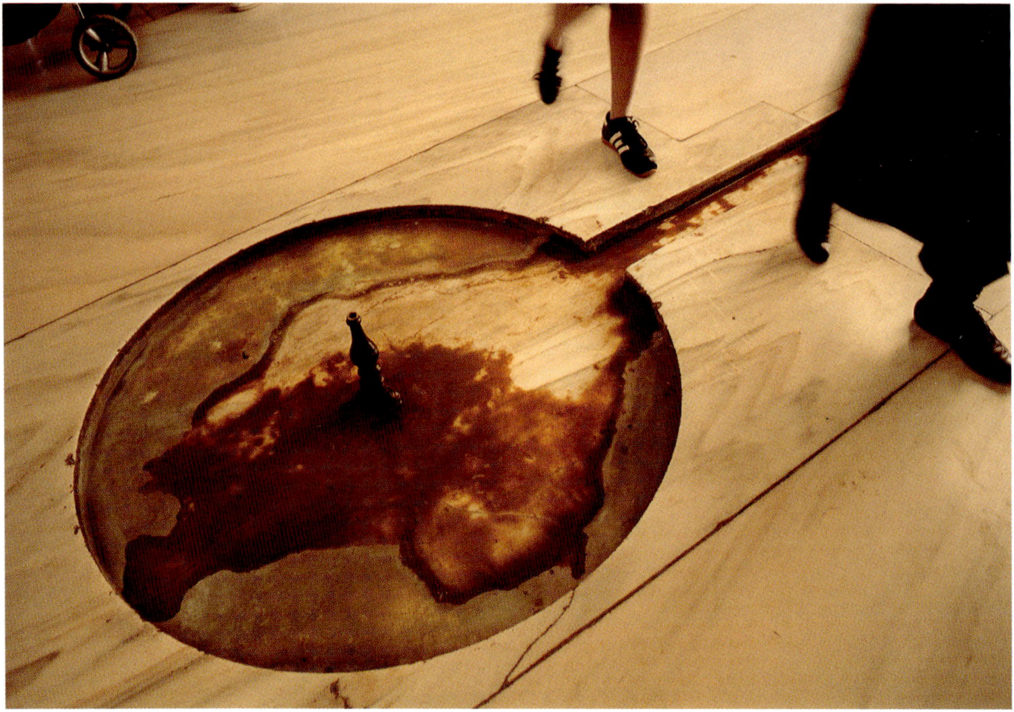

HALL OF THE TWO SISTERS
Fountain in the centre of the room.

HALL OF THE ABENCERRAJES
Dome that covers the room.

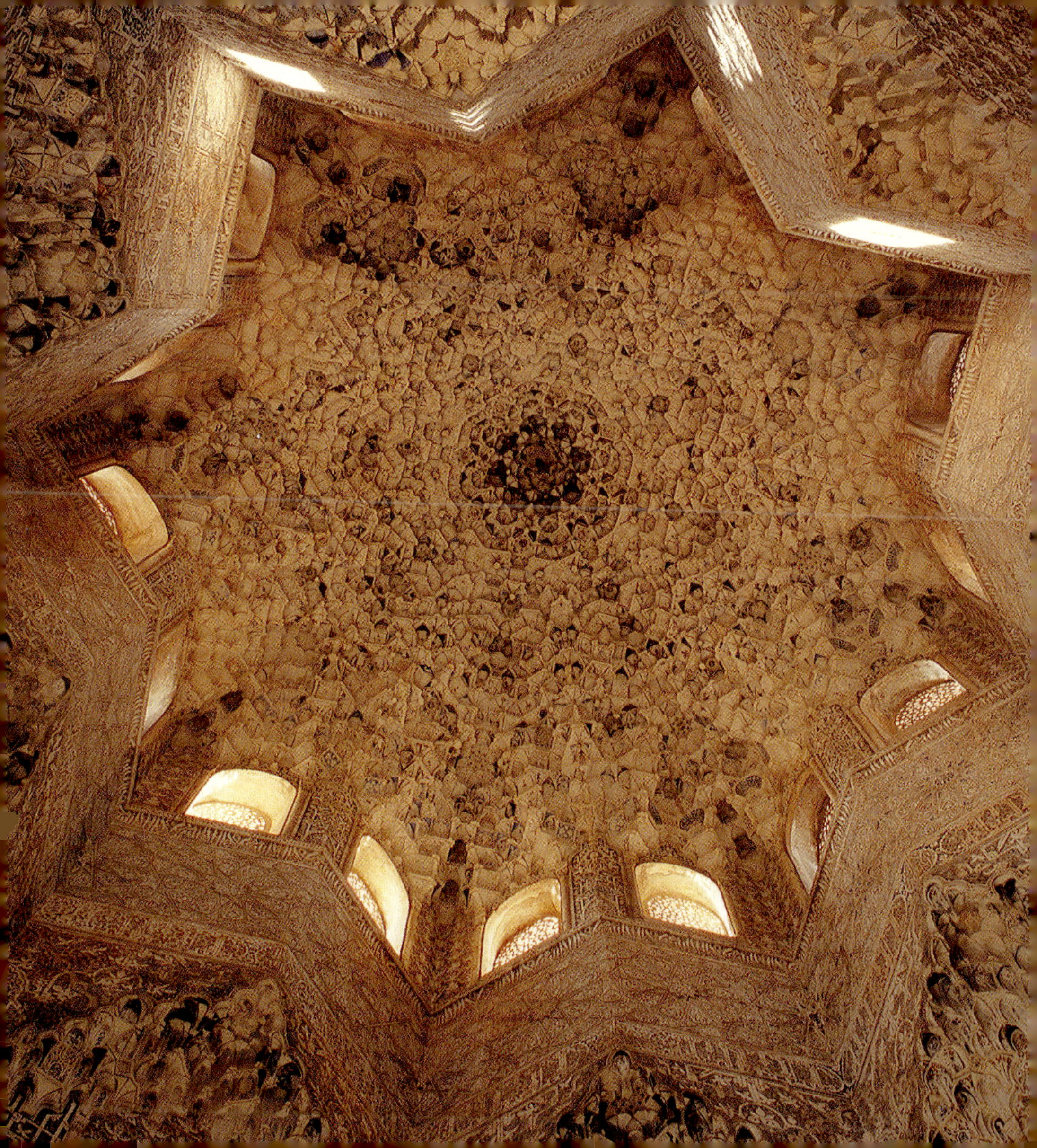

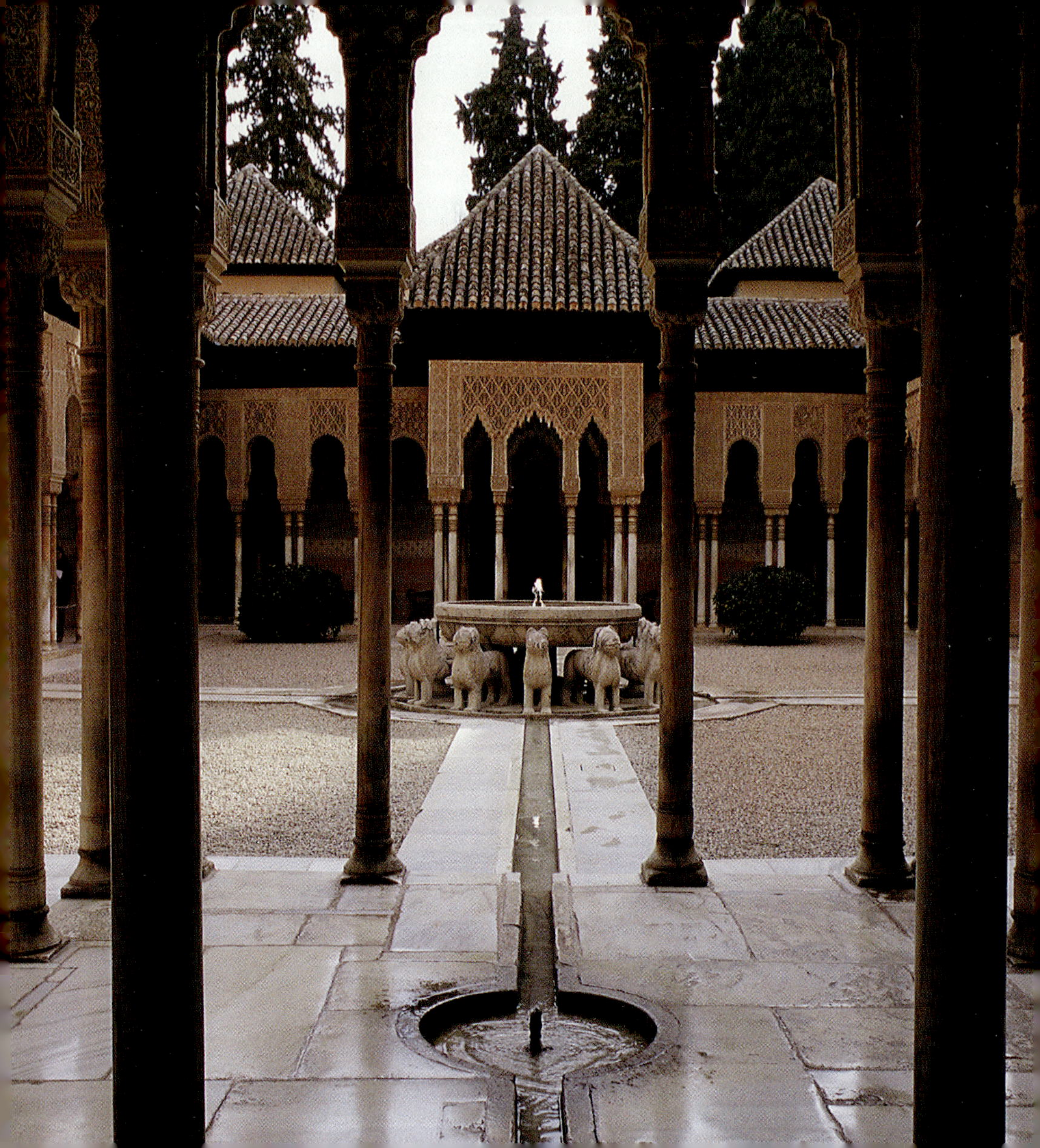

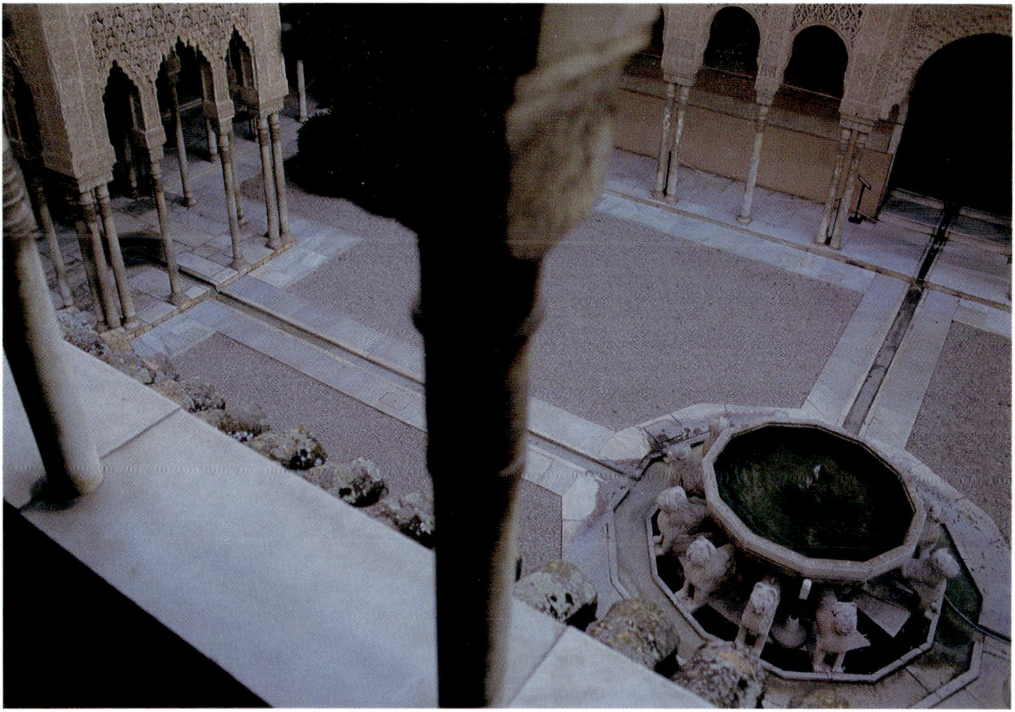

PATIO OF THE LIONS
The slenderness of the columns gives the whole space great elegance.

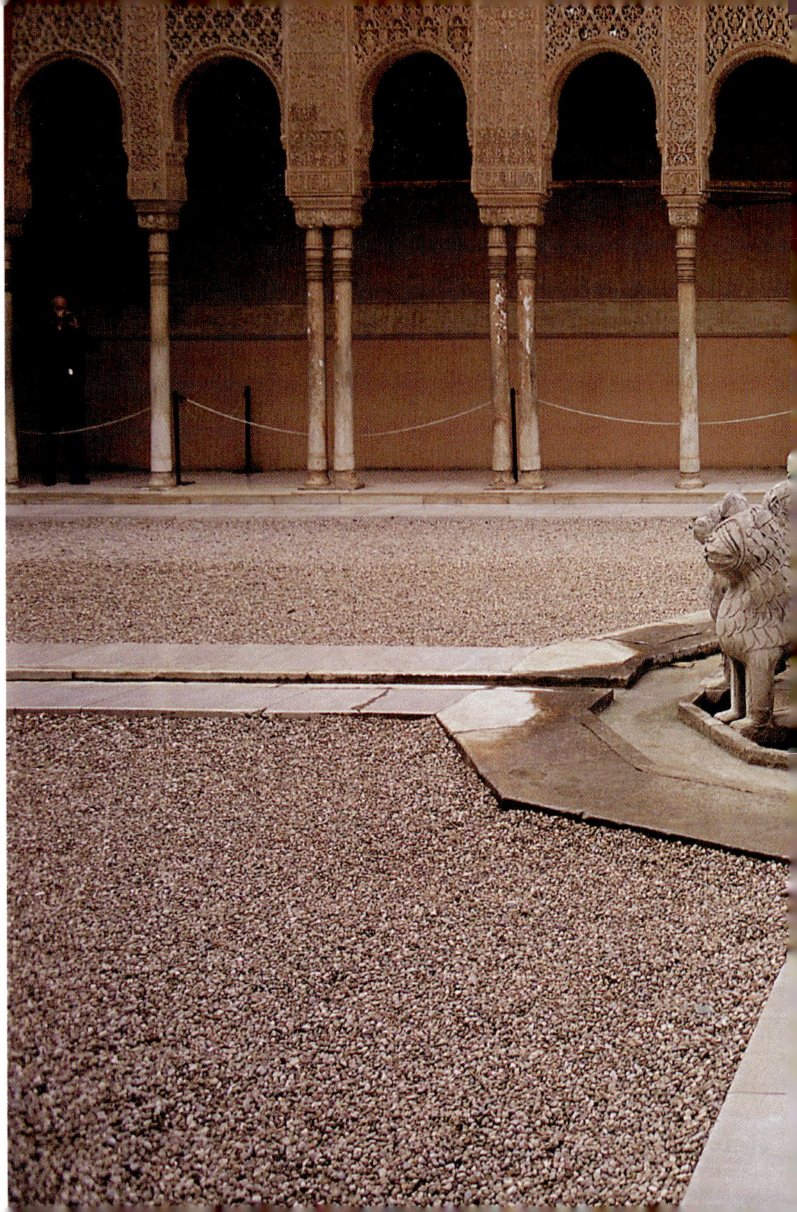

PATIO OF THE LIONS
The origin of the twelve lions in archaic forms that support the pile of the fountain is unknown. Some hypotheses tend towards the possibility that they may have come from another Hispano-Arab palace.

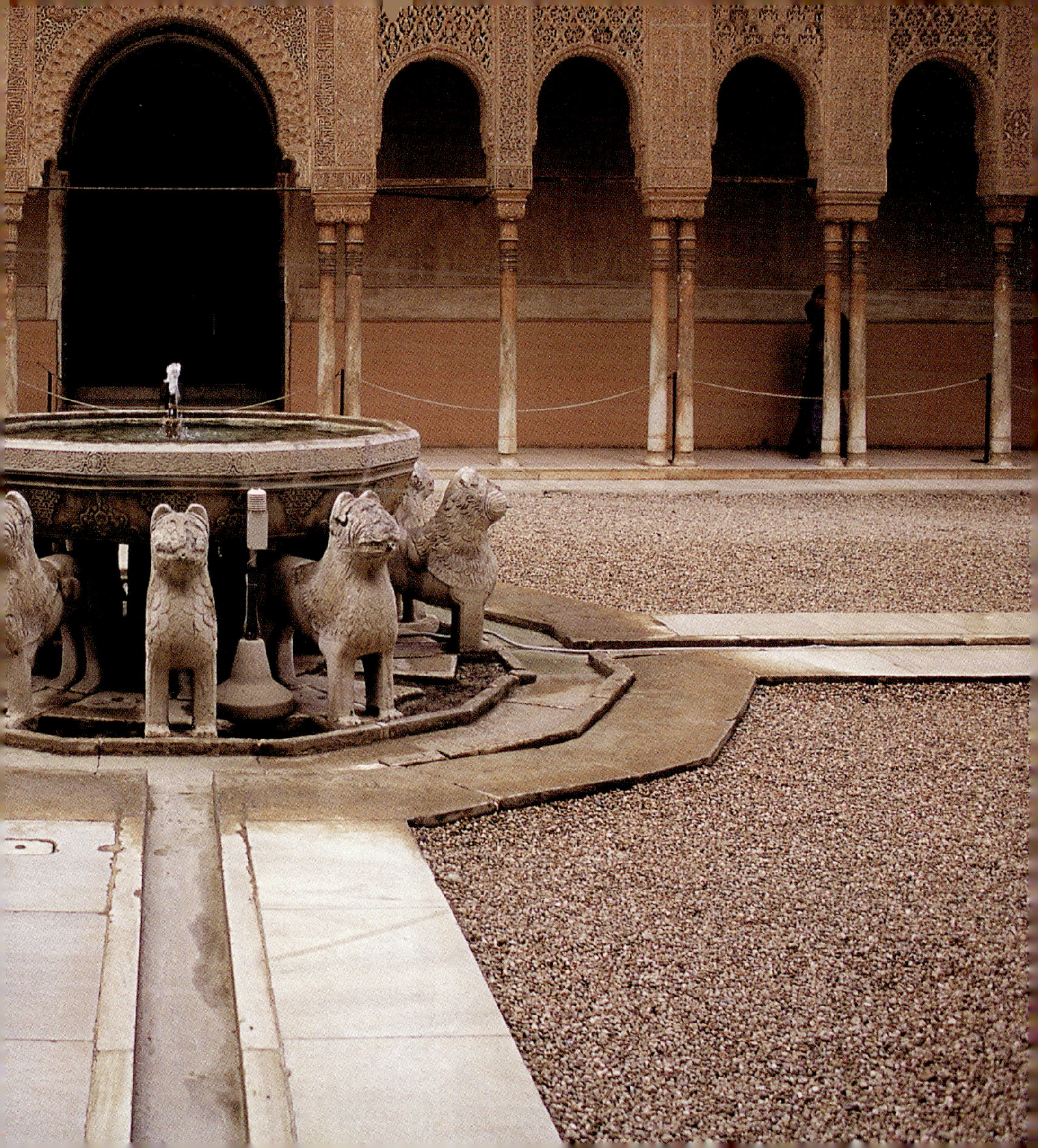

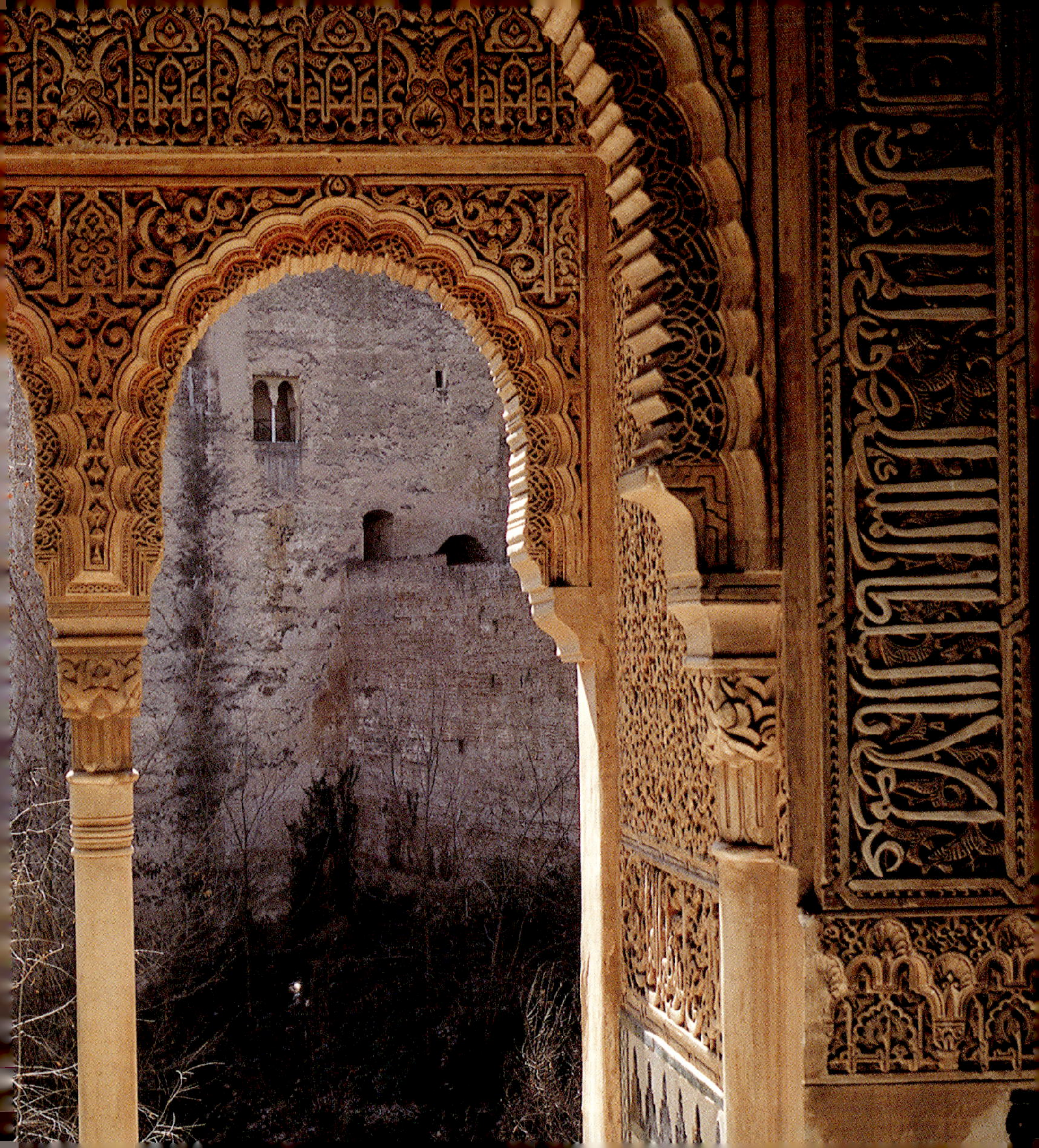

THE PARTAL AND ITS ENVIRONS

The modern Garden of the Partal occupies a space that originally housed some orchards and small palaces of the noble families settled alongside the royal palaces. Out of all the constructions the Ladies Tower is the best-preserved, with a portico of five horseshoe arches reflected in a pool that recalls the Persians. It is just one façade of the four that made up a wonderful palace.

Alongside the Tower are three houses that were almost certainly for the servants who worked in the palaces. The house closest to the wall has some interesting but badly damaged Arabic paintings, which were discovered in 1907 during some renovation work. They represent a unique example in their genre of the territories dominated by the Arabs on the peninsula.

In the highest area of the gardens there are archaeological remains that outline the buildings belonging to the Muslim elite of Granada, and the Rauda, which housed the royal cemetery alongside the Great Mosque, where today the church of Santa María stands.

TOWER OF THE POINTS
In the background, the Tower of the Captive.

Above the parapet walk of the wall, to the right of the Ladies Tower, stands the beautiful Tower of the Mihrab. The inside houses an oratory, with attractive decoration, which was almost certainly for the use of the people who lived in the neighbouring palace. Higher up, following the parapet walk eastwards, is the singular Tower of the Points, given this name because of its pointed merlons that were added by the Christians. A little further east, the Tower of the Cadi, facing the narrow street that led to the old entrance of the Generalife and the Tower of the Captive, which was inhabited by Zoraya, sultan Muley Abul Hassan's favourite wife, a Christian converted to Islam who answered to the name of Lady Isabel de Solís.

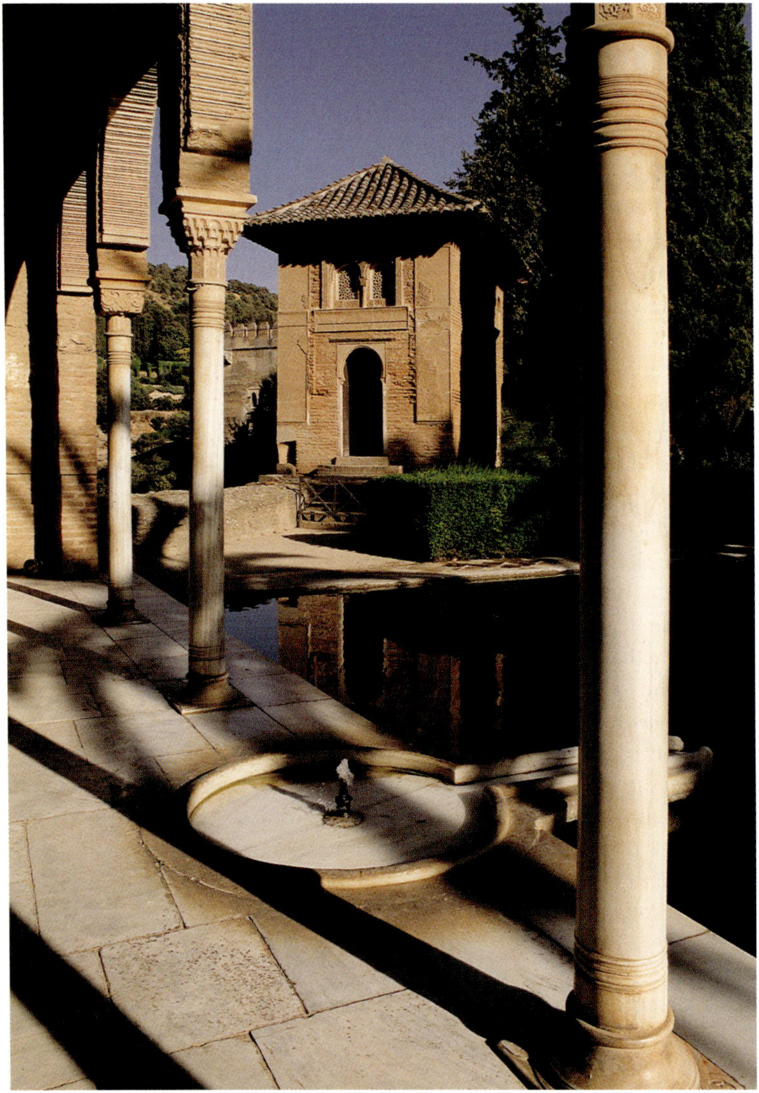

TOWER OF THE MIHRAB
Seen from the portico of the Ladies Tower.

LADIES TOWER
Previously known as the Tower of the Prince; Fernando VI, the Prince of Asturias, lived there.

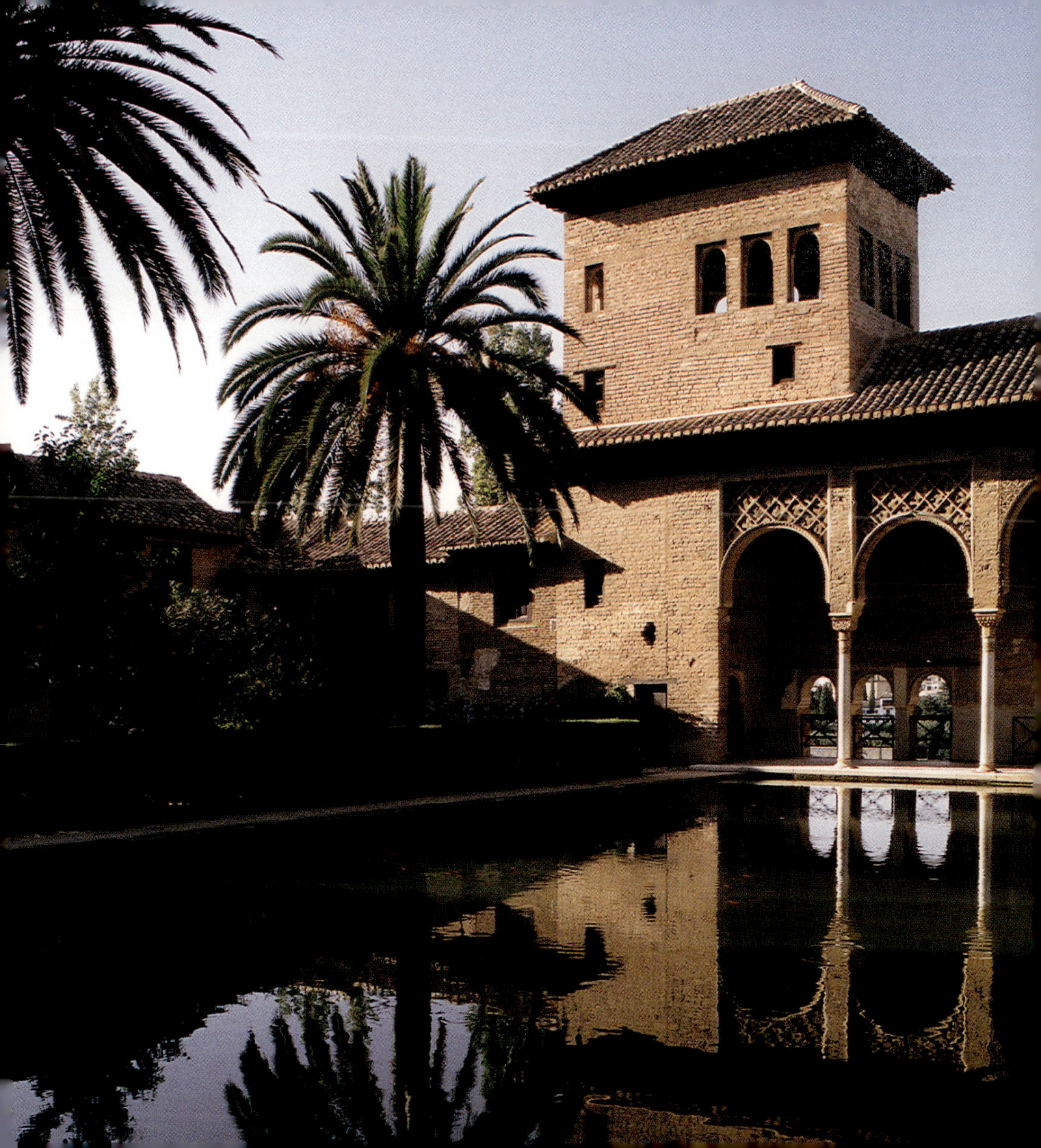

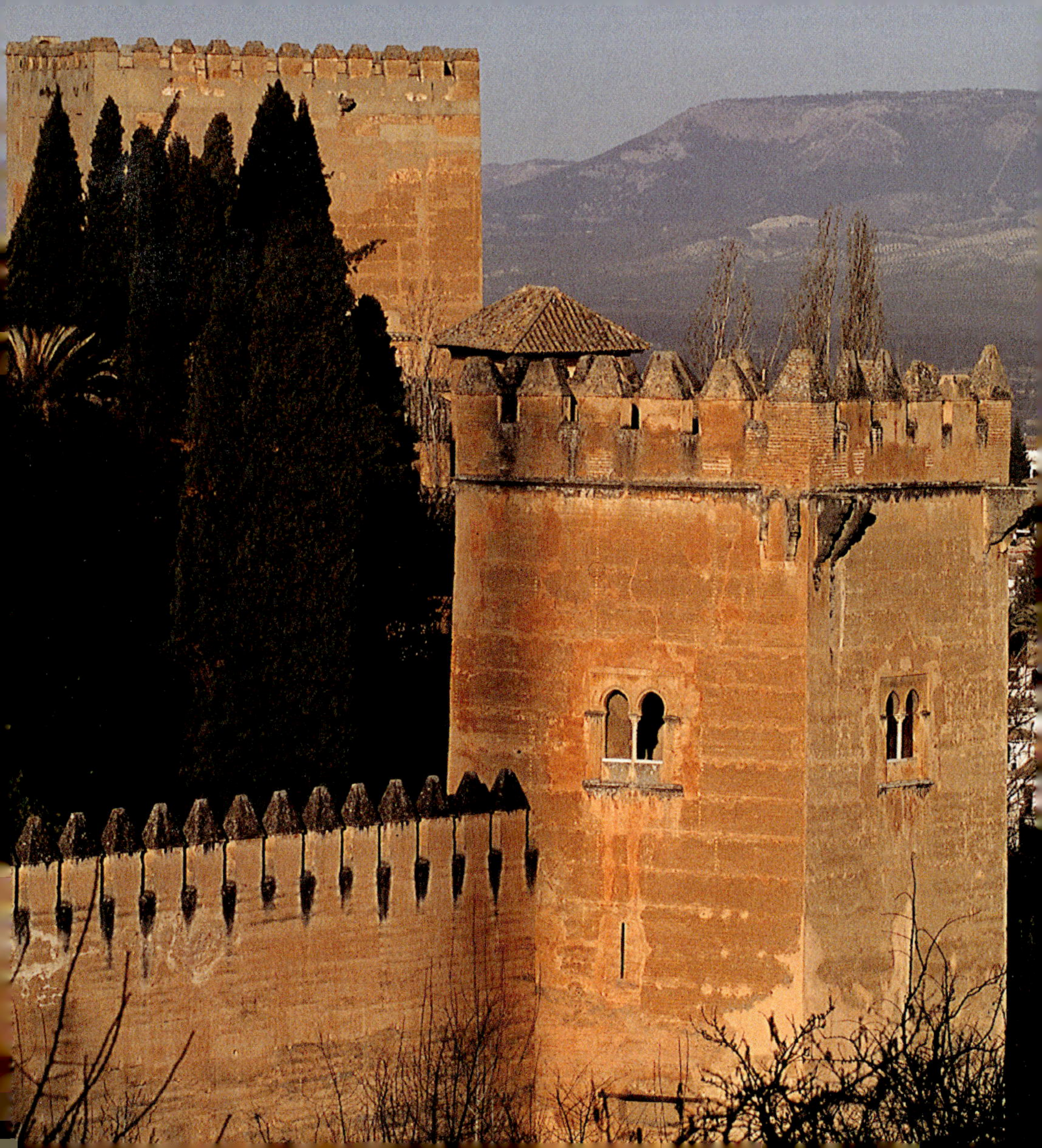

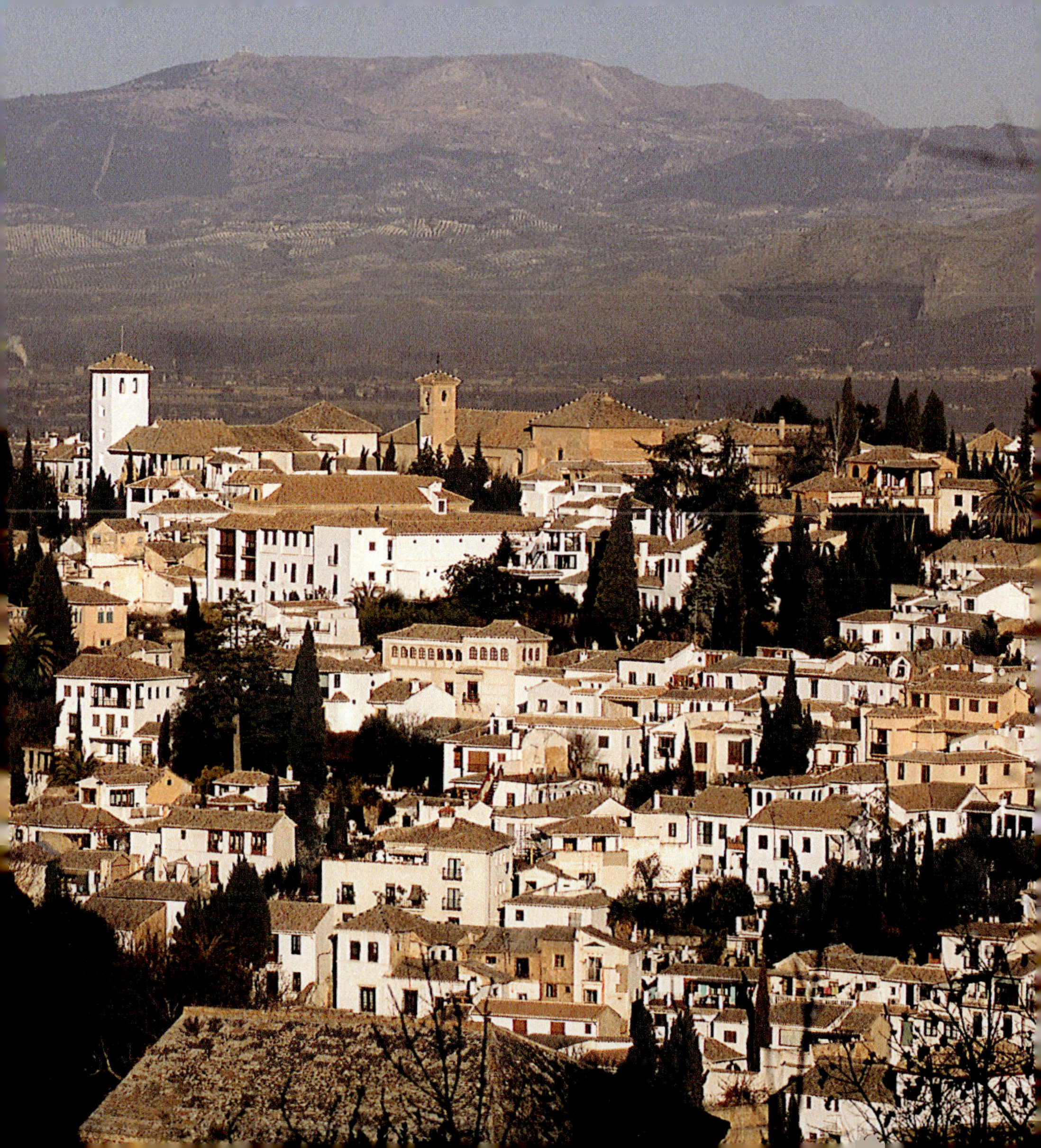

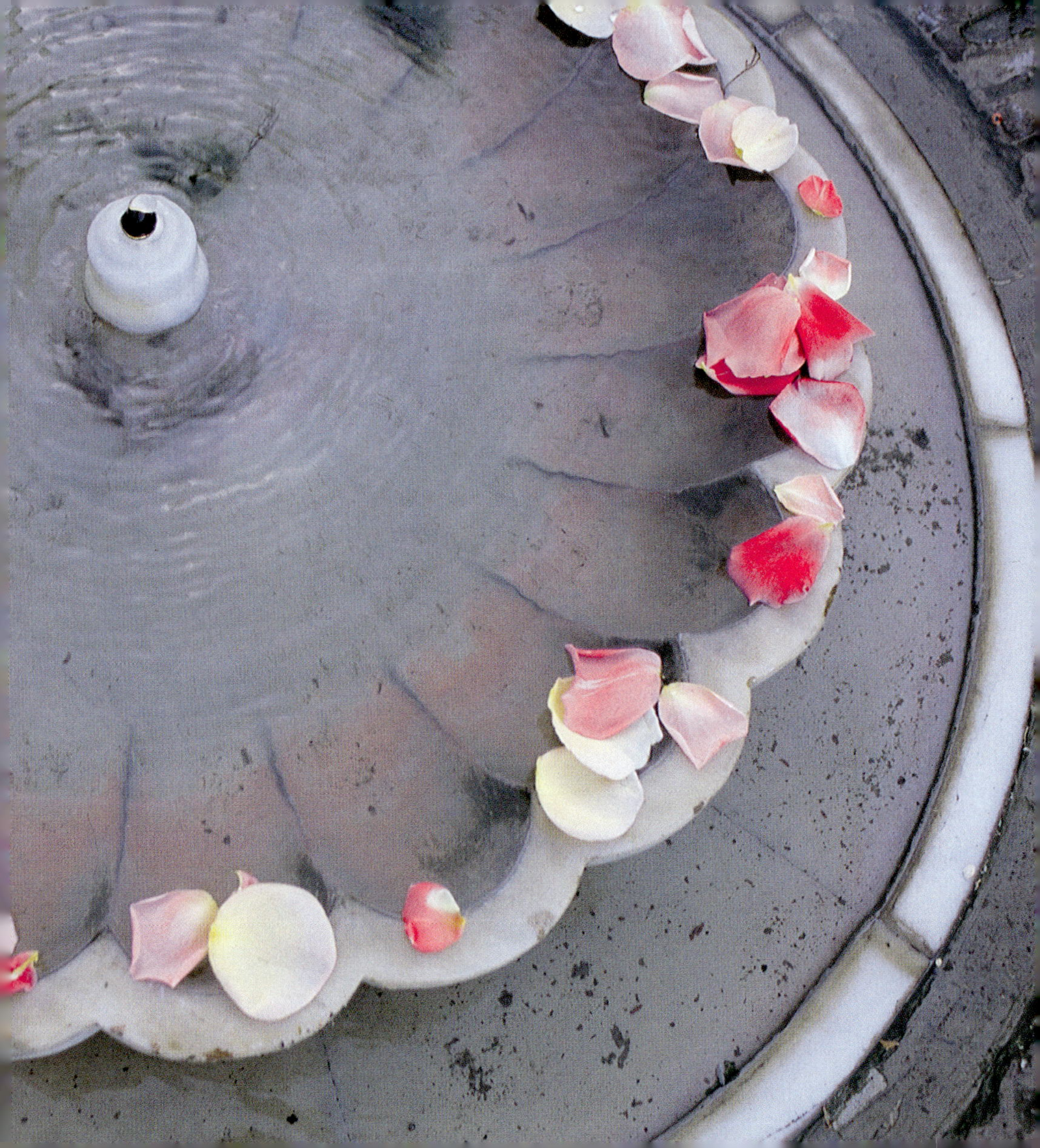

THE GENERALIFE

Spread along the side of the Cerro del Sol, to the east of the walls that surround the Alhambra and connected directly to it by the Iron Gateway, is the Generalife: the house and gardens where the sultan could cut himself off from official court life. Its name comes from *Yannat al-Arif*, "the architect's garden". According to Arab chronicles of the time it was bought from an architect to be turned into a royal villa for relaxing. Although the exact date of its construction is not known, it seems that it was there from at least the mid-13th century. Some inscriptions made during the reform work carried out in 1319 by King Abu l-Walid Ismail are proof that it must have been built during the previous dynasty.

The grounds are made up of some gardens full of quiet spaces and a palace, the original design of which is very difficult to see clearly, since it has been subject to a great many restorations and reforms since the arrival of the Christians. The purely Arab elements have been reduced to almost only a couple of porticoes, the pool, the viewpoint of the western nave and some arches, ornaments and capitals scattered around different rooms. The royal leisure palace is organised around the exceptional Patio of the Acequia (waterway), a large rectangular space divided in its main part by a pool, over which is spread an endless number of water spouts that create a spectacular visual display, embellished by the murmur of the water. Just above is the Patio of the Sultana, an enigmatic corner that has inspired passionate legends of sultanas seduced by handsome knights. We should continue climbing to reach the high gardens, a labyrinth of leafy vegetation where the surprising Water Stairway is, perhaps of Arab origin, with the water of the Royal Waterway running down the handrails.

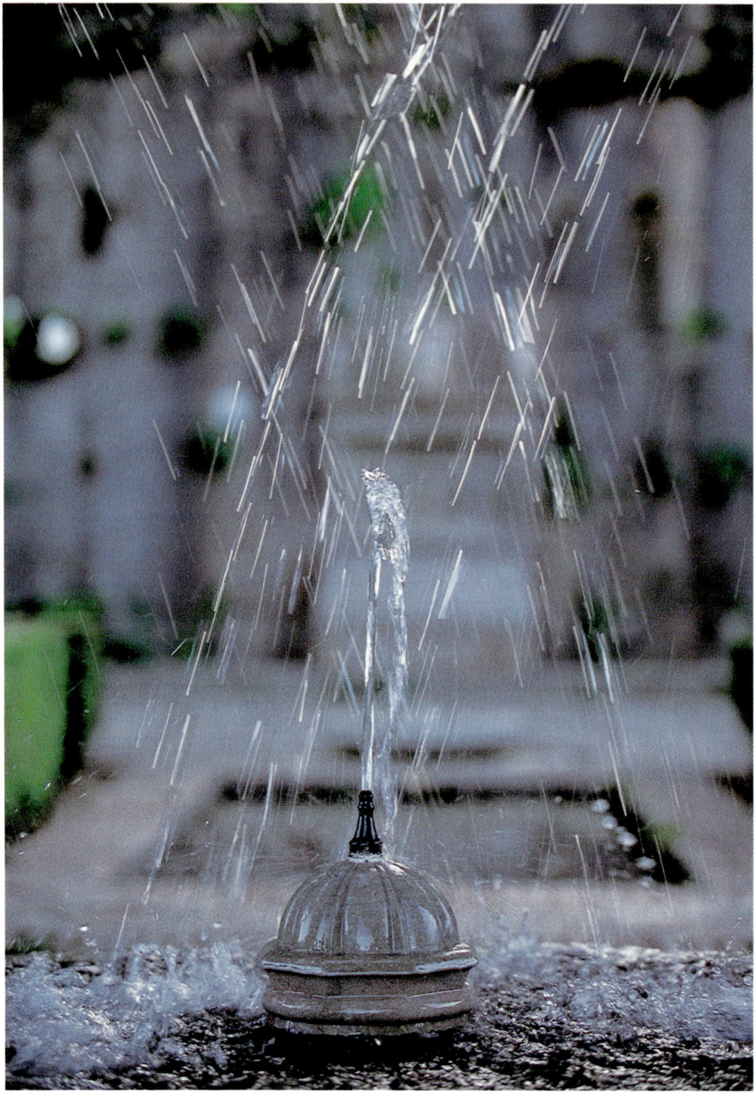

GARDENS
The murmur of water follows the visitor all around the Generalife.

In the background, the Tower of the Princesses.

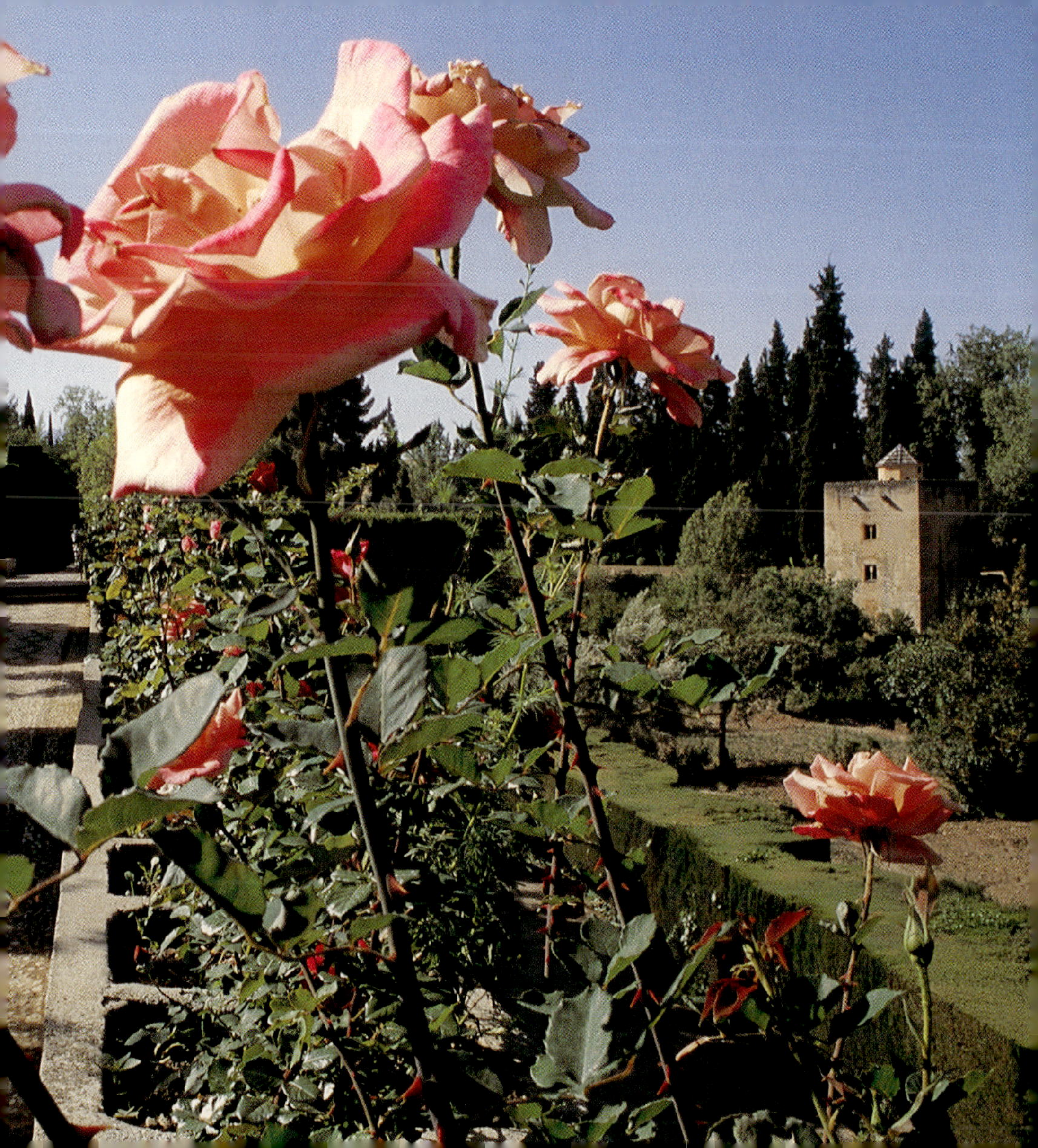

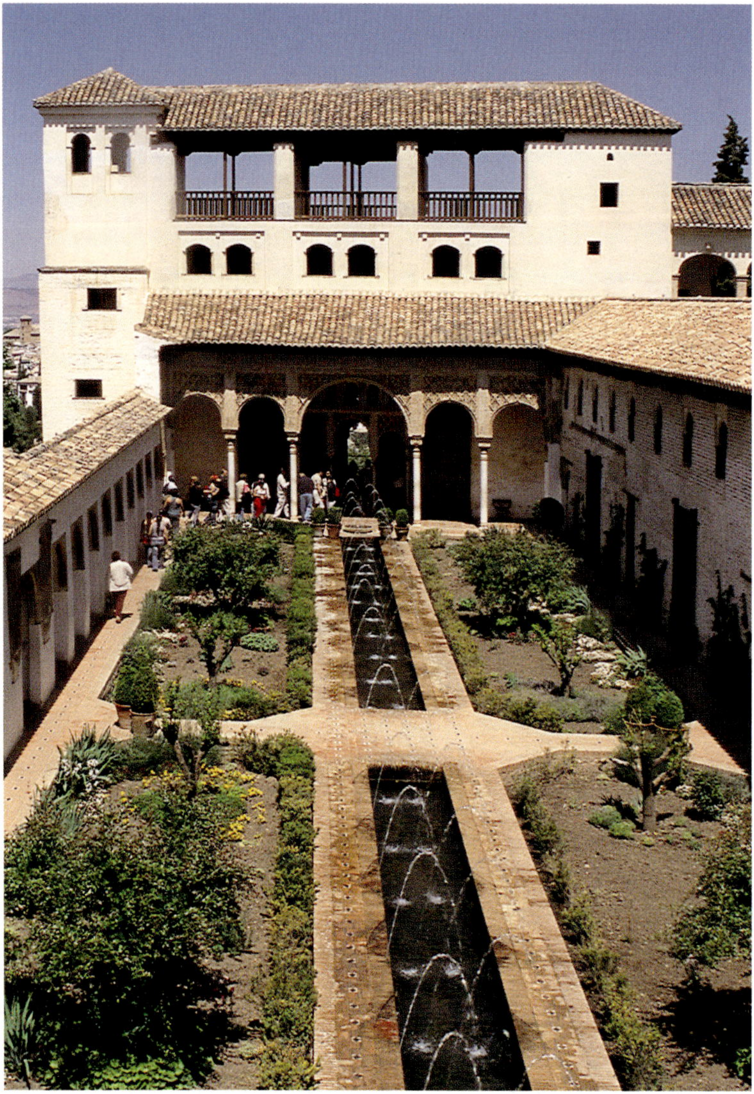

PATIO OF THE ACEQUIA
Due to its characteristics and use for leisure, it must have emulated the paradigm of the Koranic garden, a spot where water and shade form an integral part of the design.

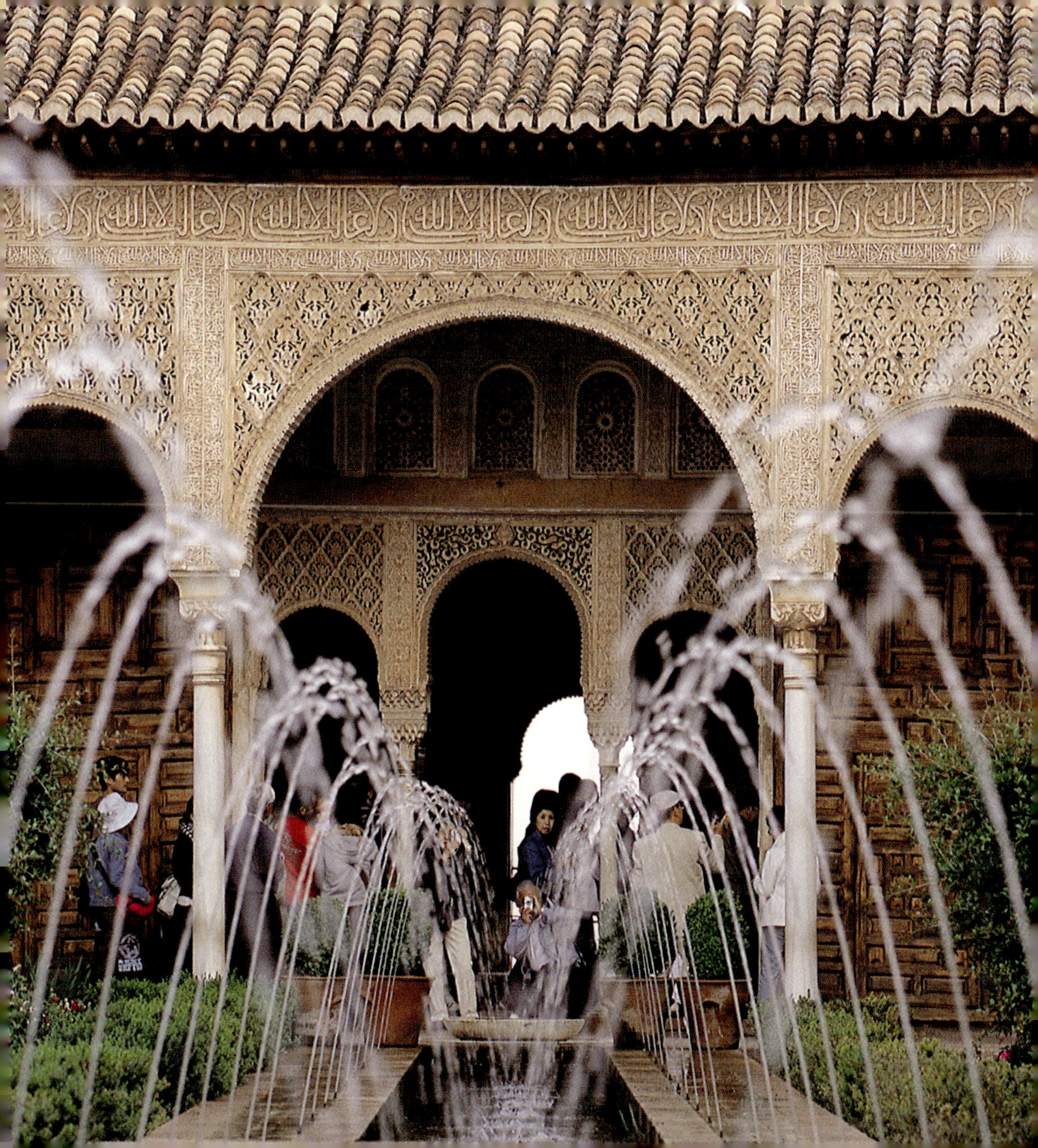

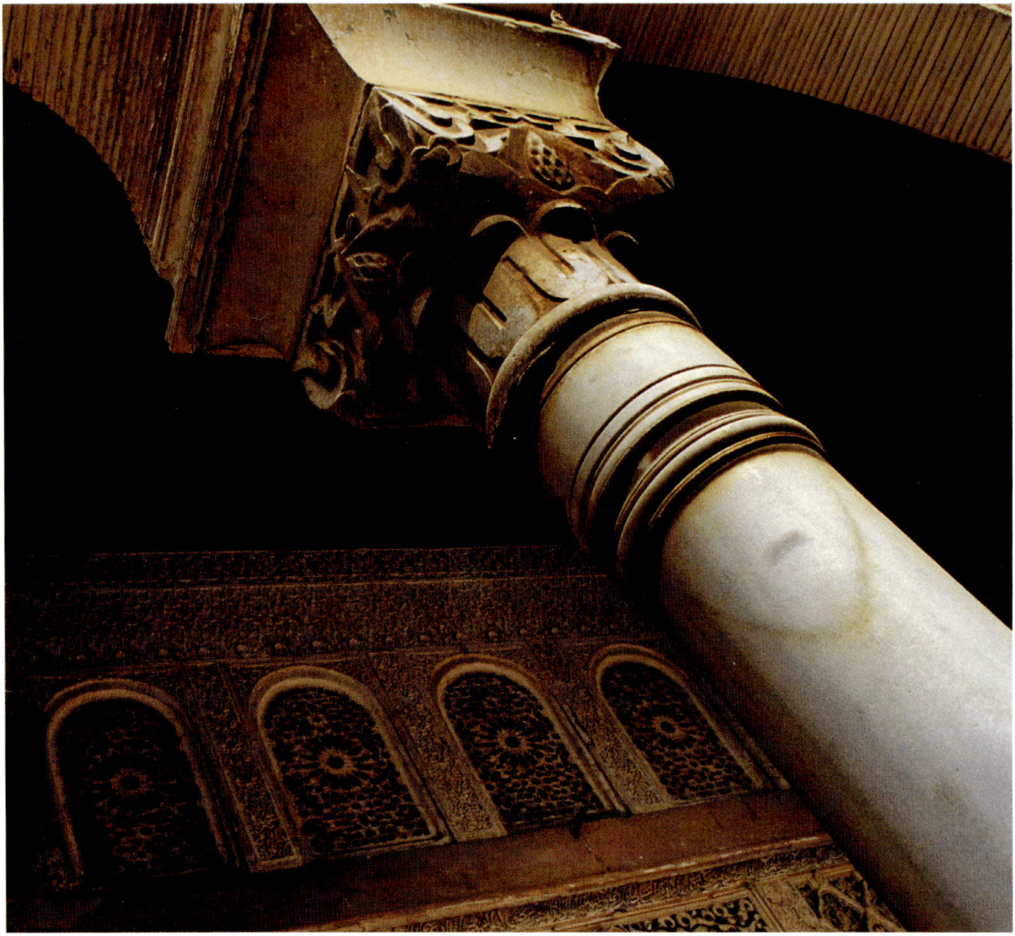

PATIO OF THE ACEQUIA
Detail of the north portico.

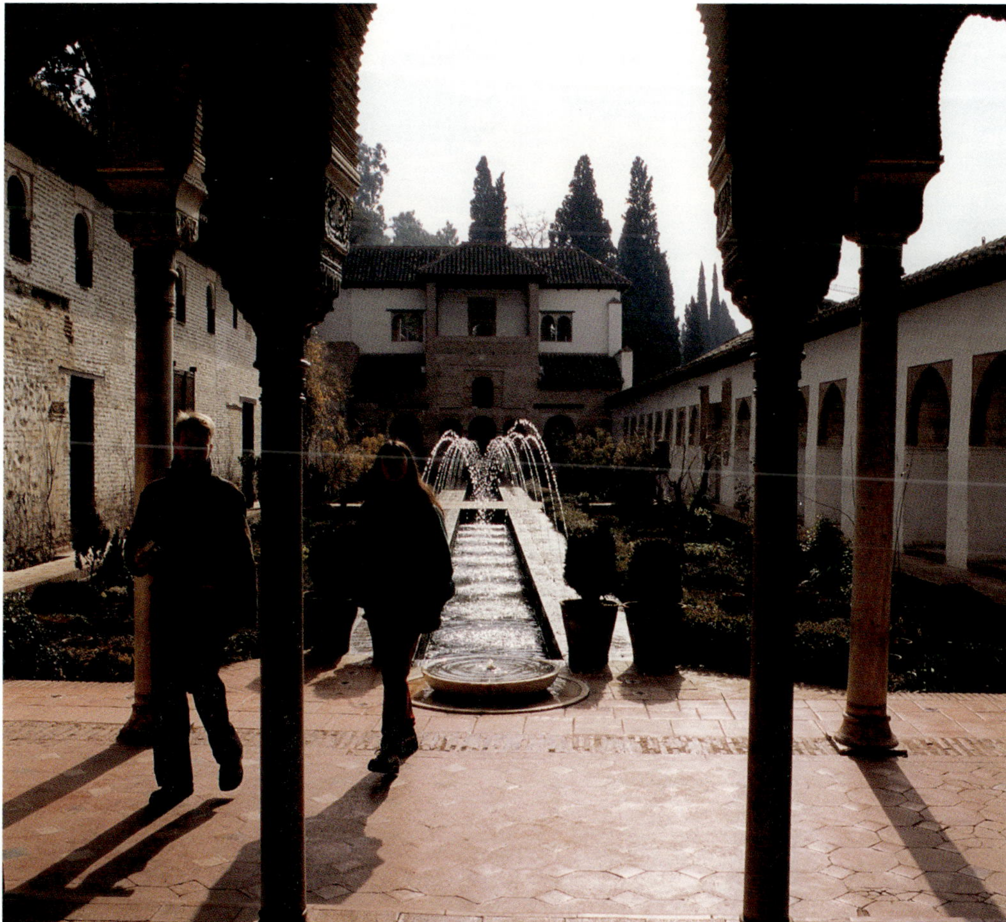

PATIO OF THE ACEQUIA
View of the pool from the north portico.

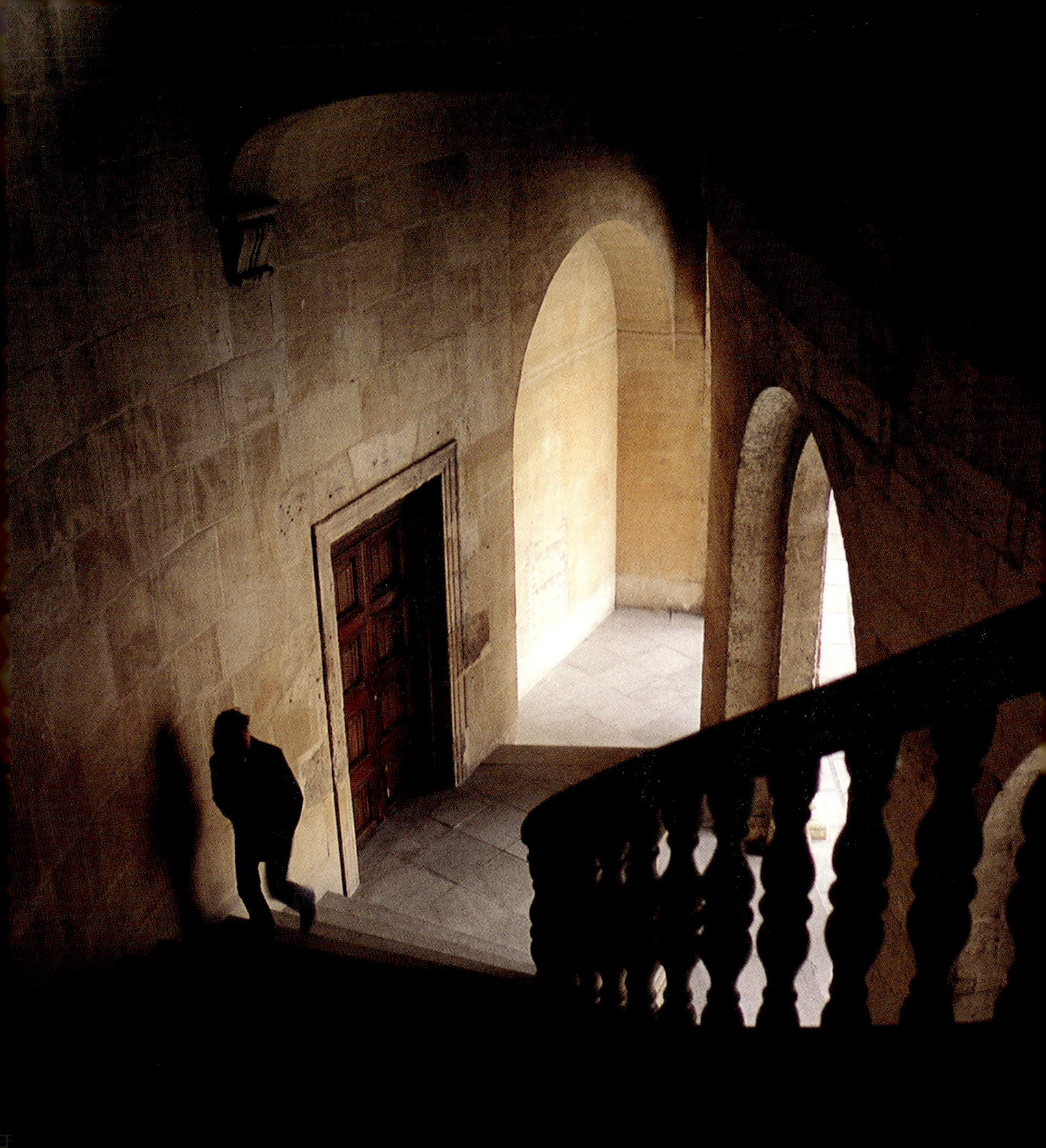

THE PALACE OF CHARLES V

In the summer of 1526, Emperor Charles V spent the first months of his married life with Isabel of Portugal in Granada. He was so fascinated by the magic of Nasrid art that he ordered a palace to be built within the Alhambra to establish one of his residences there. The construction must have responded to the requirements of a monarch at that time, since the ancient Arab royal palace did not meet those needs, but at the same time it had to be integrated into it in order not to lose its particular charms. Pedro Machuca, an architect from Toledo who studied in Italy alongside Michelangelo, is the author of the work, and the project was continued by his son and many more architects until its conclusion in 1957, when the architectural management of the Alhambra was under the direction of Prieto Moreno, who covered the second gallery of the patio.

INTERIOR PATIO OF THE PALACE
Stairs leading to the arcaded second floor.

This palace is the antithesis of the Nasrid Palaces. Before an ephemeral and sober exterior architecture, the emperor built a construction with four massive ostentatious façades in worked stone, which ensured longstanding durability of the regal Renaissance building. Outside it is divided into two sections: the lower part is of a Tuscan order with dressed stone ashlars that stand out considerably on the pilasters; and from the top section springs a large skirting with an identical arrangement to the lower area but much more refined. The central part of the two main façades has two sculptural doorways in grey marble from Sierra Elvira. The large round inner patio, with two floors arcaded by a gallery of columns, Doric in the first floor and Ionic on the second floor, leads to the rooms. Today the palace rooms house the Fine Arts Museum and the Alhambra Museum.

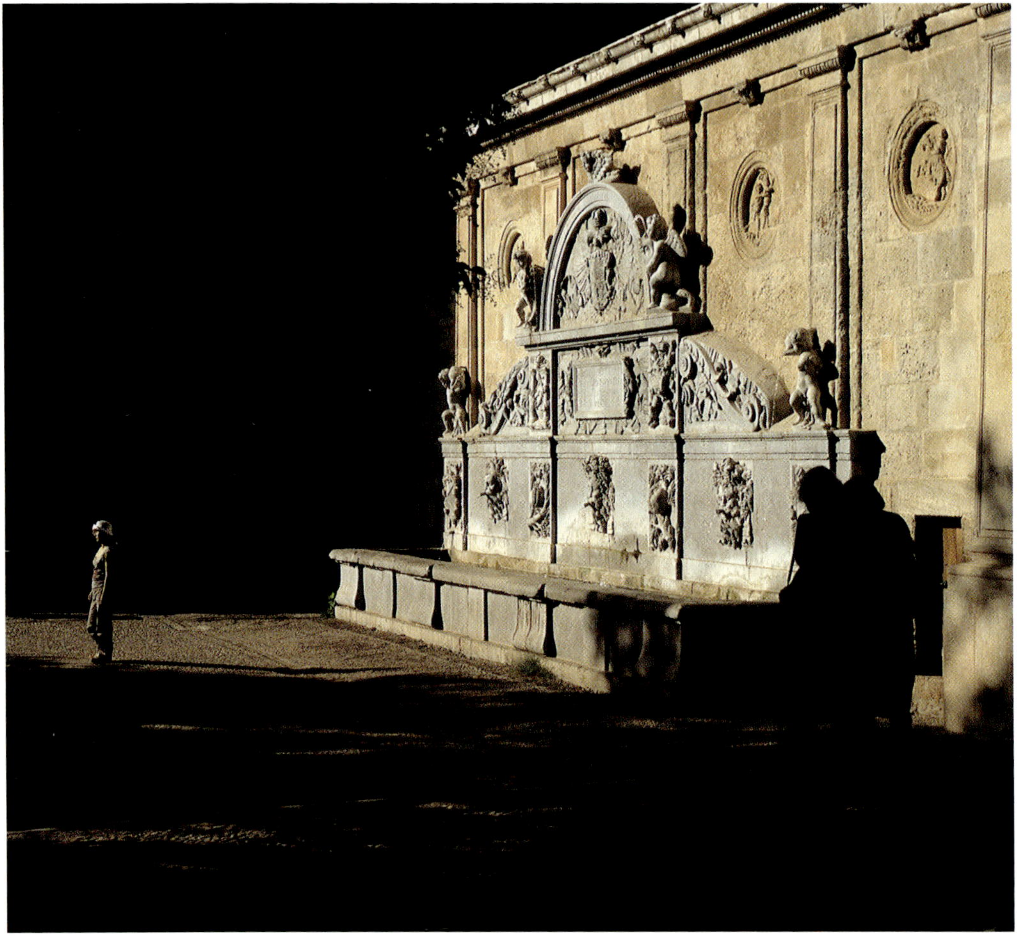

FOUNTAIN OF CHARLES V
It was ordered to be built by Count Tendilla in 1545.

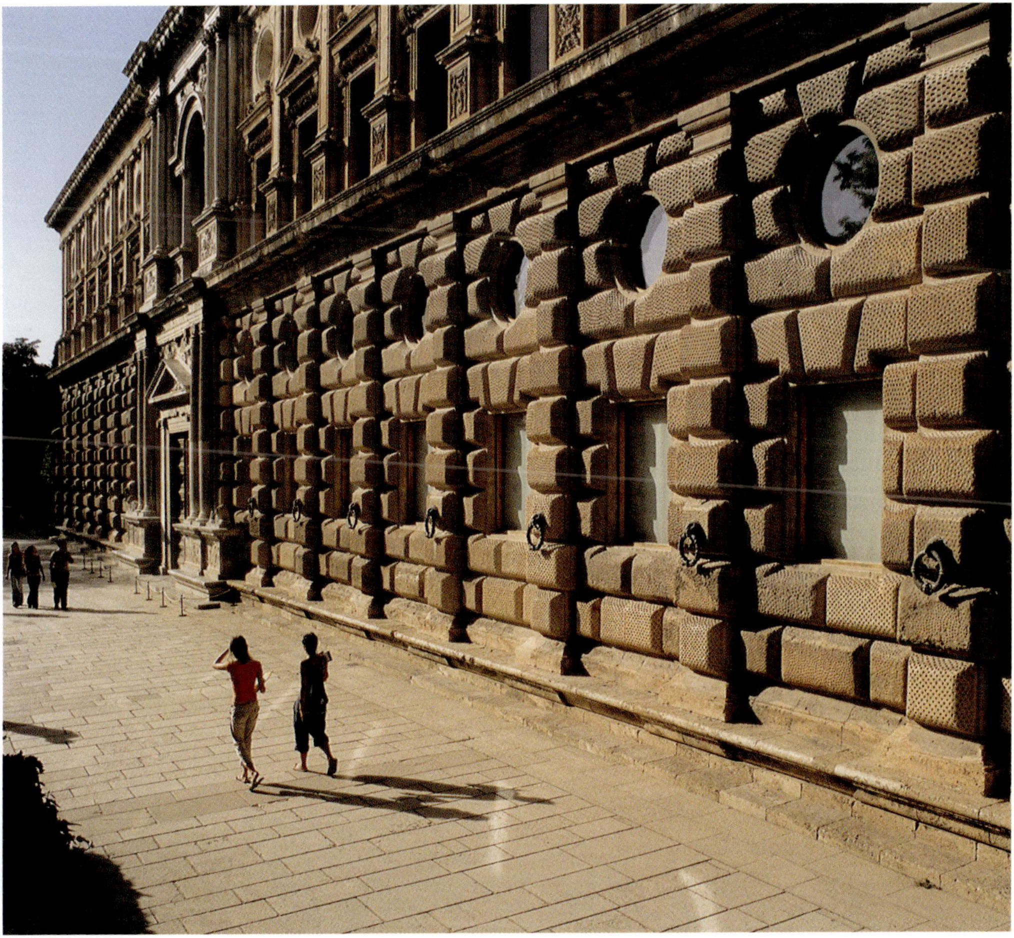

EXTERIOR FAÇADE OF THE PALACE
The building is square, measuring 63 metres in length and is 17.4 metres high.

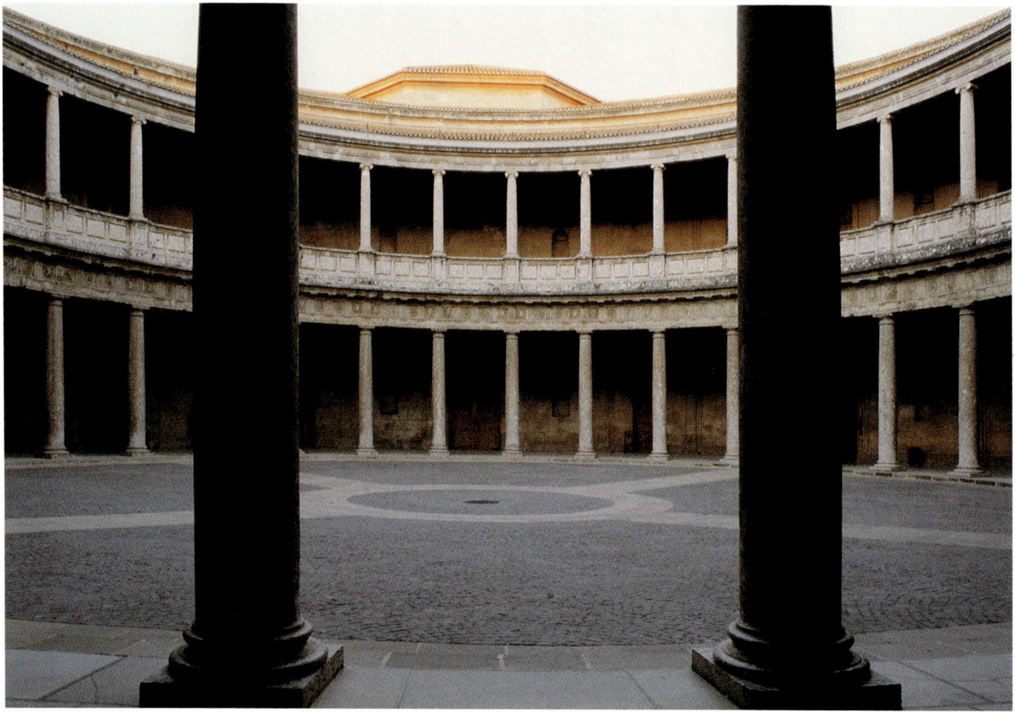

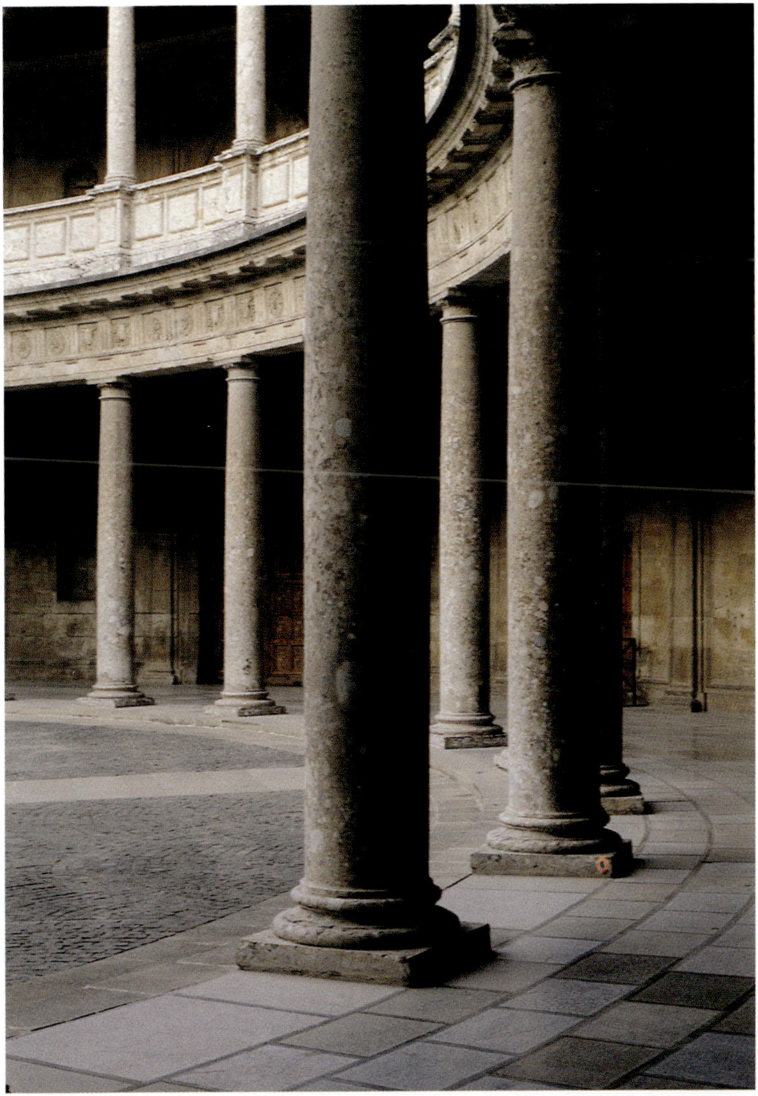

INTERIOR PATIO OF THE PALACE
Its size is quite startling. Outside of Italy, it is one of the most beautiful Renaissance palaces. The solidity of the construction is no obstacle in demonstrating great elegance.

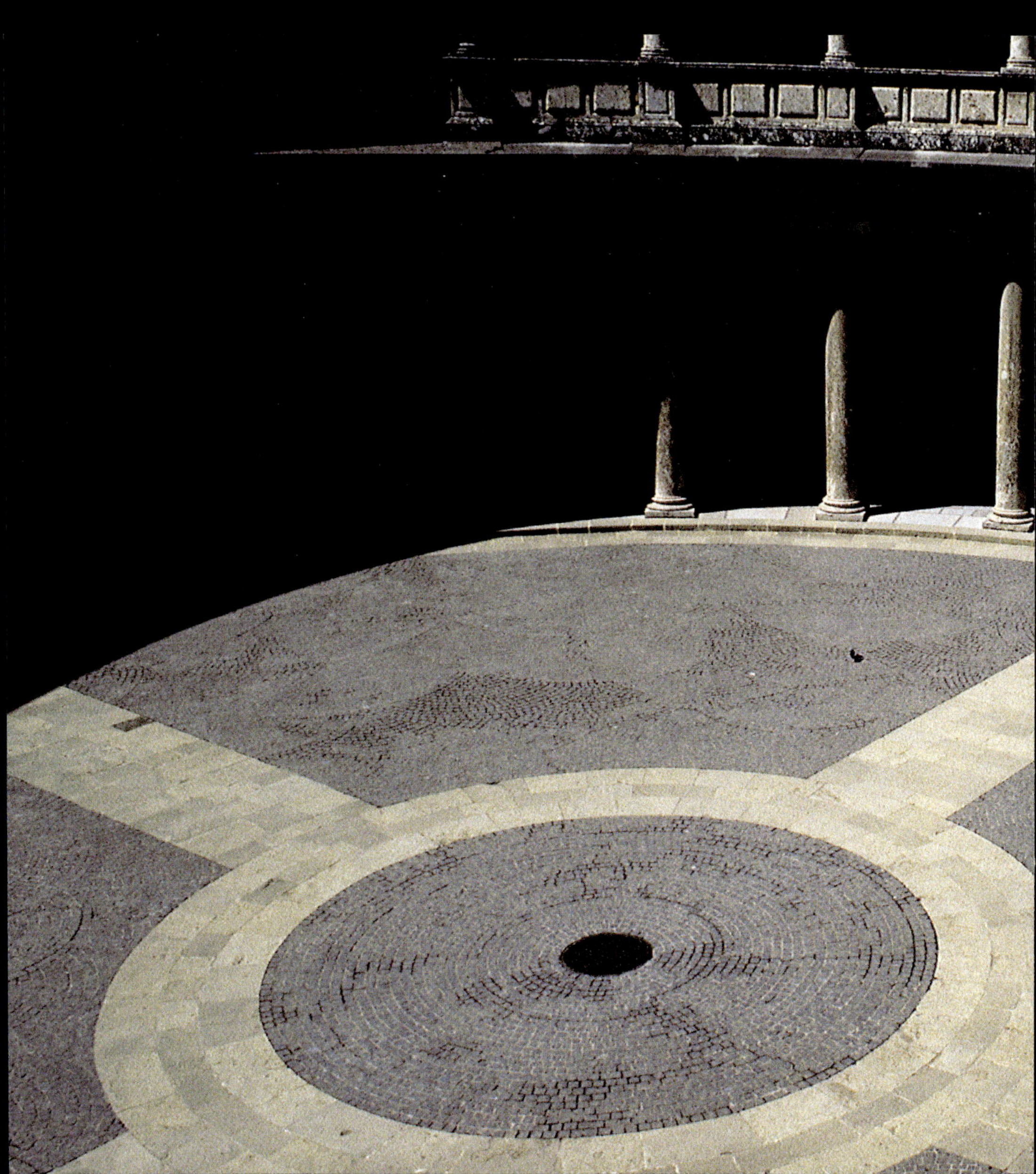

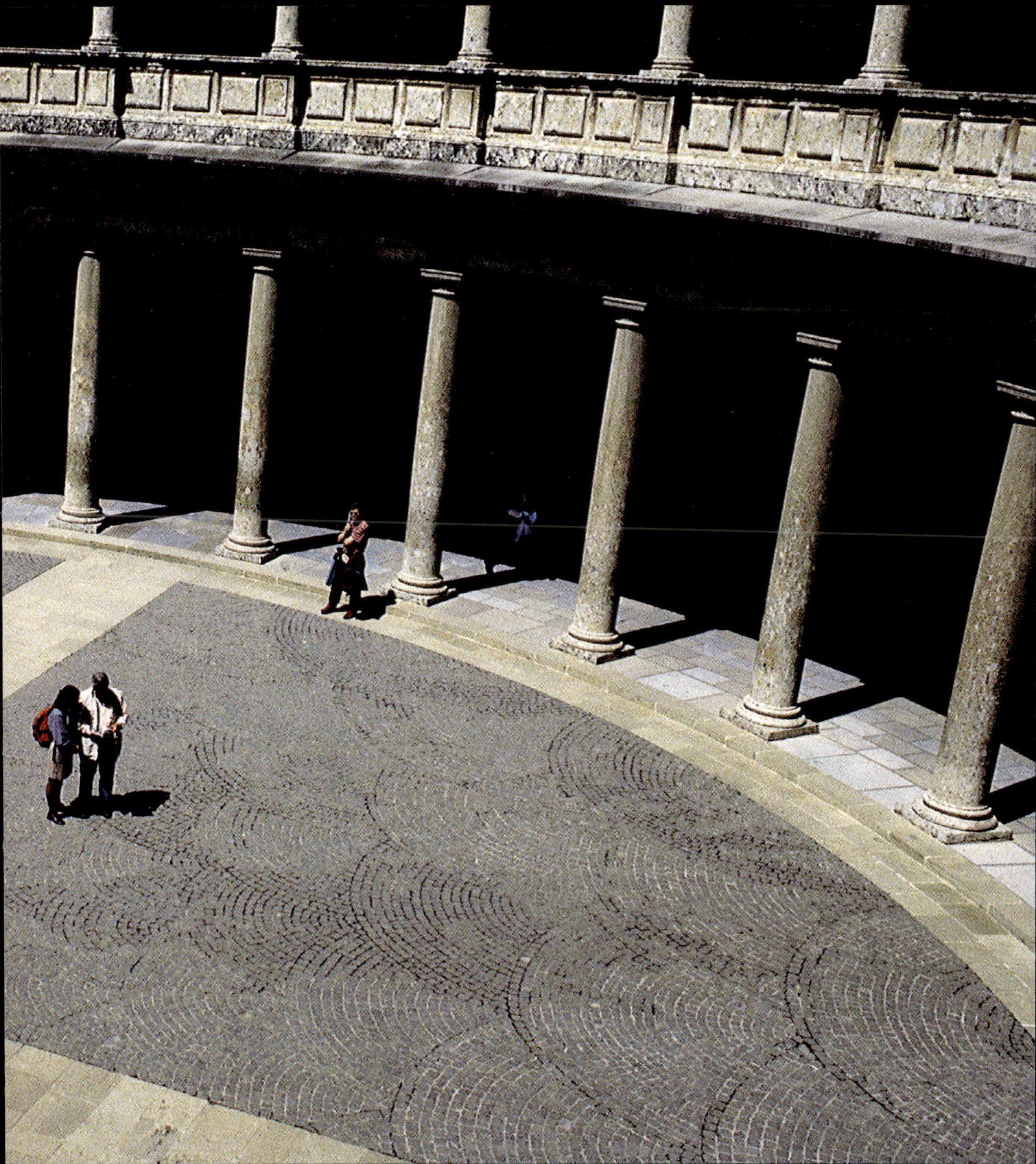

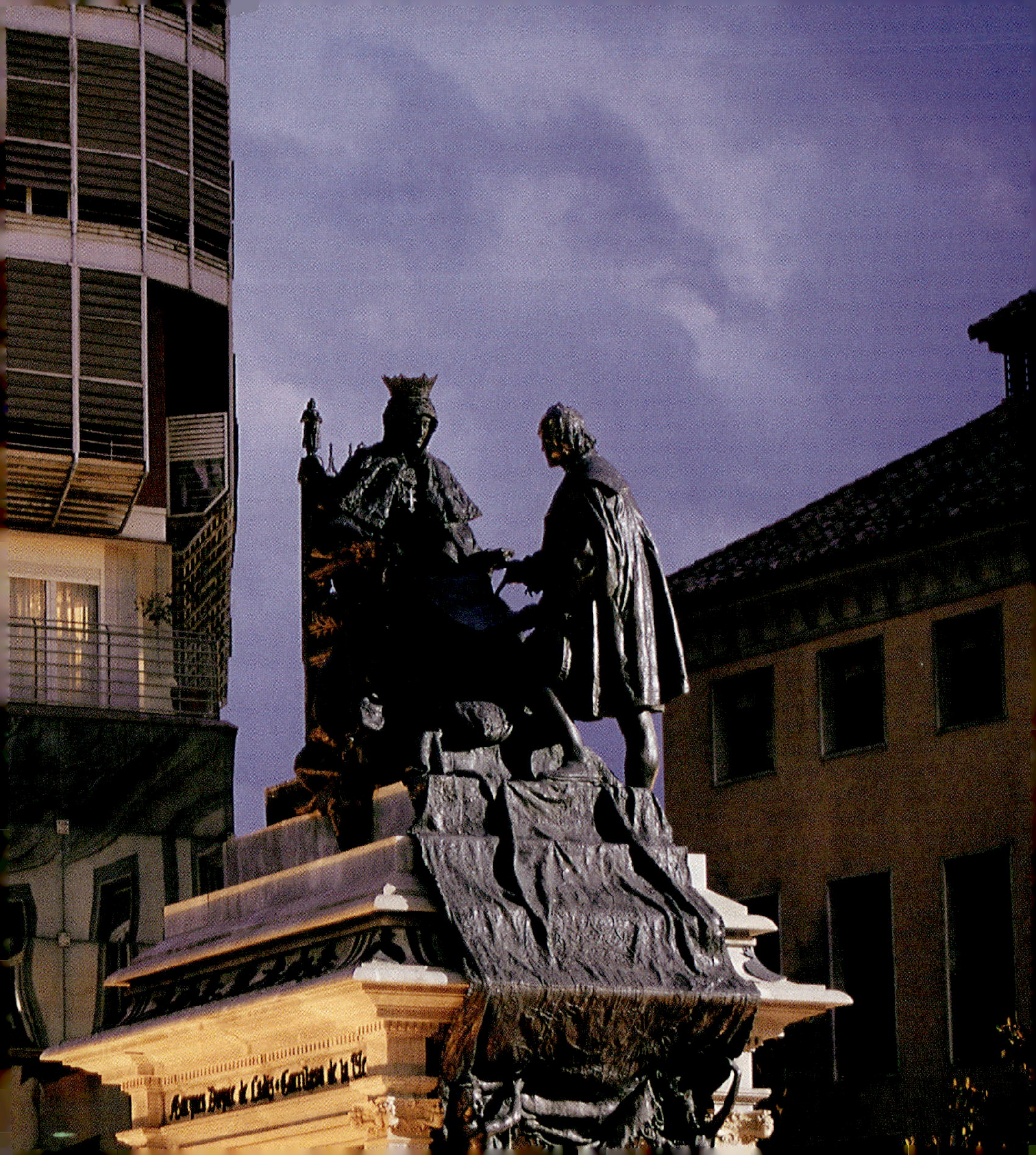

THE CITY

PLAZA DE ISABEL LA CATÓLICA
Sculpture by Mariano Benlliure that represents Christopher Columbus speaking with Isabella the Catholic.

There are few cities that reflect the passing of time as well as Granada does: it is a massive open-air museum that amazes the traveller for its hybrid and ingenious beauty. Its down-to-earth character has been shaped by experiencing crucial moments in history that have marked a country's transformation. Setting foot in Granada is to breathe in the past and present of a city open to the future. It also means experiencing the spontaneous character and cheer of the people from the south.

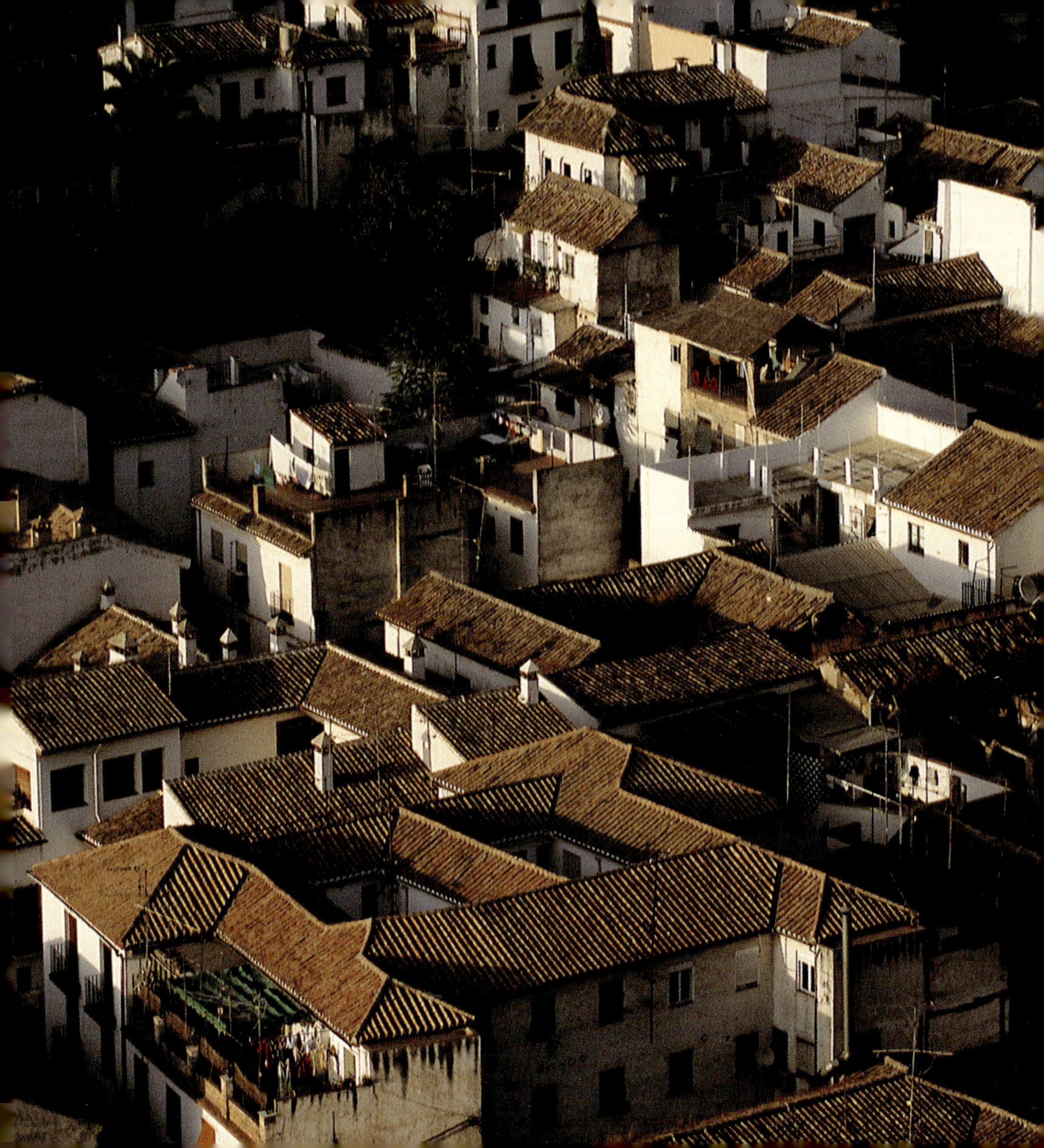

THE ALBAYZIN

Facing the Alhambra, perched on a steep hillside, is the Albayzin, a colourful district that goes from the wonderful viewpoint of San Nicolás as far as Calle Elvira and Carrera del Darro. The enclave was settled by pre-Iberians, Iberians and Romans, as can be seen from the numerous archaeological remains found there, sewing the seeds for the founding of Granada. Nevertheless, the urban layout that has survived to the present is the inheritance of what was the most important nucleus of the city during the period of Arab domain. The district had a big influence, above all under the Nasrid dynasty, on the social and political events that took place in the city.

The Albayzin is a world apart and has nothing in common with the hustle and bustle of the city centre. Life passes calmly in the streets of whitewashed façades, with flowering balconies and patios, and the layout is of narrow, labyrinthine streets where the typical house is the *Carmen*; a house with a garden or orchard, surrounded by a wall that means it cannot be seen into from outside. Since it was declared a World Heritage Site in 1994, the old Arab district has experienced a new revival, increasingly more startling. The old image of an unsafe and abandoned area is long forgotten. There is now a cosmopolitan air about the place with the Albayzin locals mixing with the new generations that have arrived in search of the charm of its cobbled streets. Even *Al-Andalus* seems to have been reborn in the marvellous souk of Caldereria Nueva or in the beautiful white mosque alongside the viewpoint of San Nicolás, which honours the 34 that existed in the Albayzin before the arrival of the Christians. This labyrinth of streets is a living museum where getting lost is a pleasure, the map becomes useless, and you must let your intuition guide you and discover the marvels it conceals: pleasant spots such as the Cuesta de María la de la Miel, spectacular view-

ROOFTOPS OF THE DISTRICT
The layout shows a tangled network of streets.

points such as that of San Cristóbal, ostentatious churches such as that of Salvador, imposing palaces such as the Royal Chancery and magnificent Arab monuments such as the Puerta Elvira, the baths known as the Bañuelo, the walls of the Albayzin, the Arco de las Pesas, the Puente del Cadí or the Palace of Dar al-Horra.

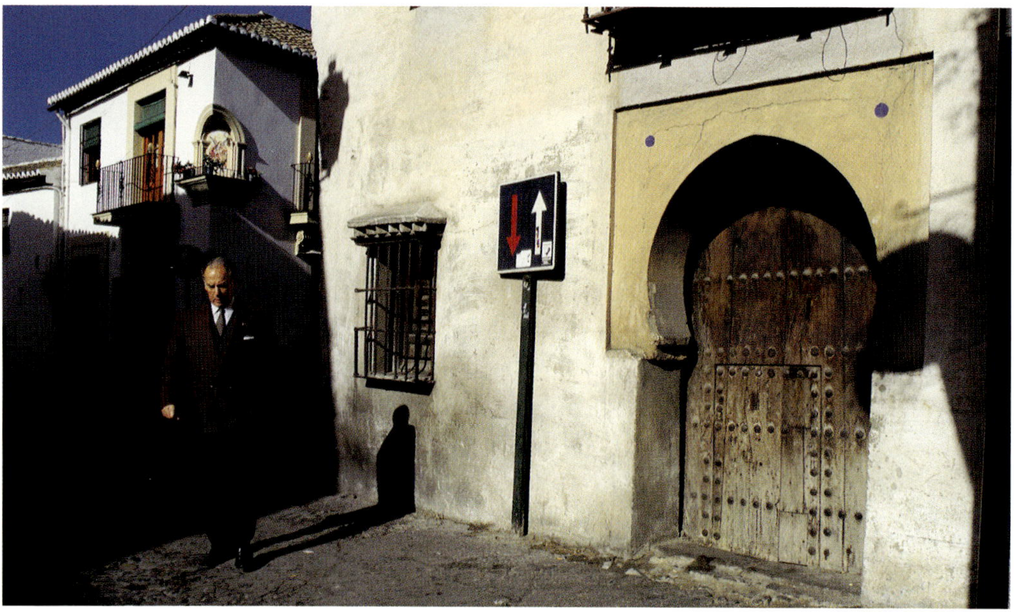

CALLE PAGÉS
Junction with Calle del Agua.

CALLE GLORIA
Opposite the church of San Pedro y San Pablo.

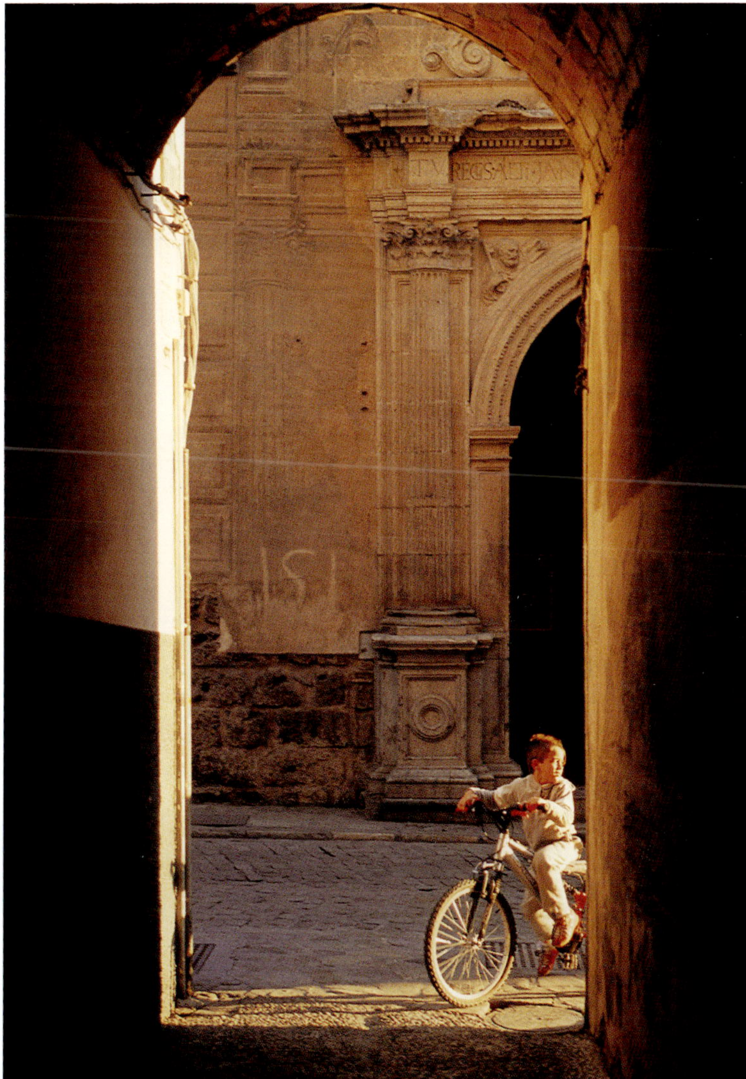

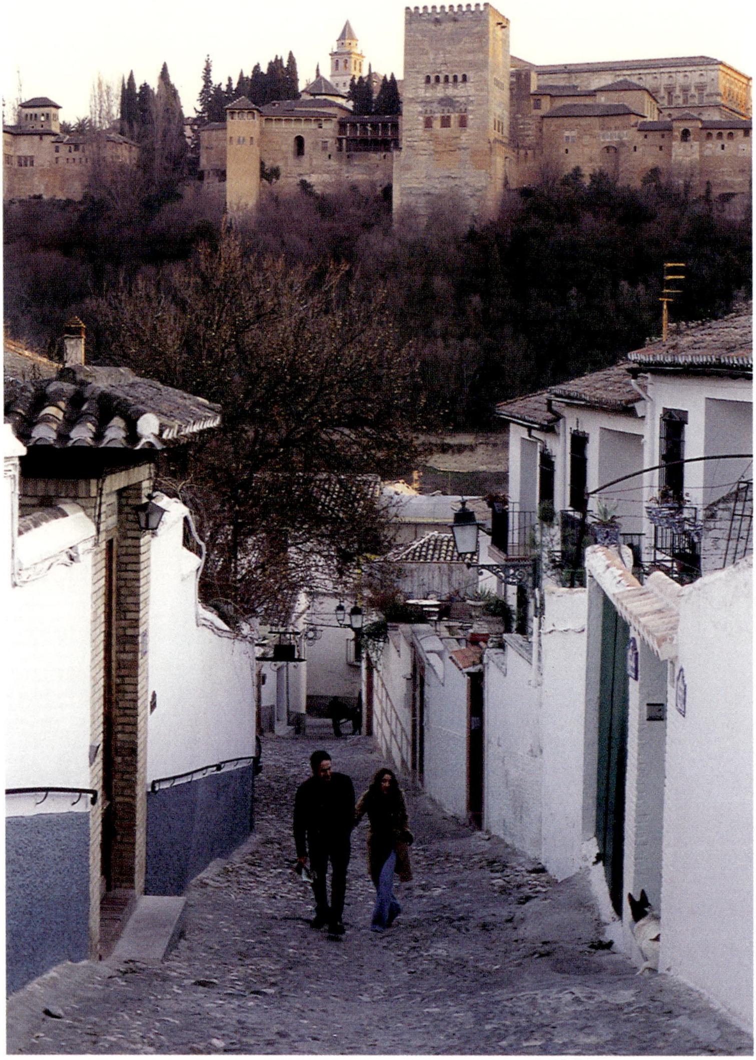

THE ALHAMBRA
From the narrow streets of the Albayzín.

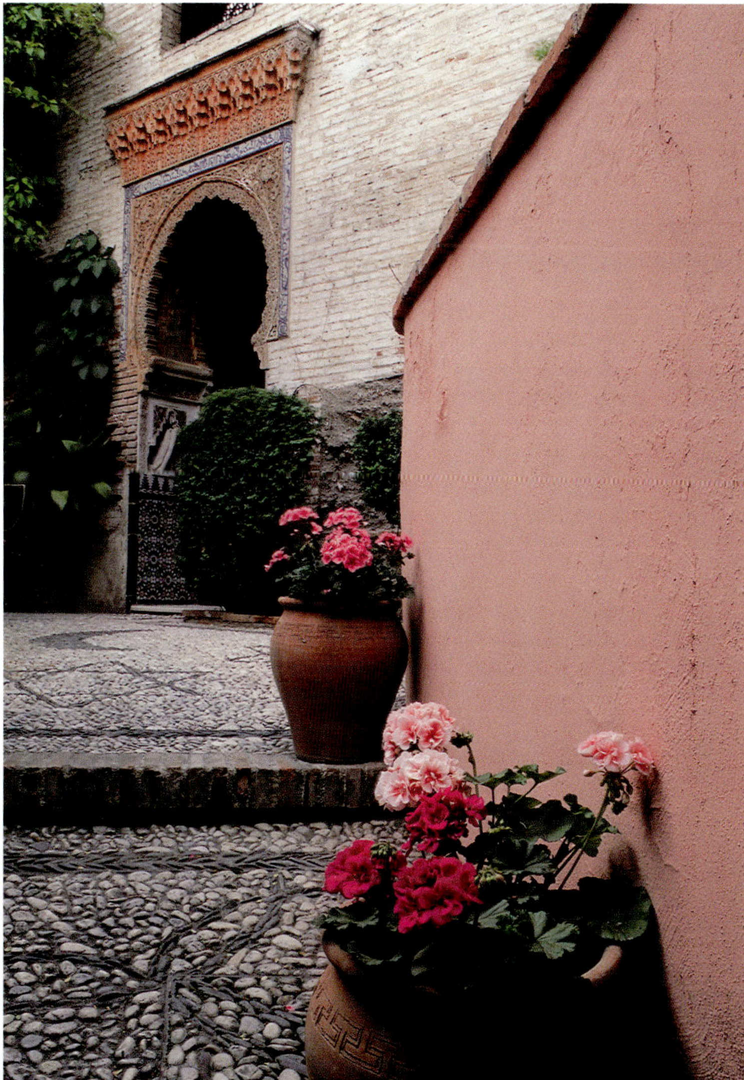

CARMEN DE LA MEDIA LUNA
Interior patio.

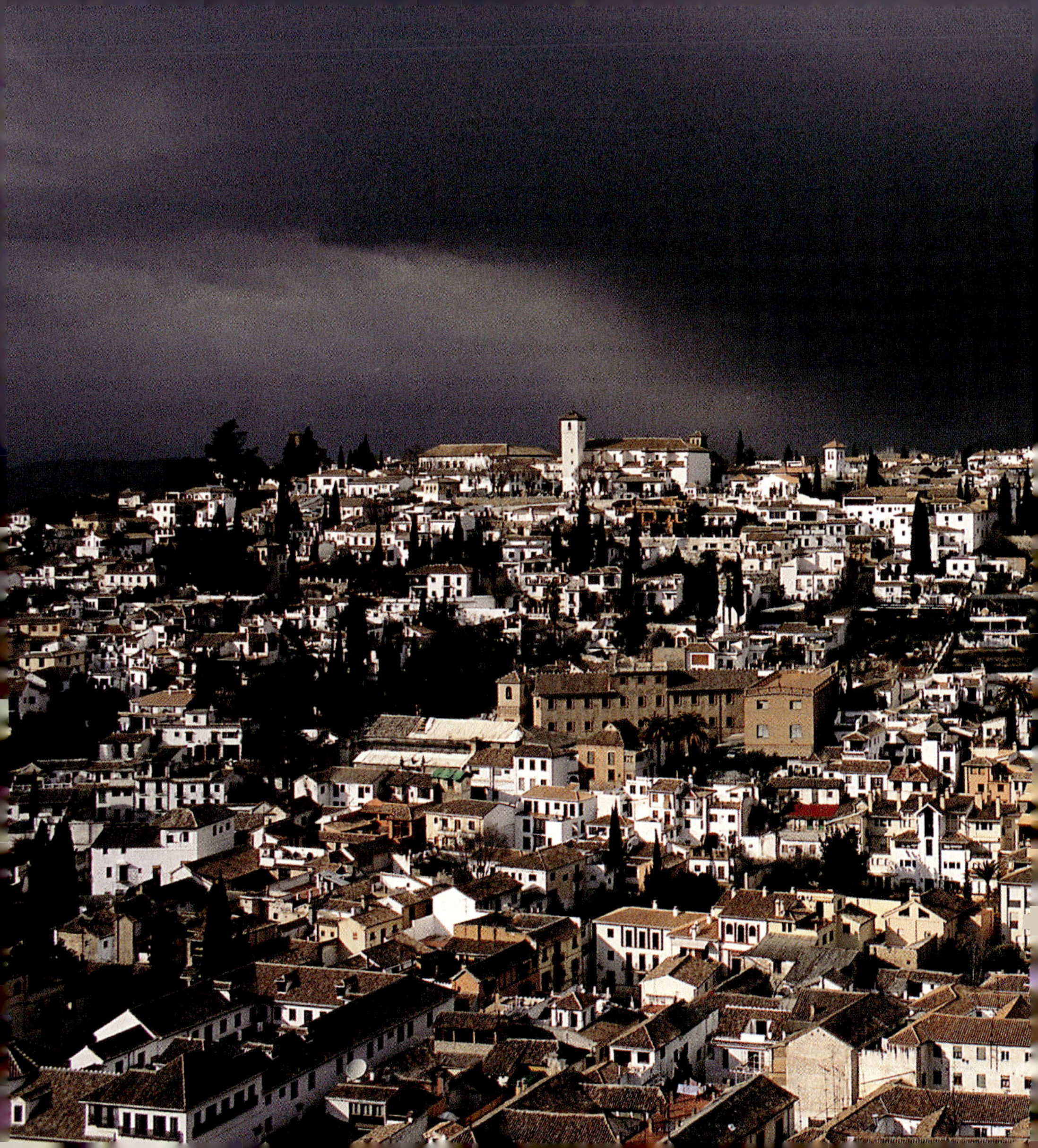

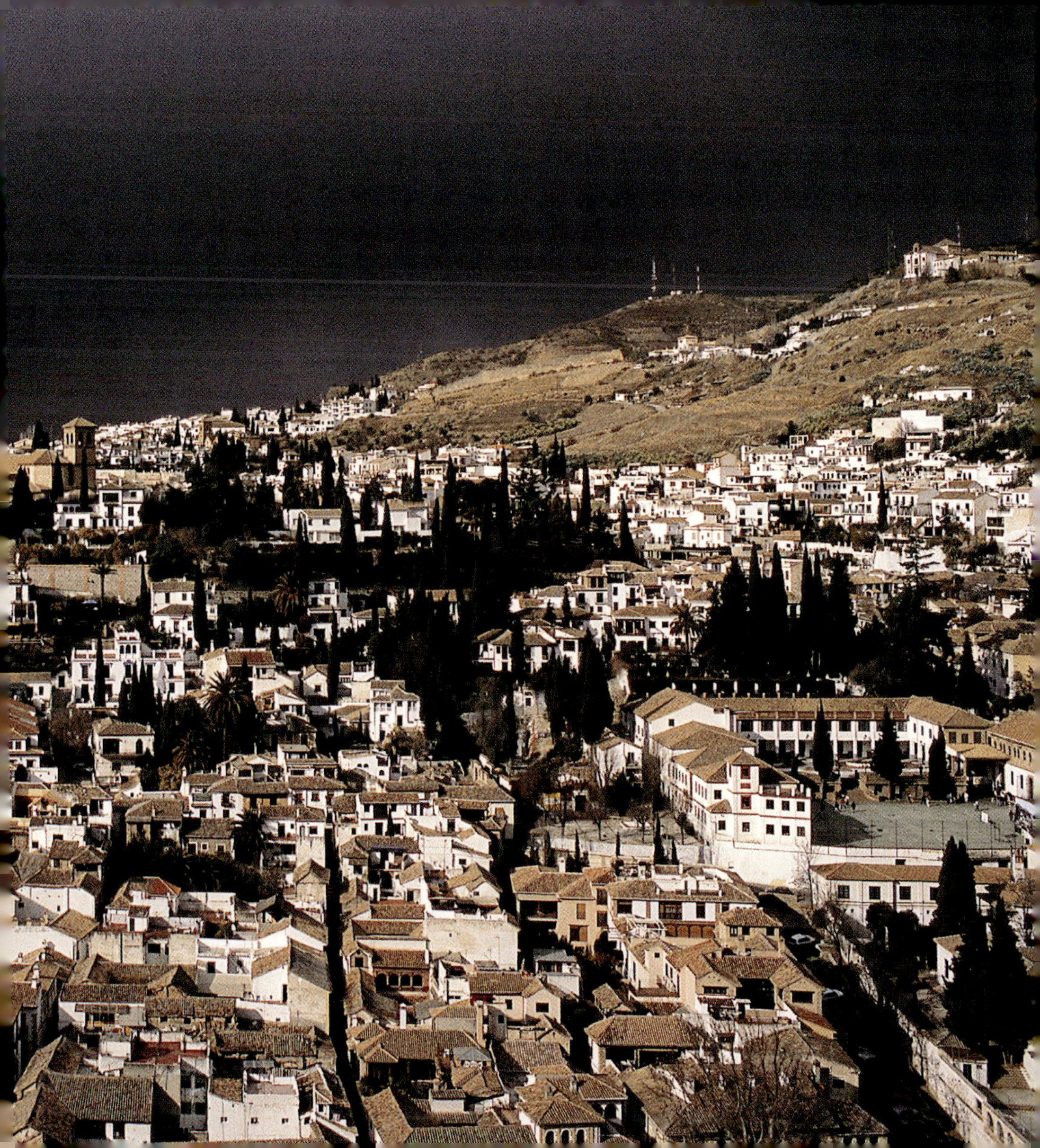

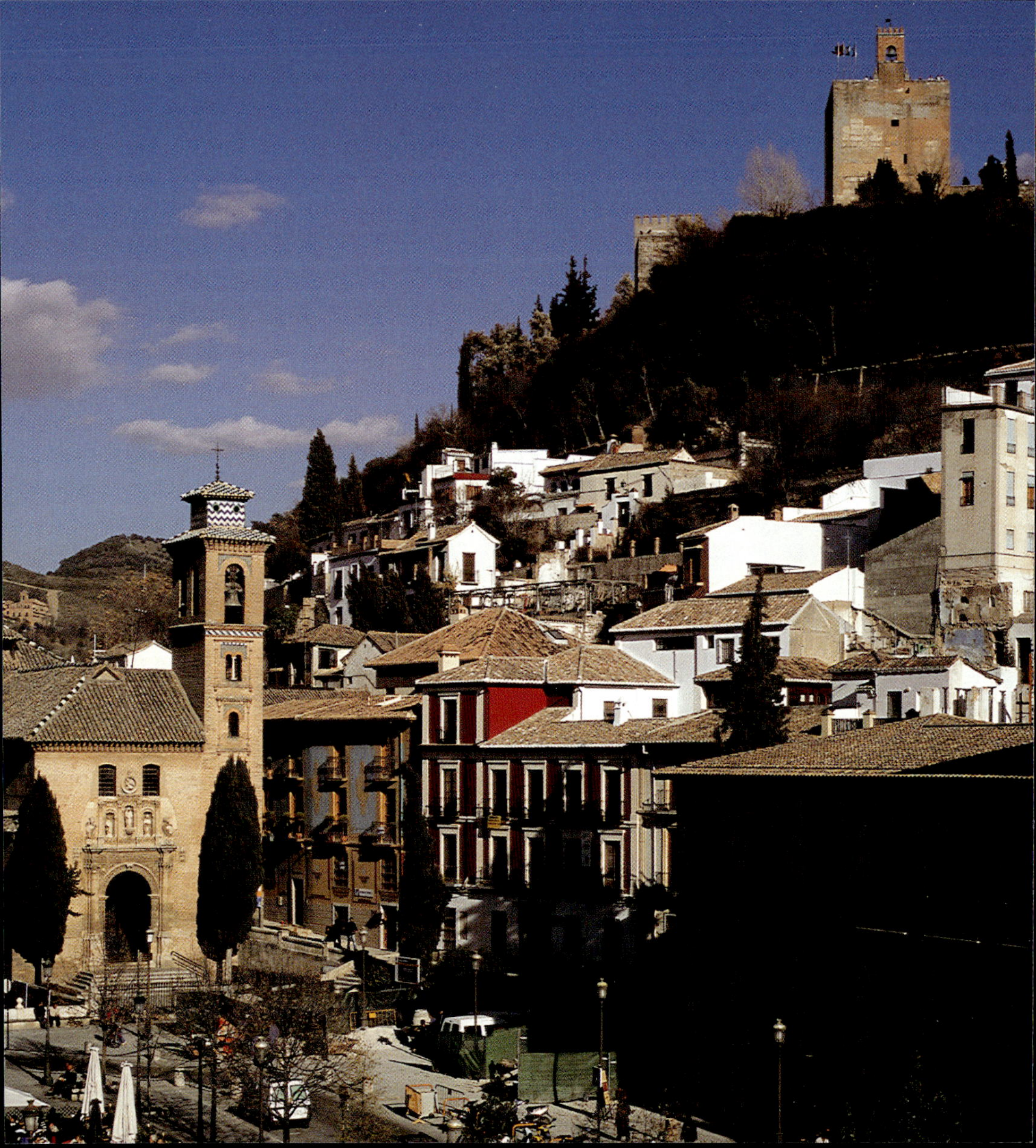

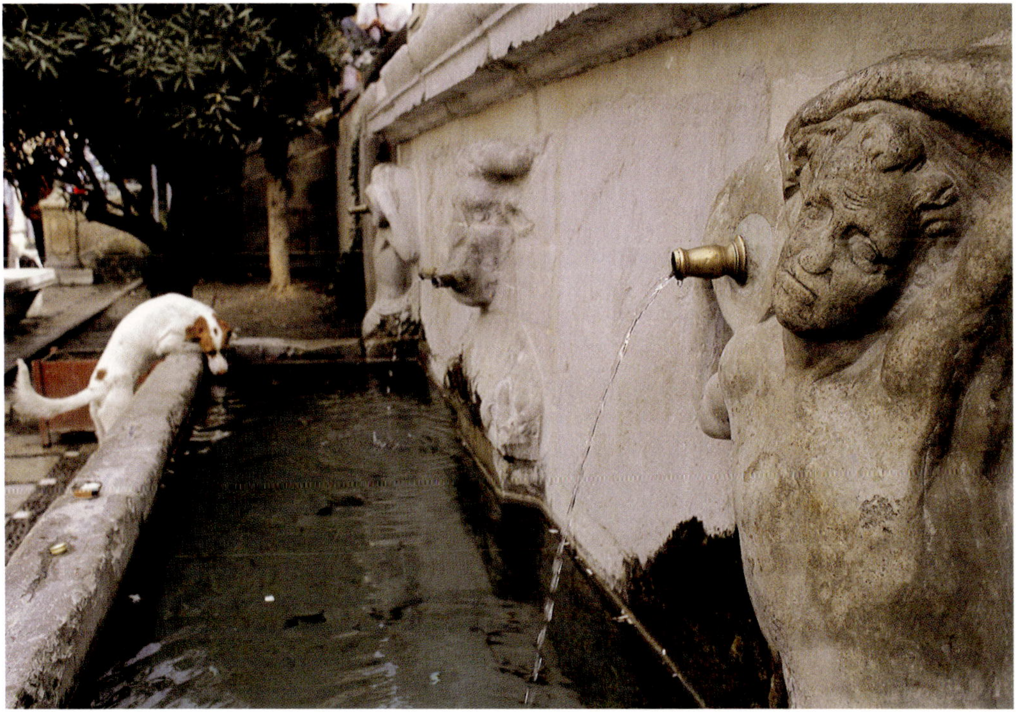

PLAZA SANTA ANA
It houses the church of the same name and is crowned by the Watchtower.

FOUNTAIN OF THE BULL
In Plaza Santa Ana.

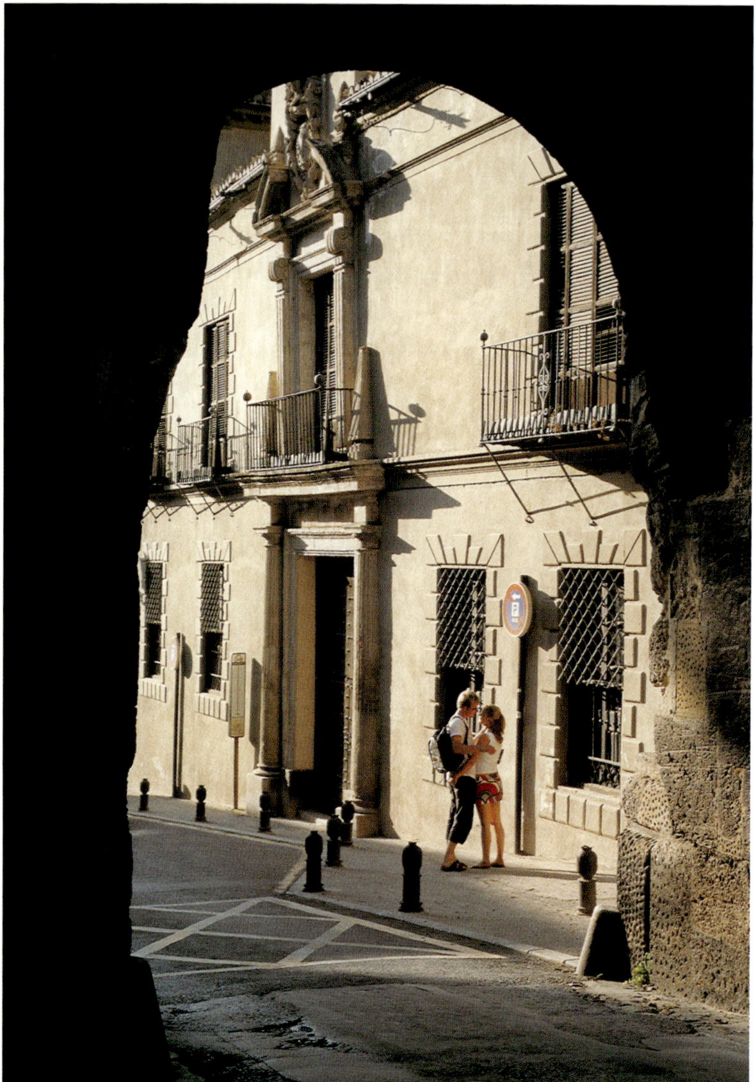

DOORWAY OF THE GRANADAS
Work by Pedro Machuca.

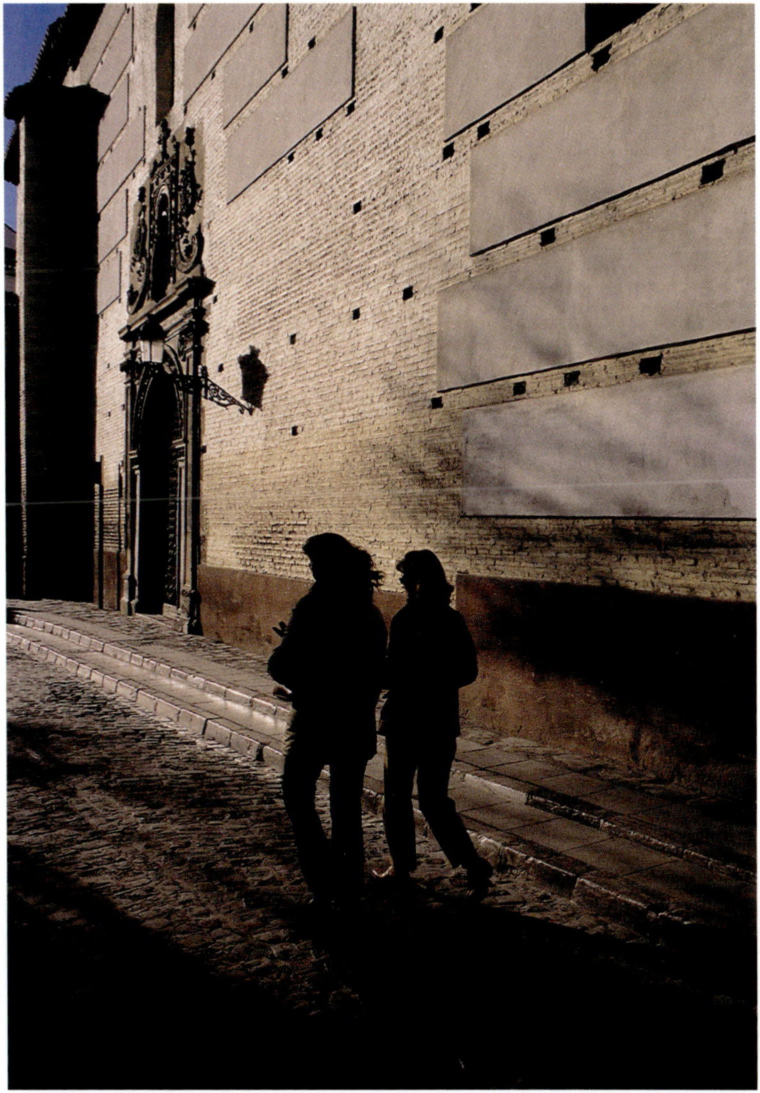

CARRERA DEL DARRO
One of the city's
most symbolic streets.

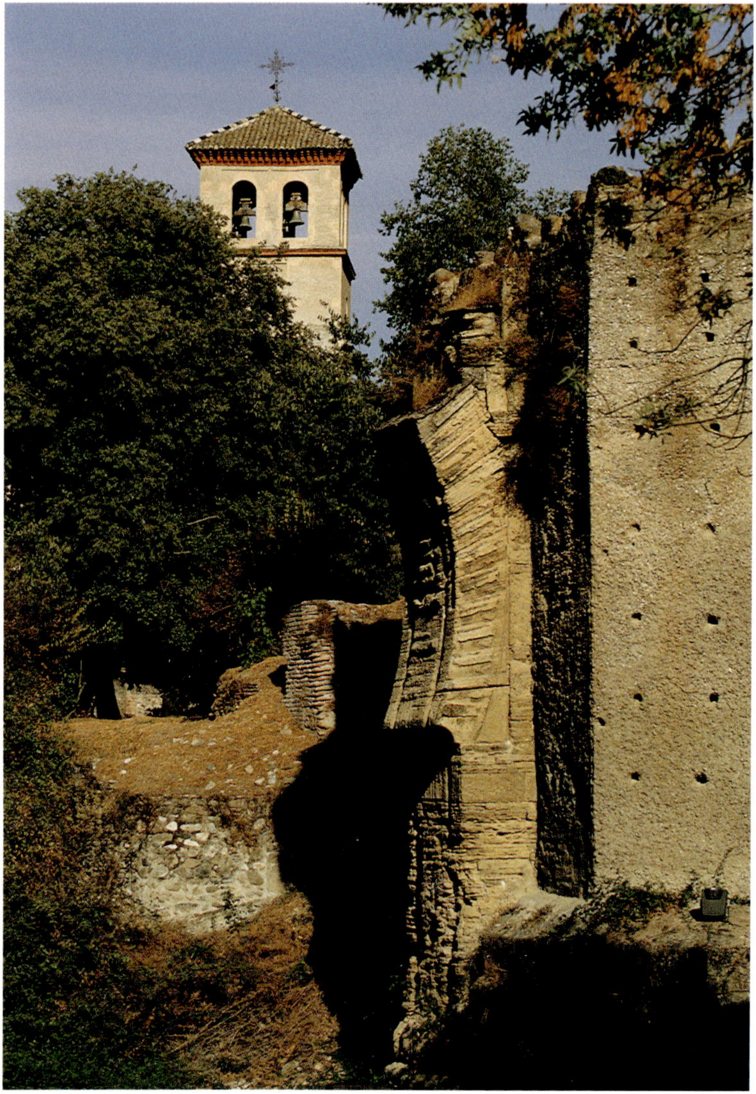

REMAINS OF THE ARAB PUENTE DEL CADÍ
In the background the bell tower of the church of San Pedro y San Pablo.

CARRERA DEL DARRO
At the end of the day.

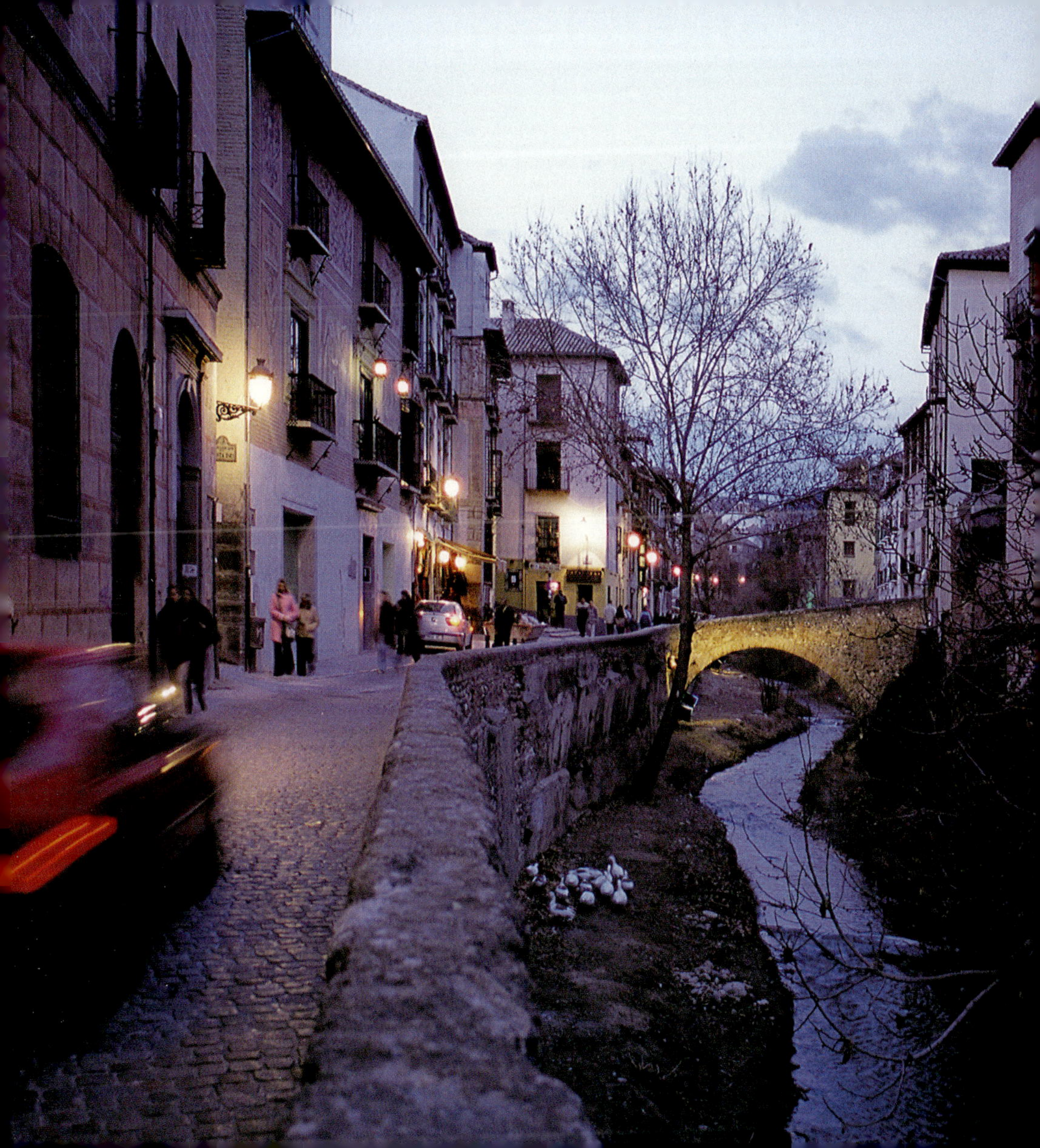

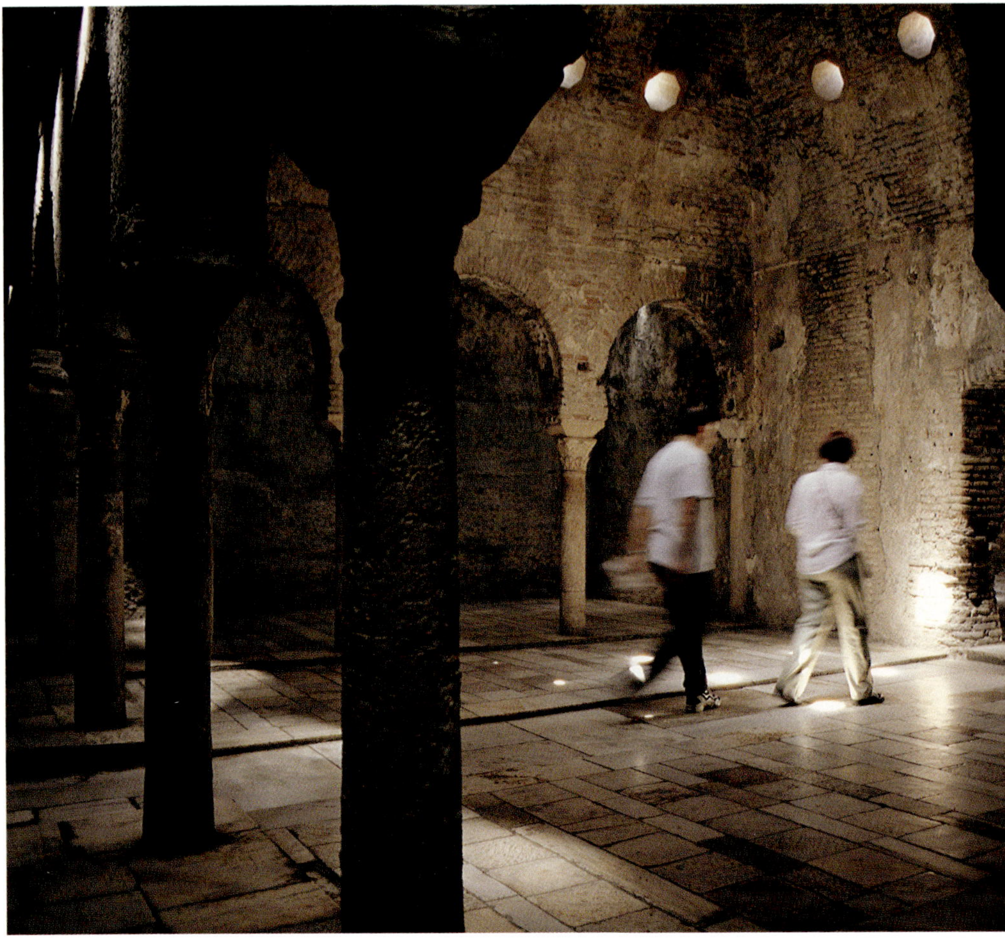

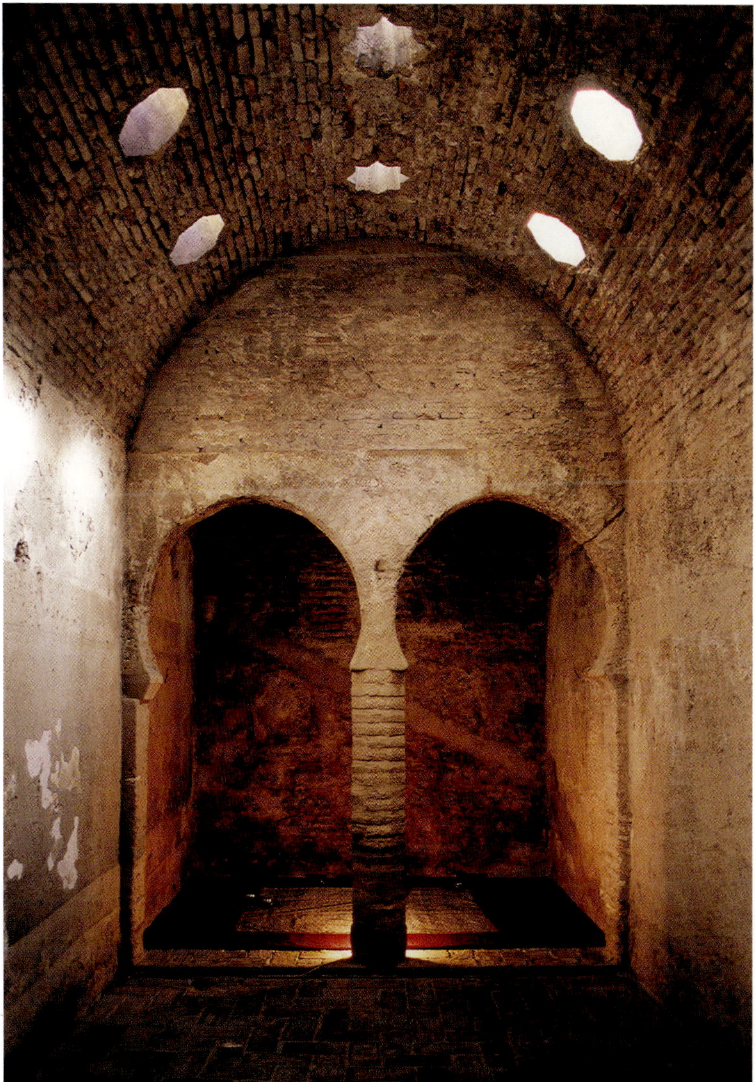

THE BAÑUELO
Arab baths situated in the Carrera del Darro, which are very well preserved.

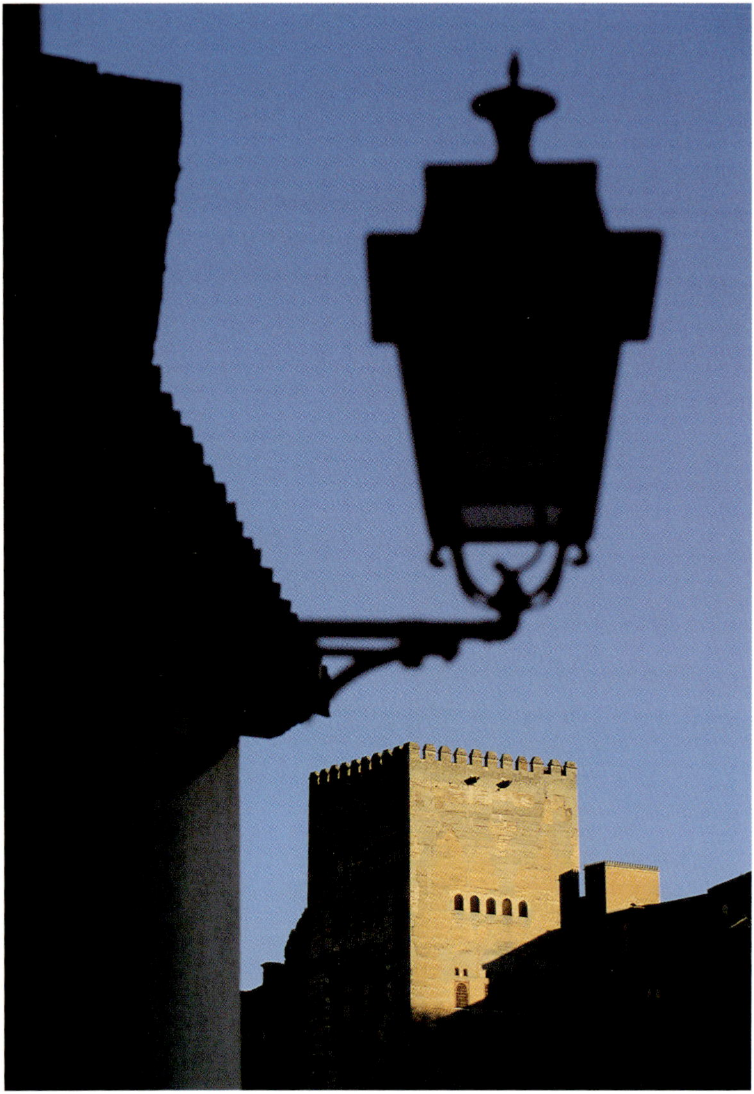

COMARES TOWER
From the Albayzín.

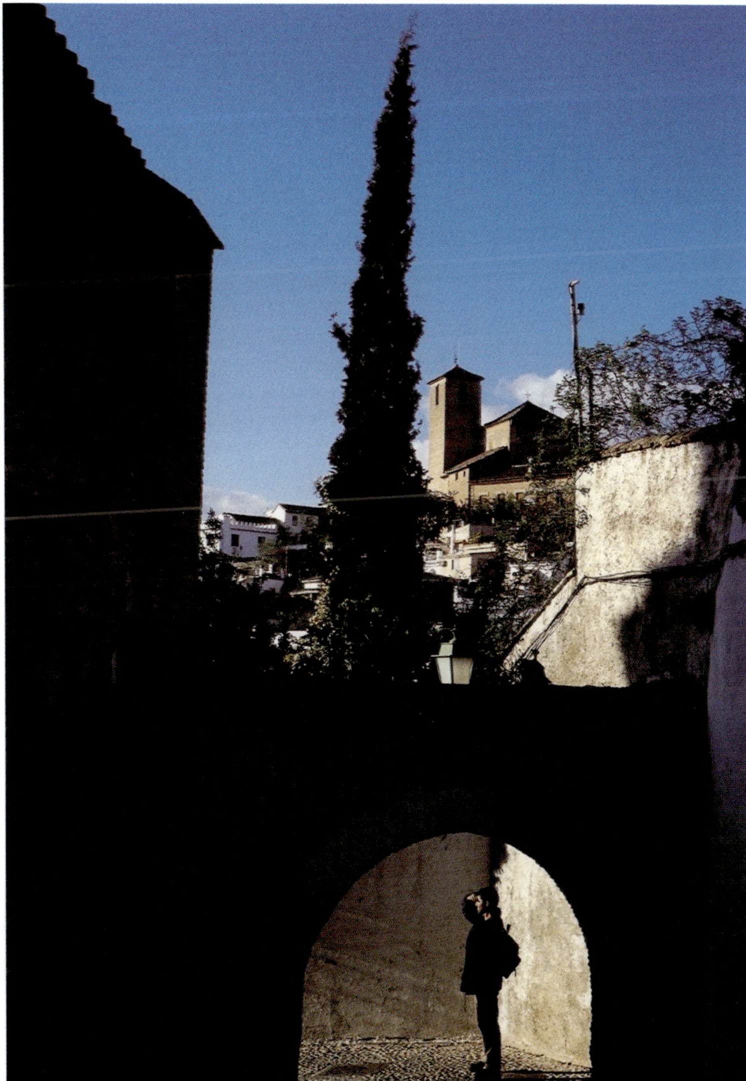

CALLEJÓN DE LAS MONJAS
In the background the church of San Cristóbal.

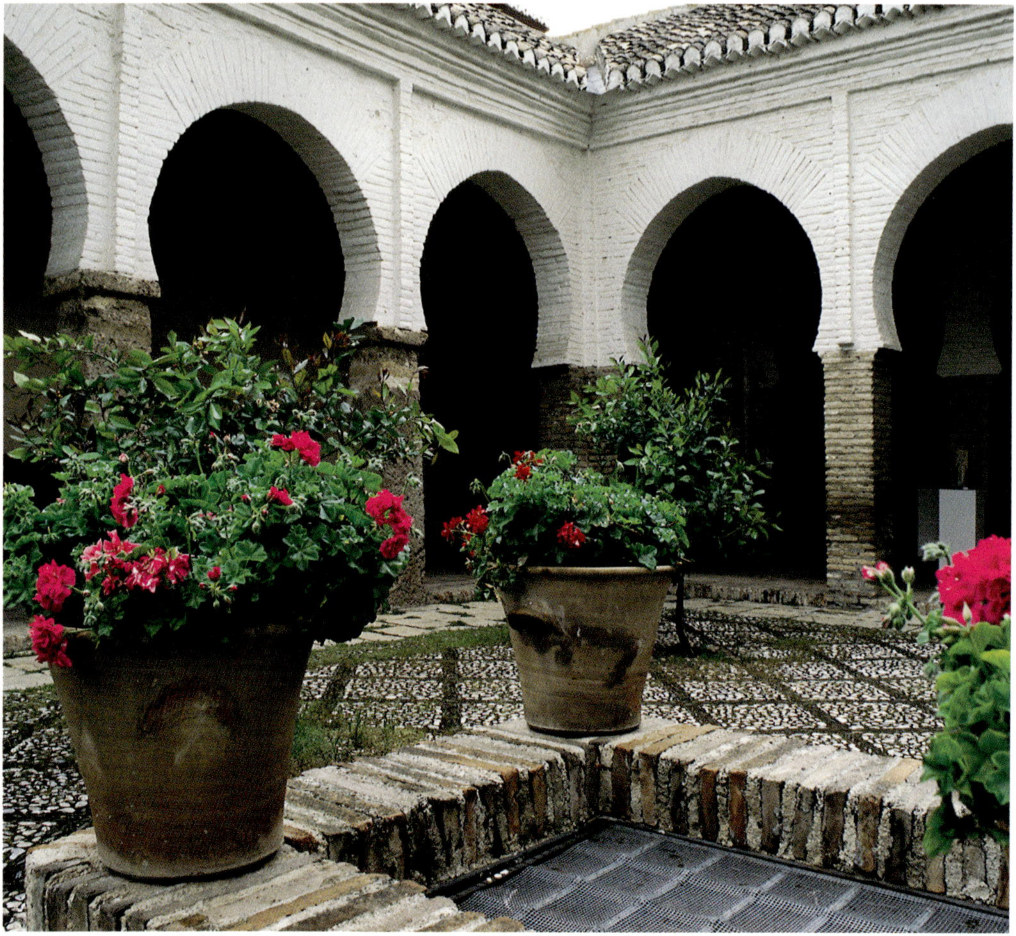

CHURCH OF EL SALVADOR
Here stood the Main Mosque of the Albayzín, of which this washing courtyard is still preserved.

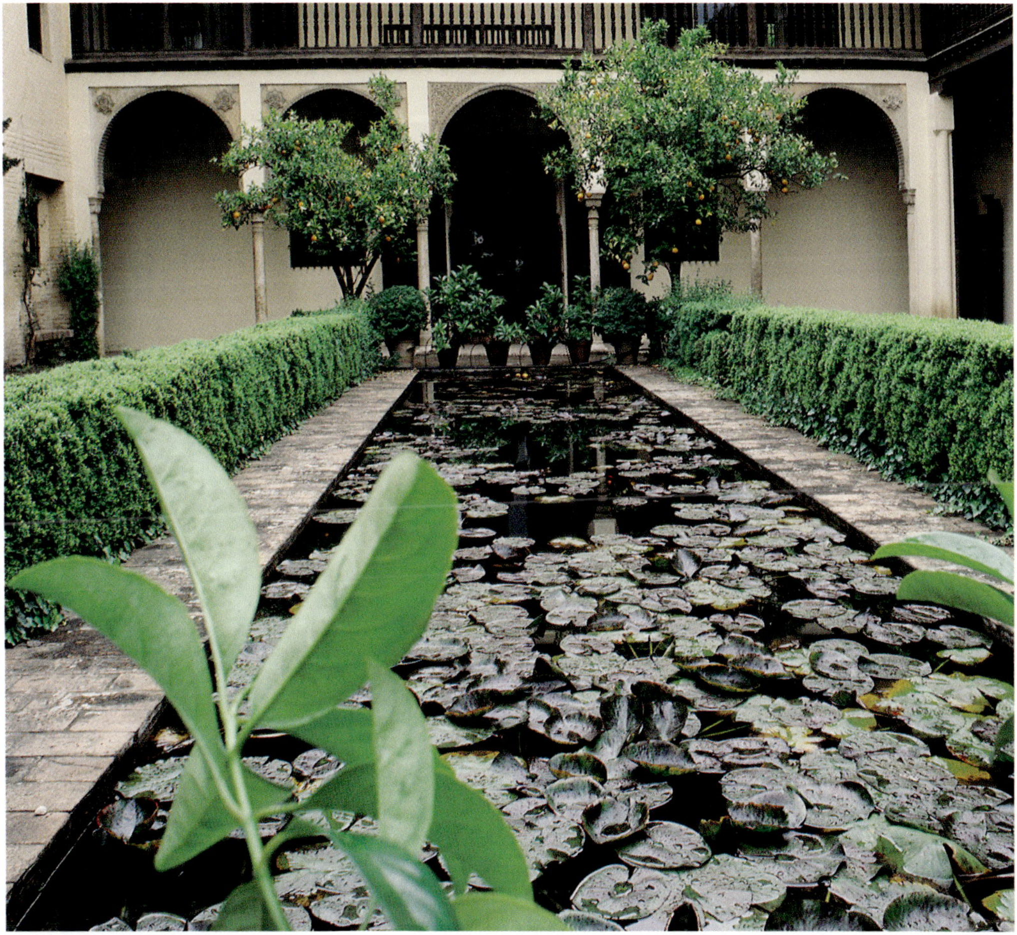

CASA DEL CHAPIZ
One of the best examples of Moorish art.

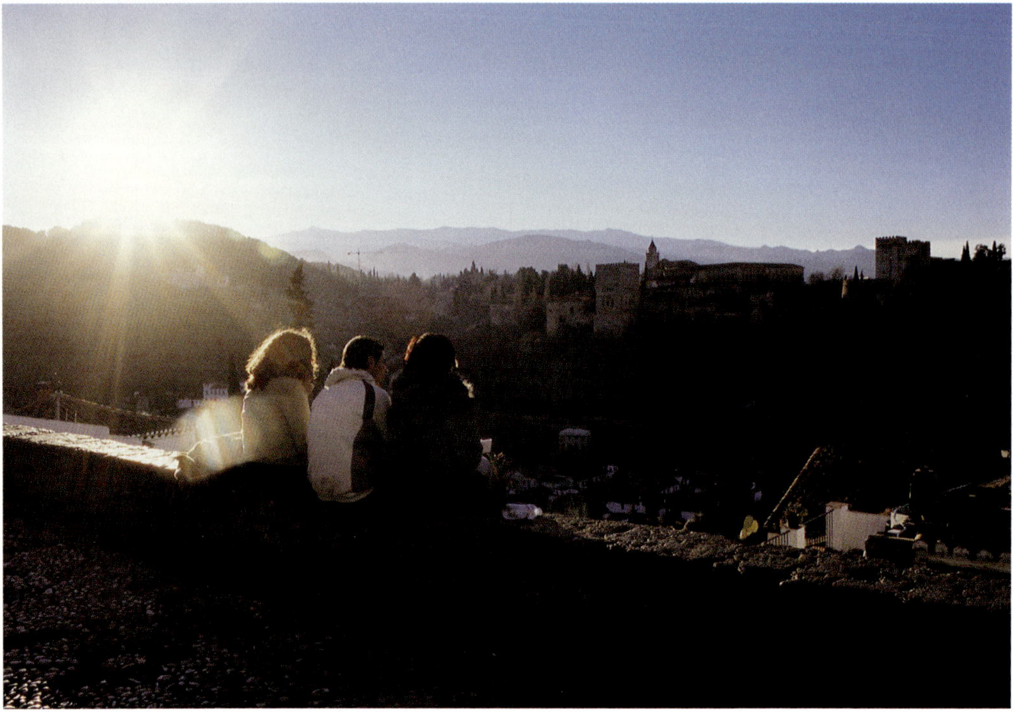

VIEWPOINT OF SAN NICOLÁS
Dawn at the viewpoint most visited by tourists.

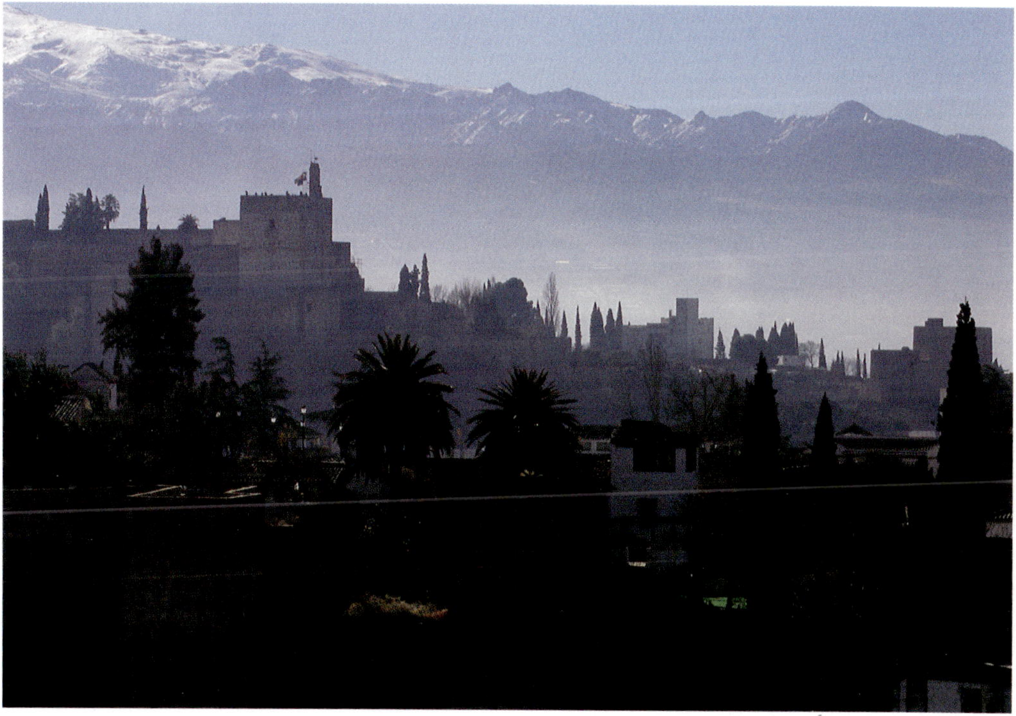

VIEWPOINT OF SAN CRISTÓBAL
Situated opposite the church of the same name, it offers us this panoramic view.

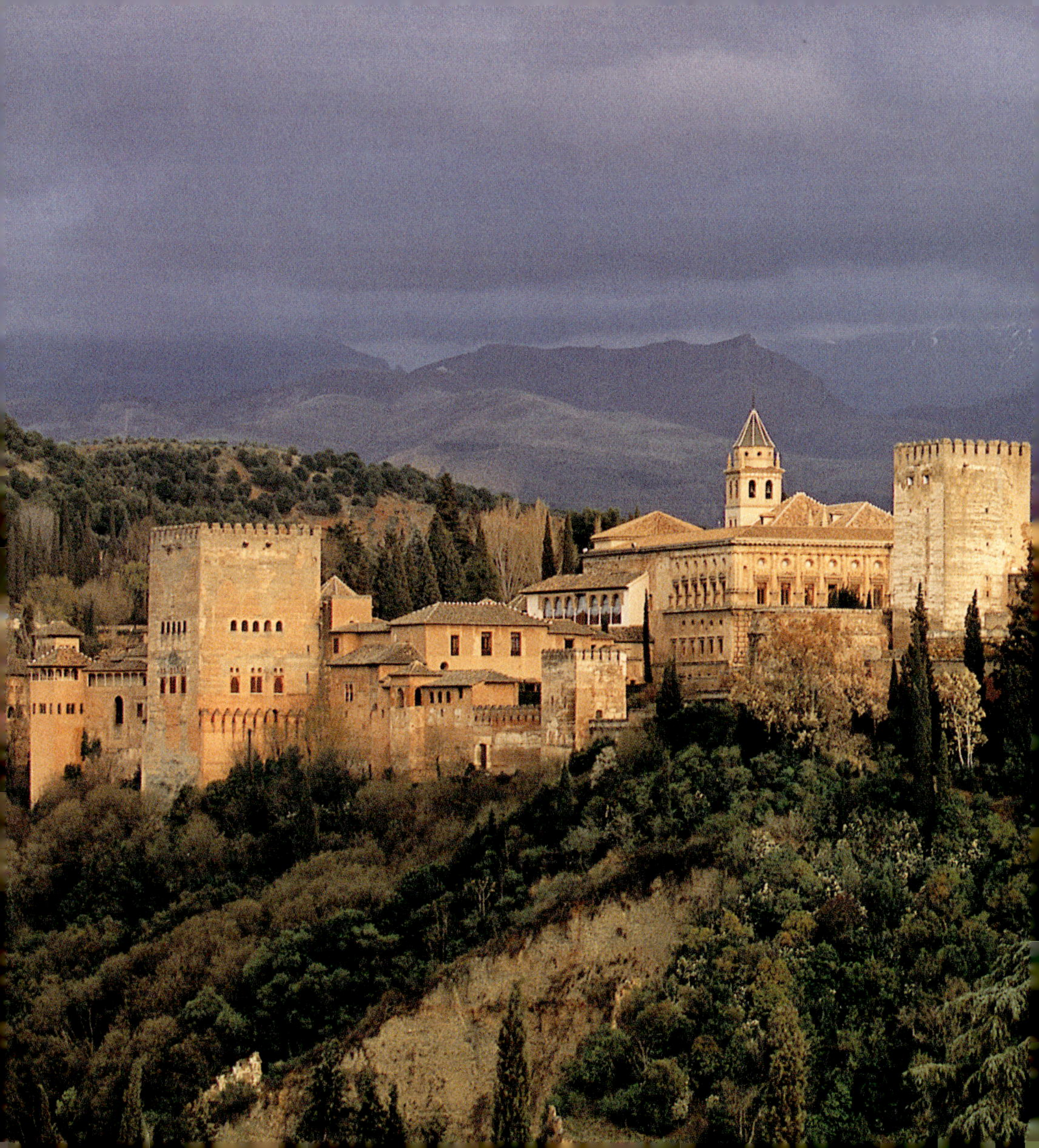

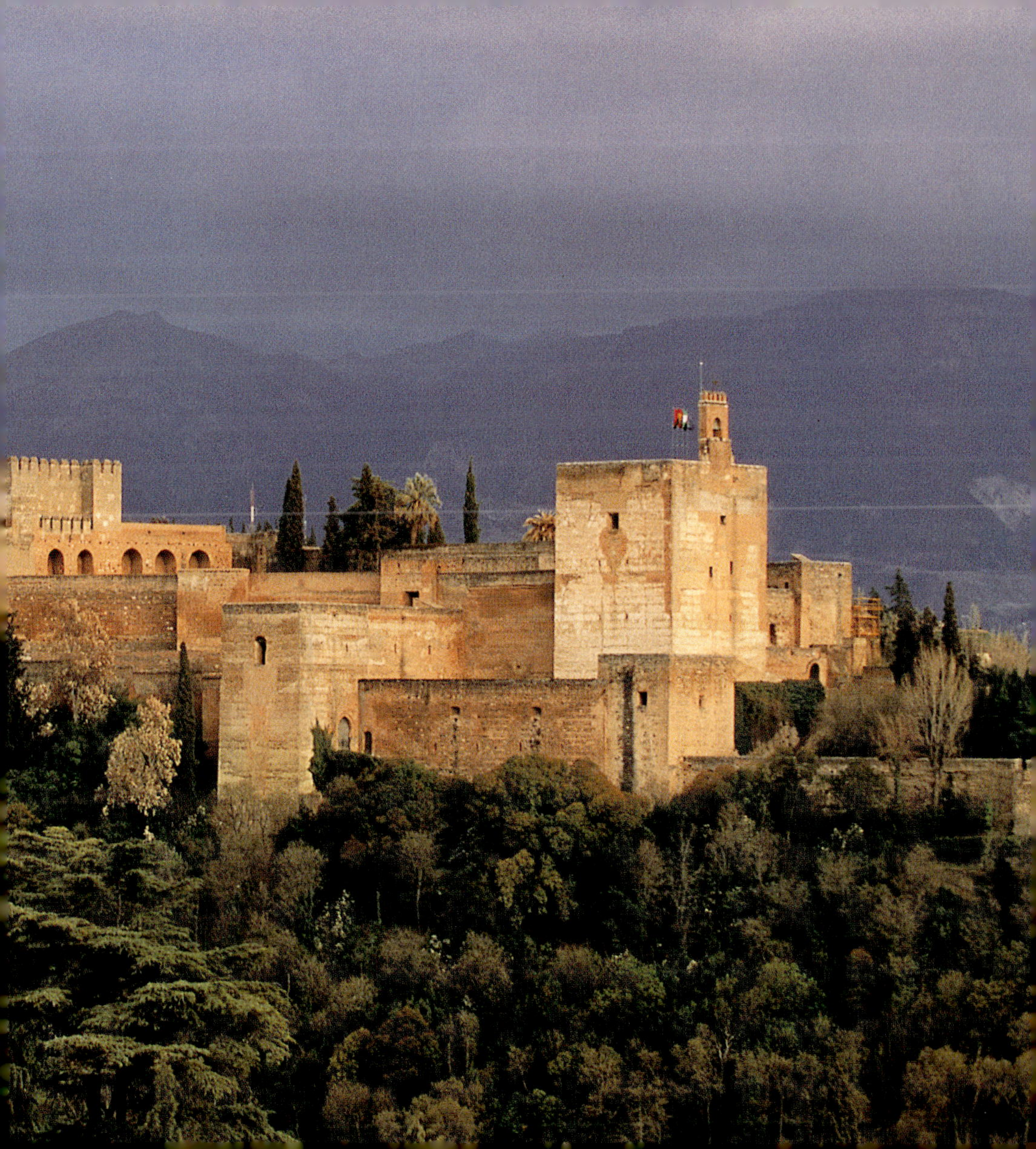

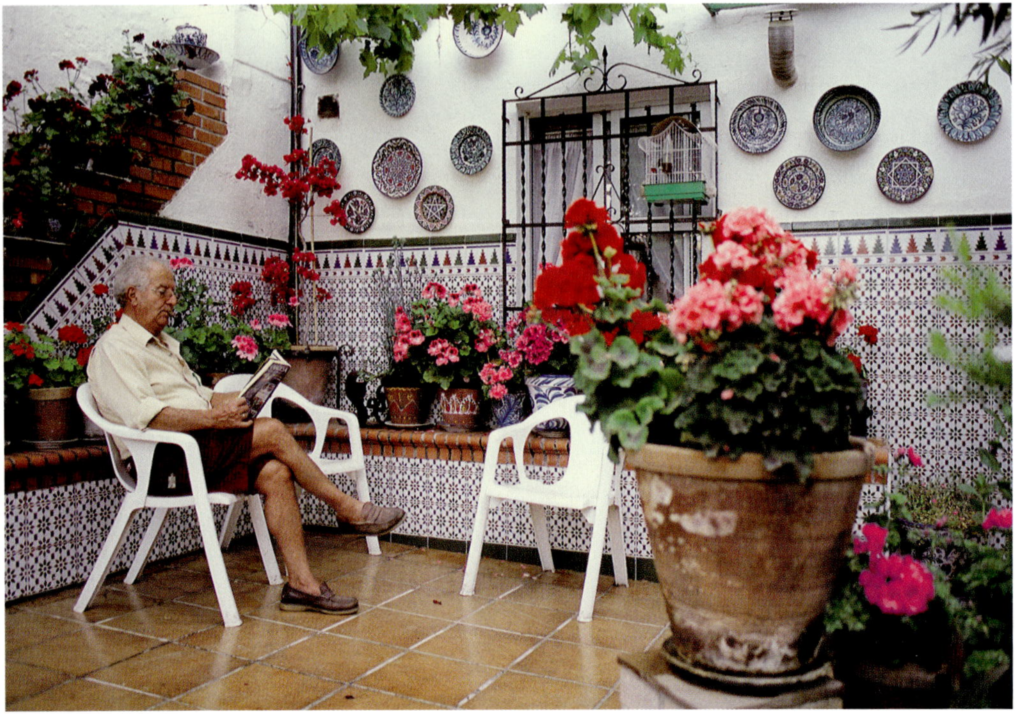

CARMEN DE LA ESTRELLA
Manuel Ocaña relaxing in the garden.

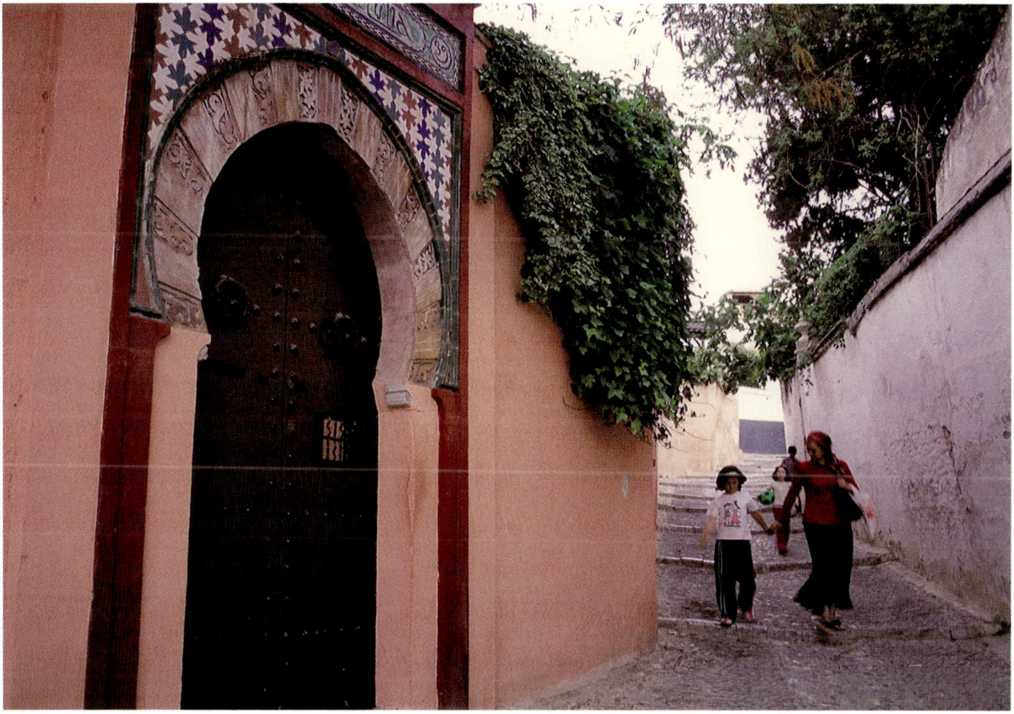

HIGH WALLS
The houses of the Albayzín, following Arab architectural rules, jealously guard their privacy.

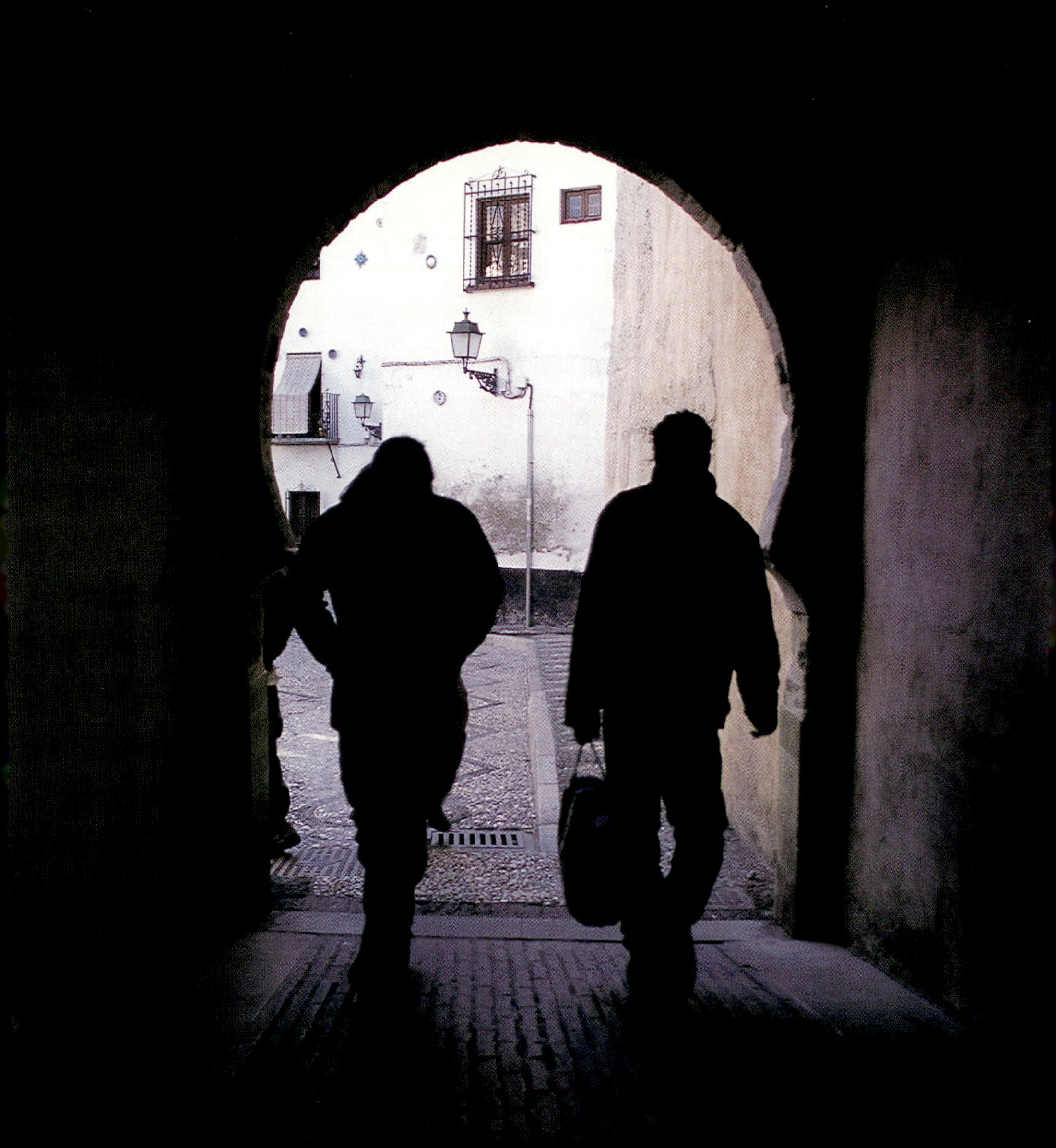

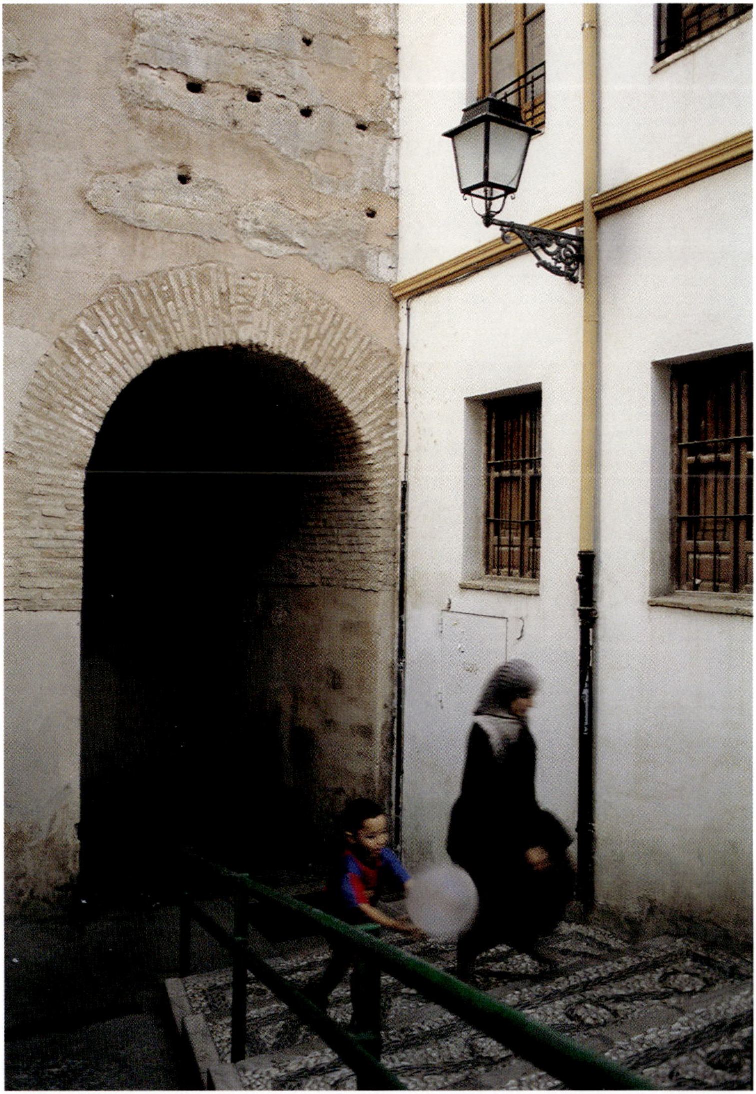

ARCO DE LAS PESAS
It is a door in the wall of the Albayzín, which connects Plaza Larga with the Callejón de San Cecilio.

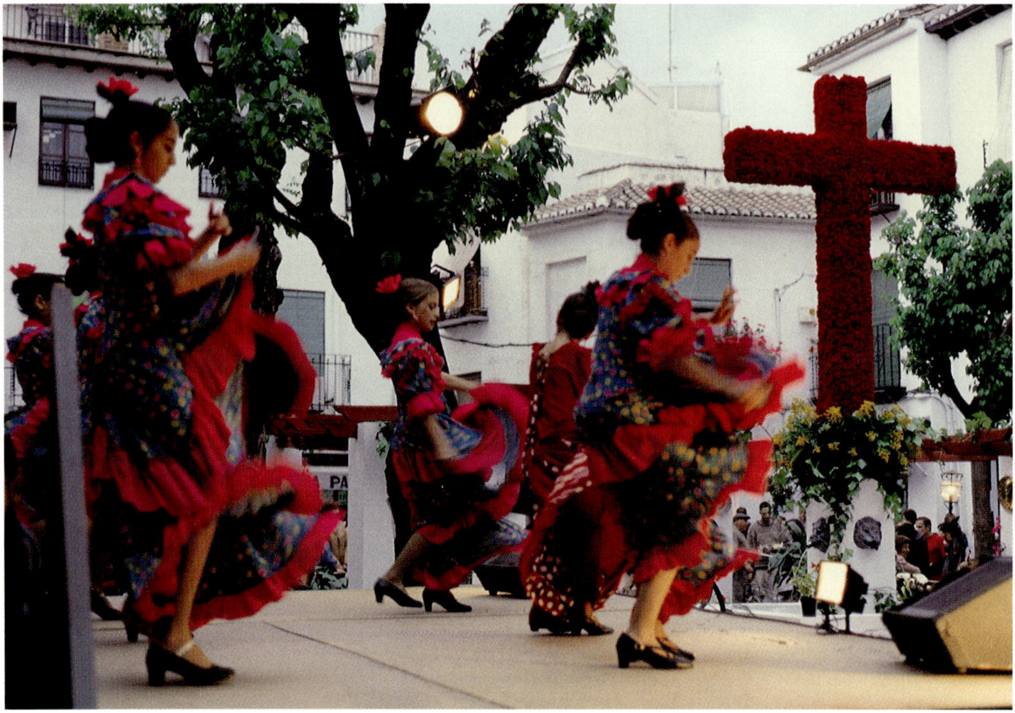

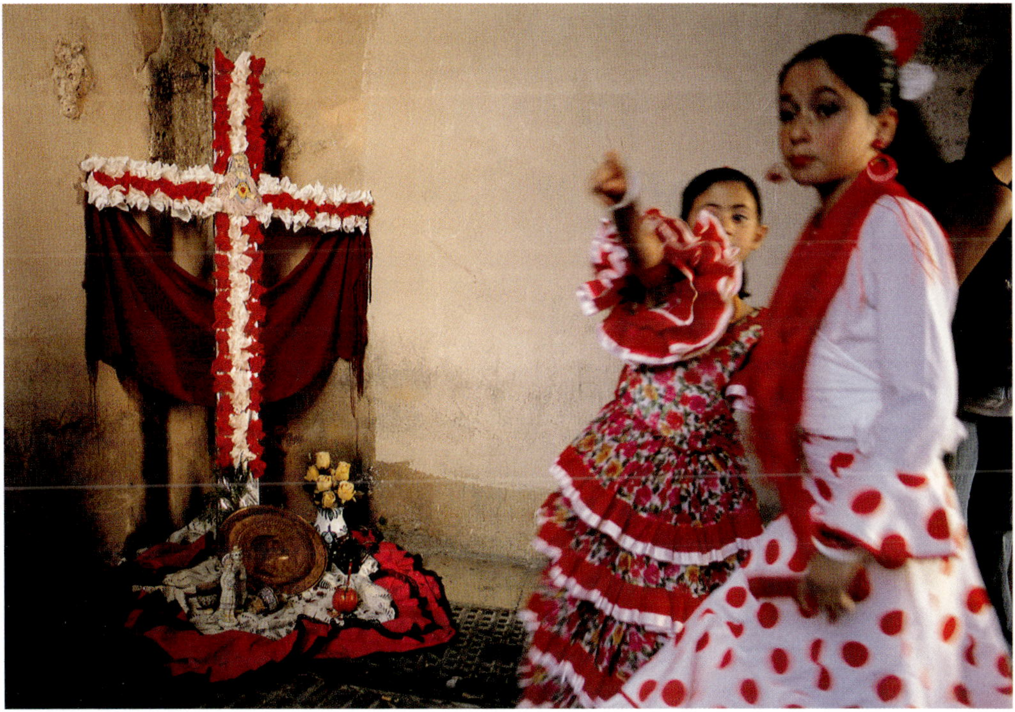

DAY OF THE CROSS
To celebrate this day the people of Granada raise beautiful crosses made of flowers which they dance around. "Give us a few pence for the cross", the children in the street ask passers-by to pay for the cost of the cross and to buy themselves some sweets.

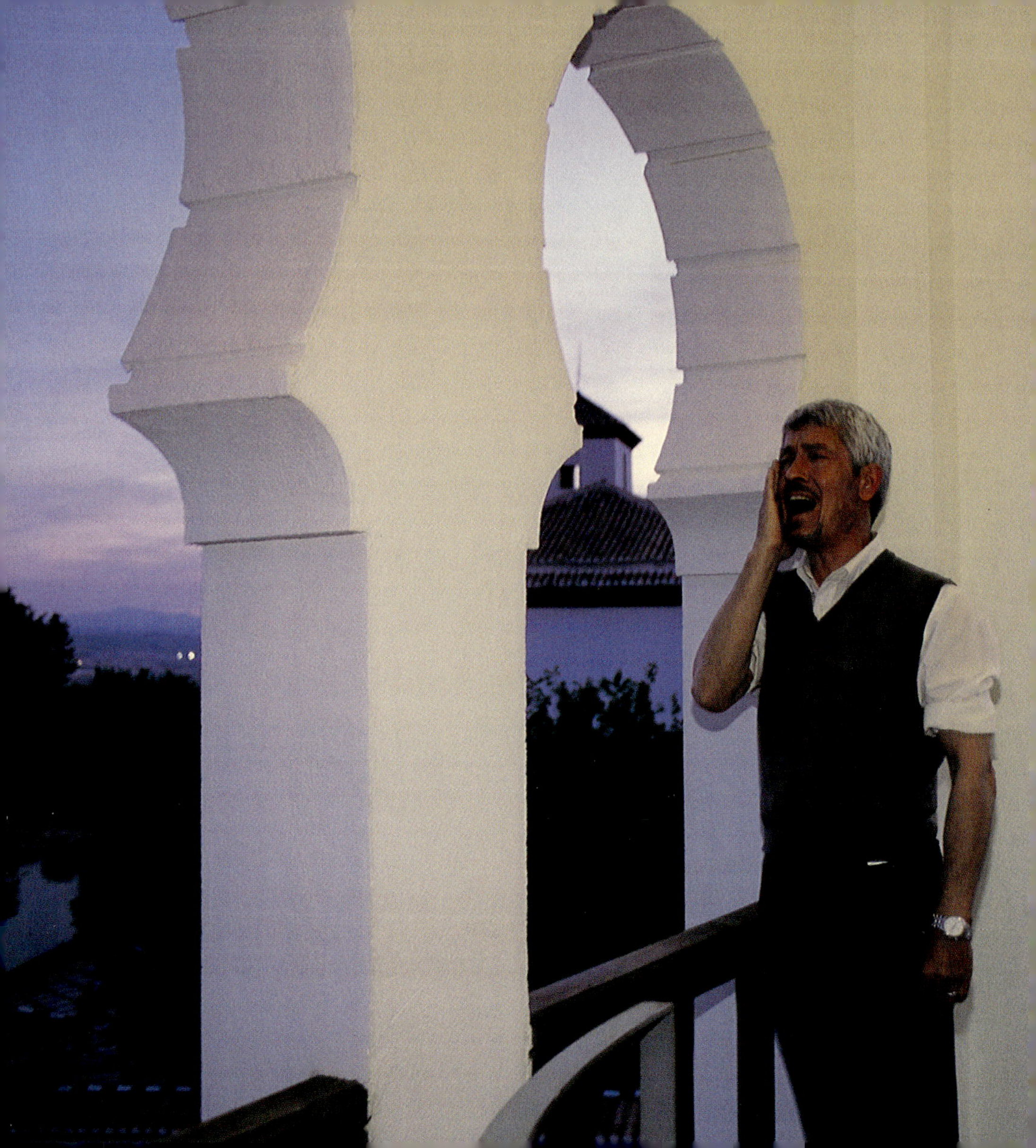

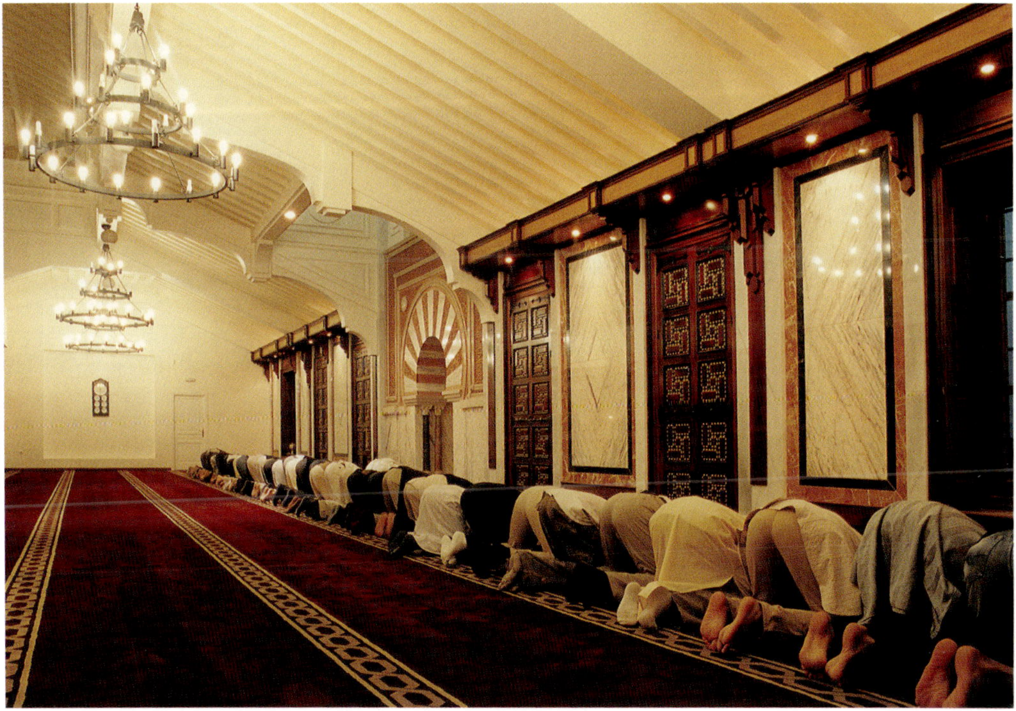

MOSQUE OF GRANADA
After 500 years, on
the 10th of July 2003
Granada once again heard
the call of a muezzin:
"Allahu Akhbar!"

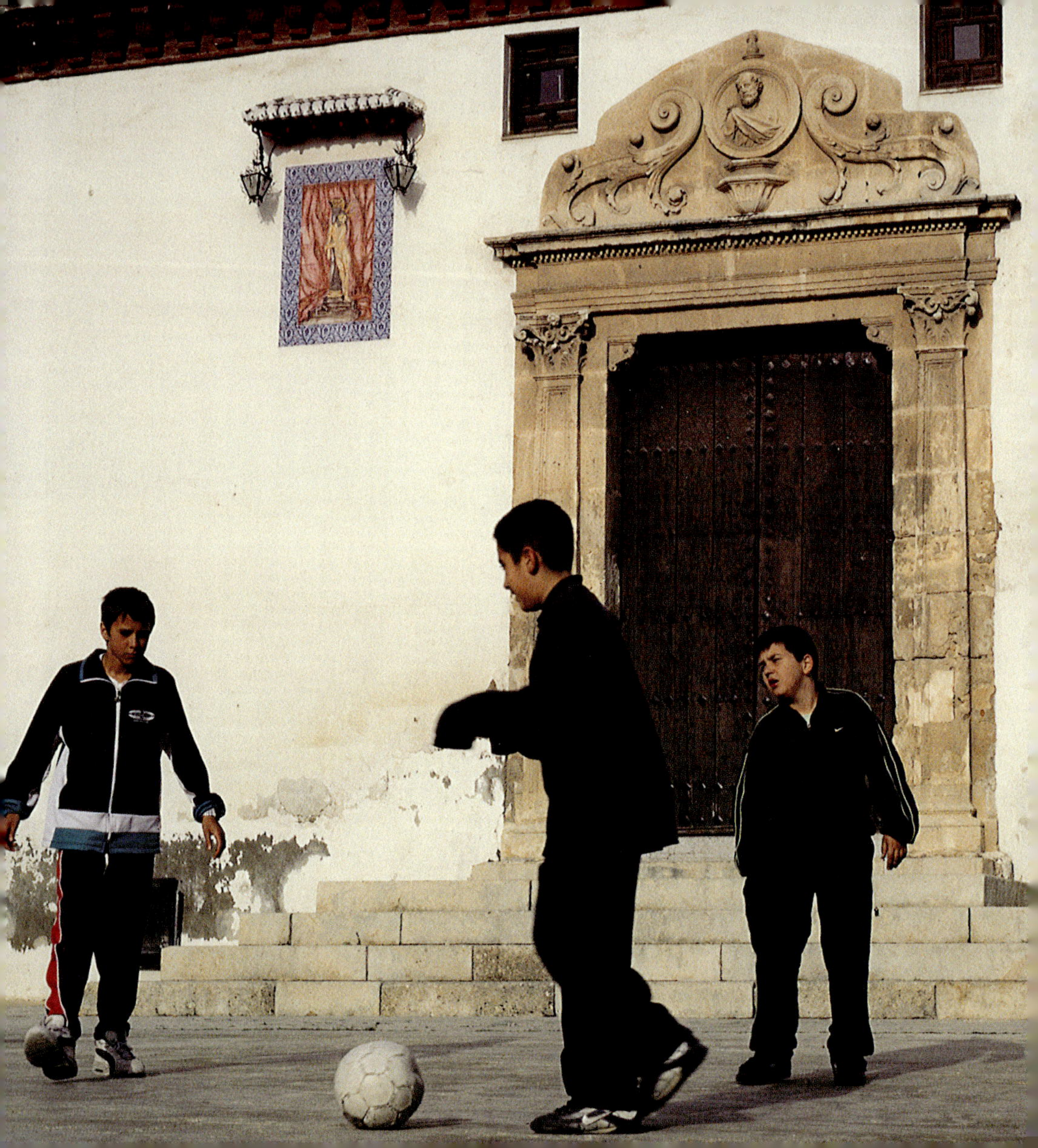

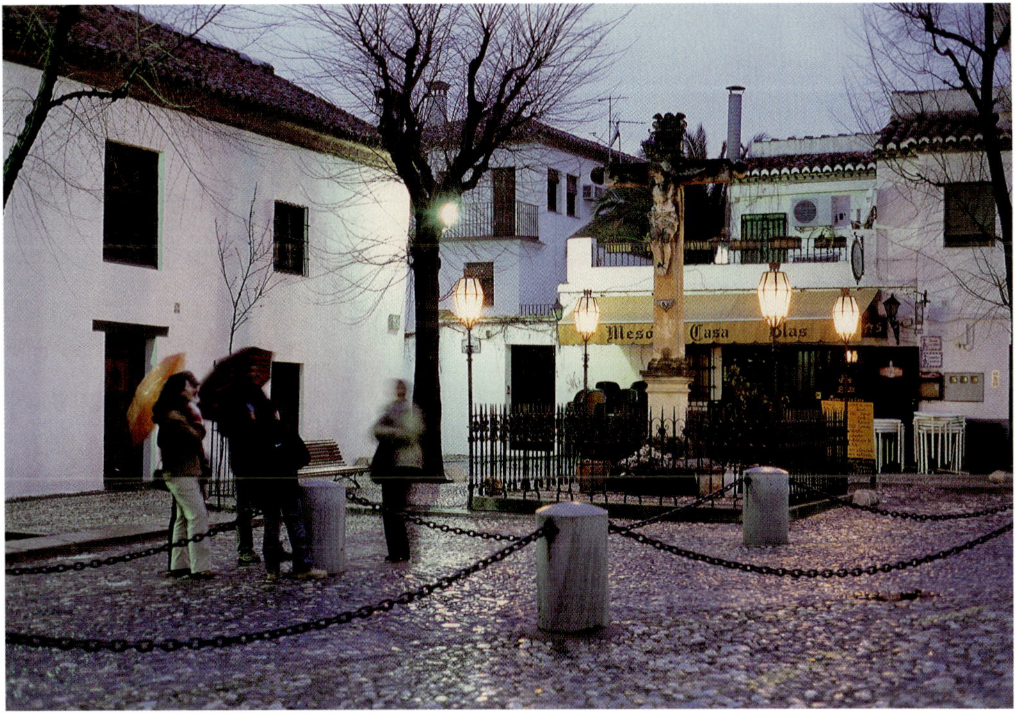

PLAZA SAN MIGUEL BAJO
On one side stands the church of the same name and in a corner the Christ of the Clamps, which was broken during the Civil War and later rebuilt with some large clamps that are easily seen in the sculpture.

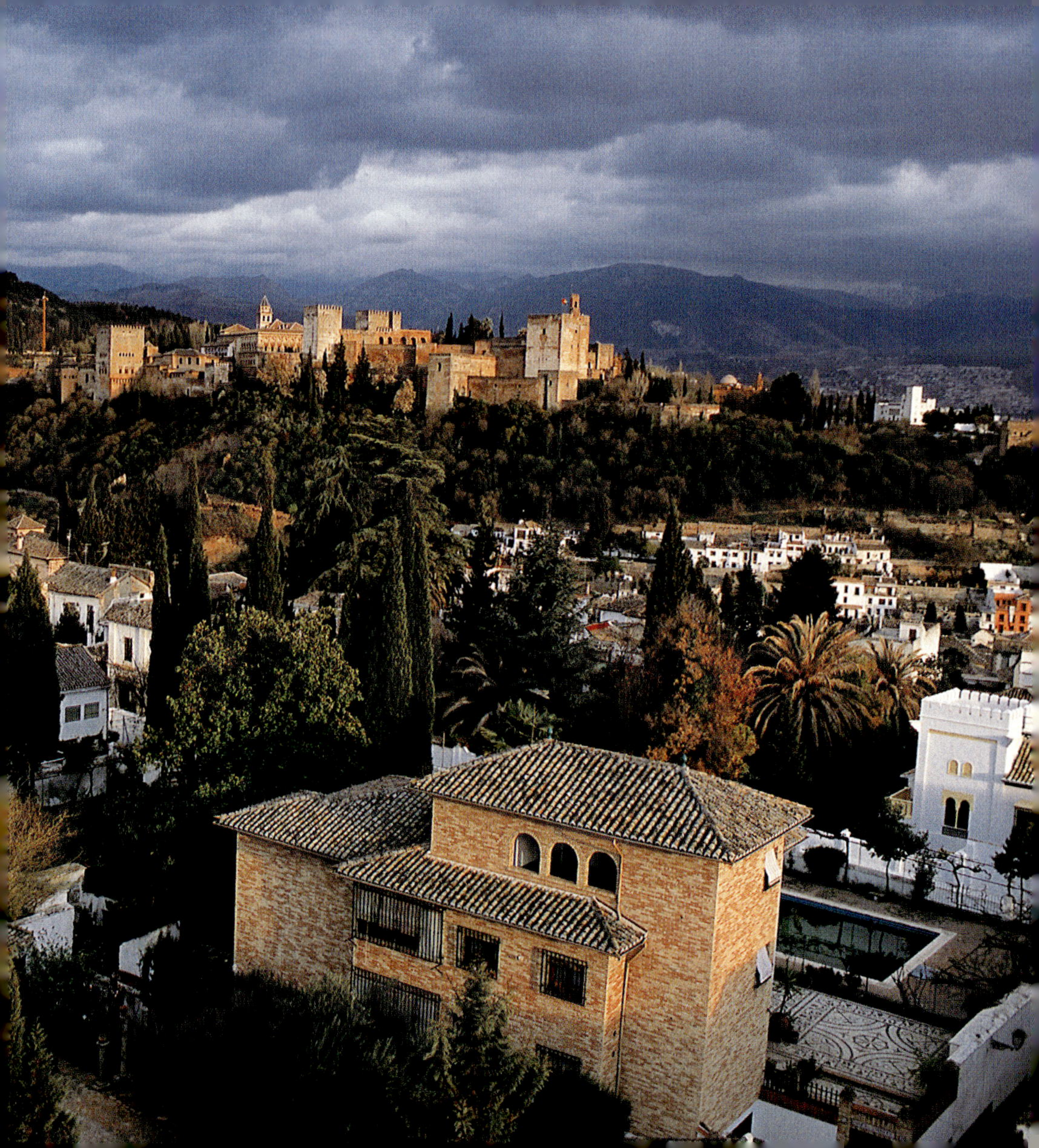

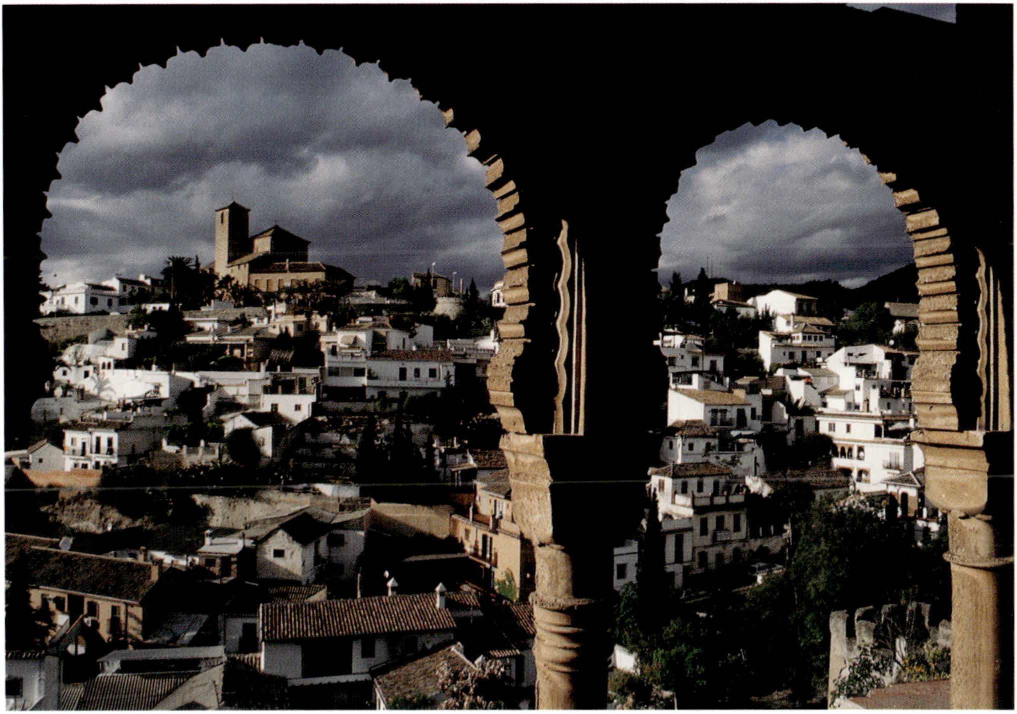

ATTRACTIVE IMAGES
The Albayzín is full of images loaded with history and romanticism.

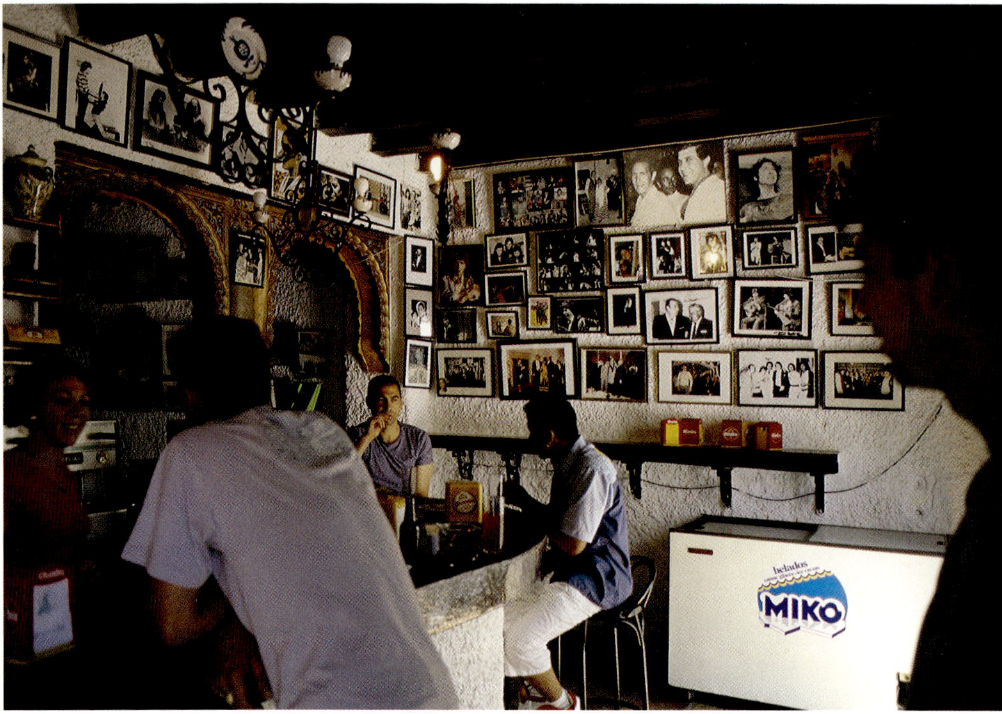

LA PORRONA
In Plaza Larga.

CALLE DEL AGUA
One of the busiest parts of the district.

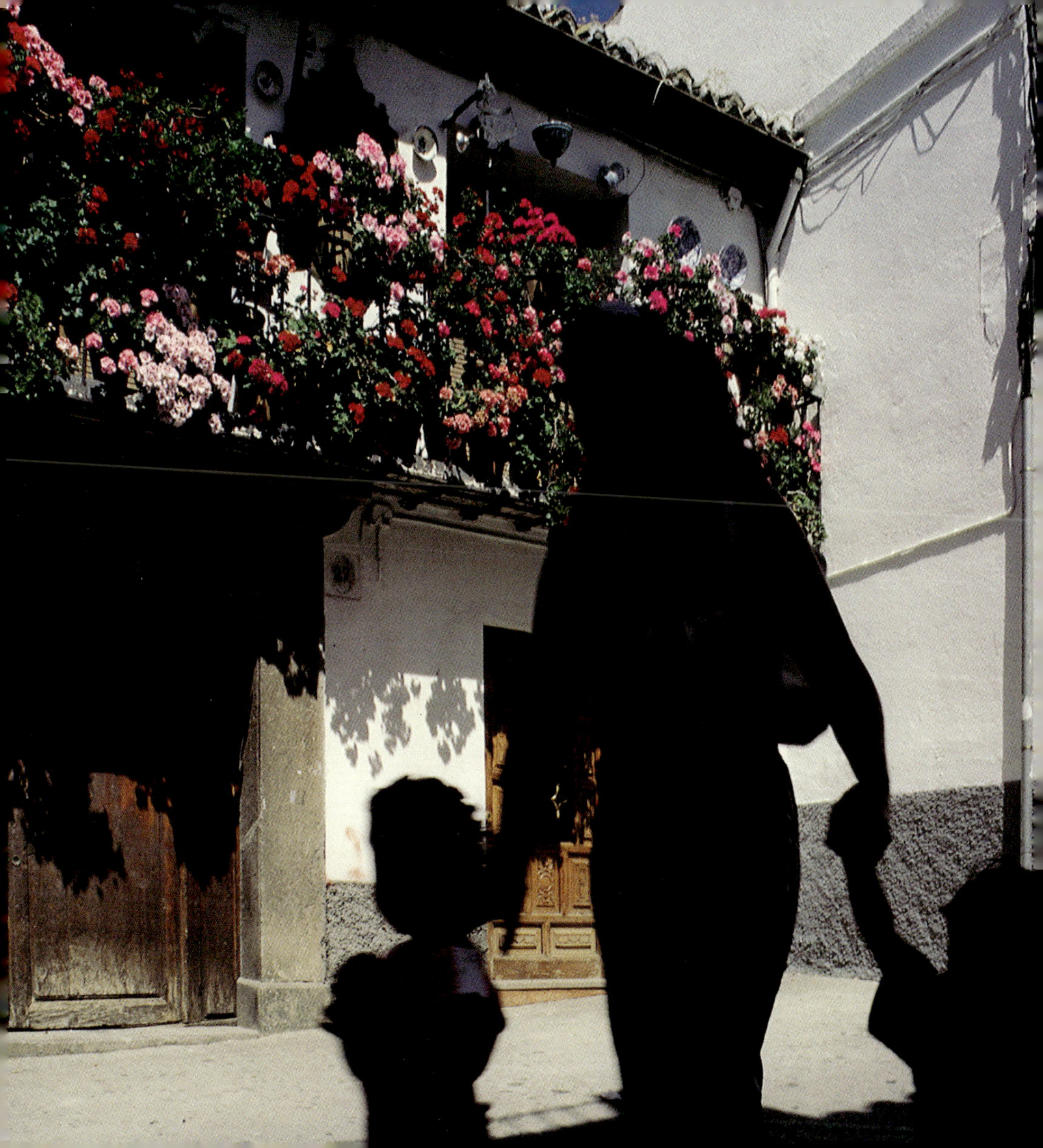

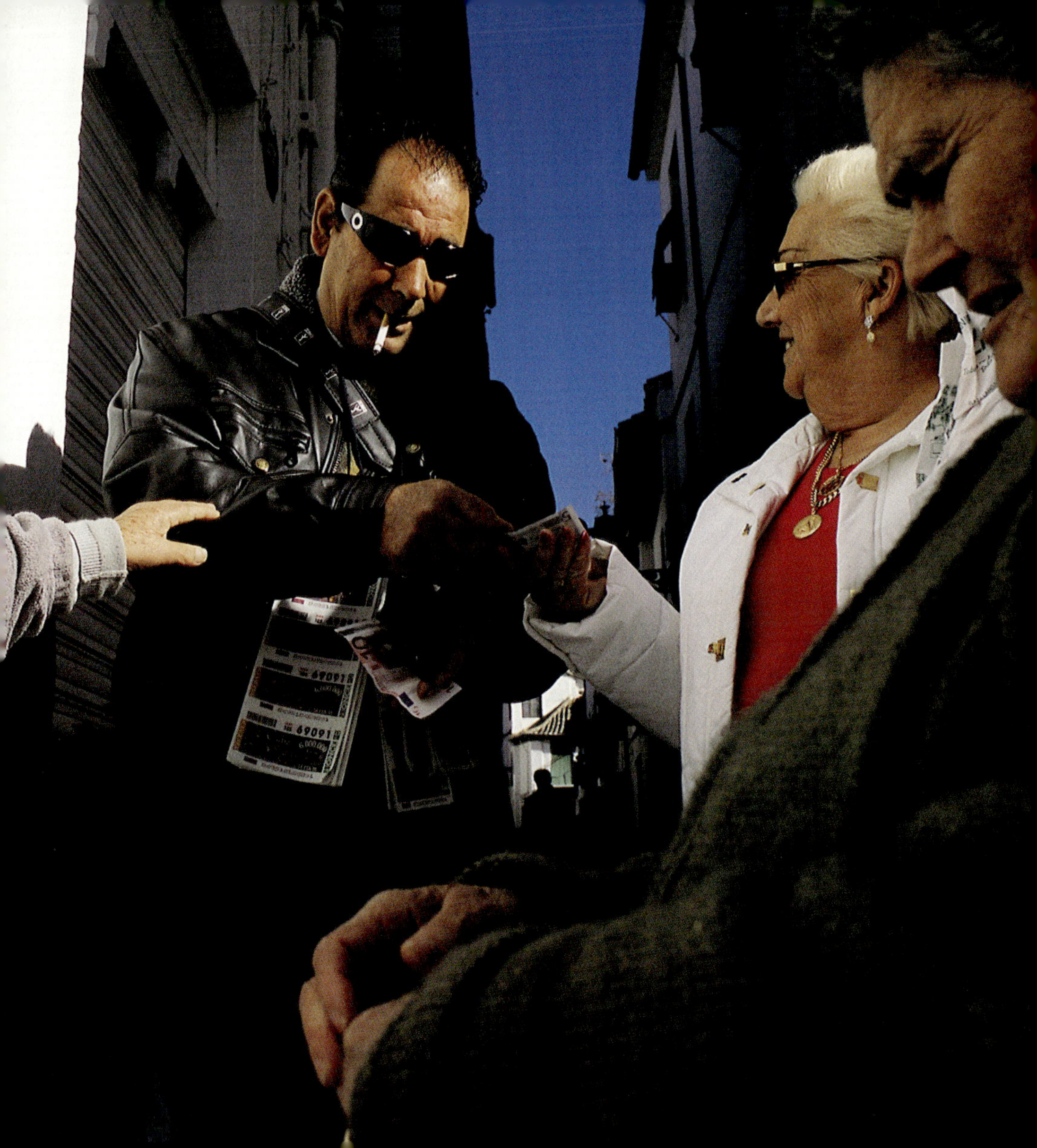
69091

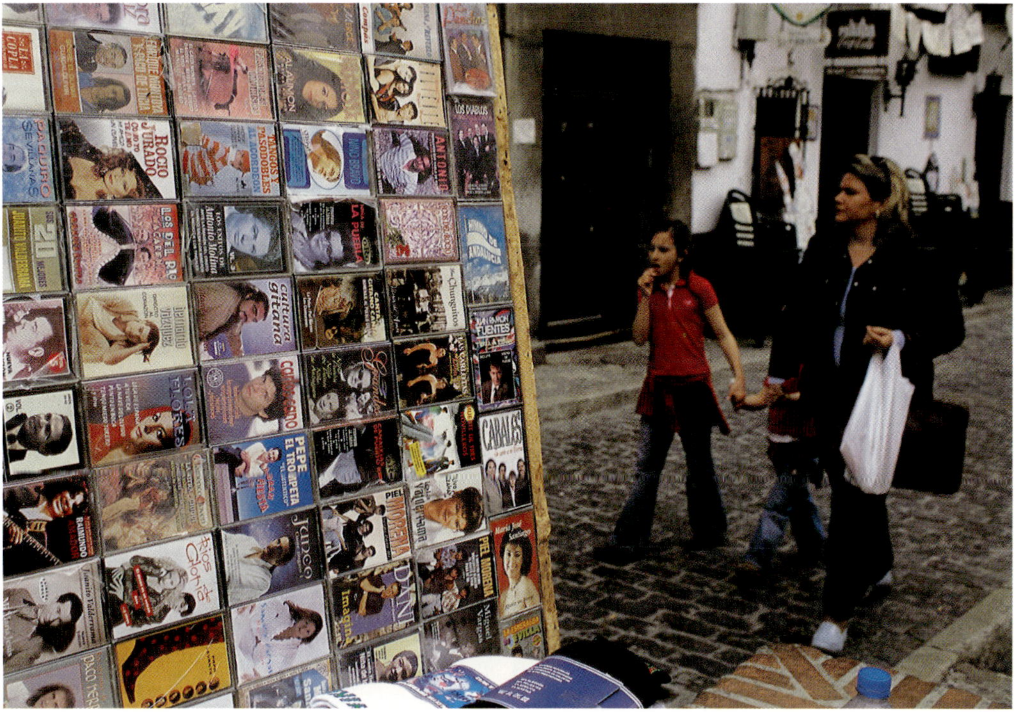

PLAZA LARGA
In the heart of the Albayzín, where there is a lively street market.

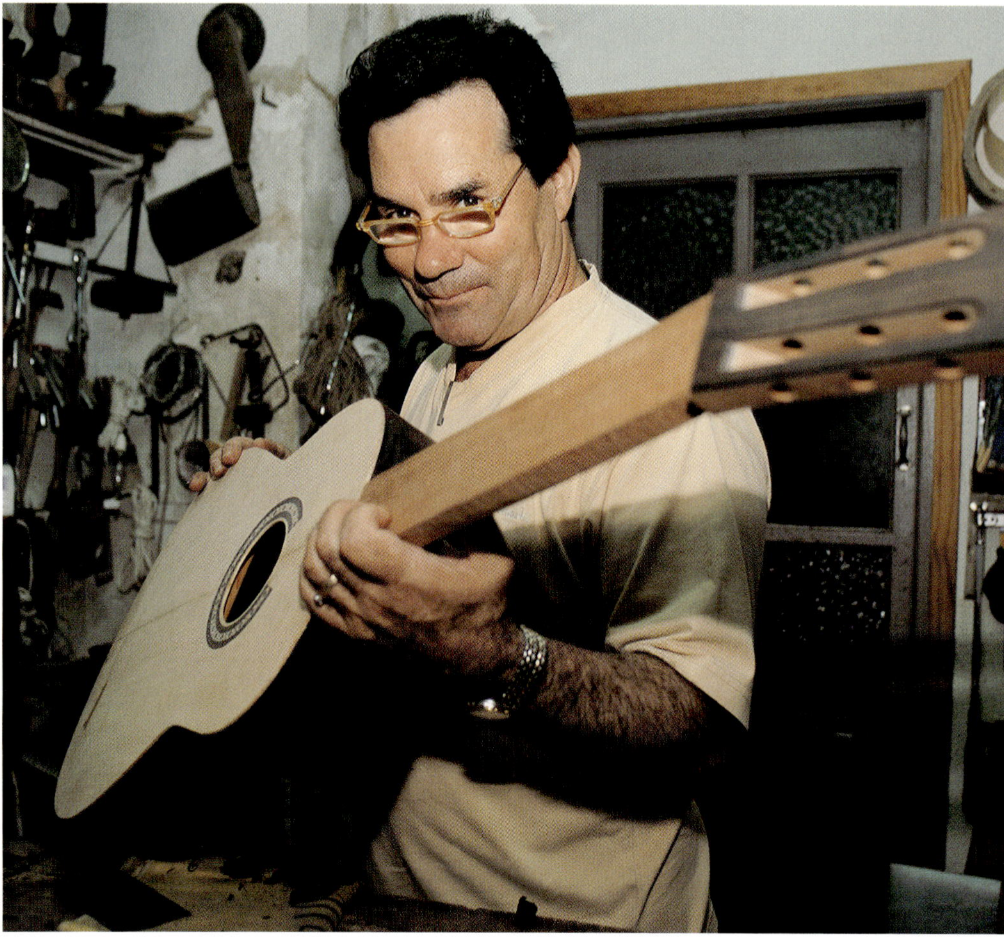

FRANCISCO MANUEL DÍAZ
Well-known guitar maker, *tocaor* or player-composer, and member of the Platería group.

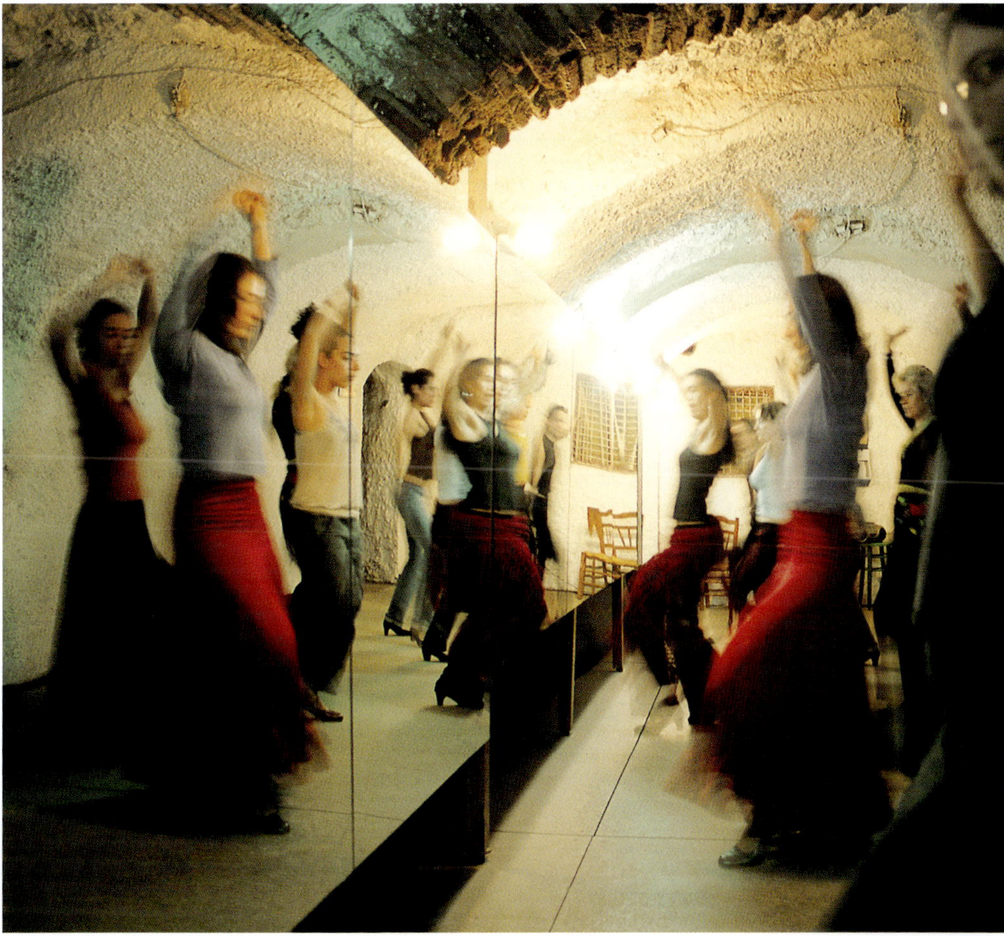

CARMEN DE LAS CUEVAS
Flamenco academy.

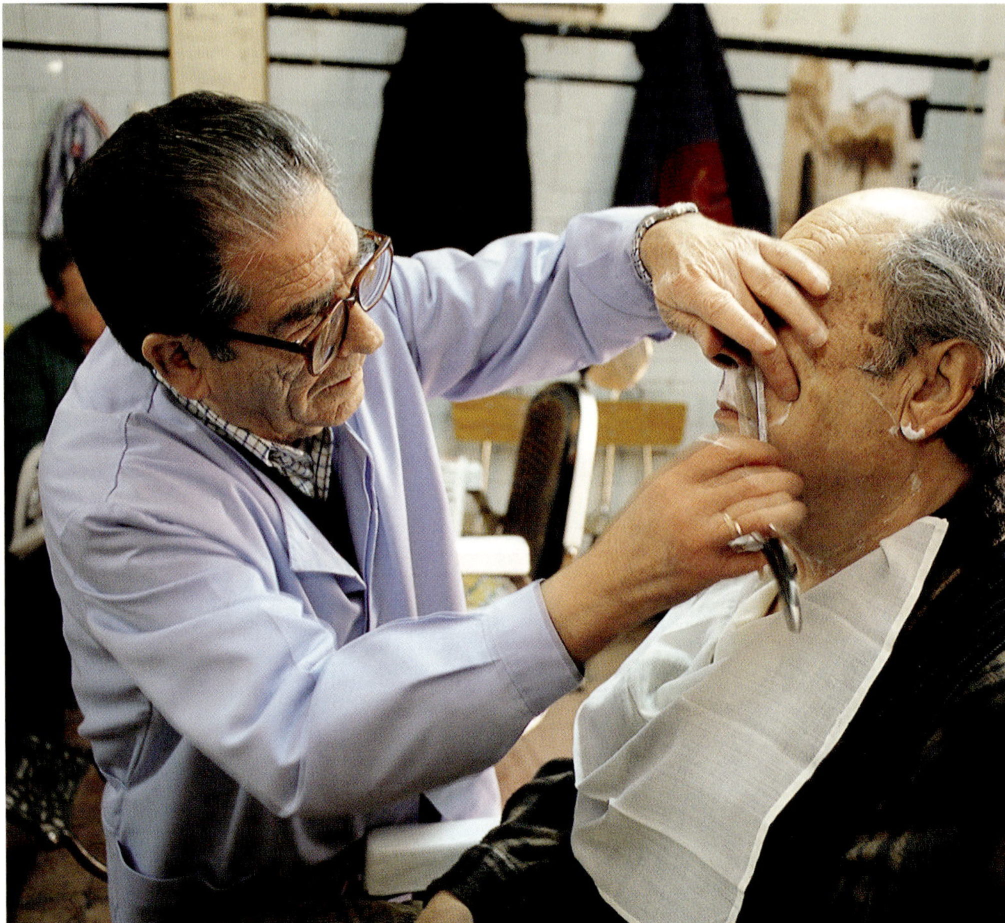

JUAN "TRUENO"
Working in his barbershop in the Plaza del Salvador.

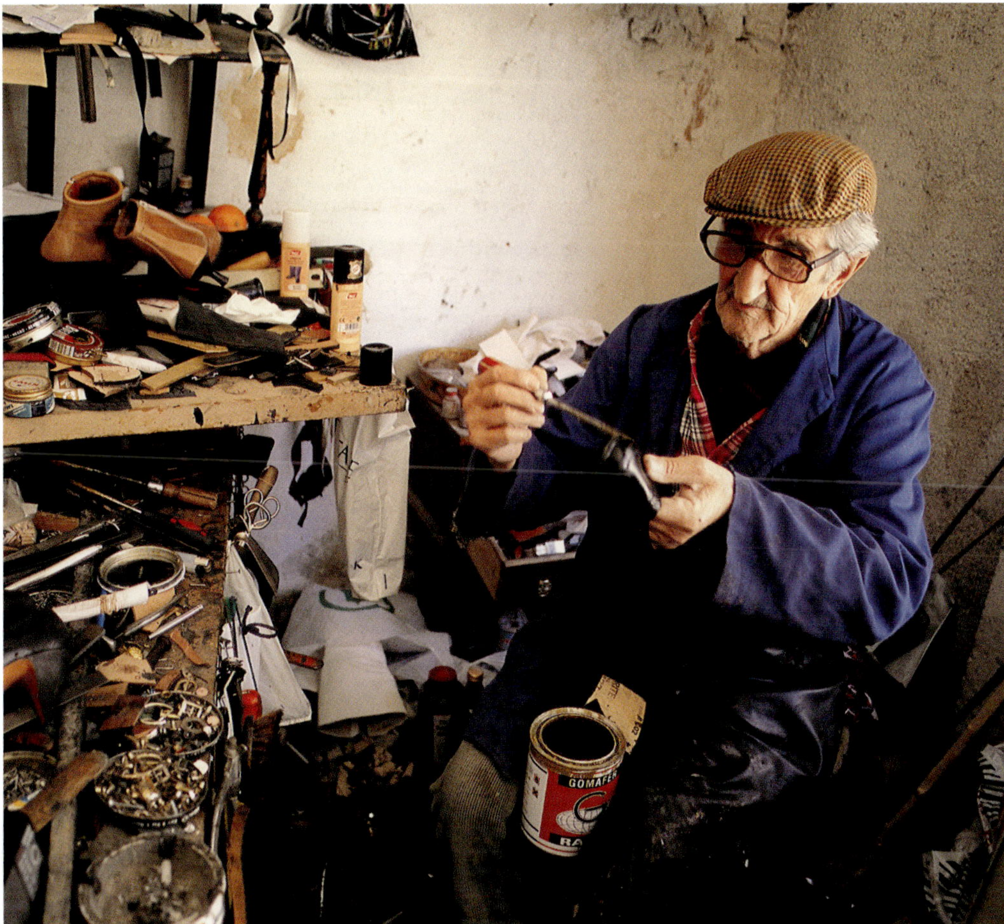

JOSÉ DOMINGUEZ
Craftsman cobbler in Calle del Horno de San Agustín.

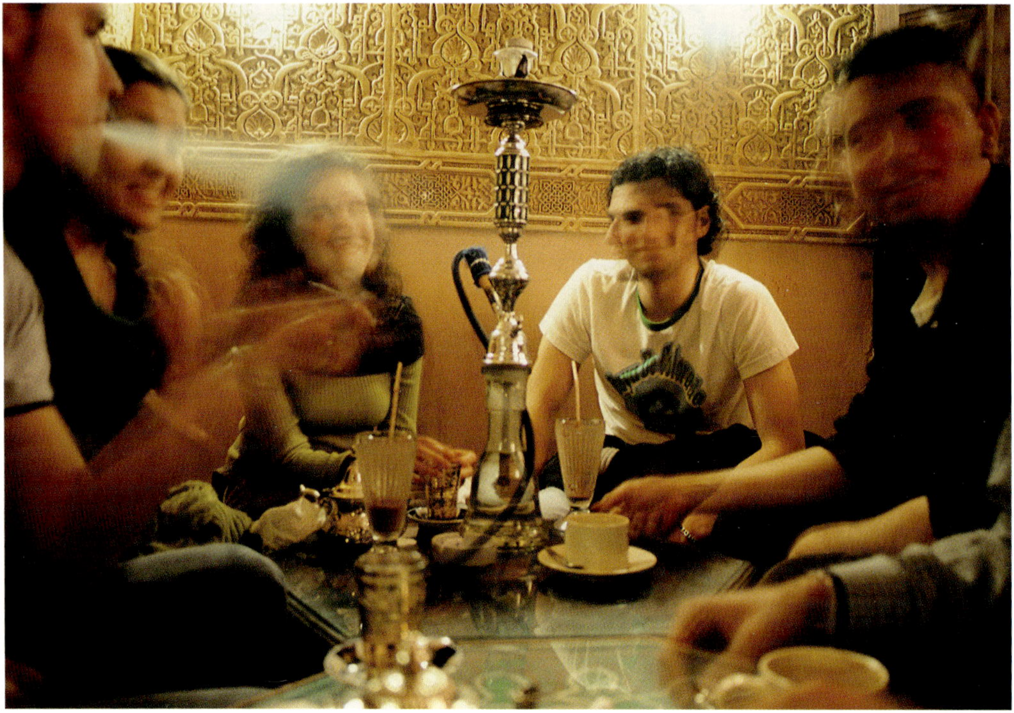

CALDERERÍA NUEVA
Dar Ziryab teahouse, one of the many sited in this street.

The coming and going of people and goods emulates a picture taken from the Medina of Fez.

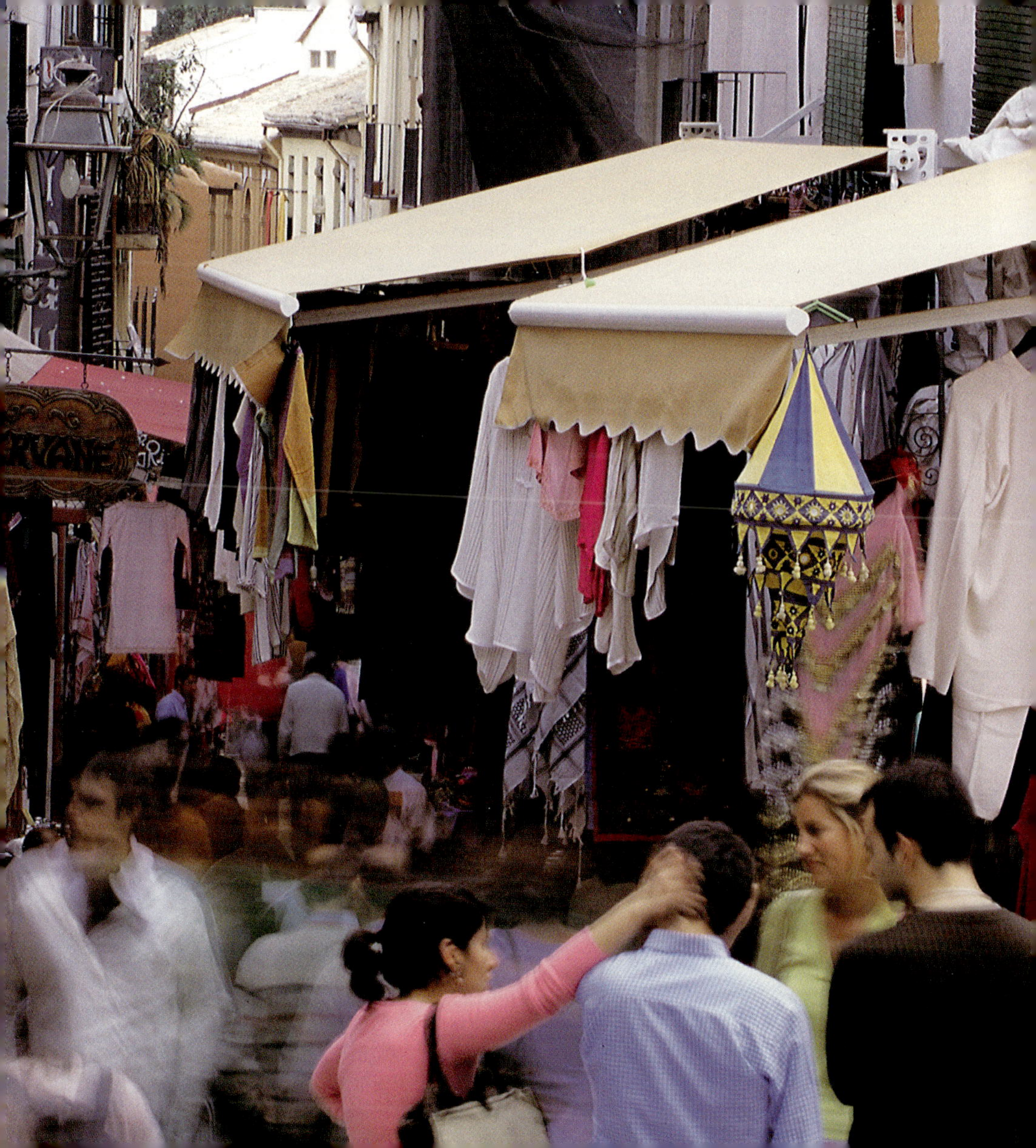

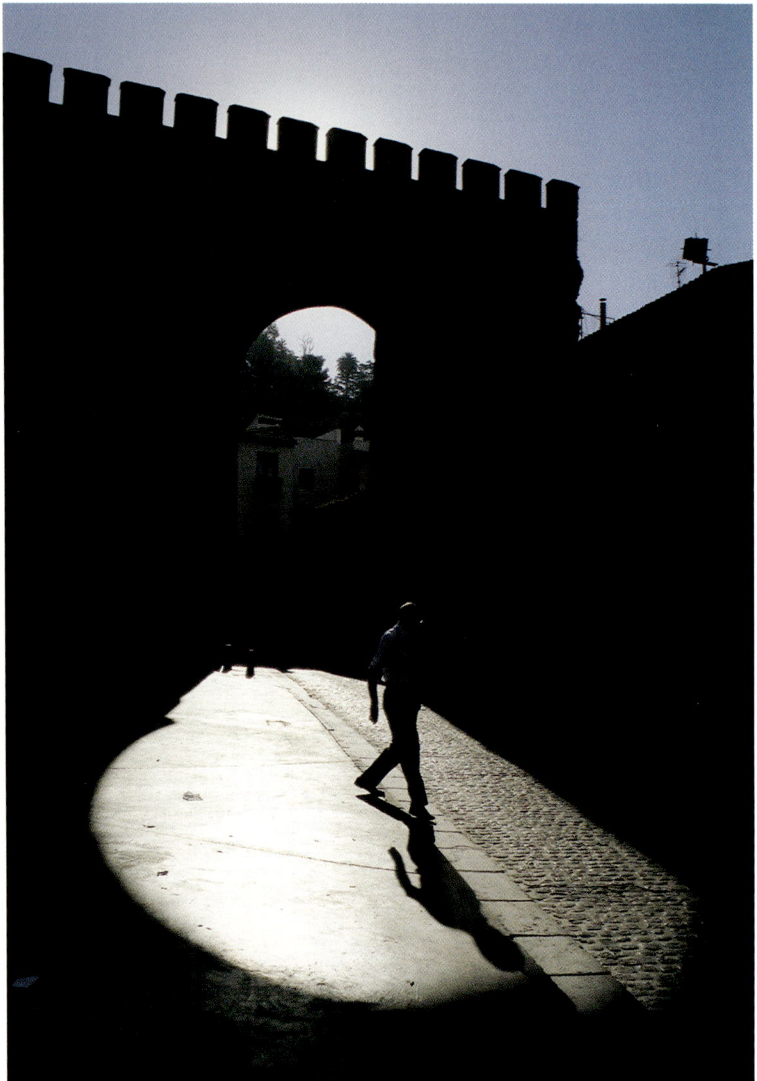

PUERTA DE ELVIRA
It was the main, and biggest, doorway of the city, and through which the Catholic Monarchs entered Granada for the first time.

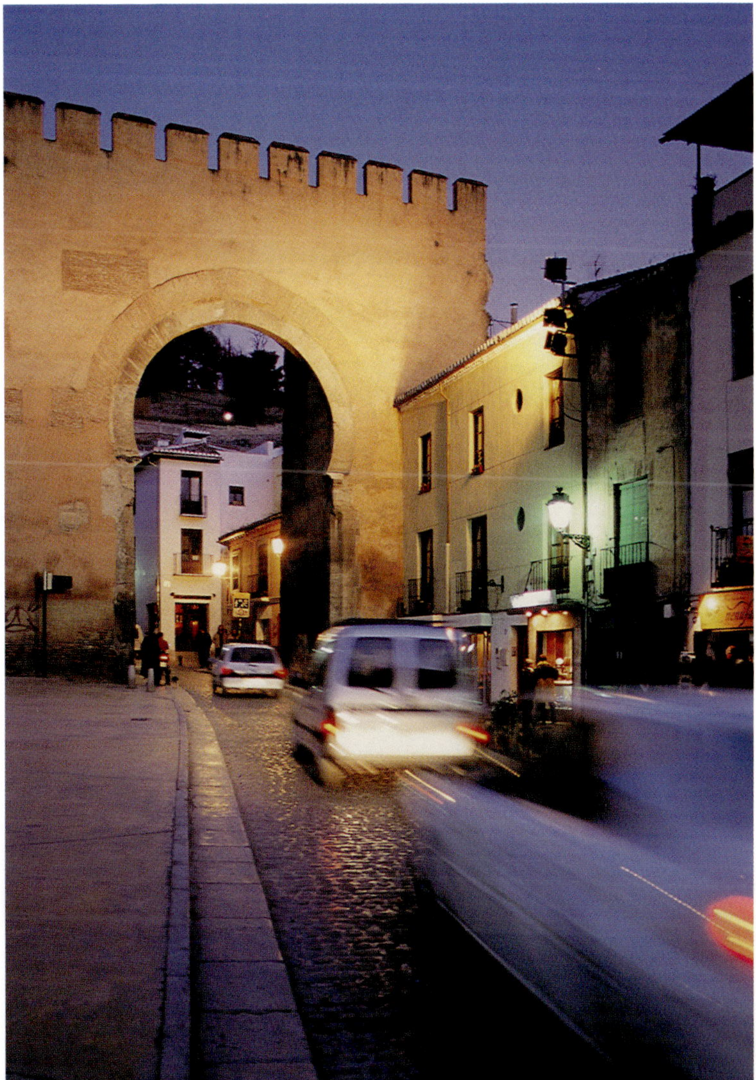

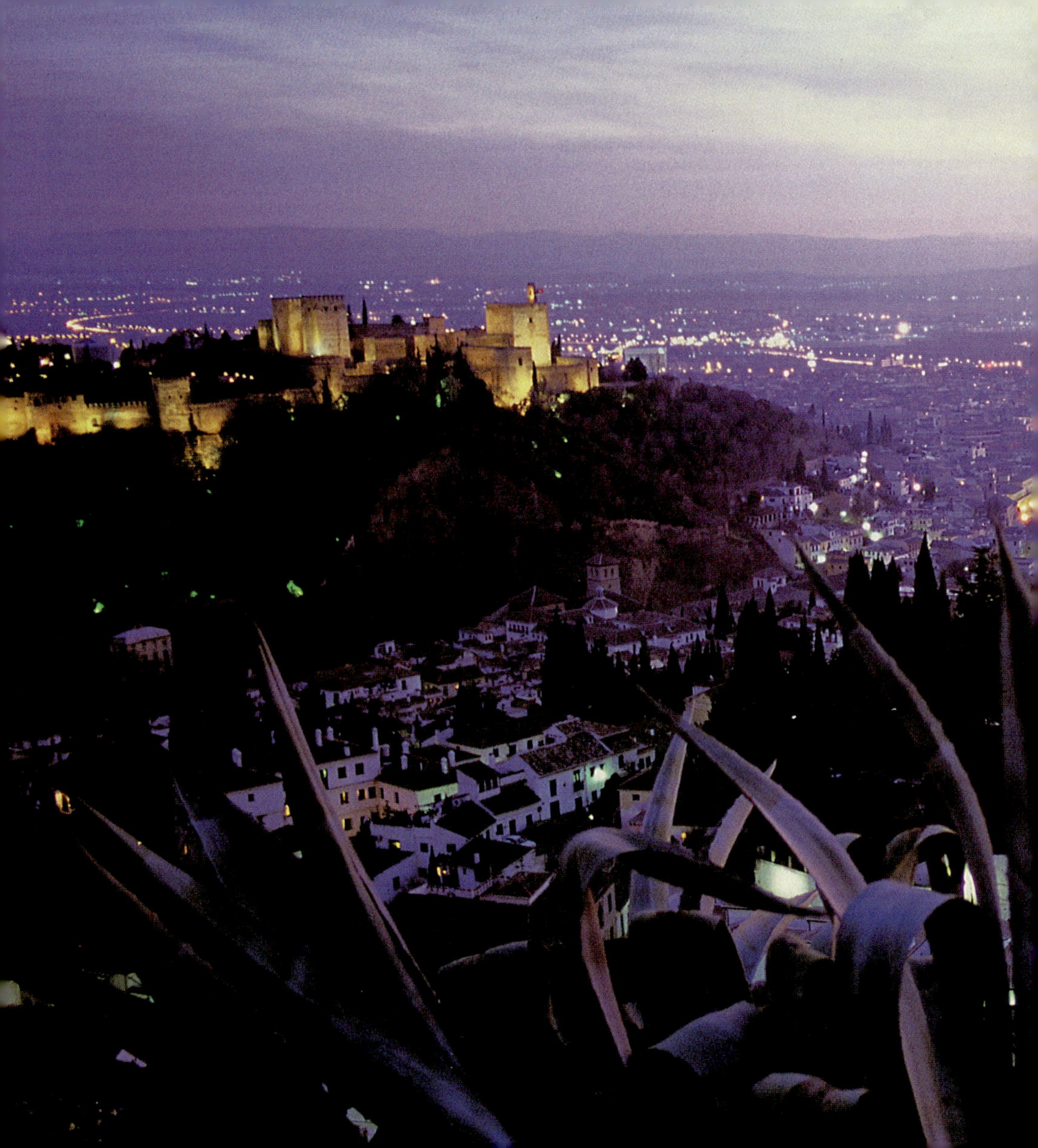

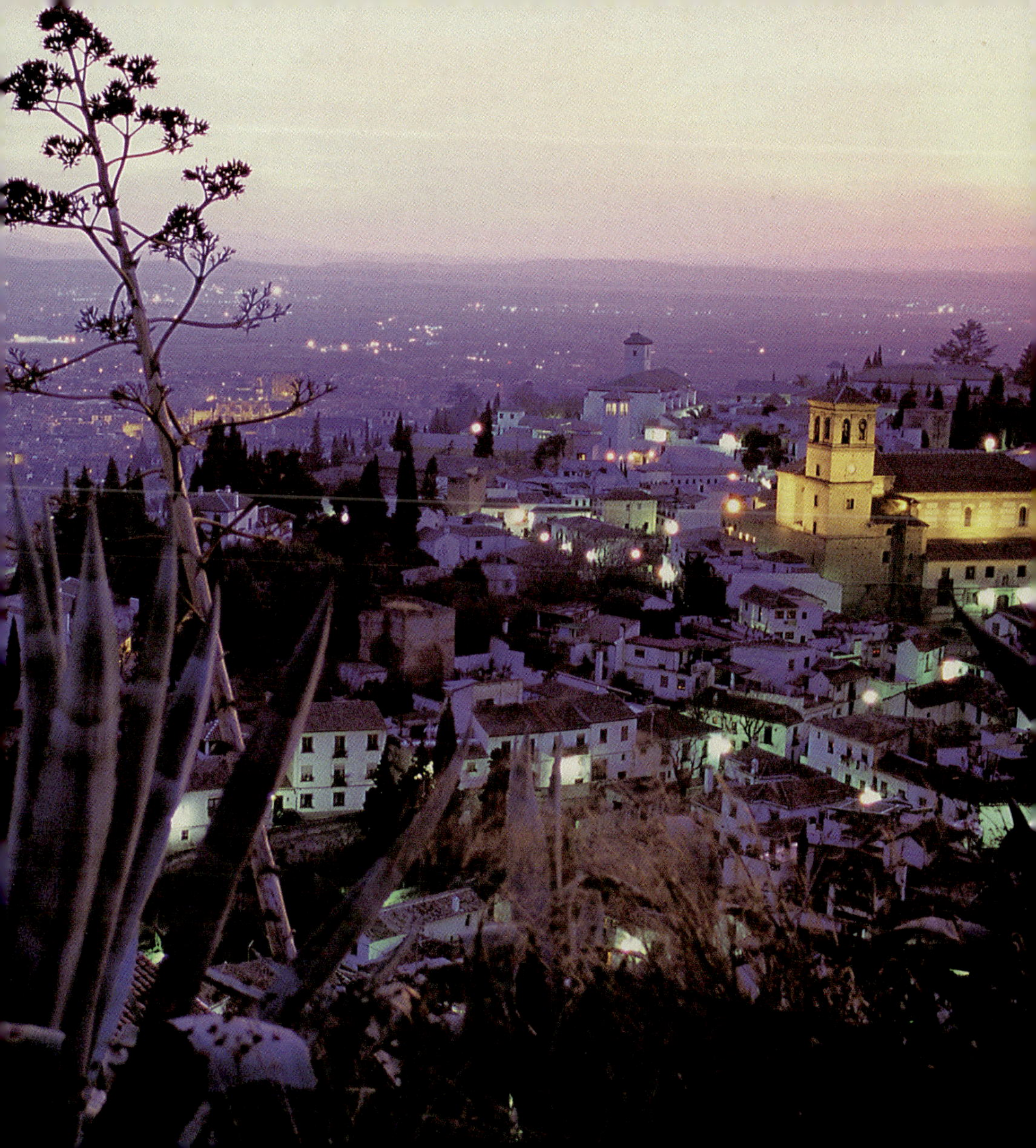

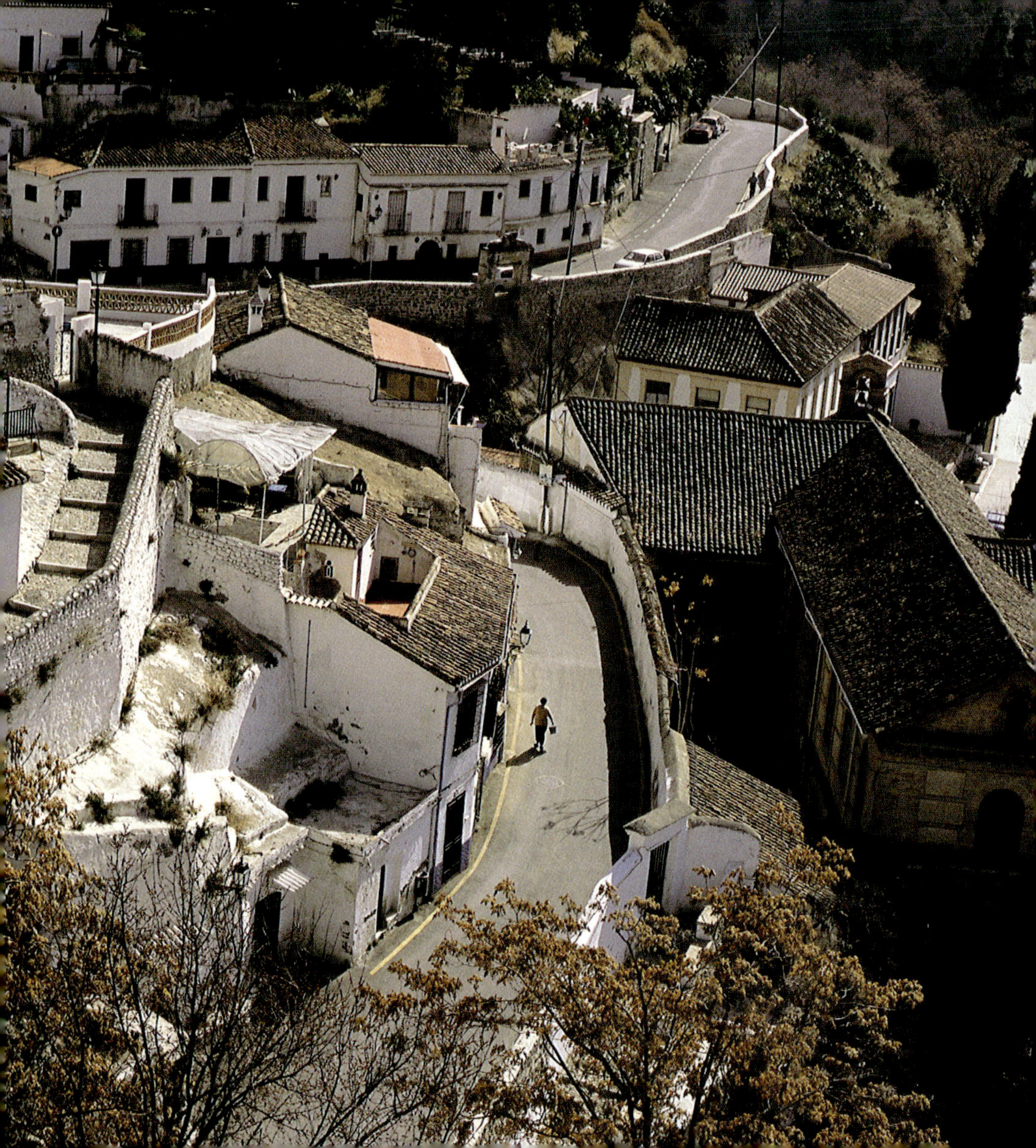

THE SACROMONTE

To the east of the wall that surrounds the Albayzin, between agaves and prickly pears are the anarchically distributed caves of Sacromonte. It is a cave-dwelling district of doubtful origin, although the leading authorities say that it was founded by the most excluded sections of Granada society in the 16th century, outside the city walls and beyond any administrative control. It is thought that the district arose as a result of the arrival at Mount Valparaíso of the Muslims and Jews expelled from Granada, who were joined by a large number of gypsies, who with the passing of time took over the area. The Sacromonte became a focus of attention of *cante jondo*, traditional flamenco singing, and around 1950, caves such as those of Manolo Amaya, La Golondrina or María la Canastera attained great artistic prestige. If the traveller wants to take in the magic that the district exudes, they should attend a flamenco festival at night, where they will be able to enjoy the performance of a "*zambra granaina*", a local *palo*, the flamenco rhythm that is accompanied by three mimic dances; "the *alboreá*", "the *cachucha*" and "the *mosca*", which symbolise moments of a gypsy wedding. For its tradition and expertise, without speaking unfavourably of the others, the mythical cave of María La Canastera is the ideal venue to go to.

CUEVAS
In the Camino del Sacromonte.

The district is crowned by the Sacromonte abbey, a religious centre founded in the 17th century as a result of the commotion caused by the finding of some human remains that the Church, among others, attributed to Saint Cecilio, the first bishop of the city and patron saint of Granada. Mount Valparaíso, called from that time on Sacromonte, became a centre of pilgrimage. The inside of the abbey houses a modest museum and the Holy Caves, with the oven where Saint Cecilio was supposedly burnt with other martyr saints under Roman domination.

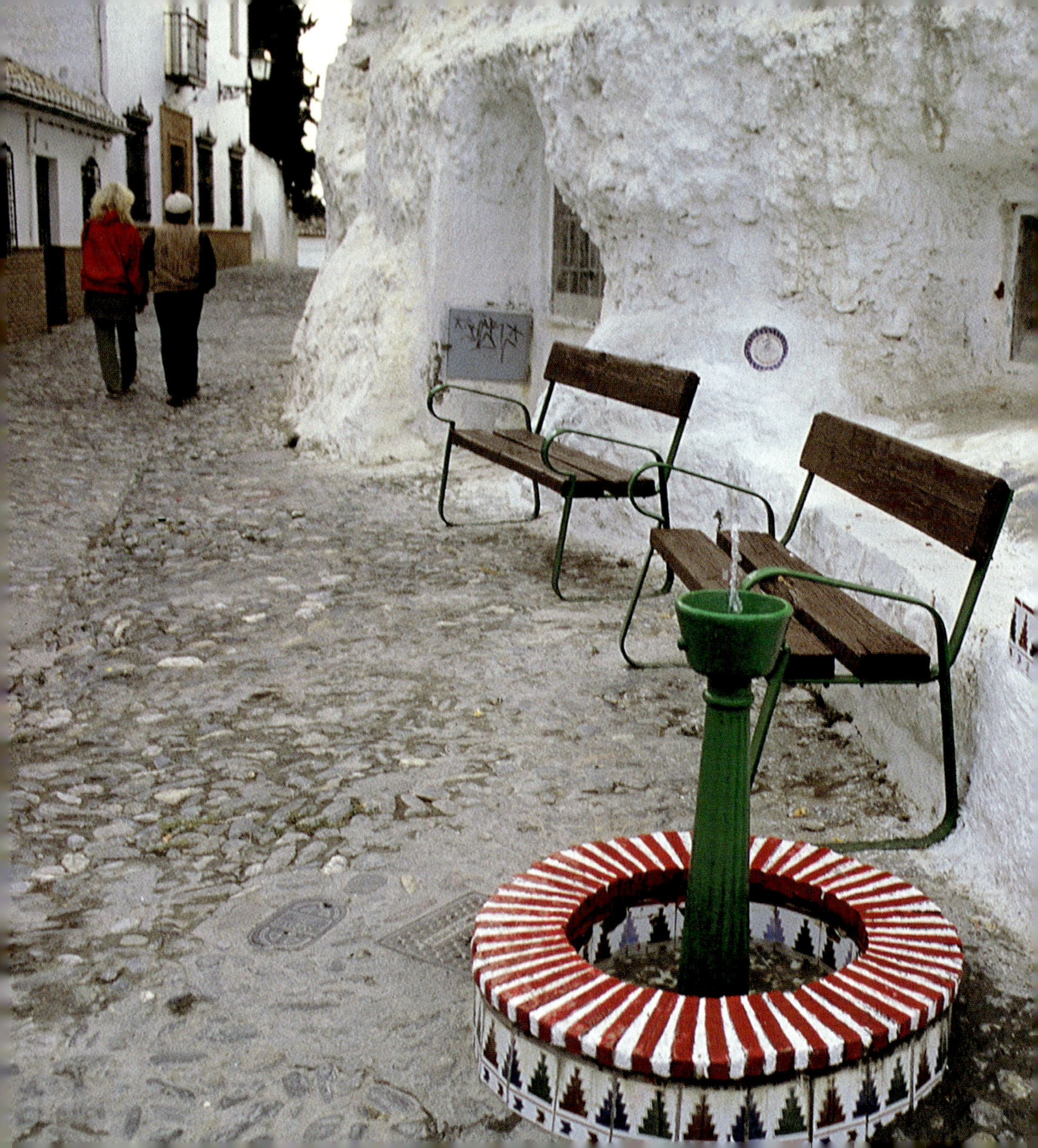

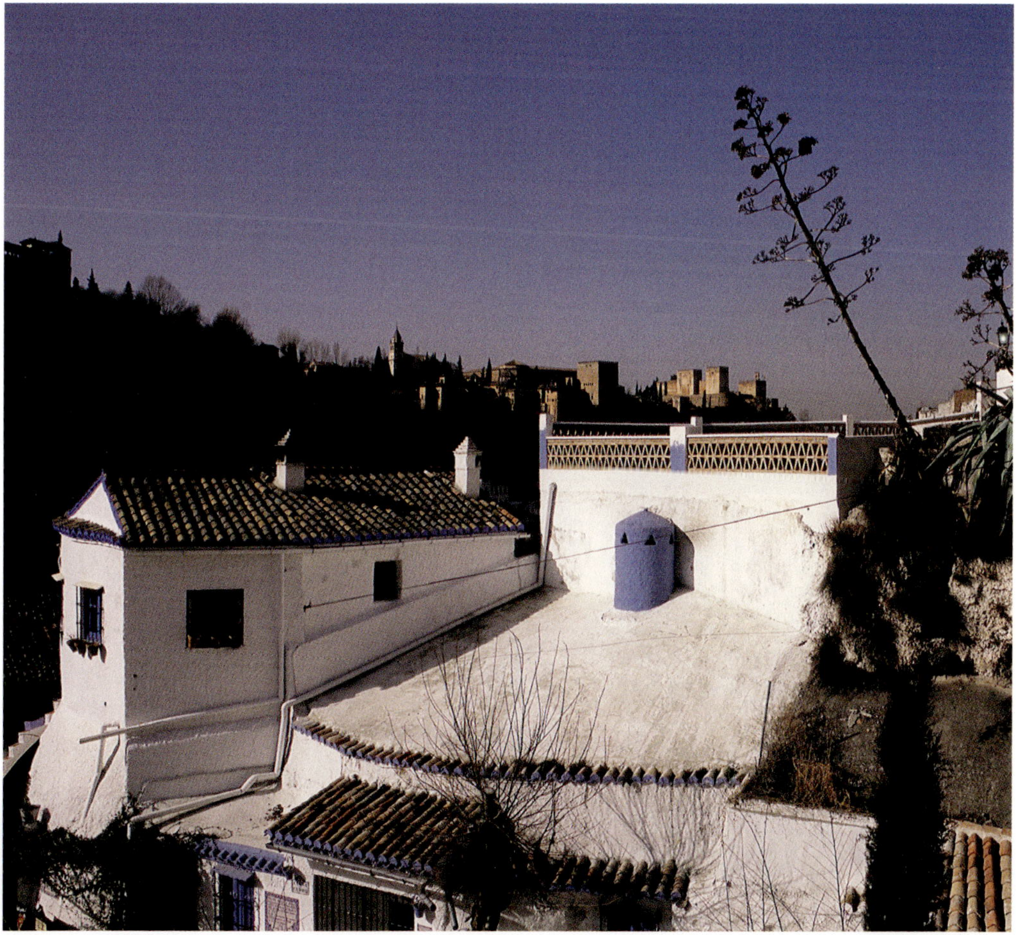

FOUNTAIN OF THE POPPY
In the "middle" section of the area.

THE ALHAMBRA
From the Sacromonte.

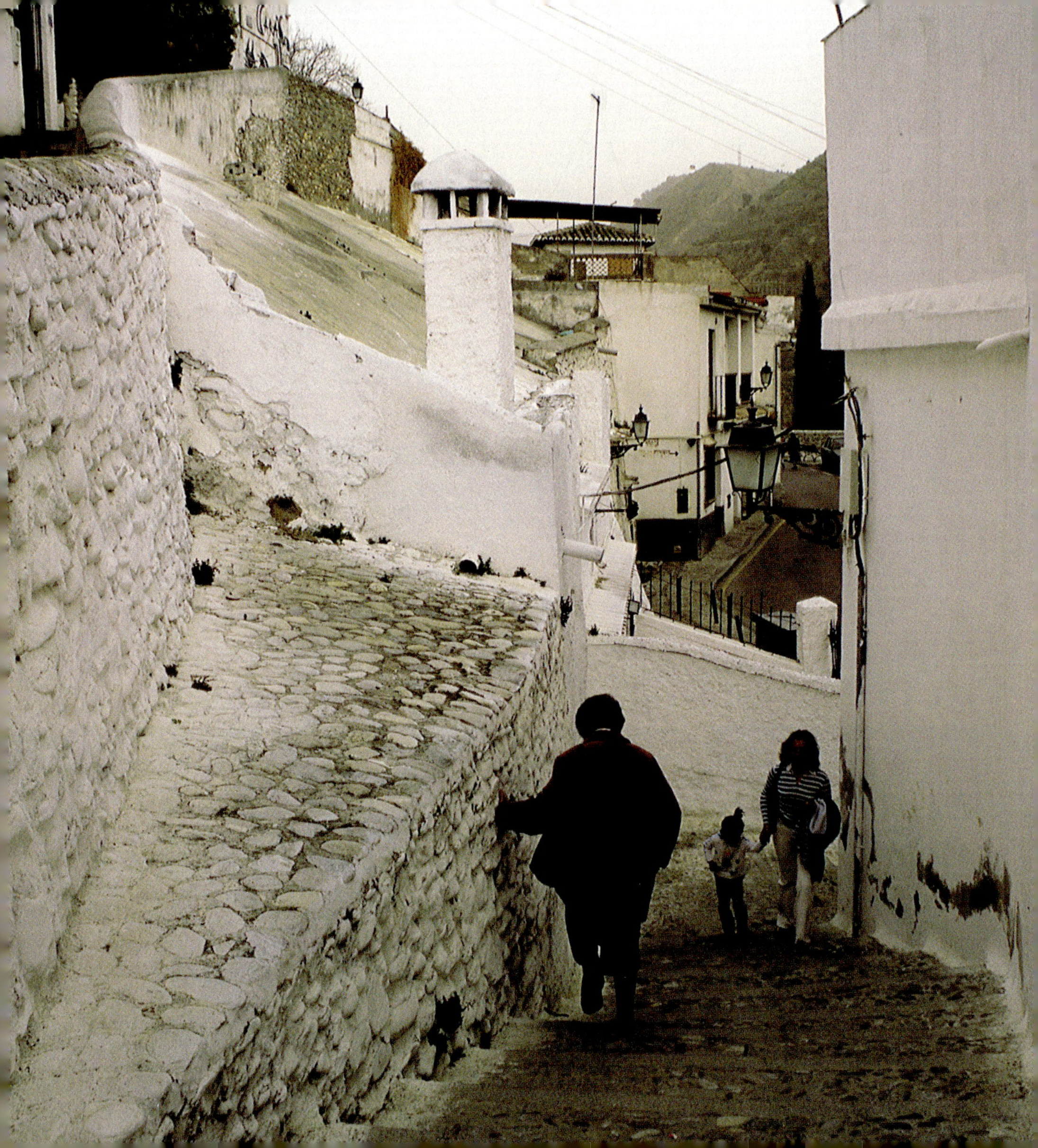

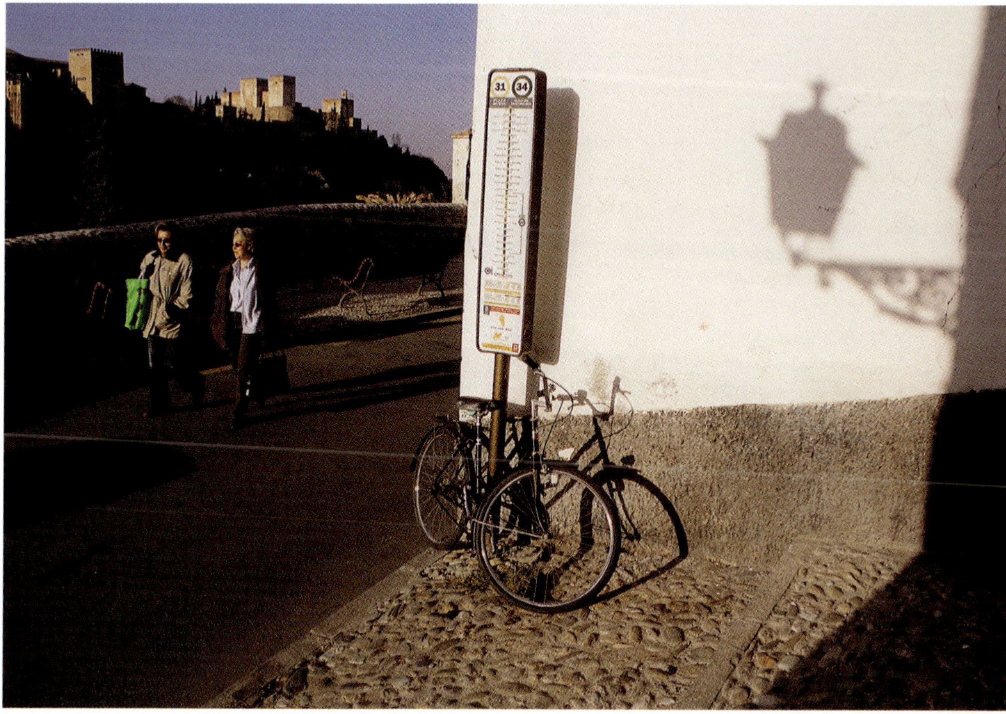

THE GYPSY DISTRICT OF GRANADA
It is the quietest part of the city: wandering around its streets means enjoying the peace and quiet.

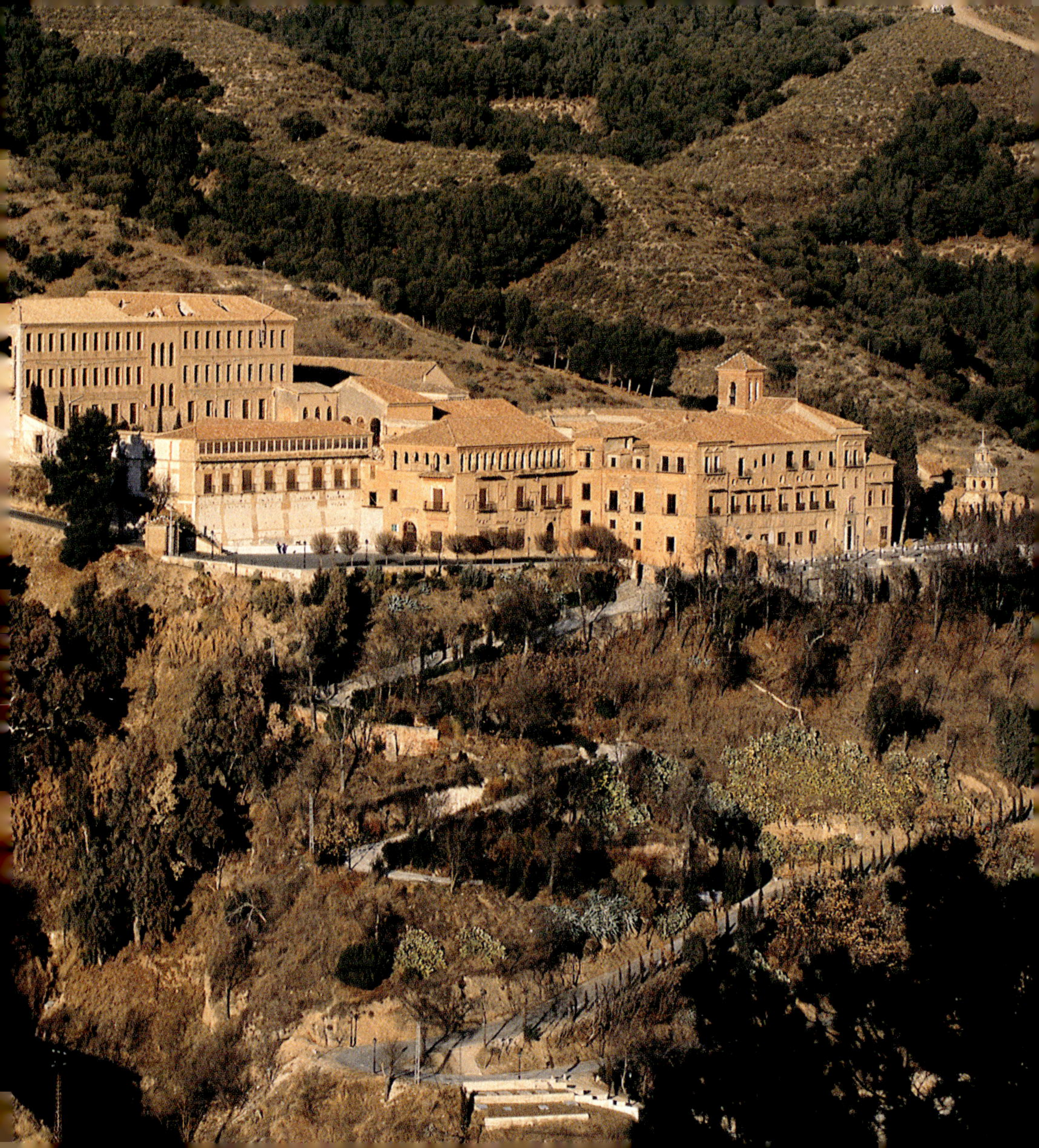

ABBEY OF THE SACROMONTE
General view.

Lantern over the chapels that house the Holy Caves.

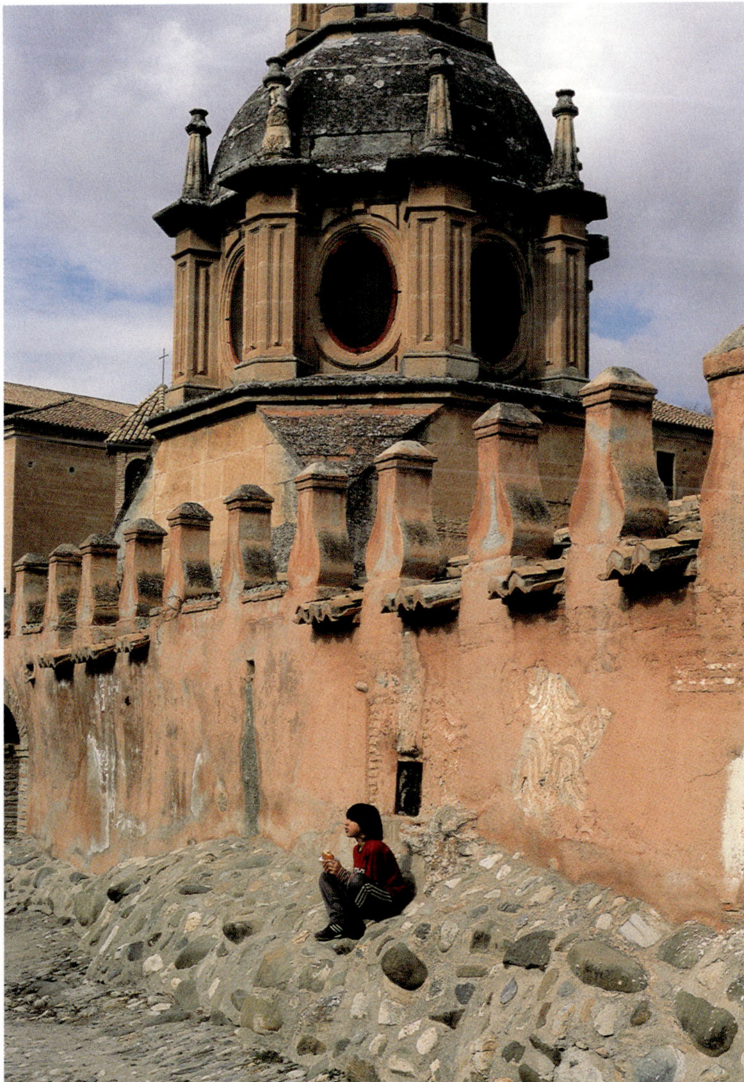

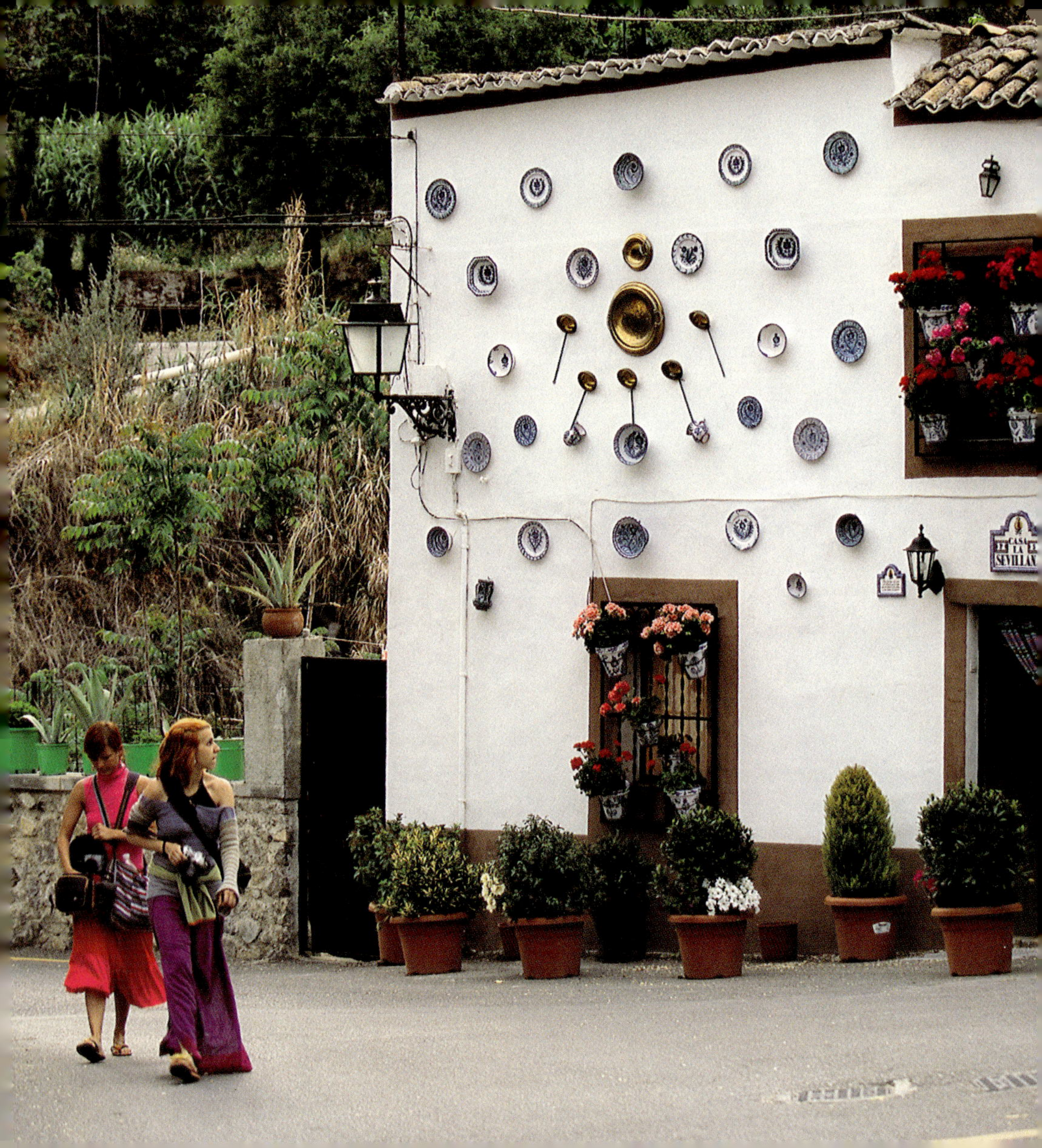
CASA
LA
SEVILLAN

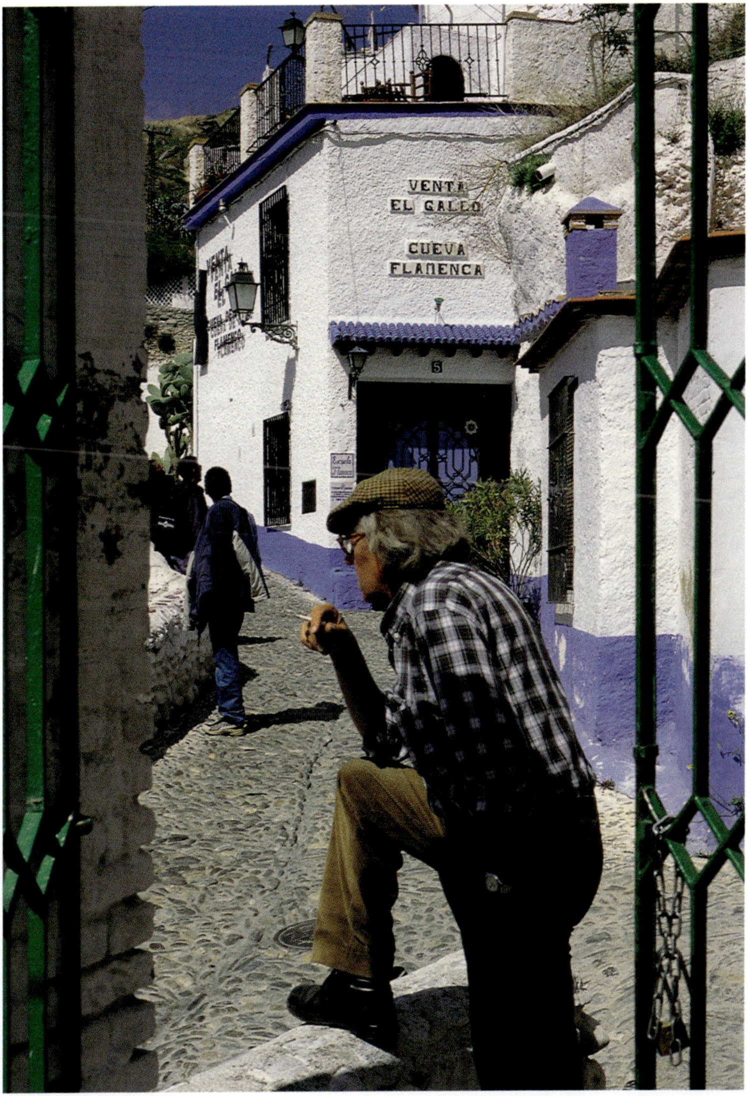

CHARMING CORNERS
The Sacromonte is full of secluded corners that ooze tradition.

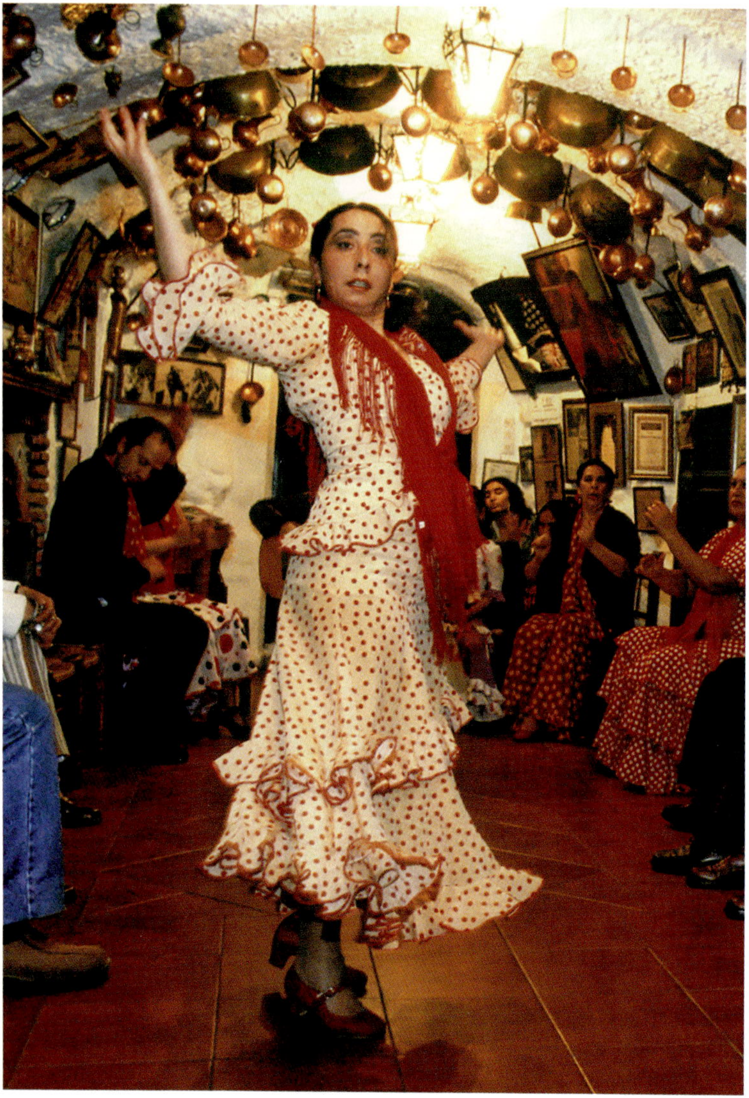

CAVE OF MARÍA LA CANASTERA
The caves that put on flamenco shows are an enormous pool of artistes.

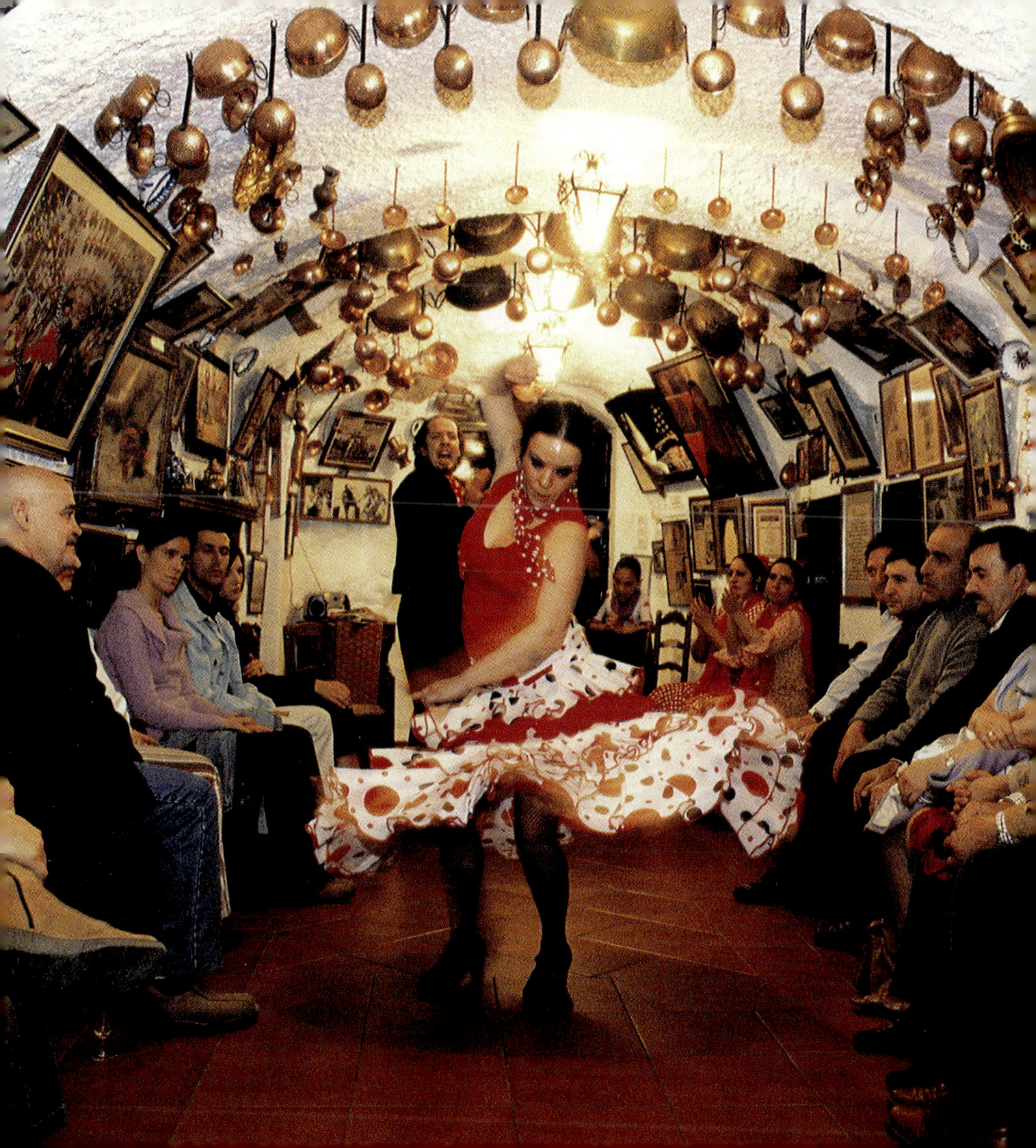

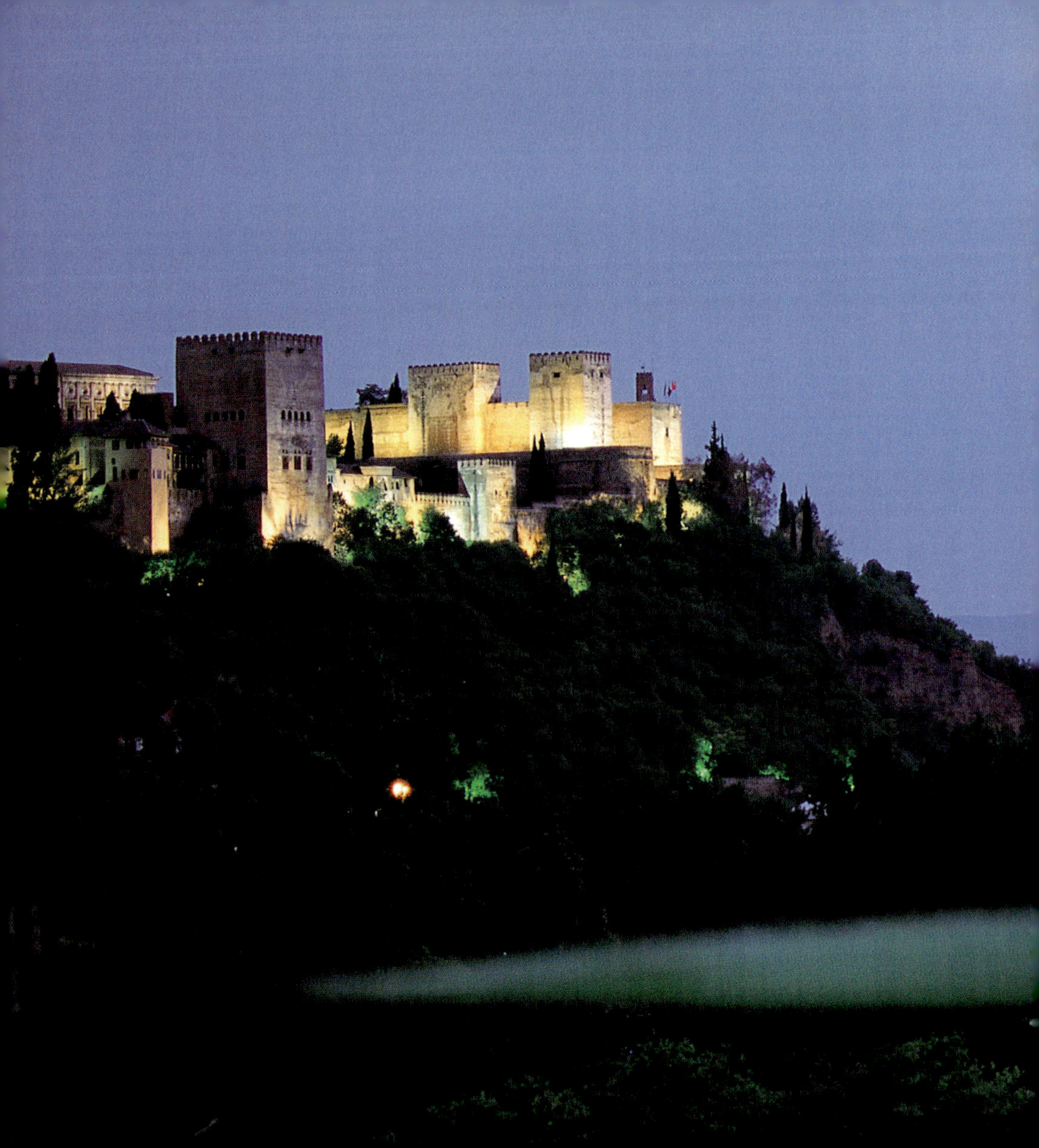

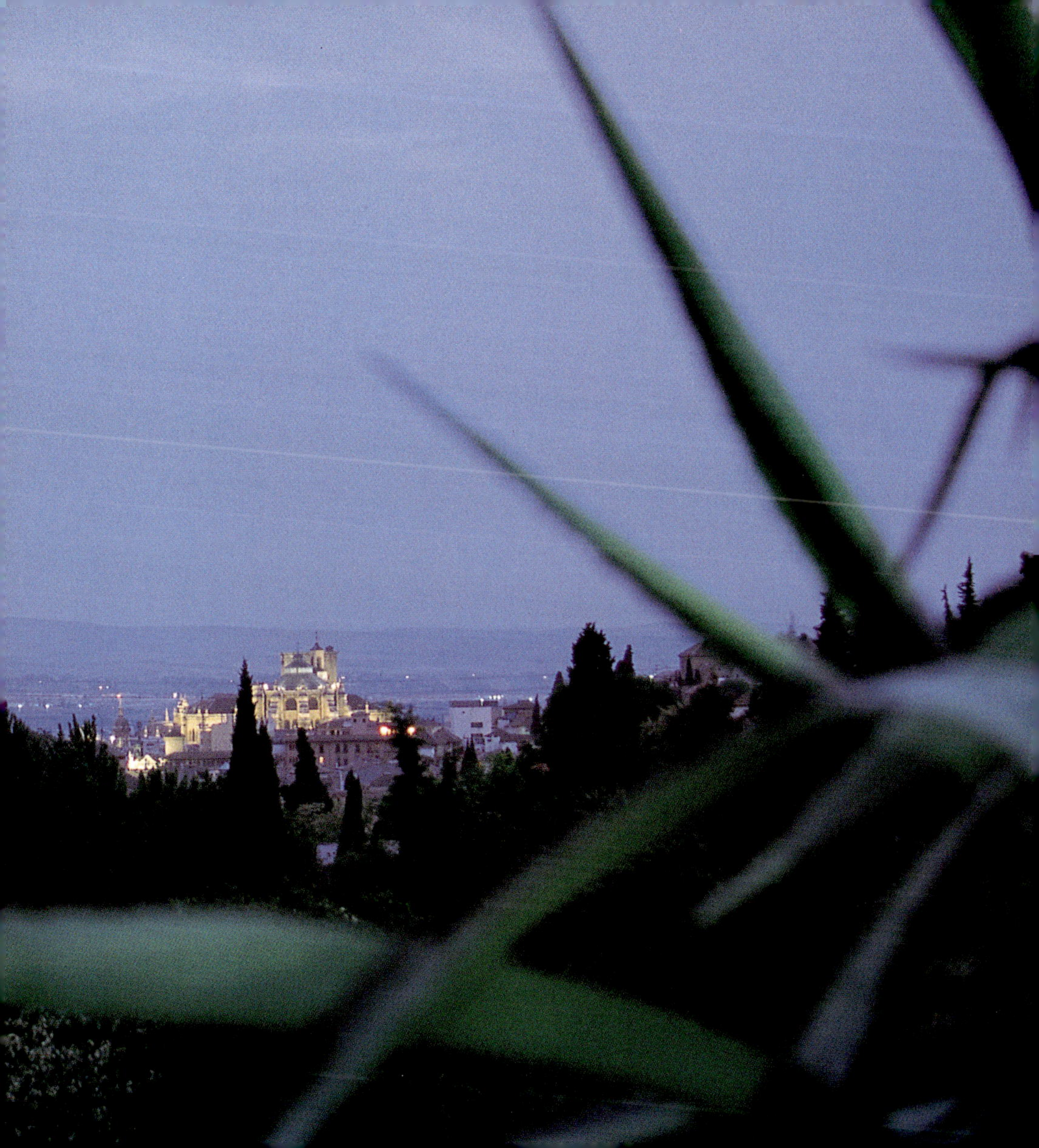

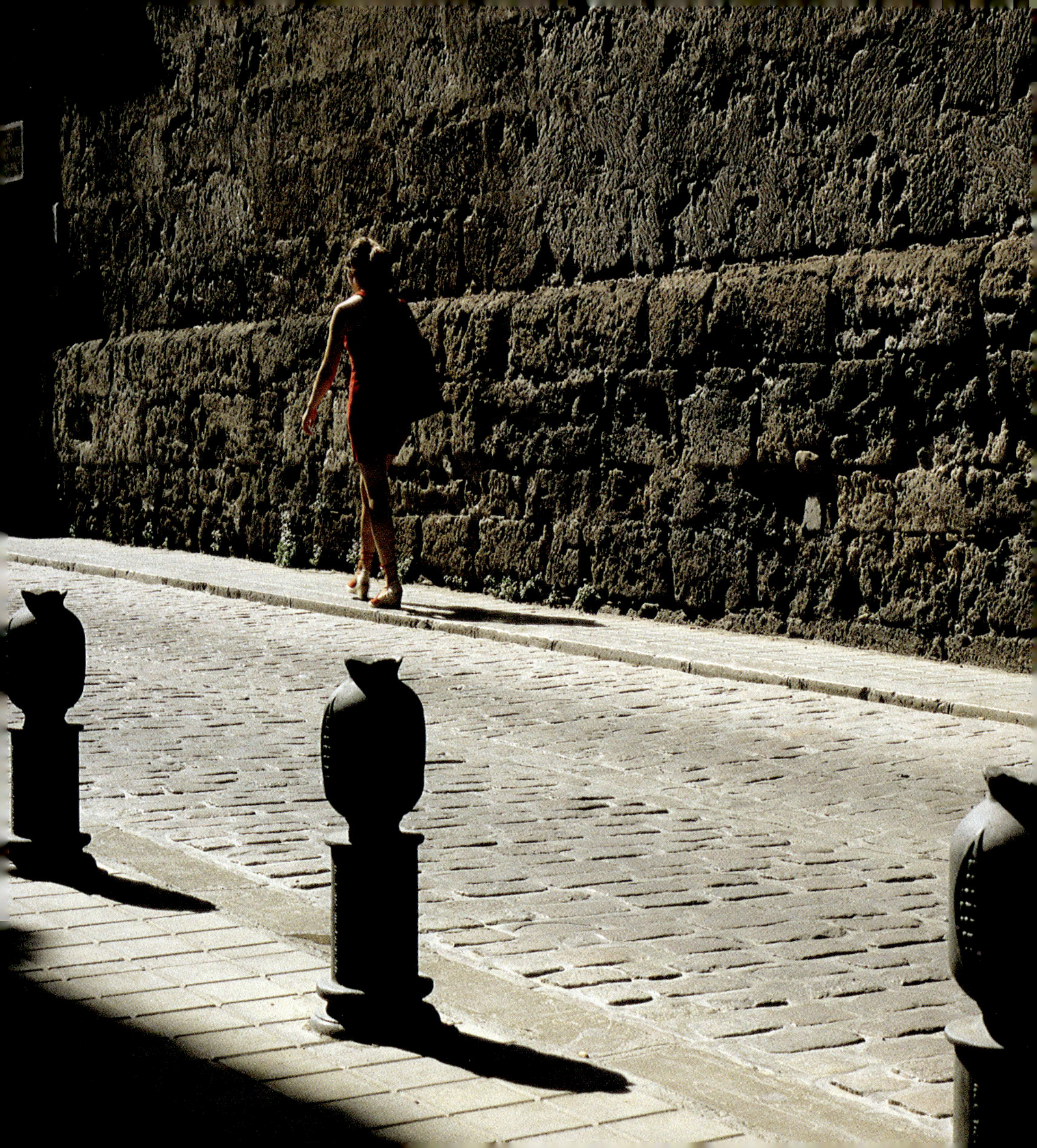

THE LOW CITY

At the foot of the hills spreads the more urban Granada, where the main squares open up and the main streets that make up the city. The layout, while maintaining Arab constructions, is to a large extent the result of reforms and extensions made over the last five-hundred years. This part, less picturesque than the Albayzin, the Sacromonte or the Alhambra, possesses big centres such as the Science Park of the Congress Hall, monuments of remarkable value such as the Gothic-Renaissance Cathedral and interesting museums such as the home of Federico García Lorca.

Perhaps the best way of starting a tour of this area is to stroll among the saints, necklaces, bracelets, gypsy costumes, marquetry handicrafts and an endless list of typical products that are piled up in the shops of the Alcaicería, one of the areas that are a big tourist attraction. The atmosphere overflows with vitality especially after twelve o'clock midday. The traveller will easily be able to imagine the throng of people who came to this ancient silk market in the times of *Al-Andalus*. Very close by one can visit the Corral del Carbón in Calle Mariana Pineda, a building that in the Nasrid era was a corn exchange, a lodging where the caravans of merchants would be provided with accommodation with space for people, animals and goods. Another monument of great artistic value is the Cartuja, one of the outstanding centres of Andalusian Baroque. It is also recommended to stop off in Calle Hospicio to visit the Hospital Real, a stunning Gothic building with Renaissance elements that is currently the rectorate and central library of the University, as well as the church of Santo Domingo, the church of Los Santos Justo y Pastor, the monastery of San Jerónimo and the basilica of San Juan de Dios, attached to the hospital of the same name.

CALLE SAN JERÓNIMO
Close to the church of San Justo y San Pastor.

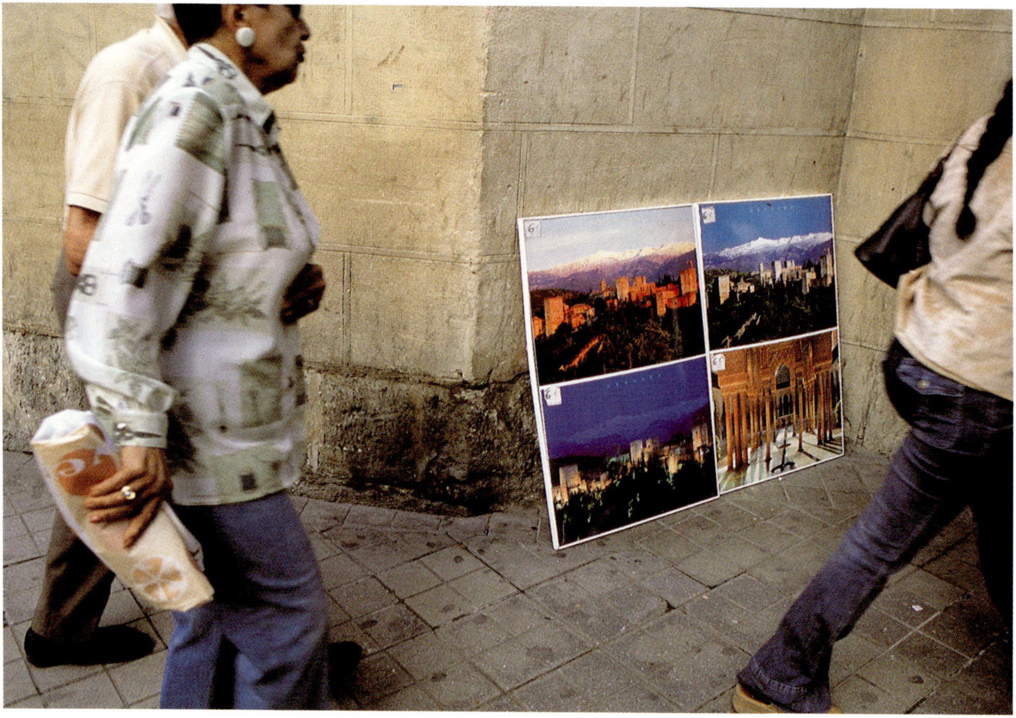

GRAN VÍA DE COLÓN
Next to the Cathedral.

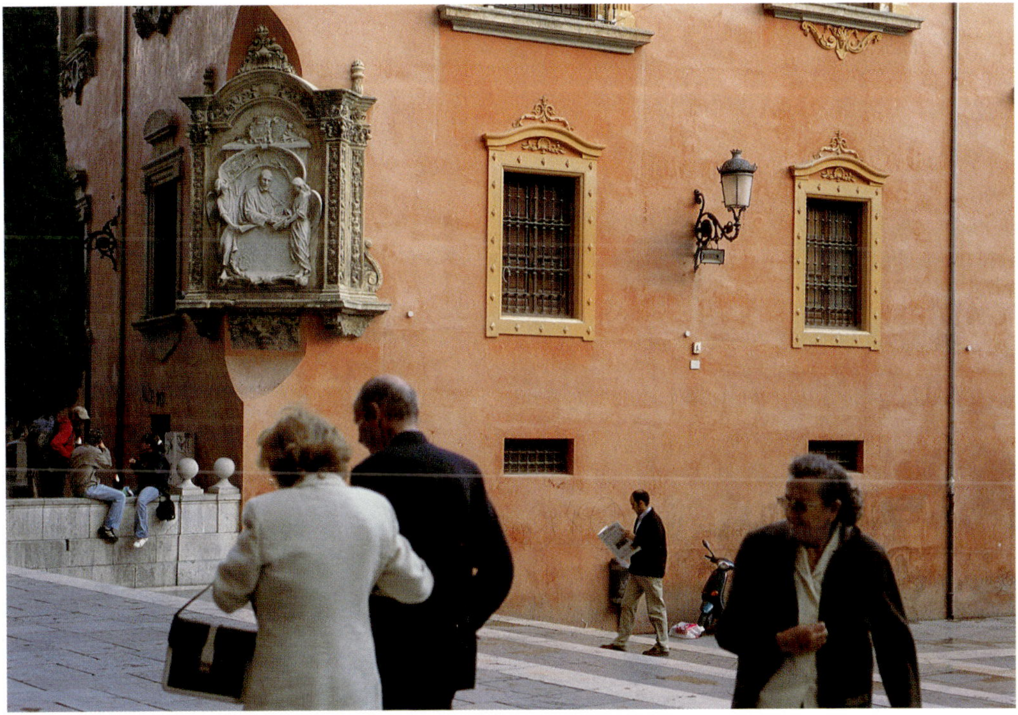

PLAZA PASIEGAS
Opposite the main façade
of the Cathedral.

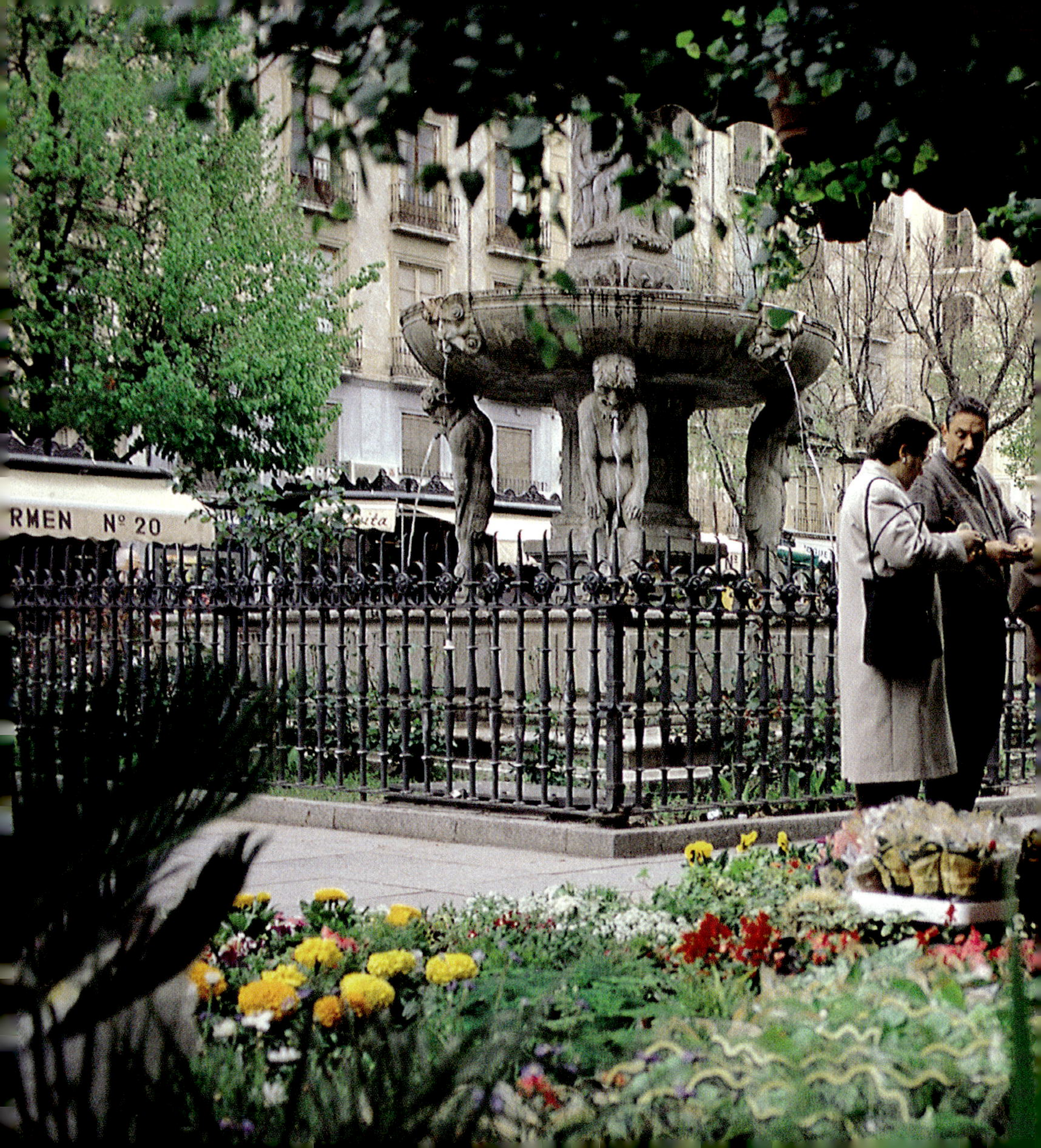
RMEN Nº 20

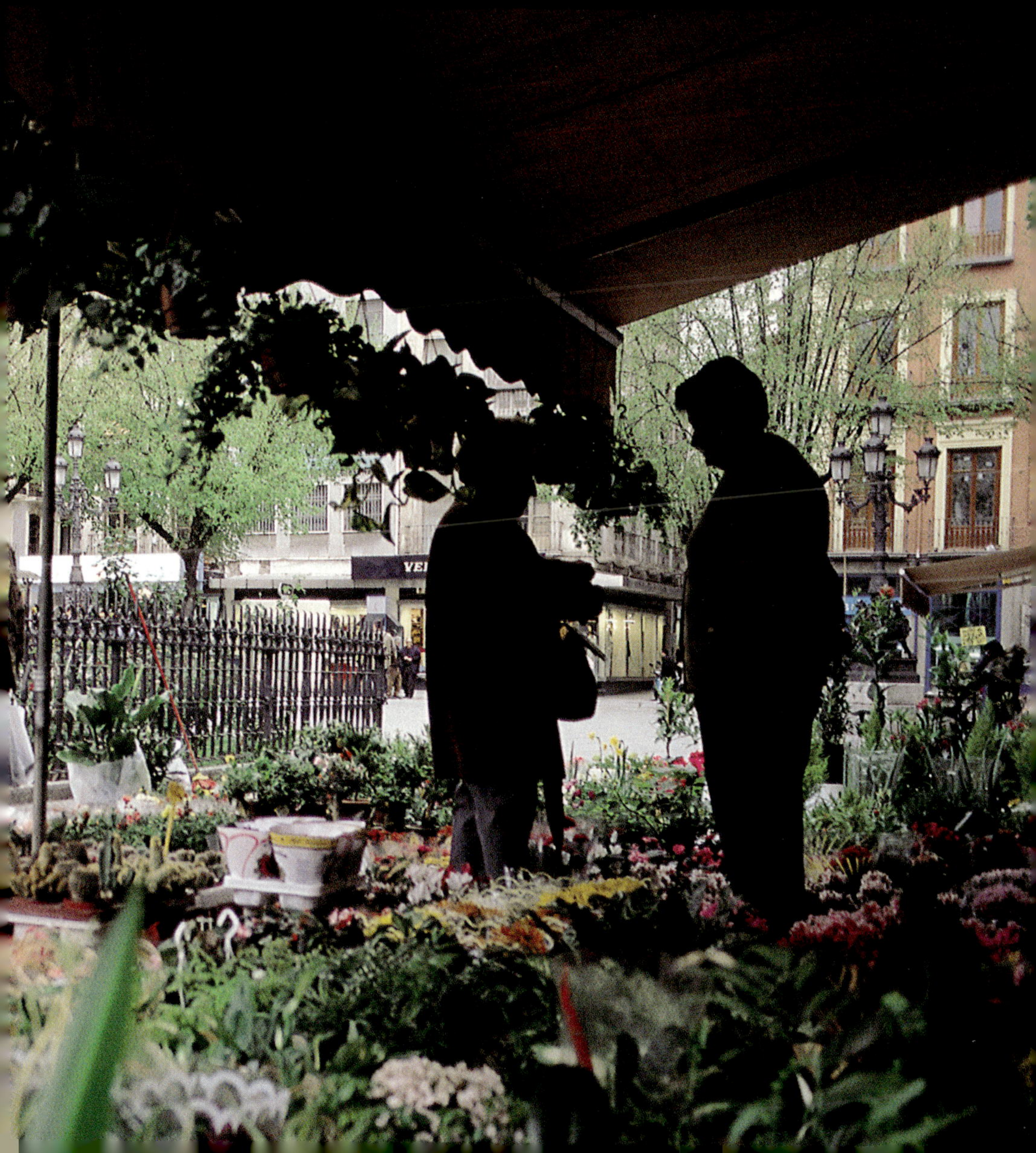

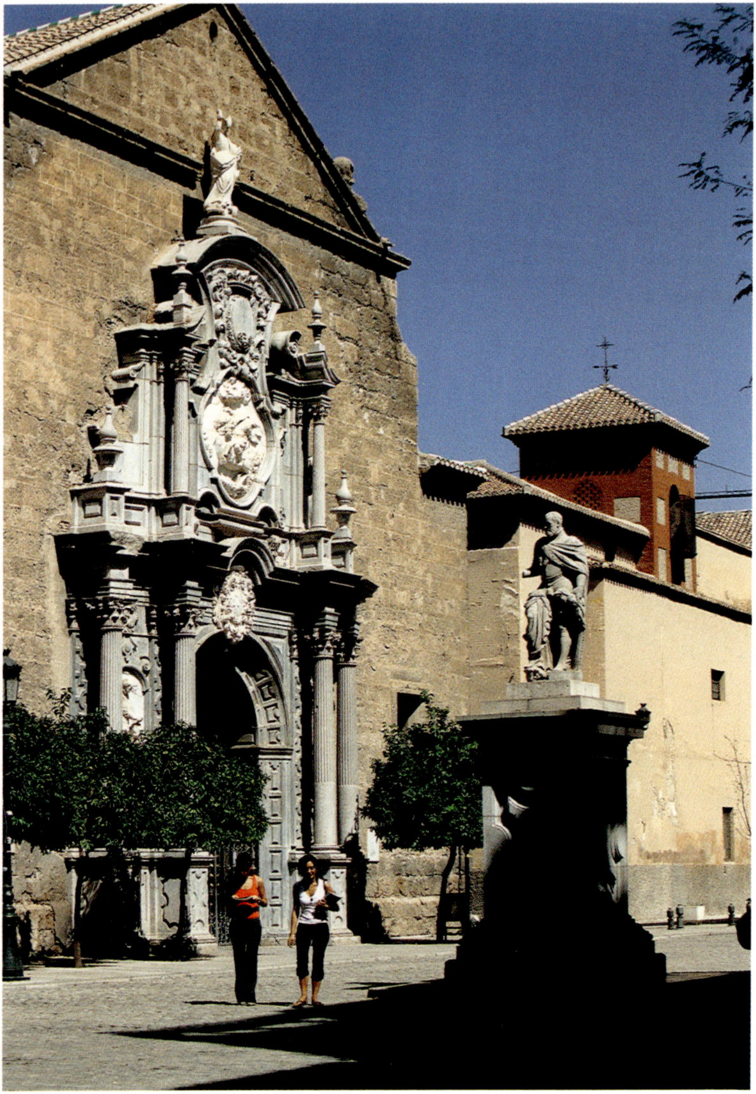

PLAZA UNIVERSIDAD
In the background the church of San Justo y San Pastor.

CHURCH OF SAN JUSTO Y SAN PASTOR
Dome covering the transept.

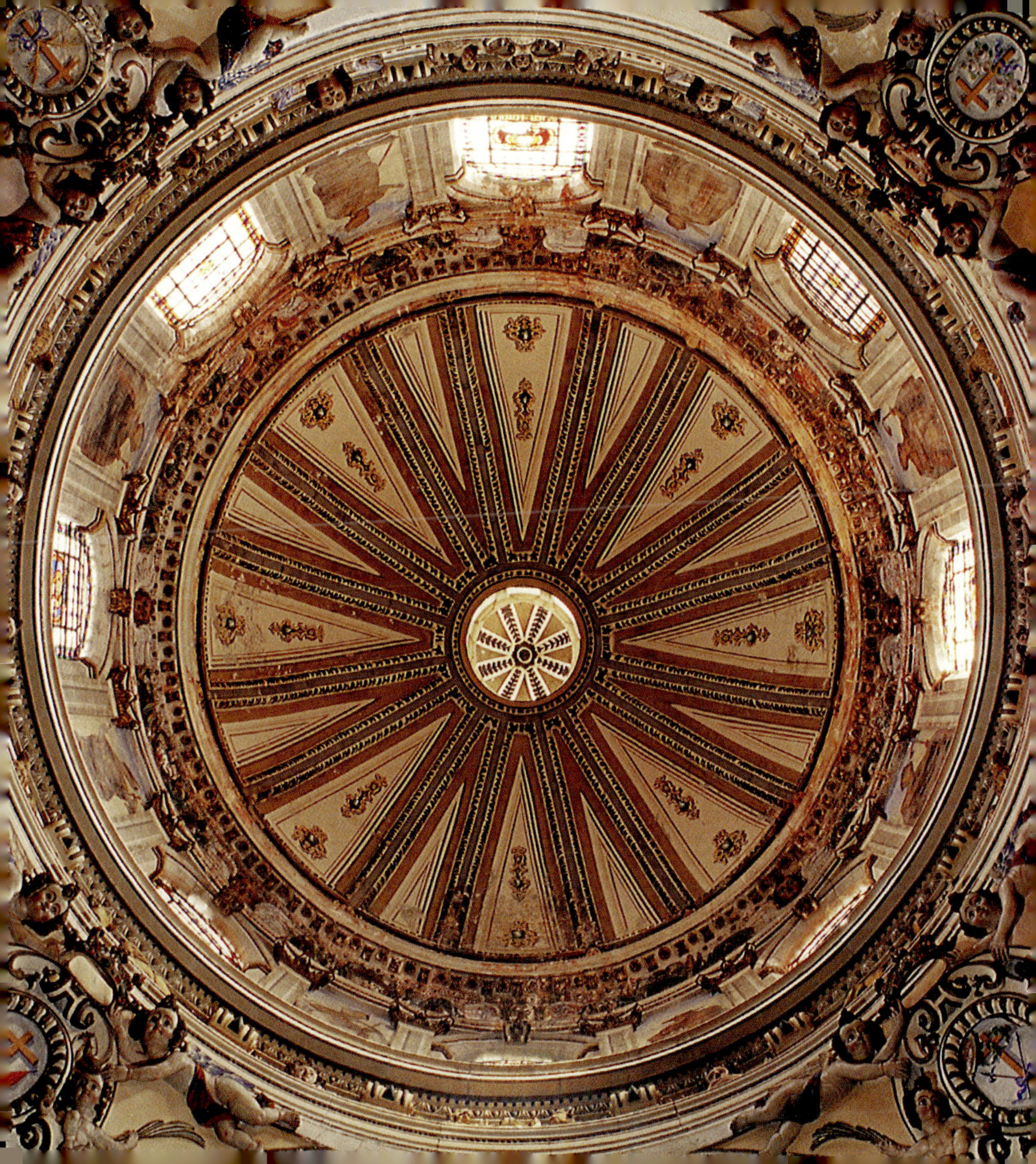

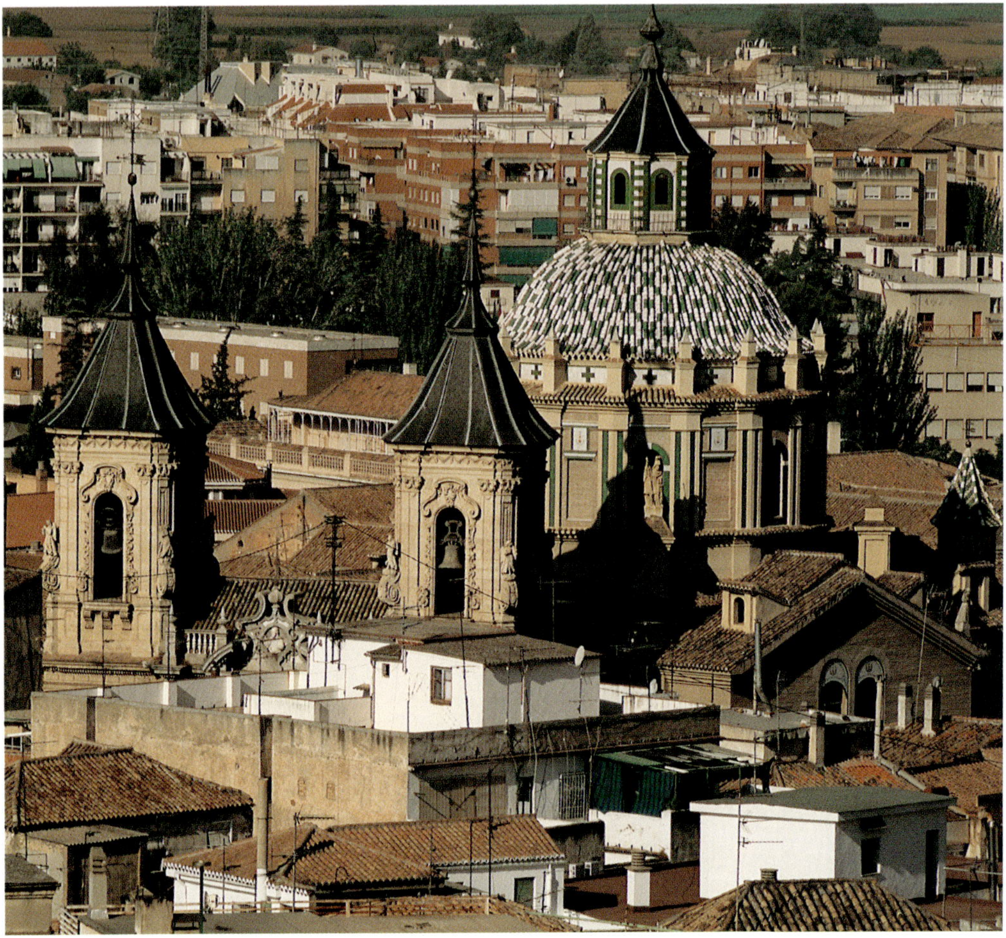

BASÍLICA OF SAN JUAN DE DIOS
One of the grand Renaissance constructions in Granada.

HOSPITAL OF SAN JUAN DE DIOS
Cloister.

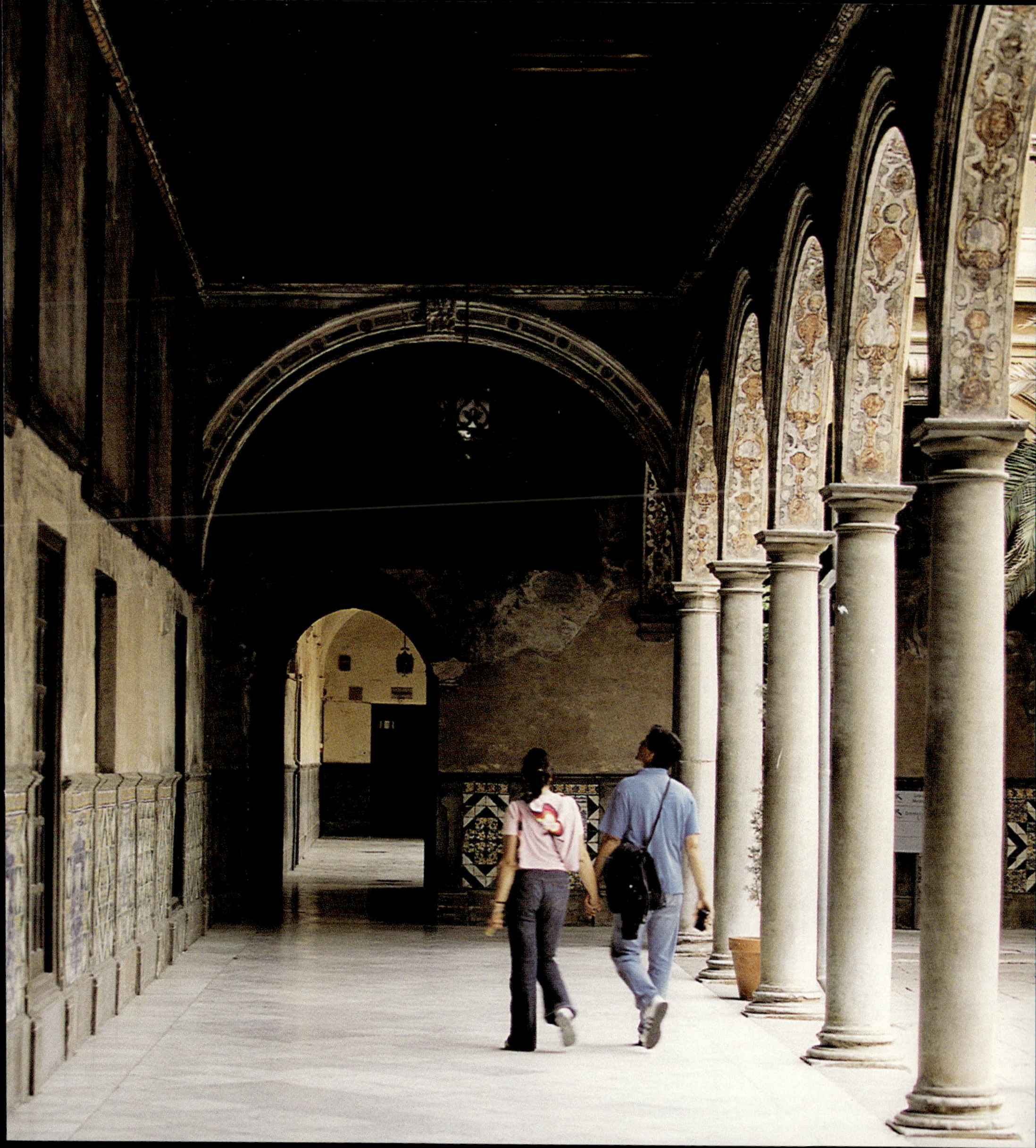

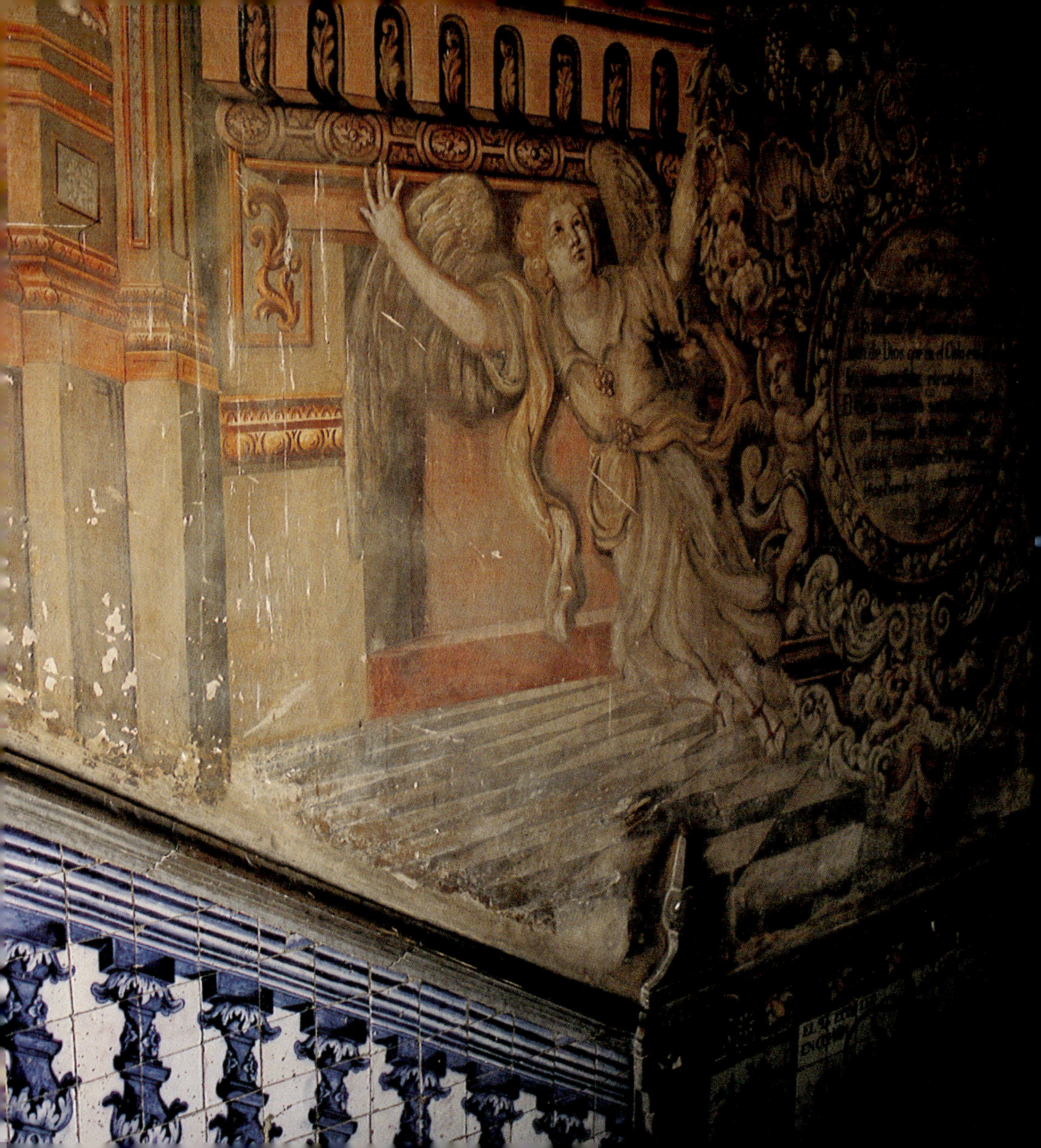

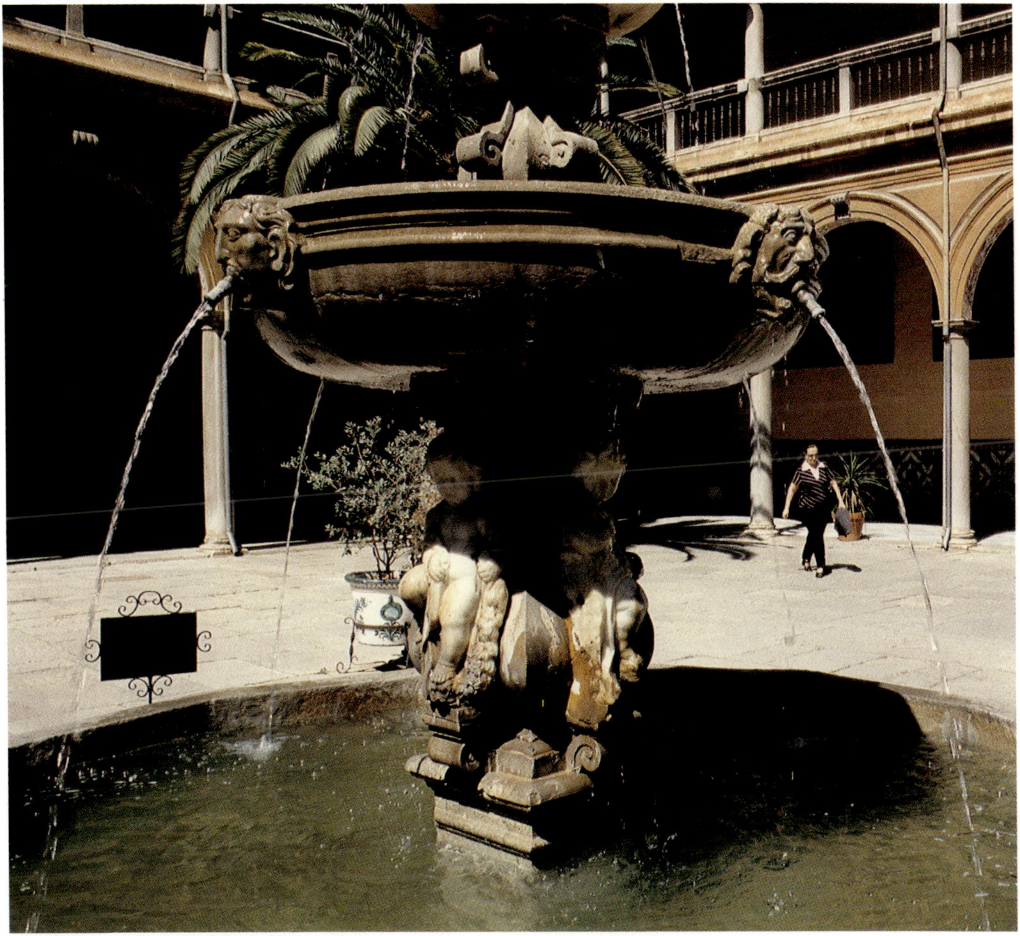

HOSPITAL
OF SAN JUAN DE DIOS
Fountain in the centre of the cloister and painting on the stairs that lead to the second floor.

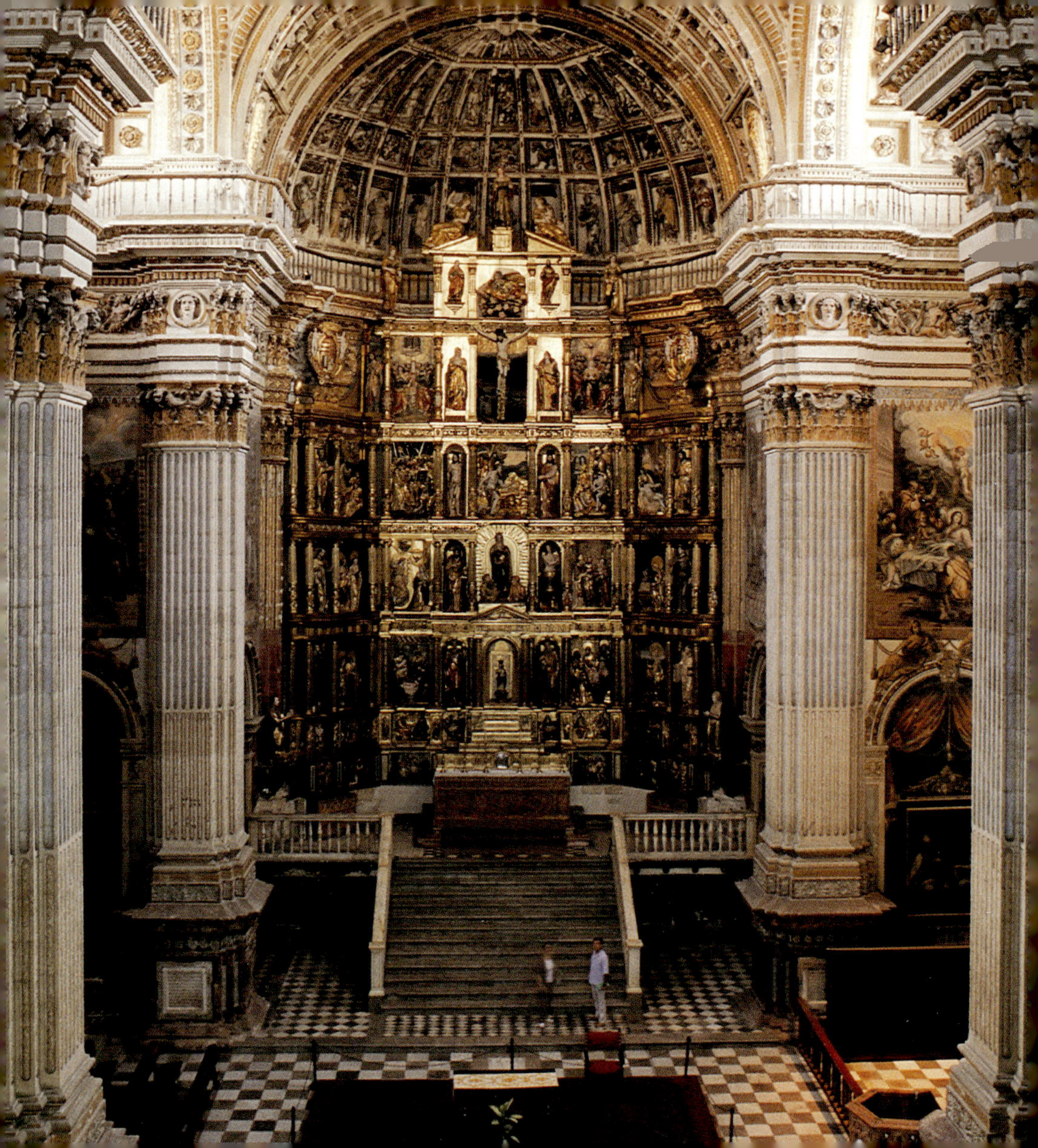

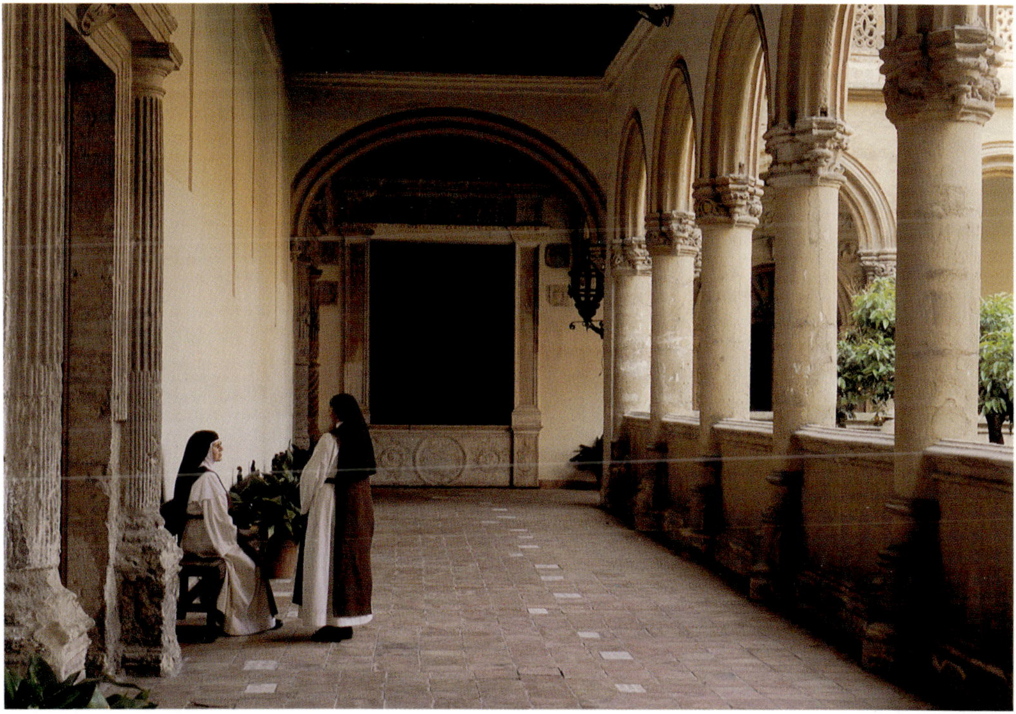

MONASTERY OF SAN JERÓNIMO
Cloister and interior of the church.

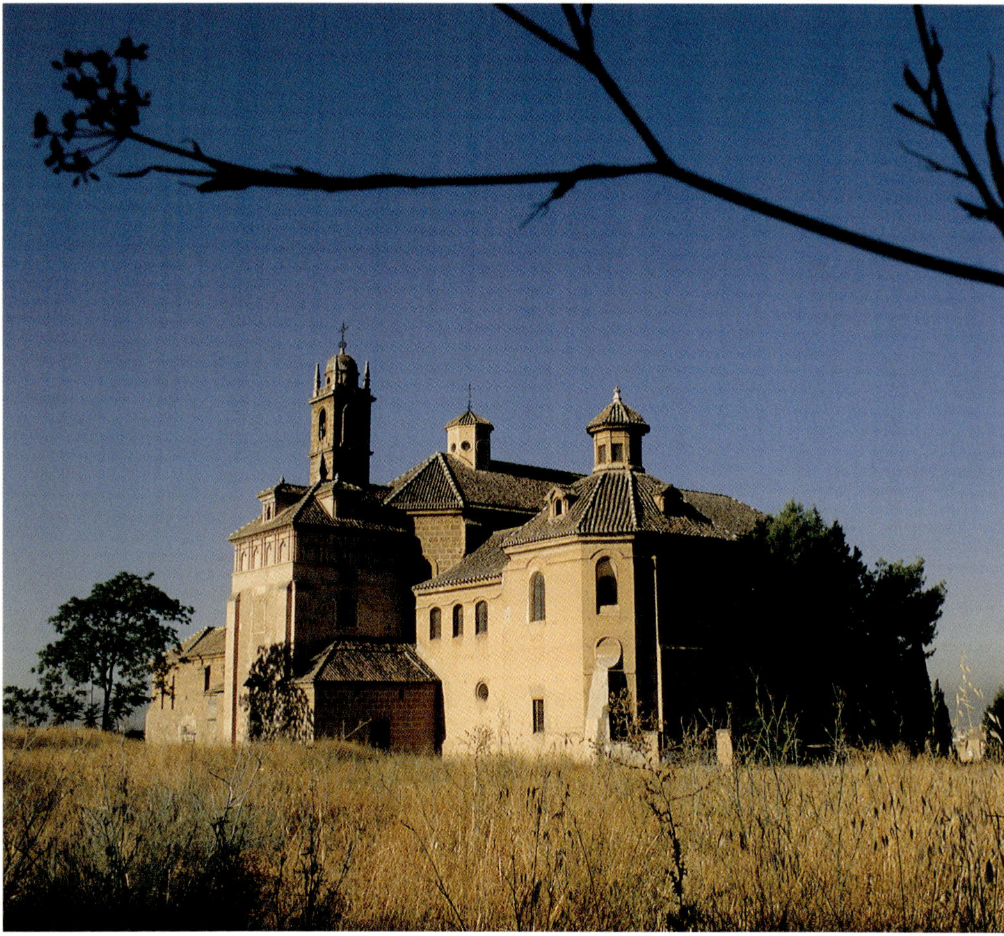

THE CARTUJA
Exterior view and detail of a sculpture that forms part of the sacrarium.

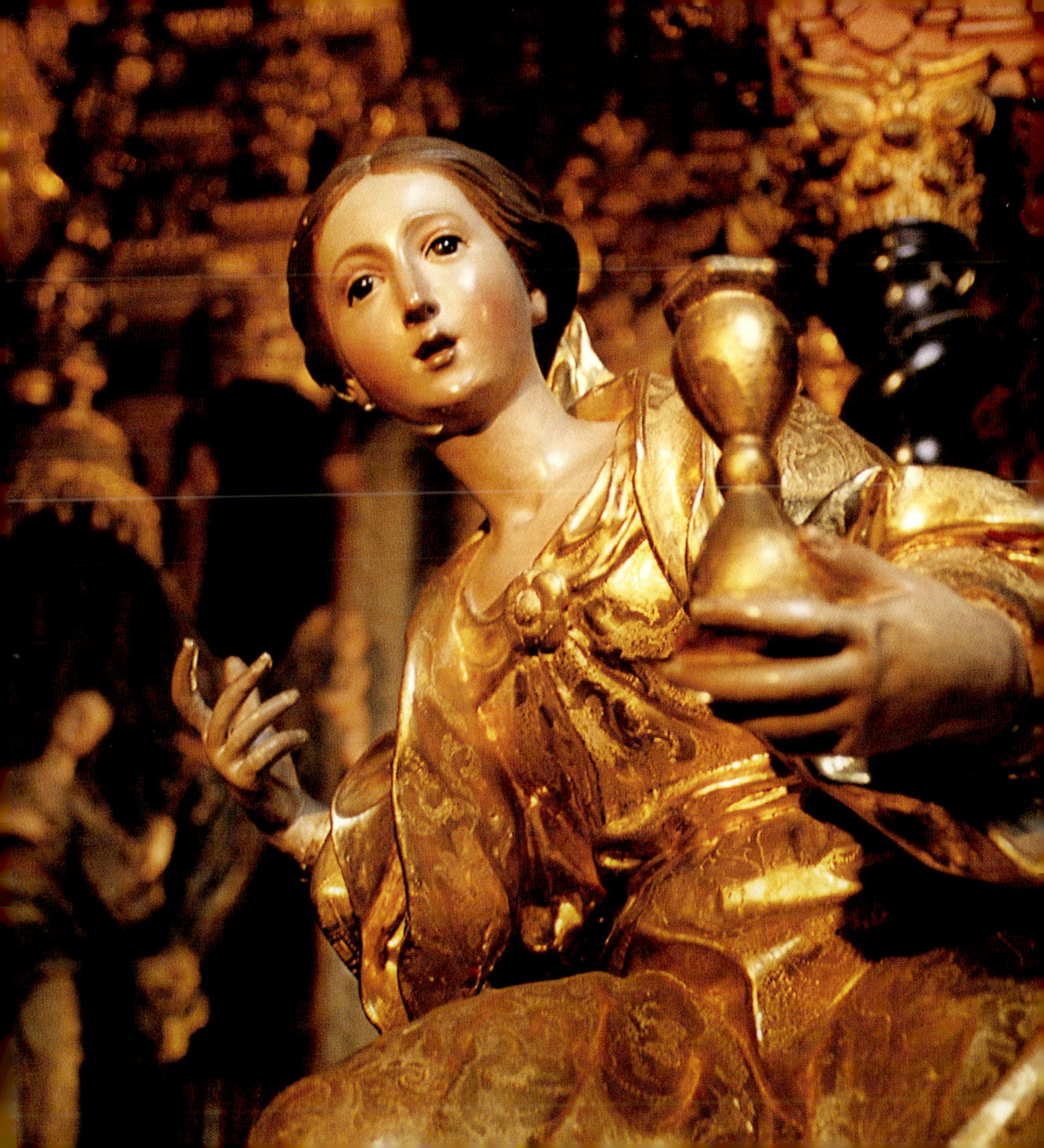

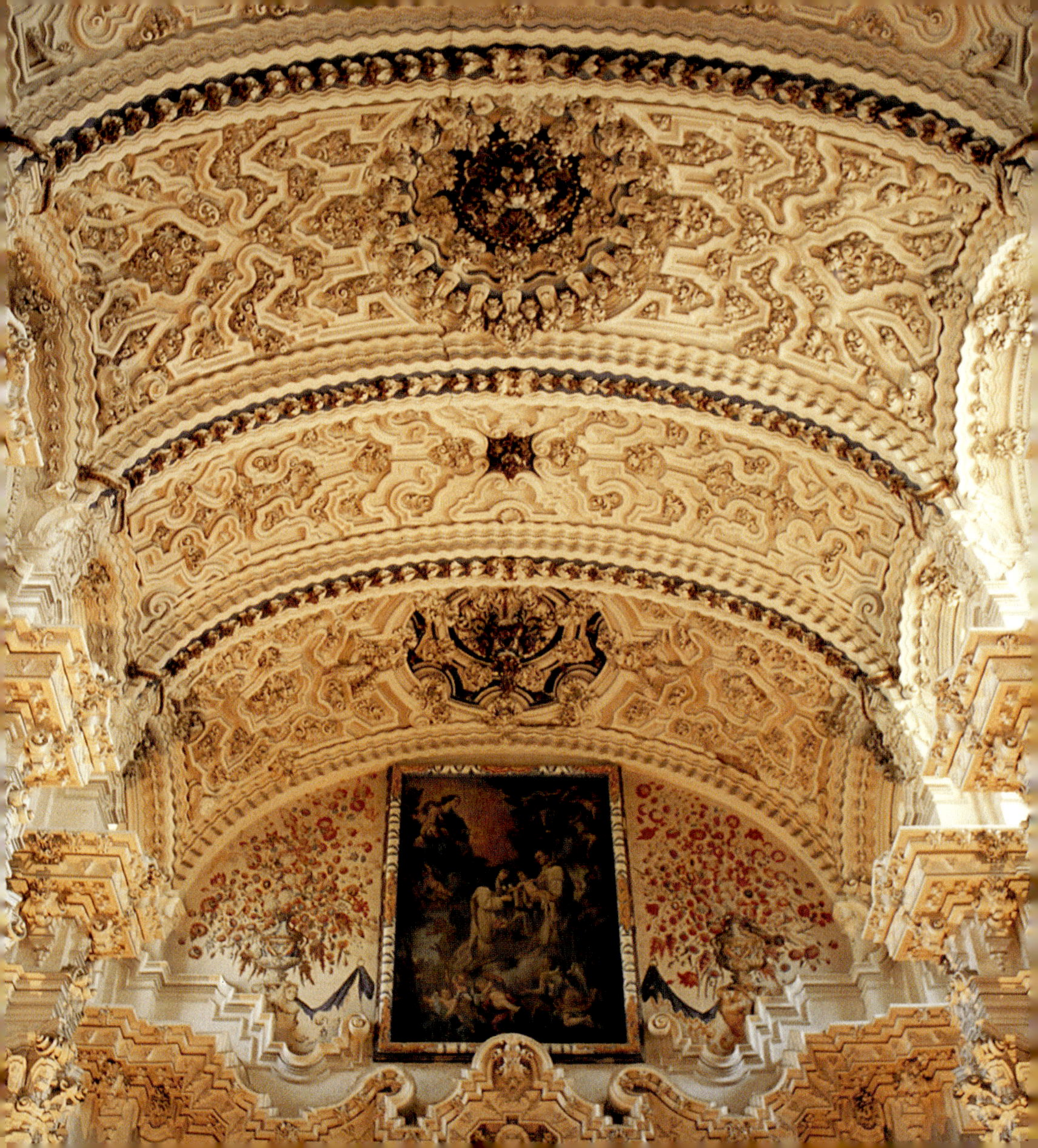

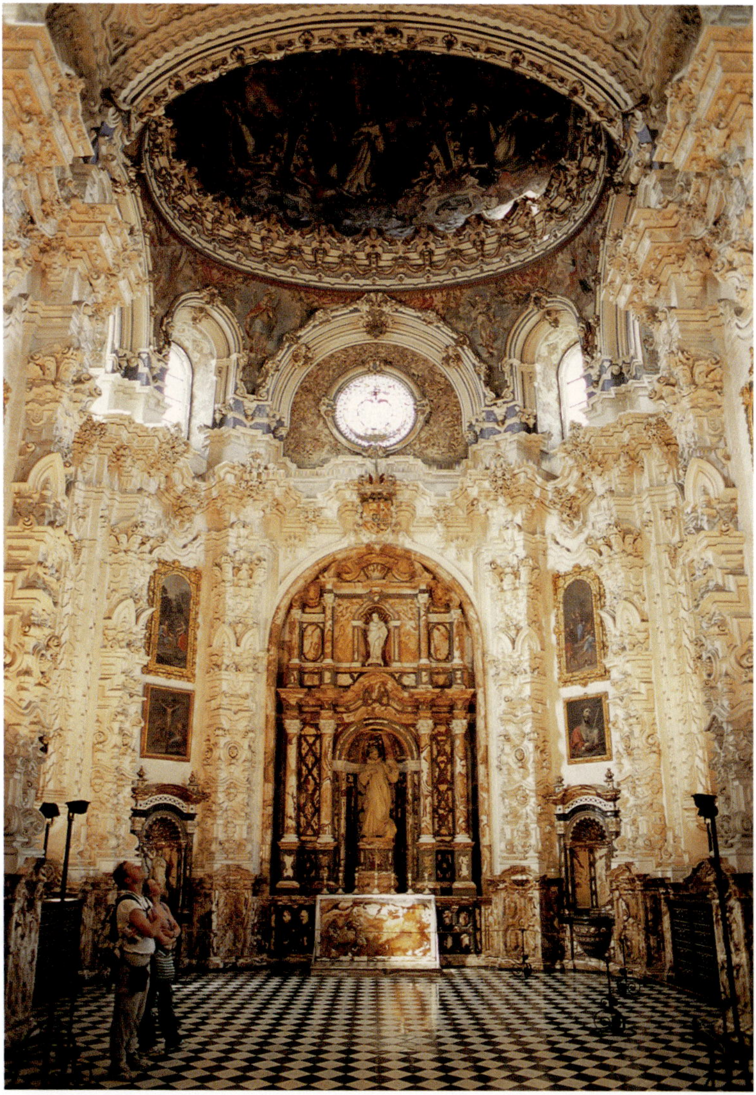

THE CARTUJA
General view of the sacristy and covering vault. Granada Baroque acquires its maximum expression in this work.

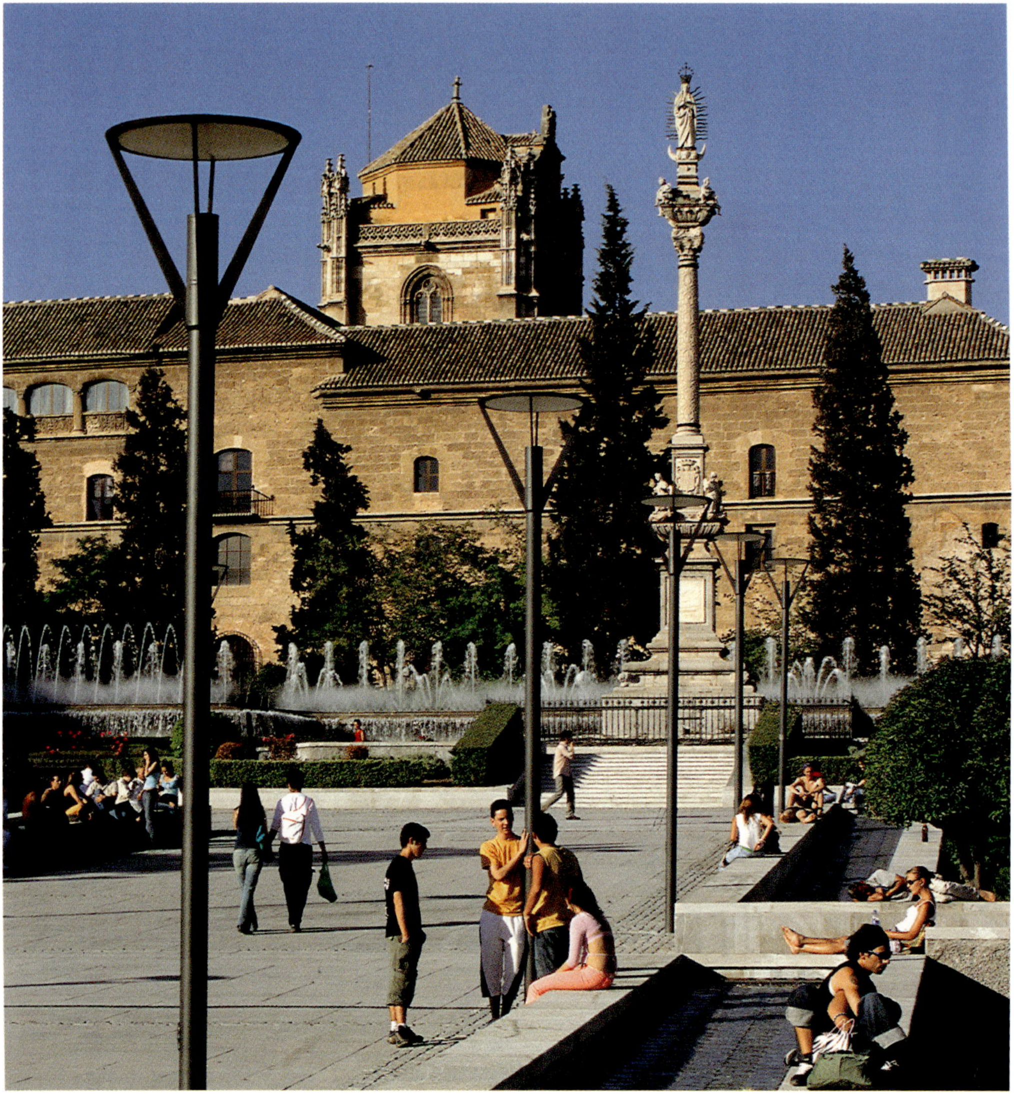

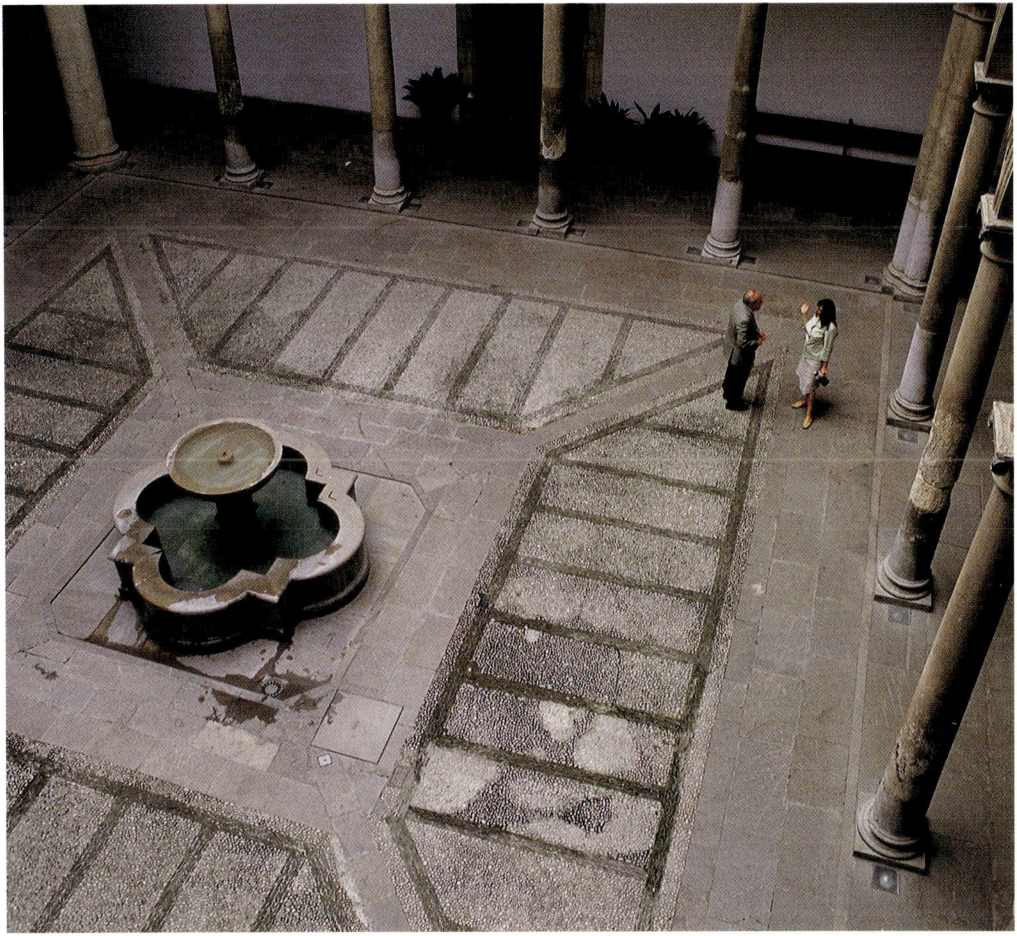

FUENTE DEL TRIUNFO
In the background
the Hospital Real.

HOSPITAL REAL
Patio of the Chapel.

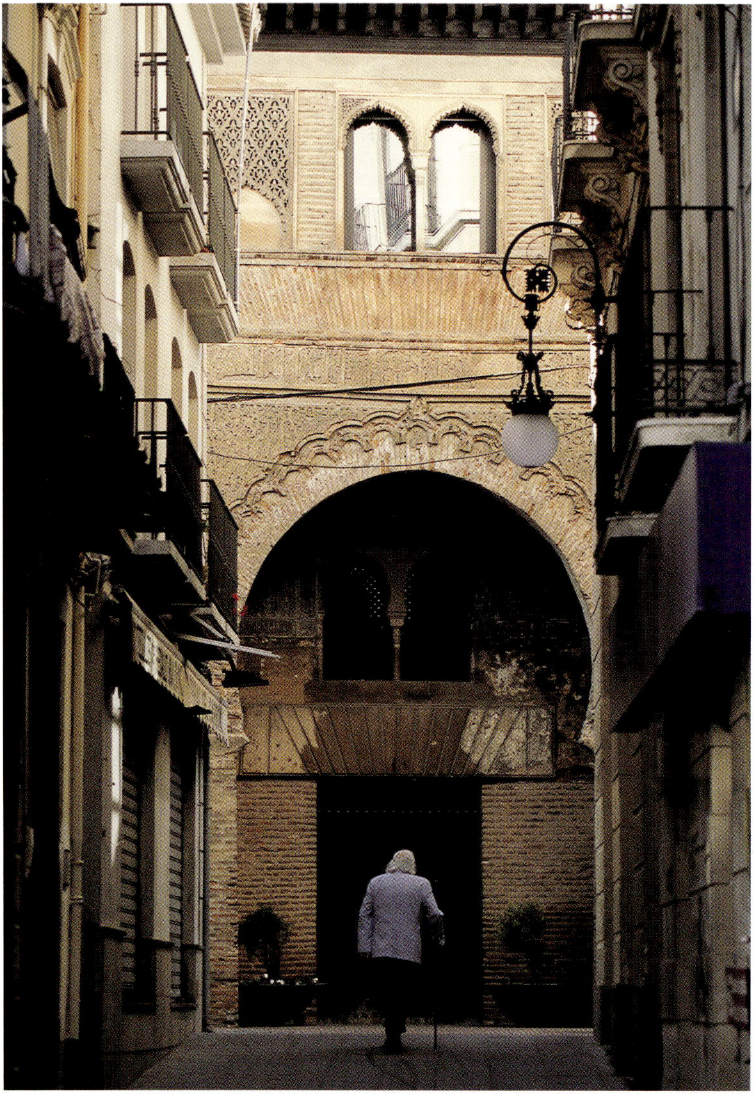

CORRAL DEL CARBÓN
Interior patio and entrance door. Named *Alhóndiga Yidida* or new by the Nasrids, it is a construction unique in Europe, similar to the Asian *hans* or African *fondaks*, dating from the early 14th century.

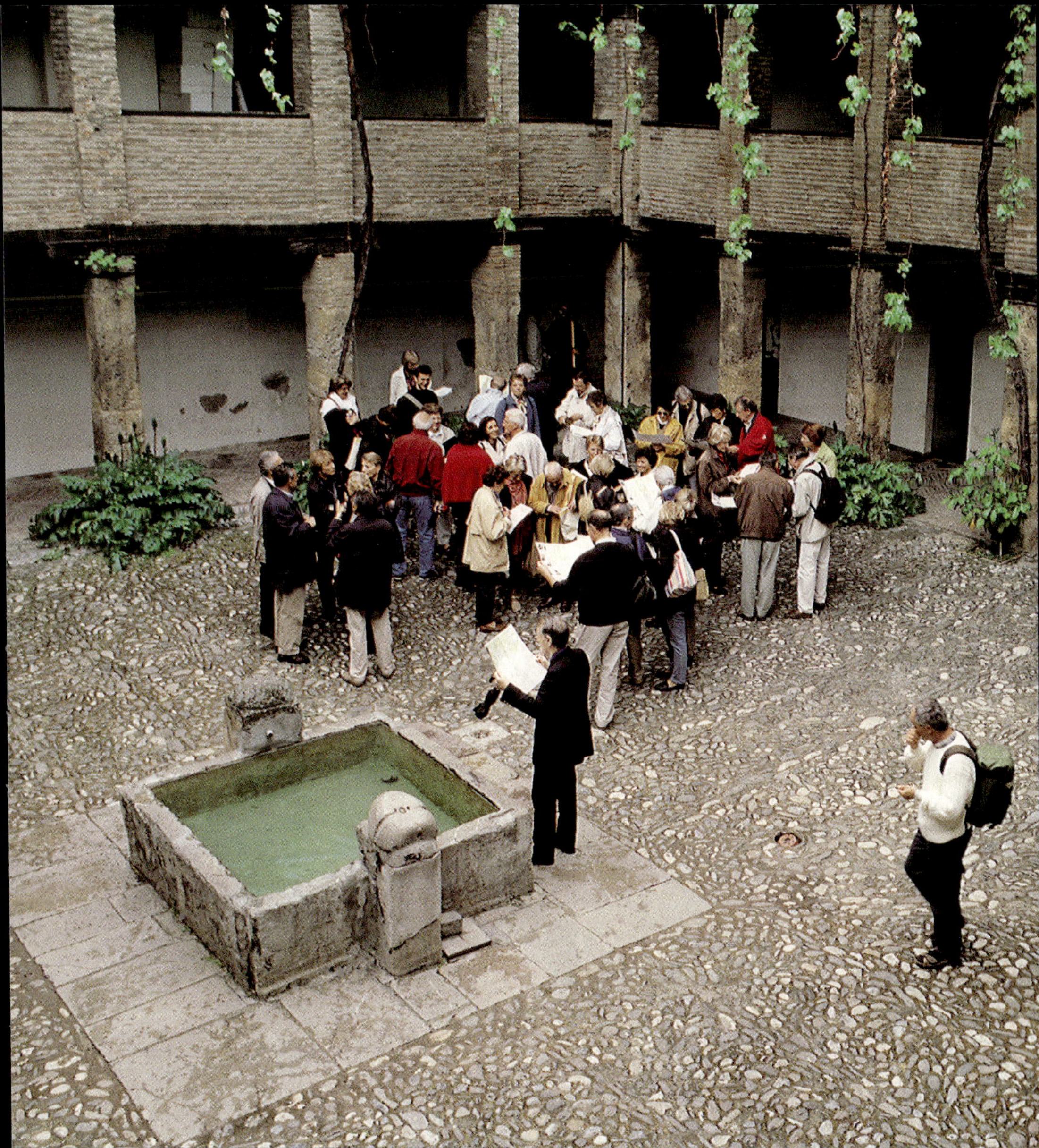

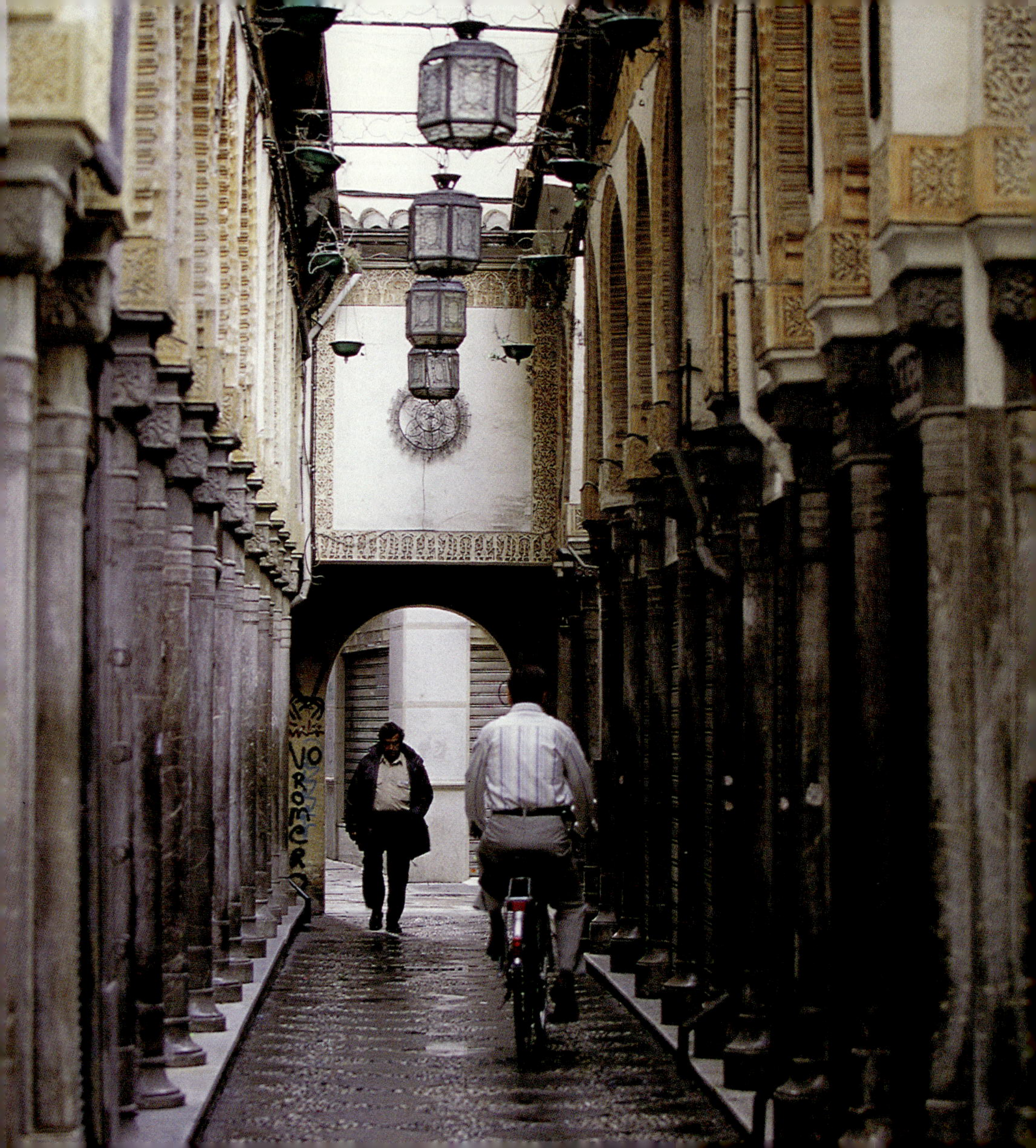

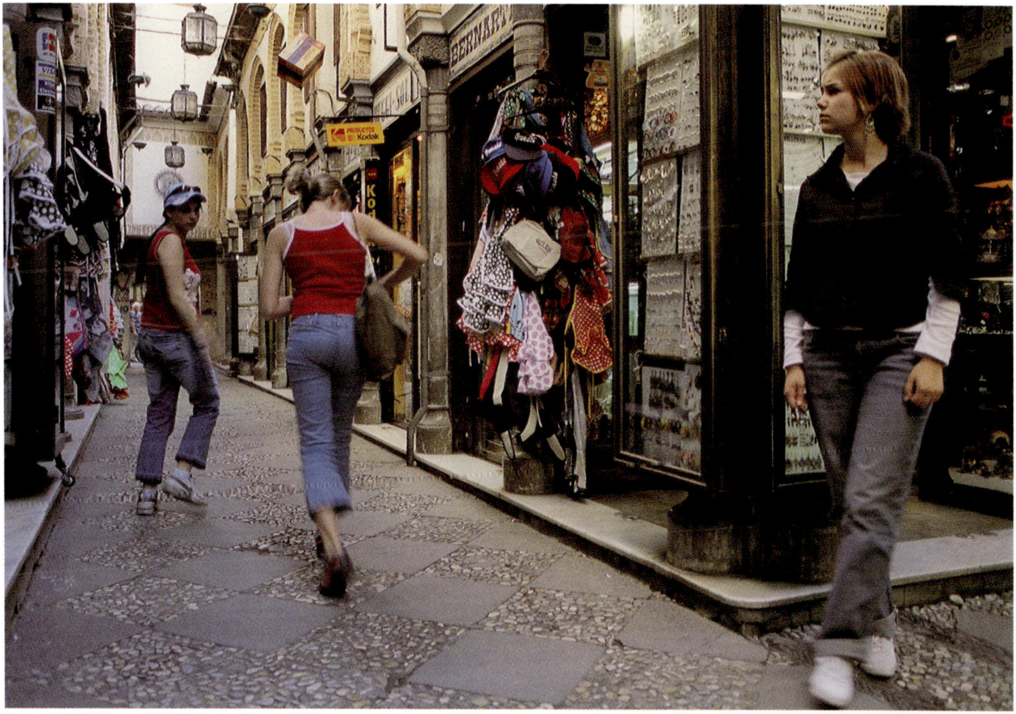

THE ALCAICERÍA
An old Arab market that preserves its early layout and continues housing many shops.

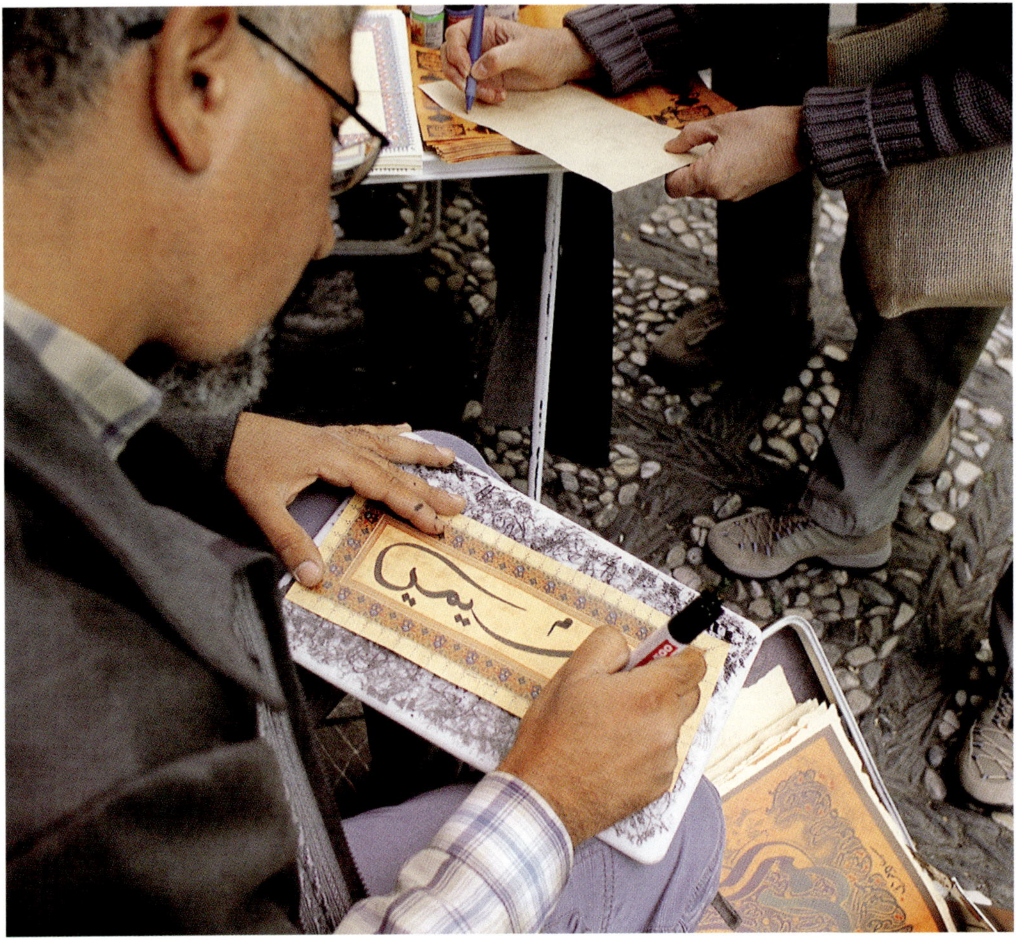

CALLE OFICIOS
For a few coins, your name in Arabic.

CALLE CÁRCEL
Spice shop.

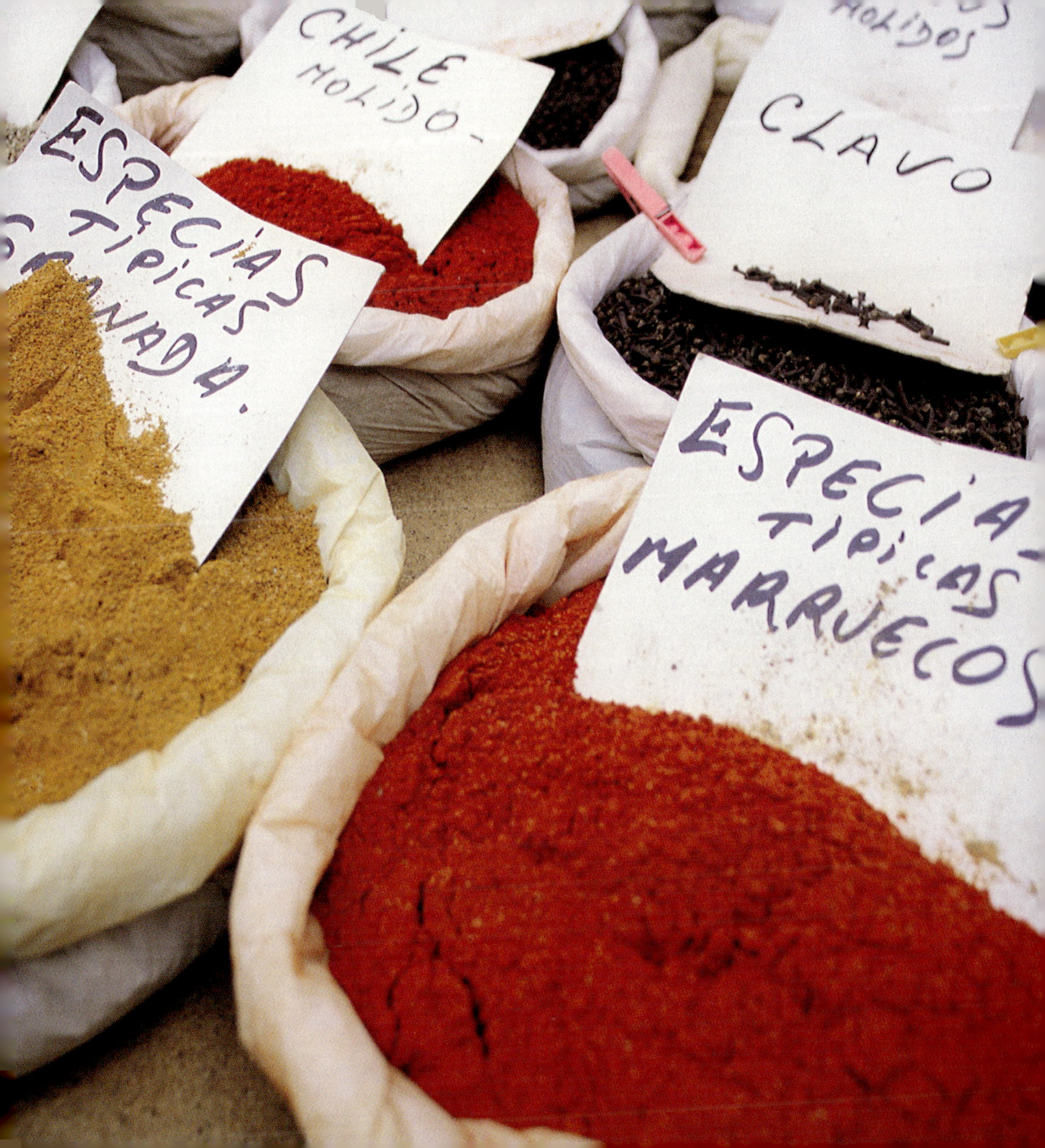
ESPECIAS TIPICAS
CHILE MOLIDO-
CLAVO
ESPECIA- TIPICAS MARRUECOS

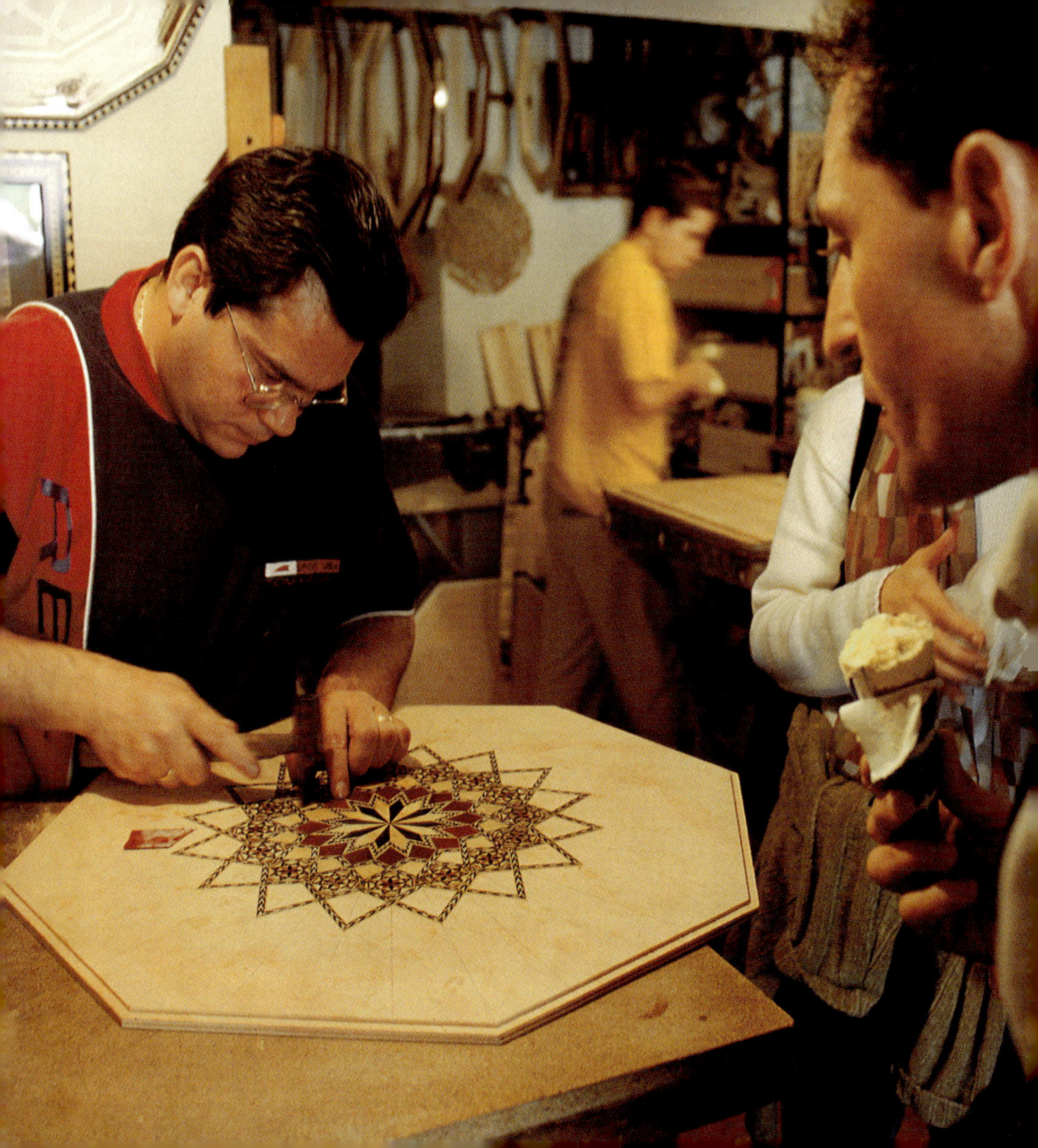

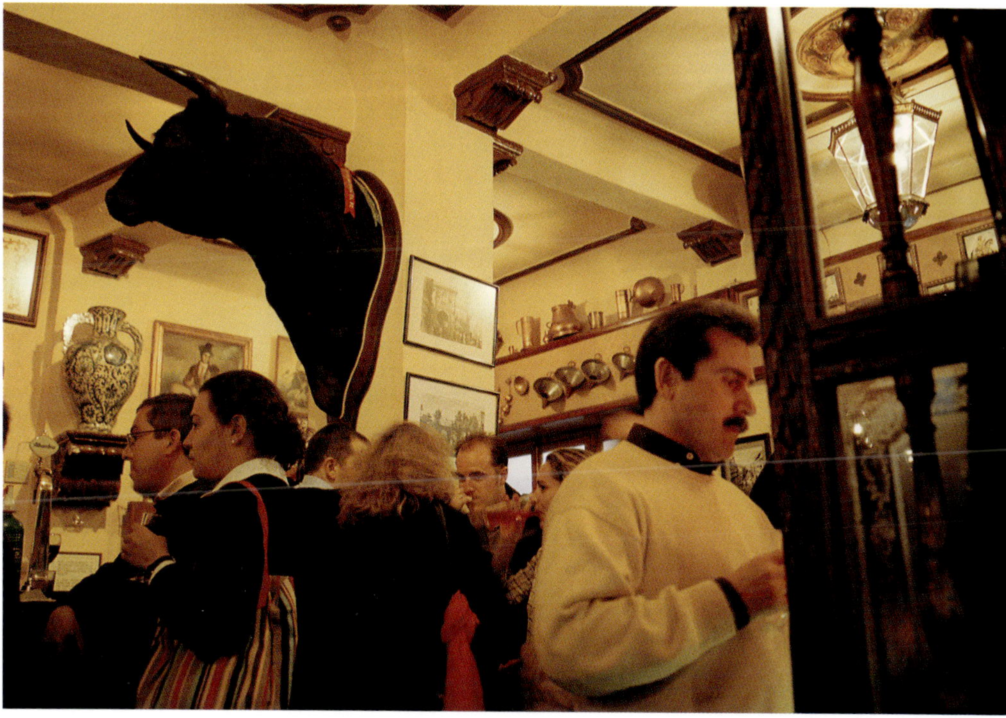

CRAFTSMAN
Making marquetry.

BODEGAS CASTAÑEDA
A classic spot in
Calle Almiceros.

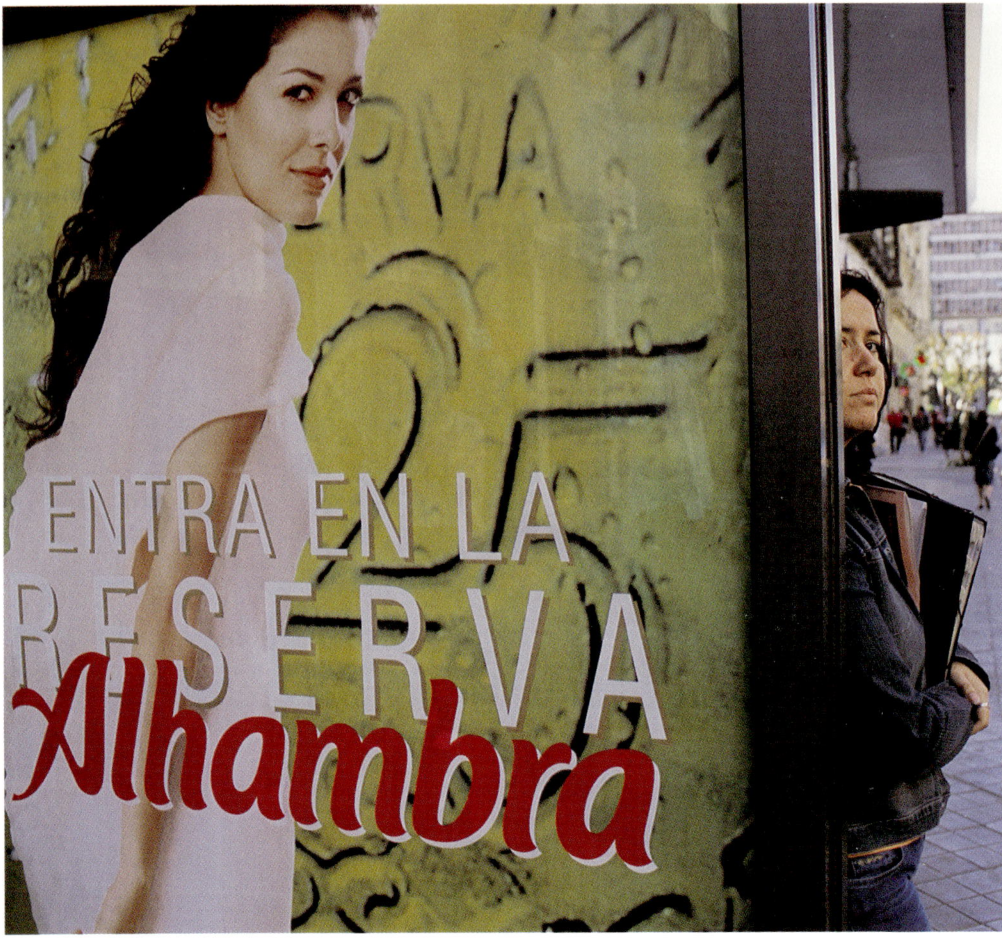
ENTRA EN LA
RESERVA
Alhambra

GRAN VÍA DE COLÓN
Bus stop.

CALLE MARQUÉS DE GERONA
Café.

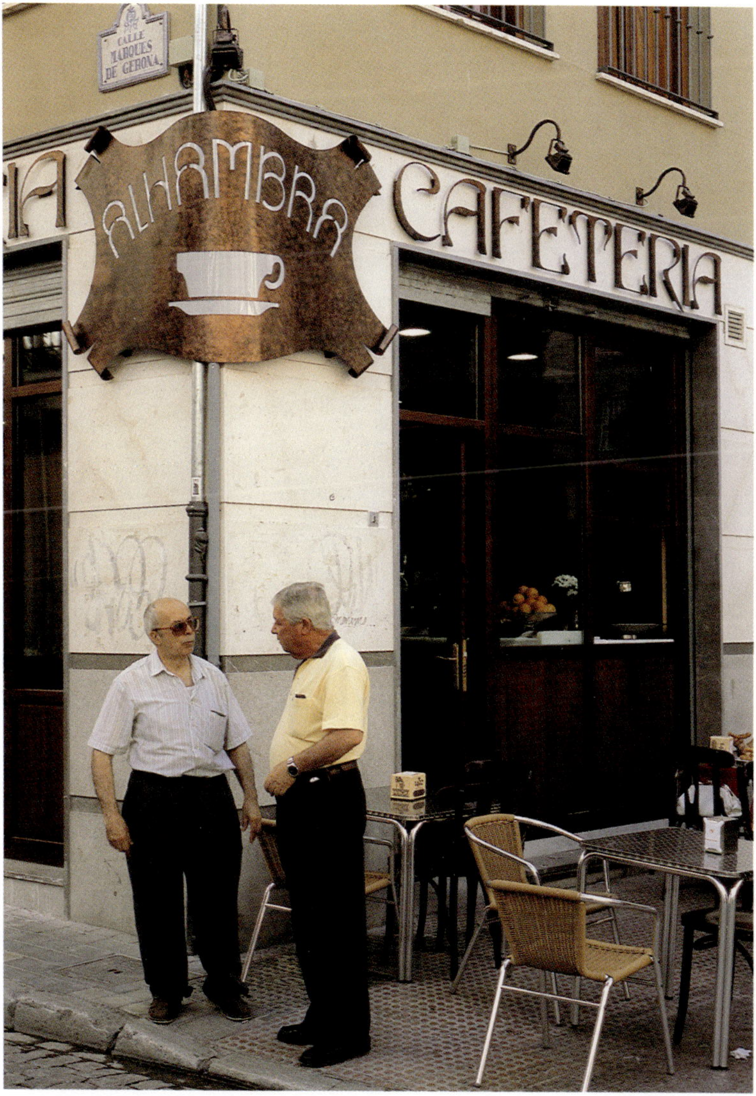

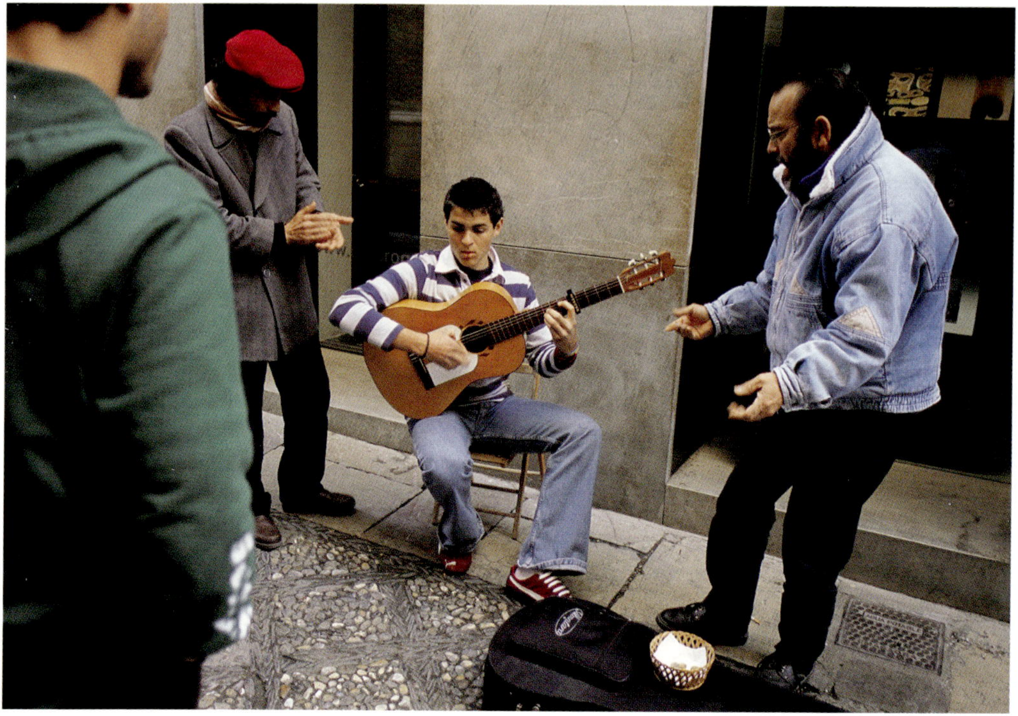

CALLE OFICIOS
Street musicians.

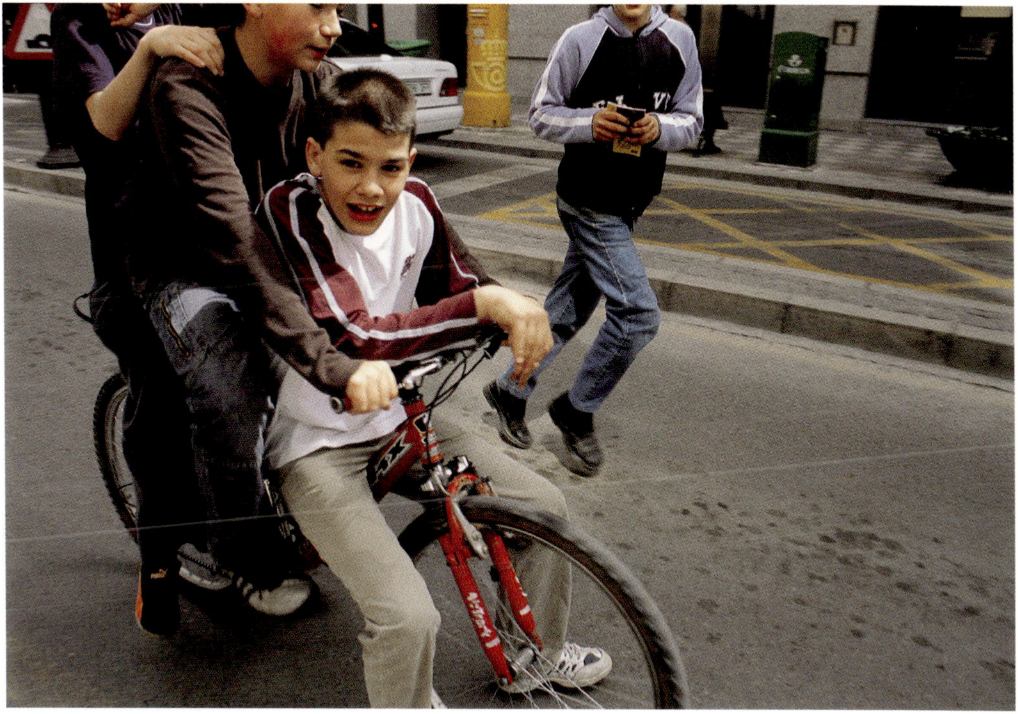

CALLE REYES CATÓLICOS
Children cyclists.

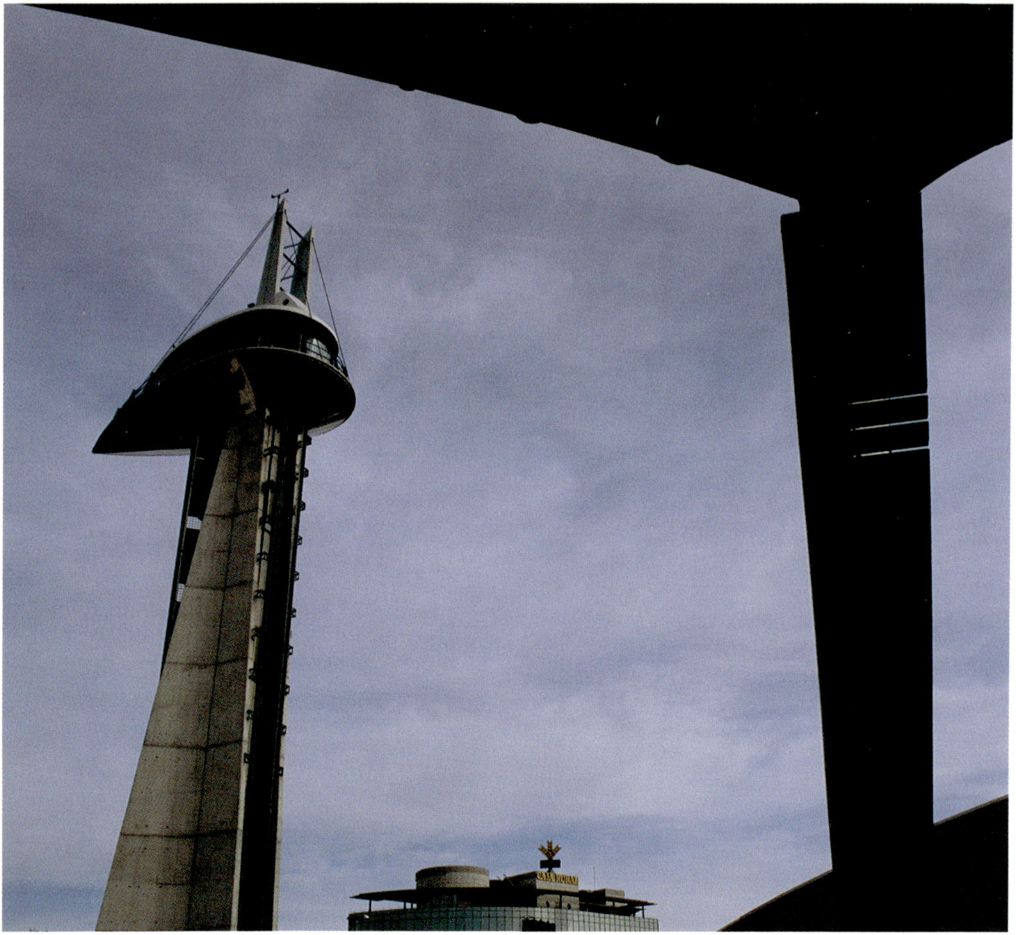

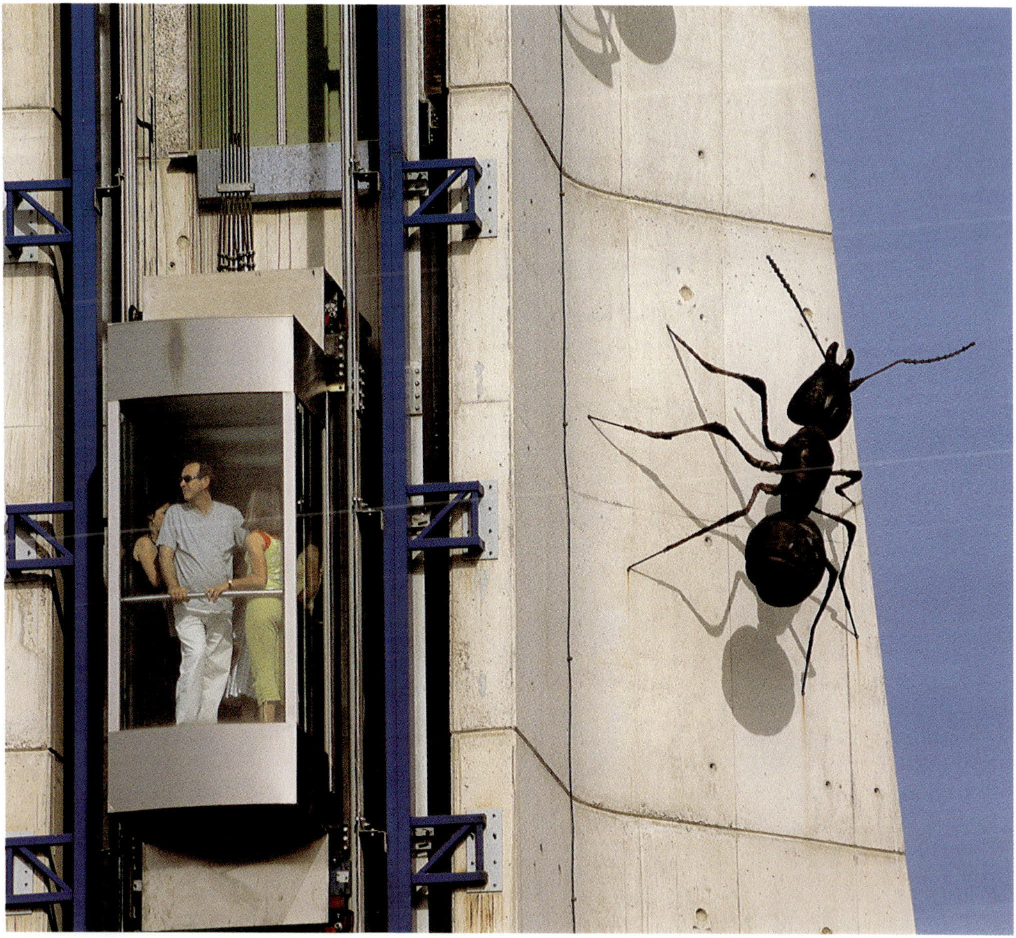

SCIENCE MUSEUM
Viewpoint tower of
the museum and lift.

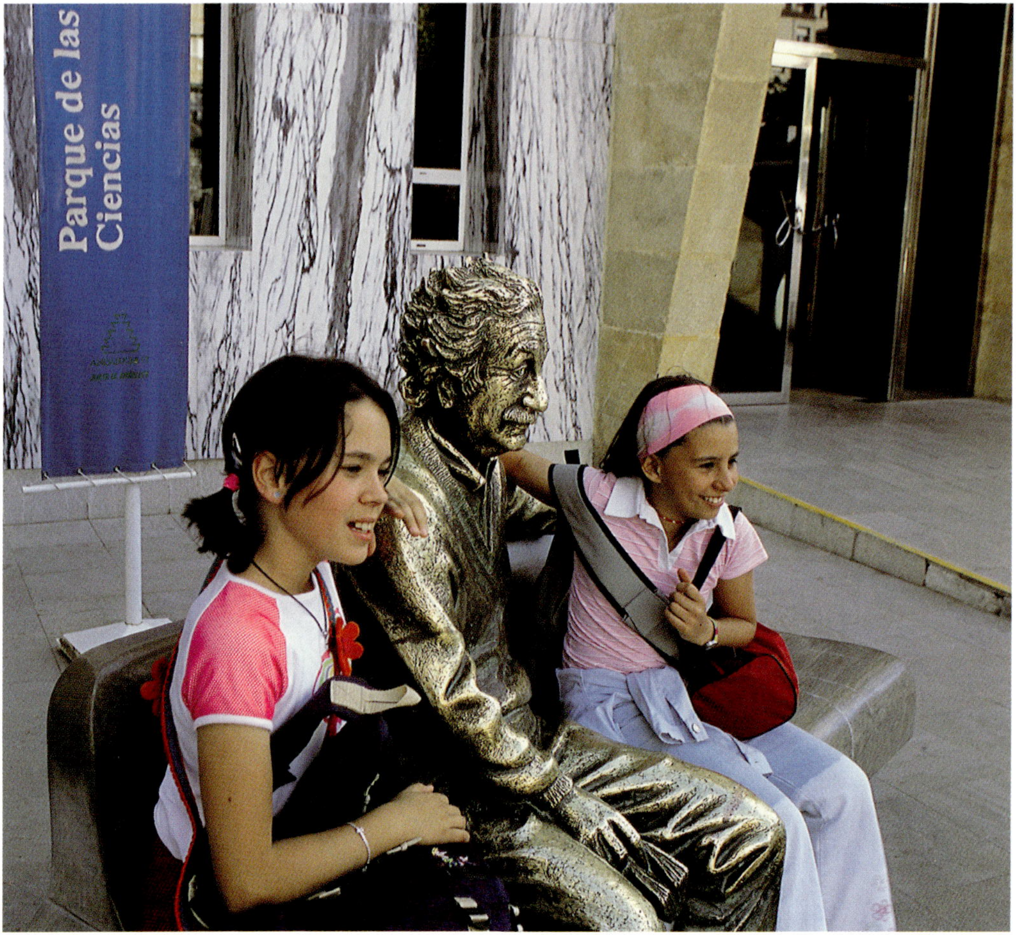

SCIENCE MUSEUM
Homage
to Albert Einstein.

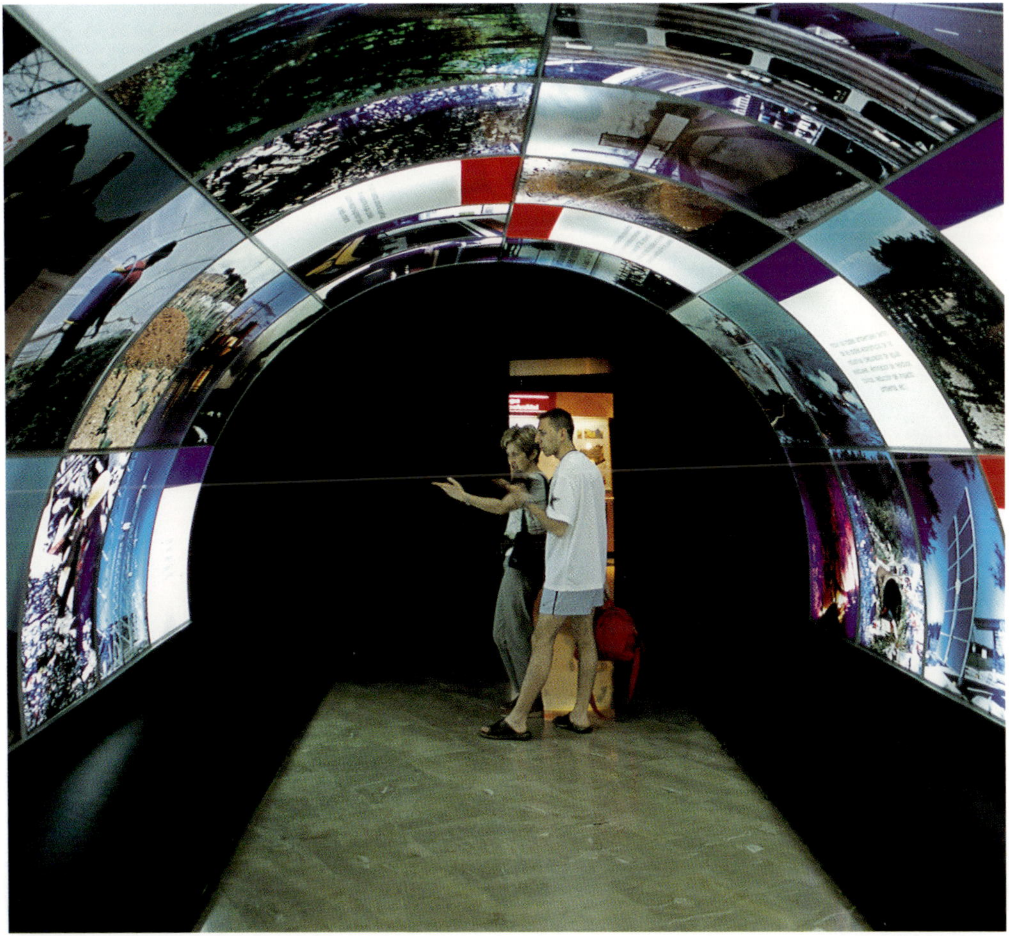

SCIENCE MUSEUM
Biosphere Hall.

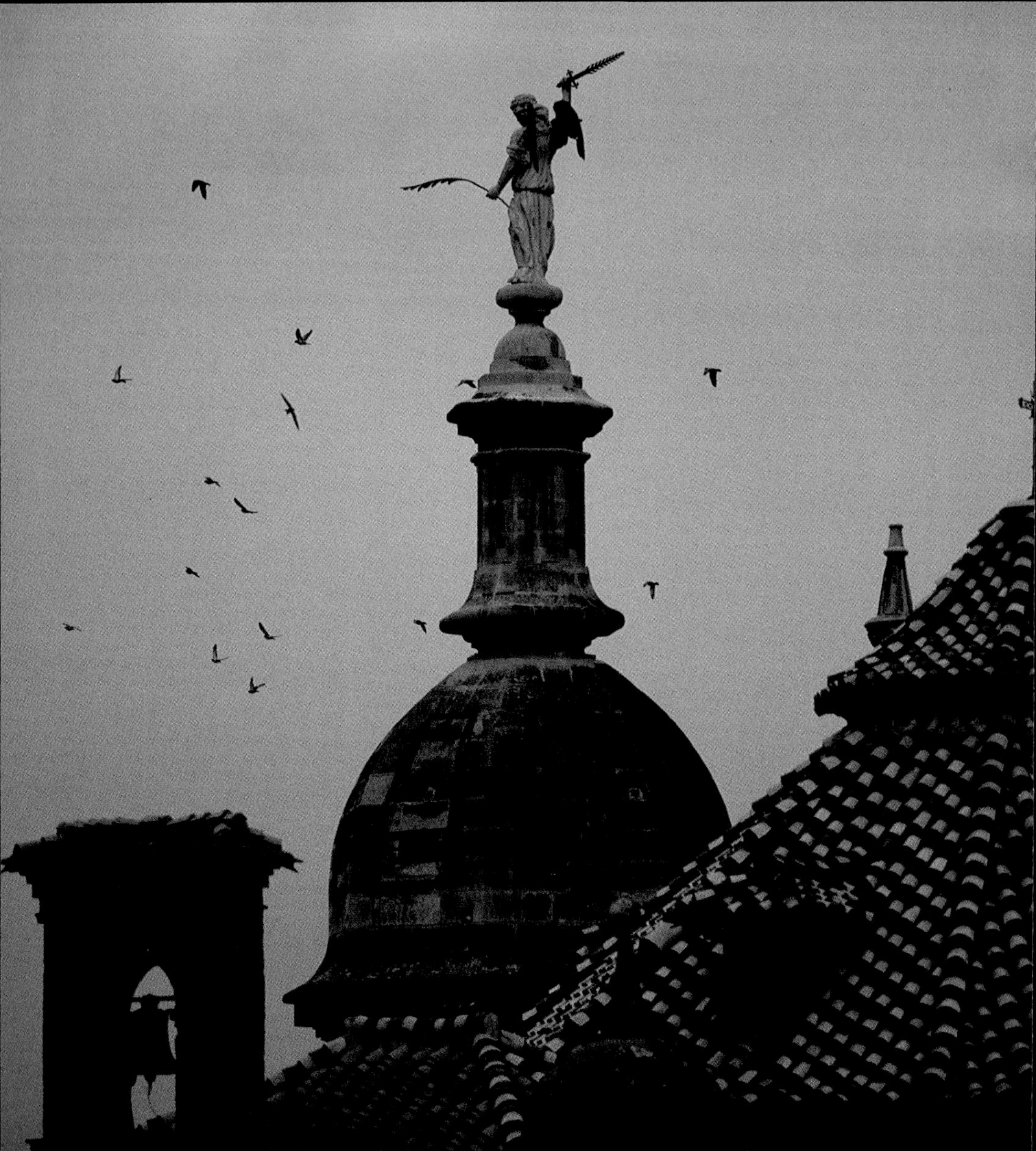

THE CATHEDRAL AND THE ROYAL CHAPEL

Since it was the last Arab bastion on the peninsula, the conquest of Granada meant a great deal to the Catholic Monarchs. So much so, that they ordered an exceptional cathedral to be built in the old part of the Hispano-Muslim city, considered an important referent in Spanish Renaissance, and a solemn Royal Chapel where their bodies would be buried.

The first stone of the cathedral was laid on the 25th of March 1523 under the direction of the architect Enrique Egas, who was a very unlucky man indeed: shortly after work had to be stopped for a year because of the havoc wreaked by the plague, and he was later dismissed due to the Chapter's displeasure at the line that the cathedral was taking, and was replaced by Diego de Siloé in March 1528. It thus underwent big changes with regards to the initial project. The new architect redesigned the building, but adapting it to an already-started Gothic plan. The cathedral was completed one-hundred and eighty years later by the architects Francisco Otero and Francisco Rodríguez Navajas, who closed off the roof. And this is how the profile that we still see today over the rooftops of Granada was drawn, where a sober tower that remained half completed and the dome of the head project out. The outside of the church features the elegant simplicity of the main façade in Plaza Pasiegas, designed by Alonso Cano, and the Pardon Doorway, the most pompous of them, in Calle de la Cárcel. The inside of the sanctuary possesses a Gothic ground plan, with lots of chapels and ambulatory at the head, over which is raised a Renaissance structure with five naves supported by twenty pillars, each made up of groups of four Corinthian half-columns attached to a square core. This fantastic space has its treasure in the Main Chapel, opposite the transept, where Diego de Siloé and his team deployed all their inventiveness in its 45 metres height: it is assembled by two superimposed orders, entablatures with relief work and crowned by a dome supported by ten arrises; on the first there are statues representing the apostles, and on the second seven magnificent paintings by Alonso Cano that show scenes from the life of the Virgin Mary, above

CATHEDRAL
Roof.

which are stained glass windows by Juan del Campo and Theodore of Holland that describe the incarnation of Christ.

Isabella I of Castile (1451-1504) and Ferdinand V of Aragon (1452-1516) decided that they would be buried in Granada, changing their earlier intention of being buried in the Franciscan monastery of San Juan de los Reyes in Toledo. To do this, they had the Royal Chapel built over the land the old Great Mosque had occupied, a work that was designed and directed by Enrique Egas, the Catholic Monarchs' favourite architect for large-scale works. The building, a Gothic construction, is of special artistic interest in the ornamentation and the Renaissance-style works that it houses, such as the sepulchres. Neither of the two monarchs could see the completed project, the queen dying a year before work began, and the king a year before they were finished. Both were buried provisionally in the Convent of San Francisco de la Alhambra to be finally moved to the crypt in the Chapel on the 10th of November 1521. Today the Chapel contains the remains of the Catholic Monarchs, their daughter Juana I and her husband, Felipe the Handsome. Also resting here is the son of Manuel the Fortunate and Isabella, the eldest daughter of Isabella and Ferdinand, who died at the age of two when he was heir to the crowns of Castile, Aragon and Portugal.

CATHEDRAL
Entry via Calle Oficios.

The Royal Chapel has a Latin cross ground plan covered by ribbed vaulting. A massive grille, the work of several authors, among which feature Bartolomé de Jaén, separate the head and the transept from the rest of the temple. The transept is occupied by two extraordinary mausoleums carved in Carrara marble: that of Juana "the Mad" and Felipe "the Handsome", was made by Domenico Fancelli, Pietro de Carona and Bartolomé Ordóñez; that of the Catholic Monarchs is the all the work of Fancelli. Just below, a strictly austere crypt houses the royal coffins.

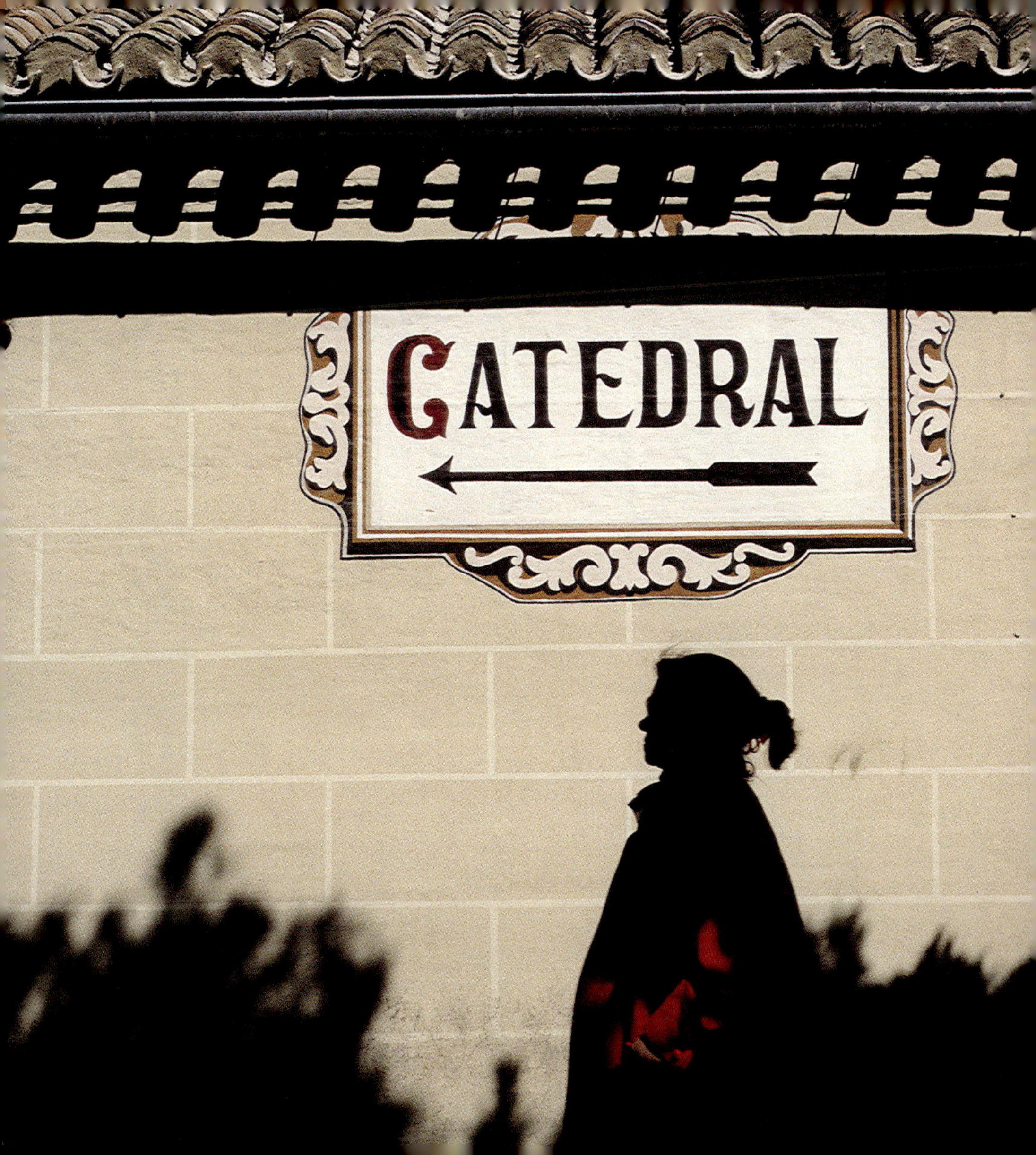
CATEDRAL

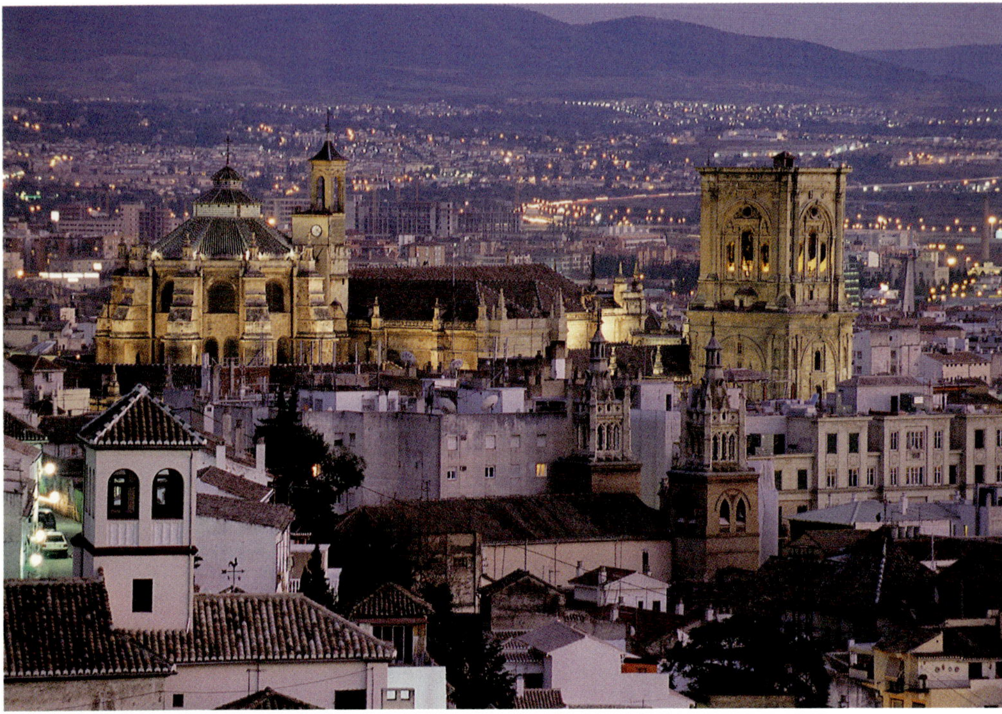

CATHEDRAL
View over the rooftops of the city and the main façade that faces Plaza Pasiegas.

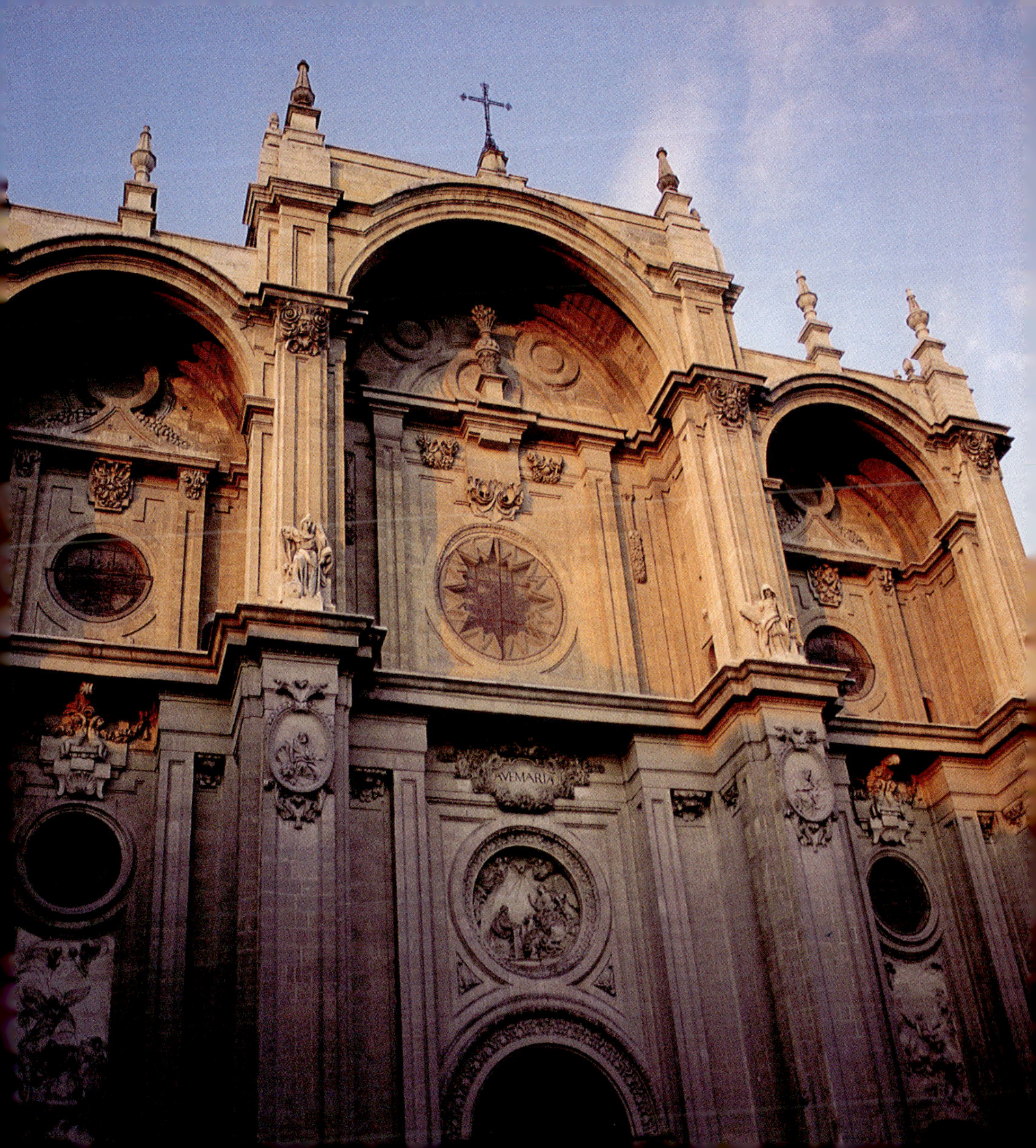
AVEMARIA

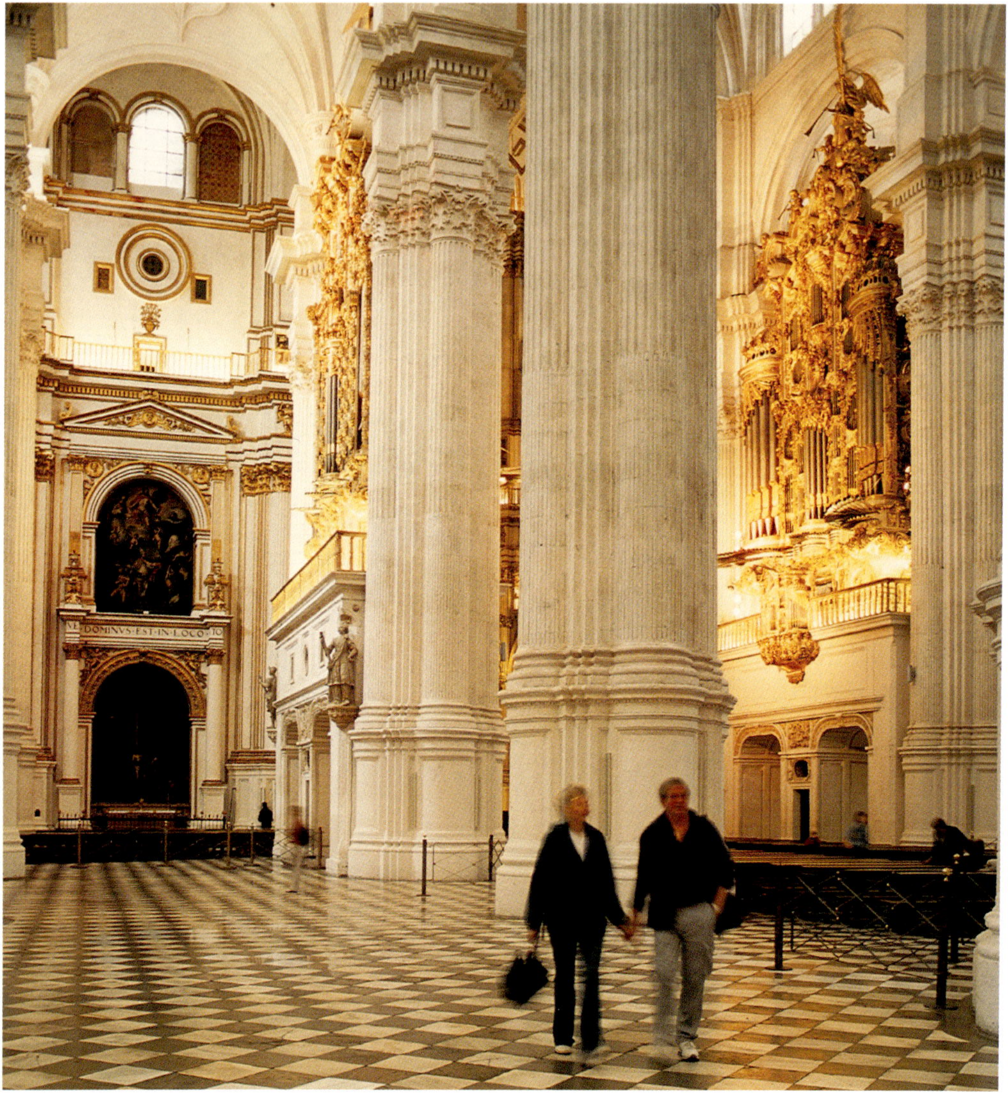
DOMINVS·EST·IN·LOCO

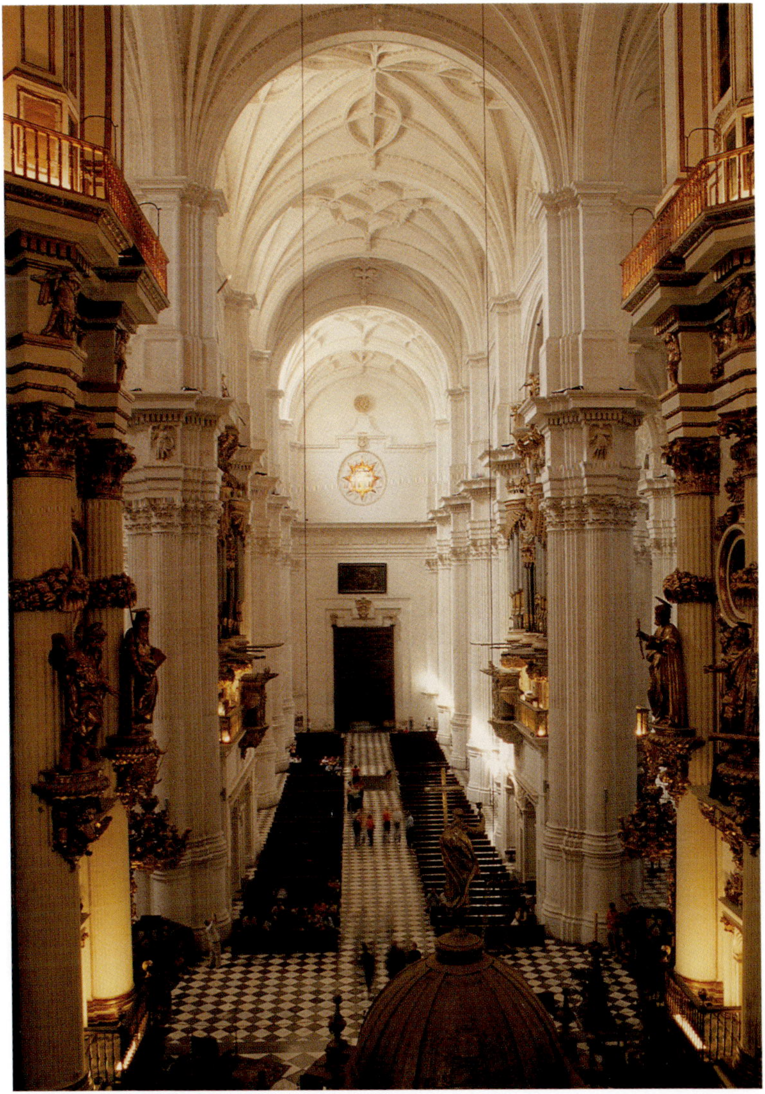

CATHEDRAL
The white naves inside are a surprise.

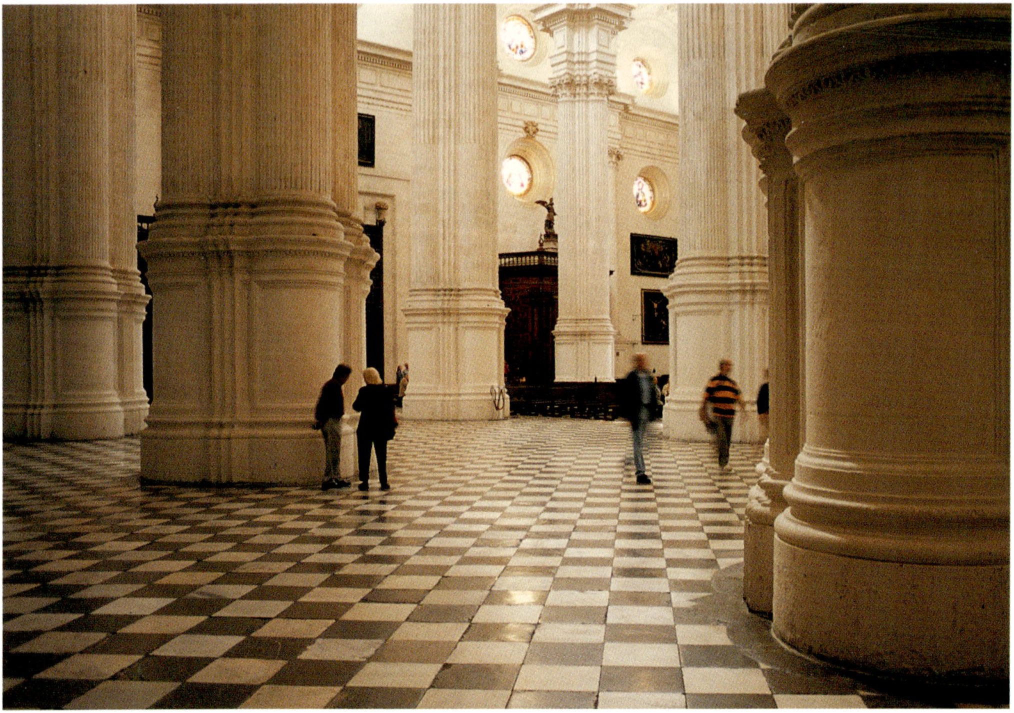

CATHEDRAL
Left-hand aisle and sculpture of Adam alongside a painting representing the Incarnation, both by Diego de Siloé.

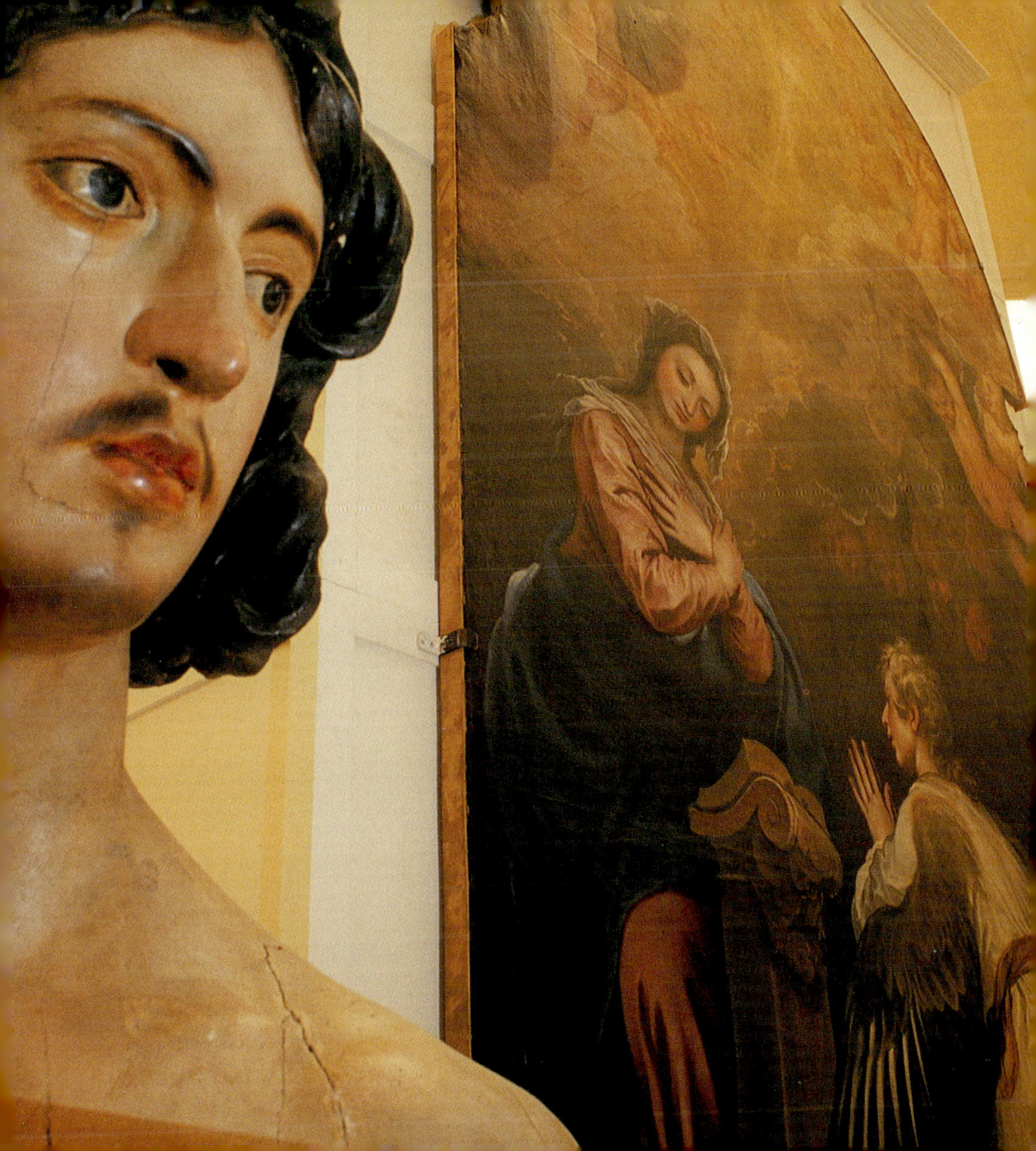

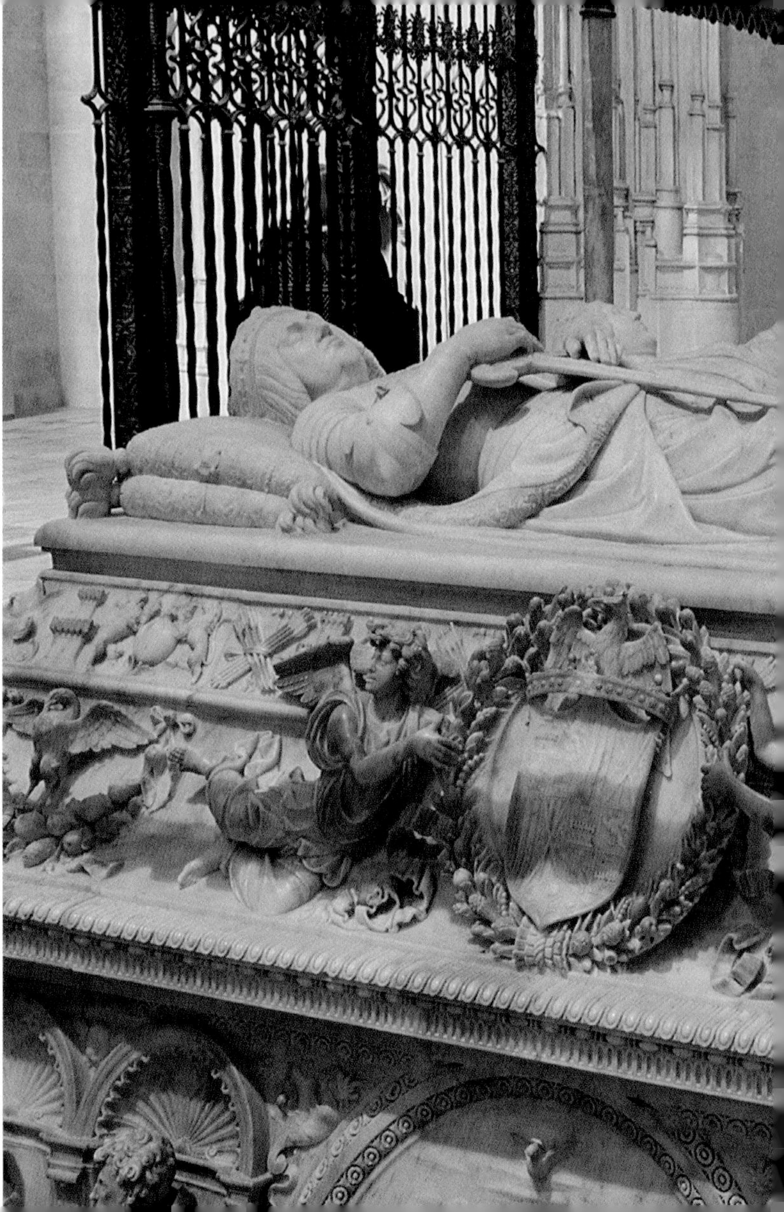

ROYAL CHAPEL
Royal Mausoleums.
In the foreground
the Catholic Monarchs
and in the background
Juana "the Mad" and
Felipe "the Handsome".

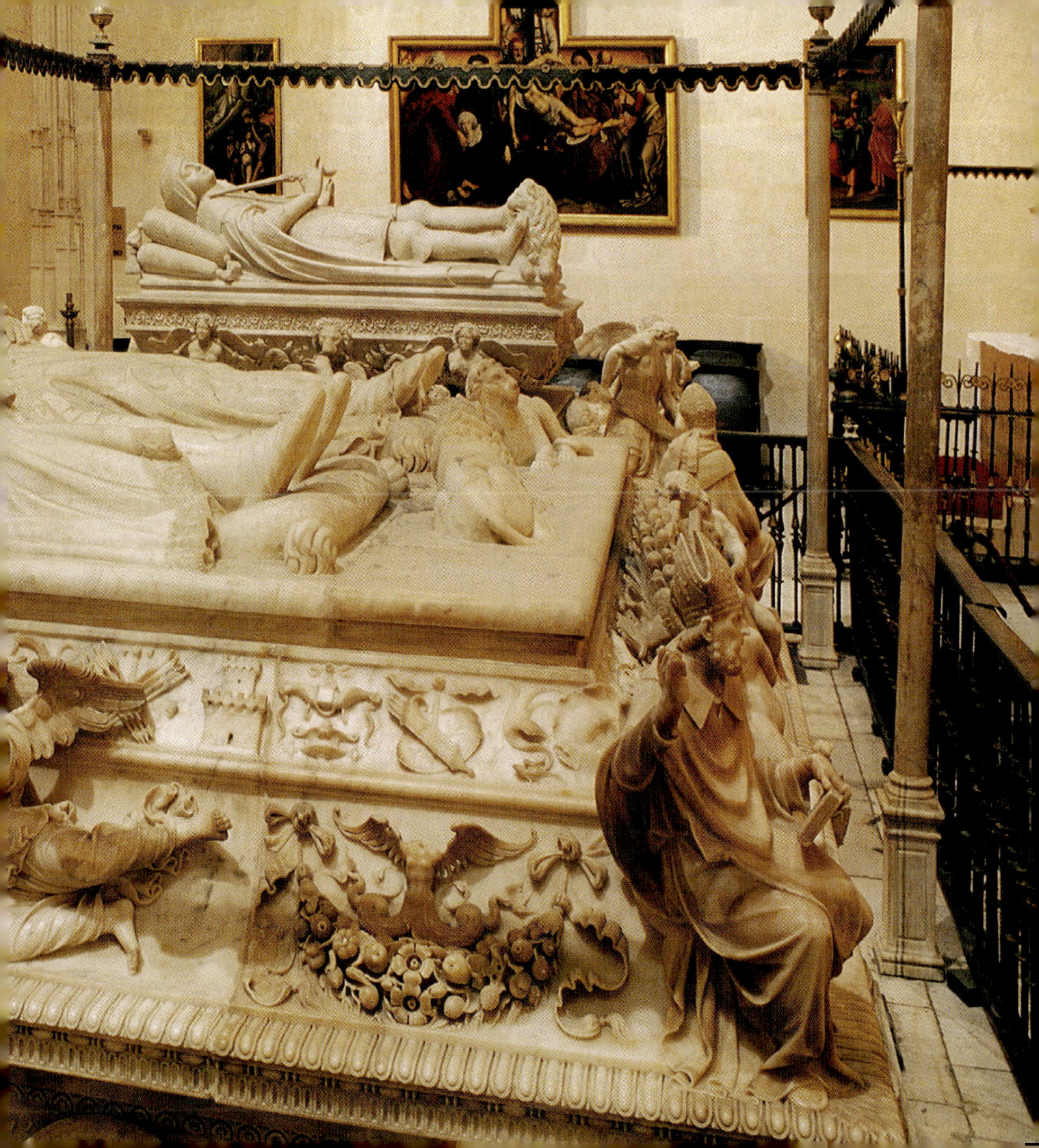

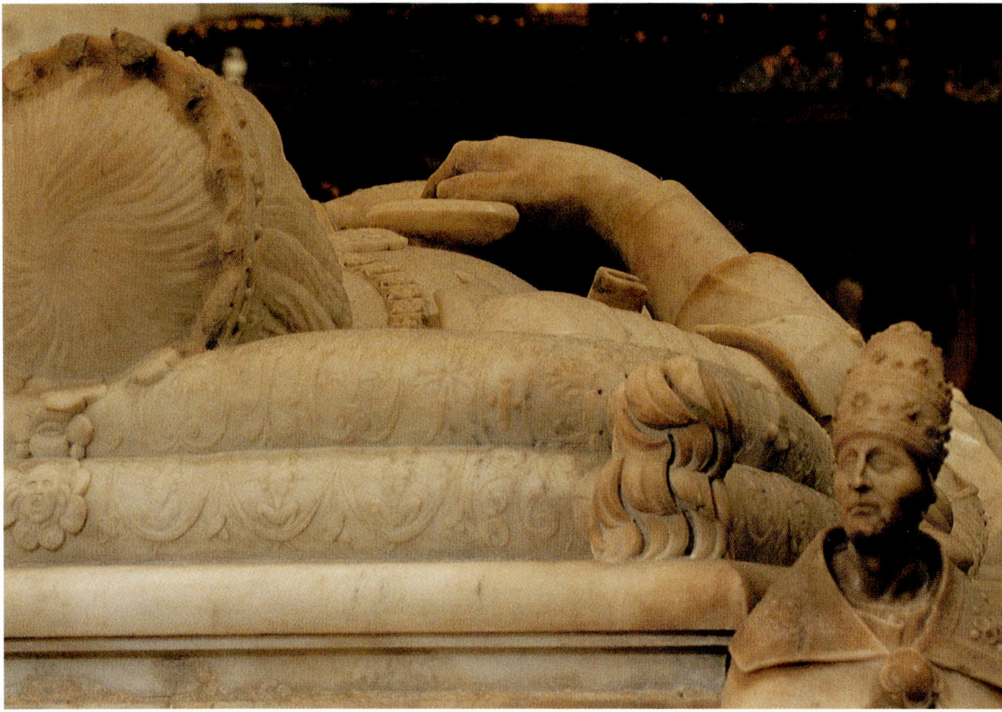

ROYAL CHAPEL

Detail of the Mausoleum of the Catholic Monarchs.

Mausoleum of Juana and Felipe.

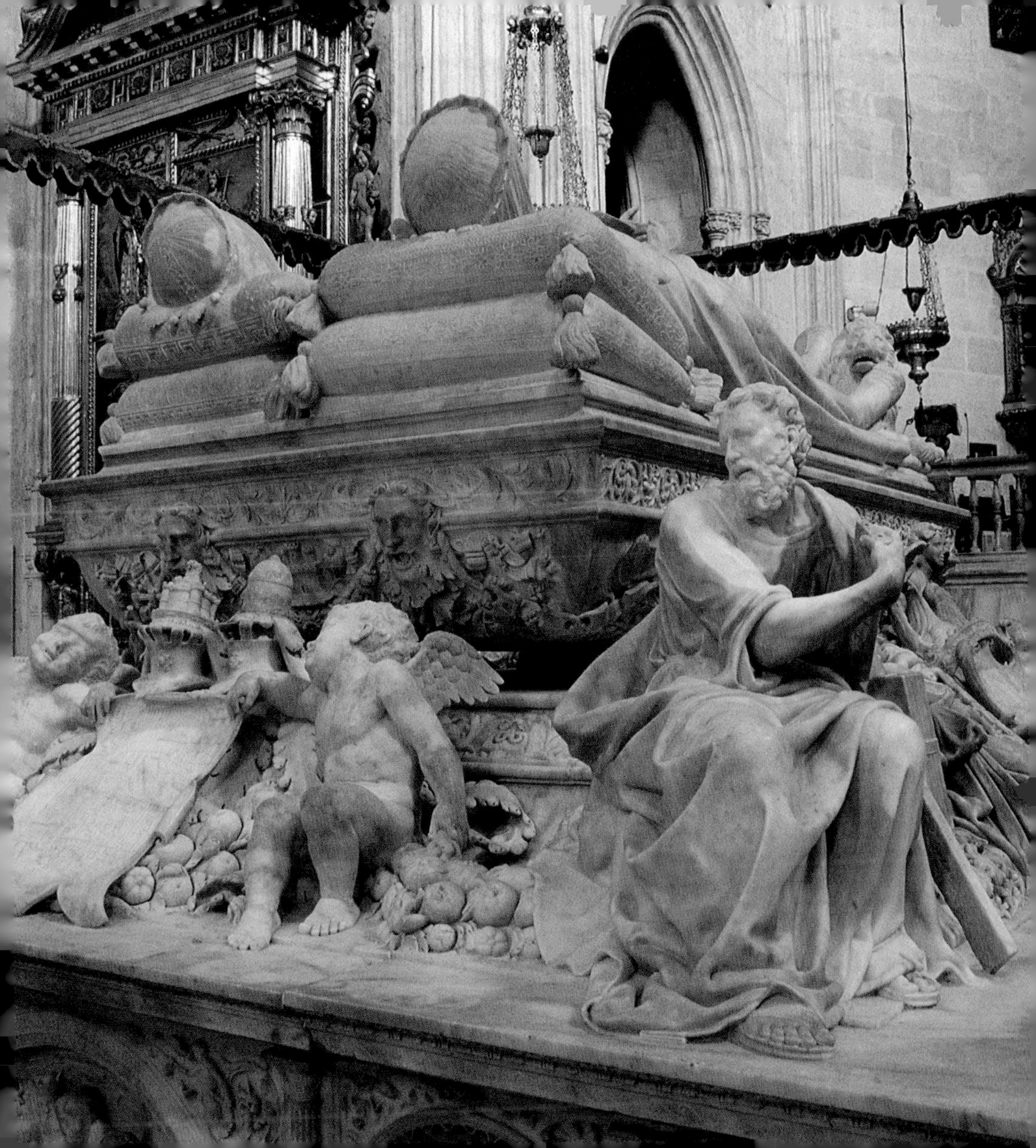

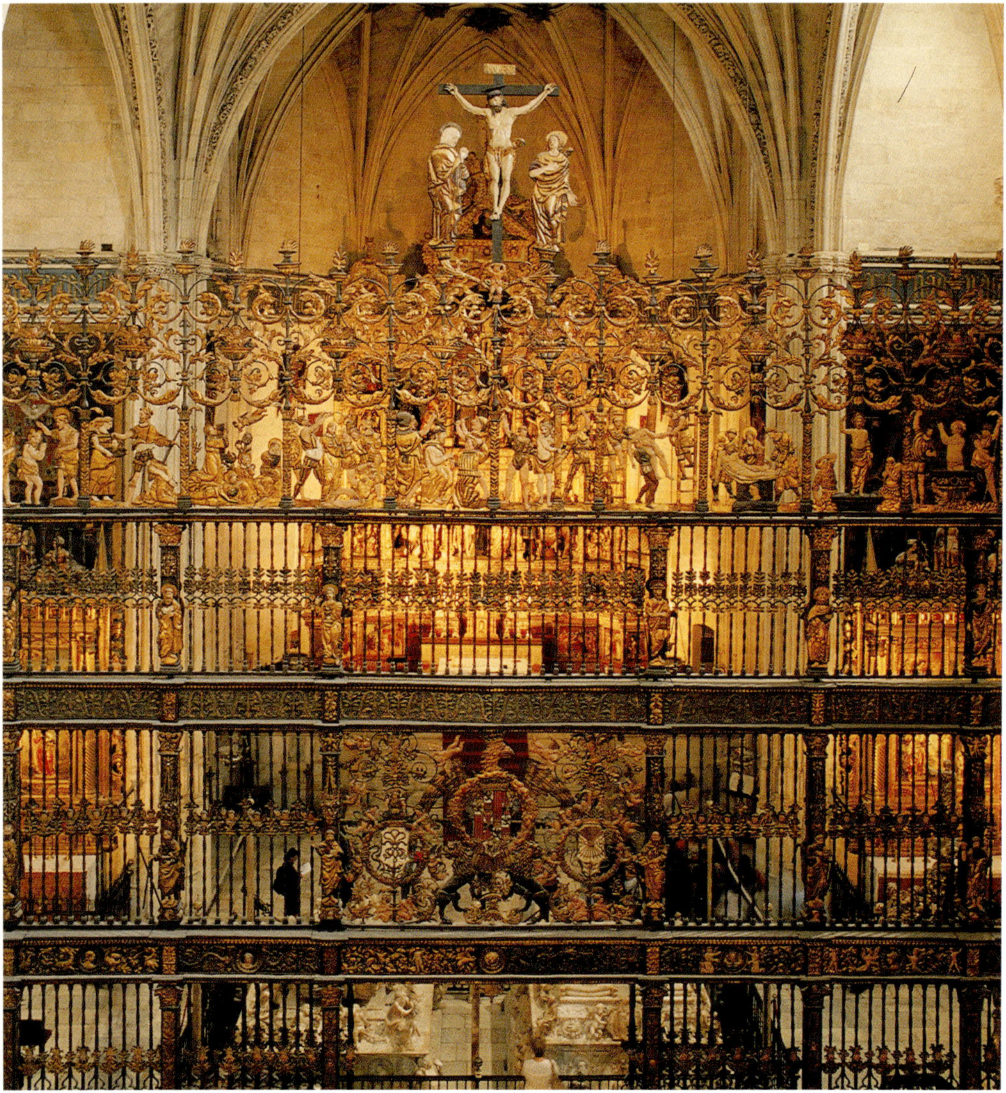

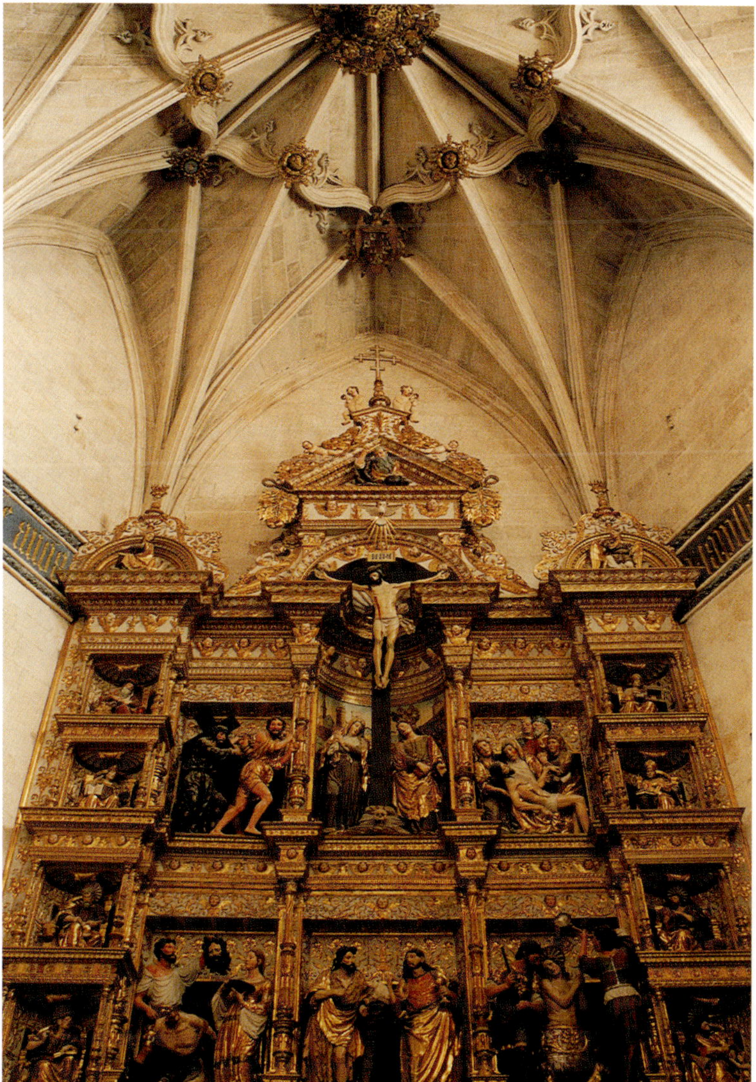

ROYAL CHAPEL
Grille separating the head and the transept from the rest of the church and the high altar.

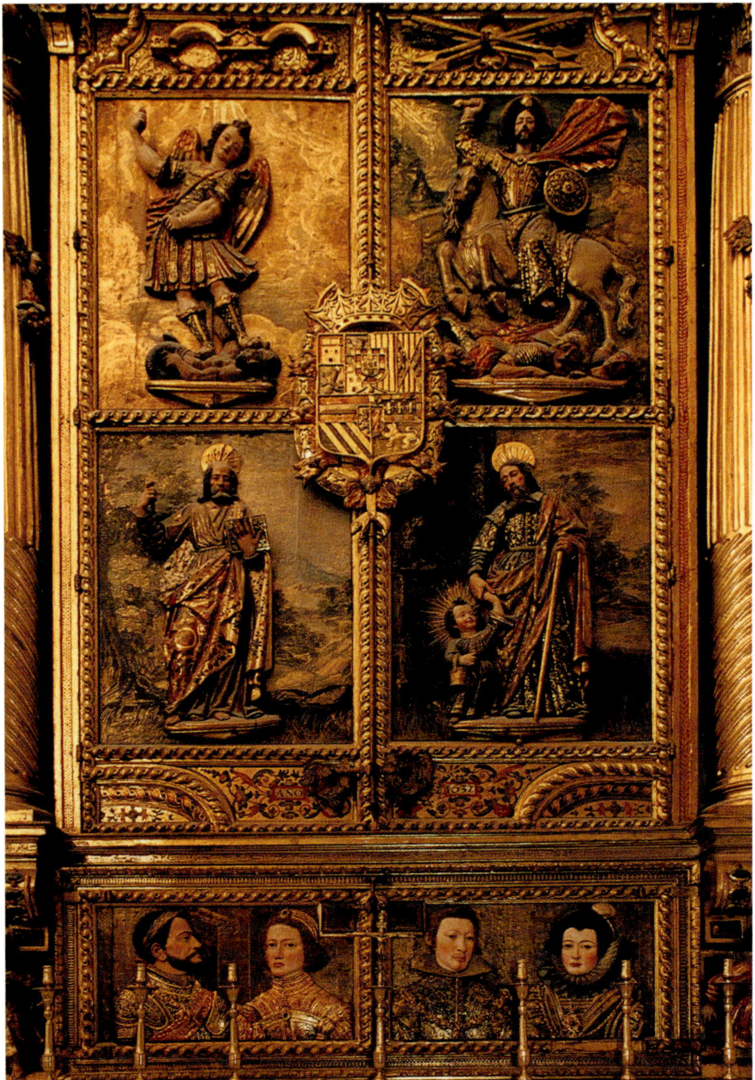

ROYAL CHAPEL
Altarpiece of the Reliquary and Crown of Isabella the Catholic.

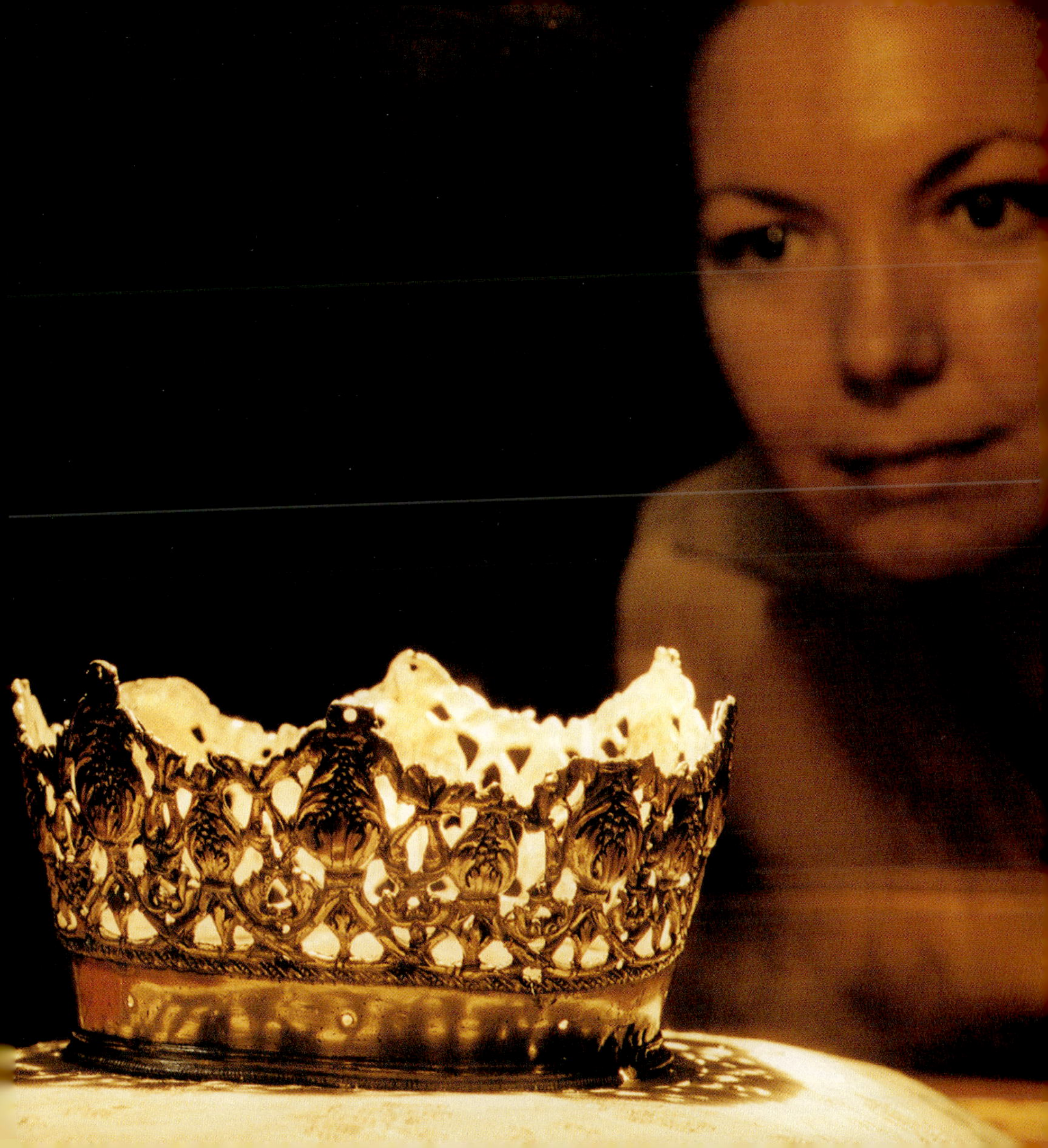

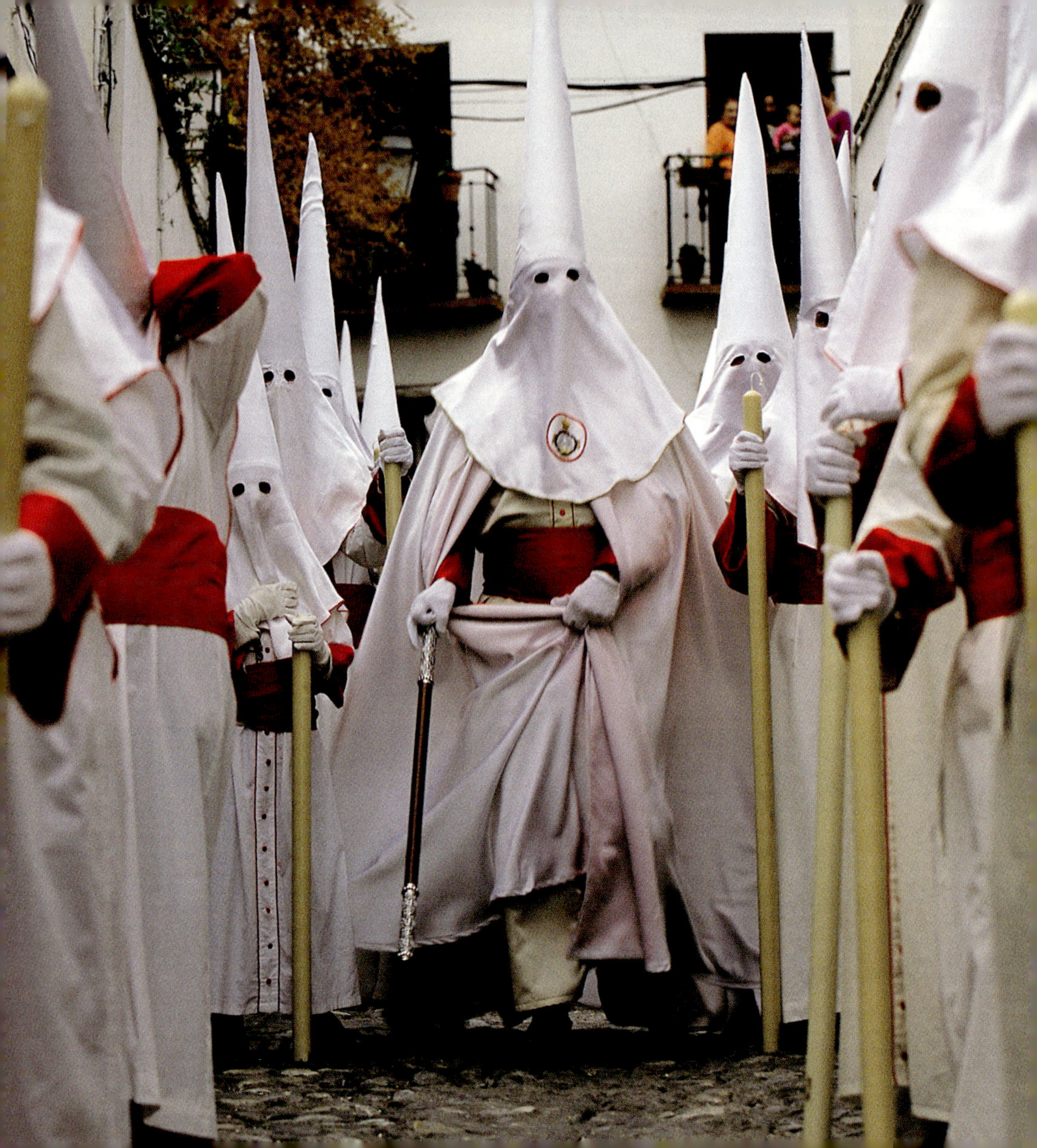

EASTER IN GRANADA

Granada has a busy calendar of popular festivals that are deeply rooted in history. The most exciting one of all, for the massive number of people it attracts, is the Easter festival, which paralyses the city from Palm Sunday until Easter Sunday. With the arrival of the Christians, the church must have established the representation of the Passion of Christ in order to spread Catholic values, although there are no documents that account for its existence until 1573, when the congregations of penitents were prohibited, and which were not allowed again until 1611. The majority of the current *cofradías*, lay brotherhoods, date from the first half of the 20th century, after almost disappearing entirely in the late-19th century, an age of splendour that has lasted until the present.

THE AURORA
In Calle San José Alta.

This festival involves many months of practice and personal sacrifice so that during the days of the festival everything operates to perfection. The beginning is marked by the popular association of the "Borriquilla", which with its arrangement opens a week that fills Granada with processions packed with fervour and the smell of incense. There are moments and days that are particularly emotive, such as the climb of the "Christ of the Gypsies" to the Sacromonte Abbey, on the night and morning of Ash Wednesday and Maundy Thursday, between bonfires and traditional singing that the gypsies provide for him; Maundy Thursday, when the main brotherhoods parade around the Albayzin forming beautiful images in the winding narrow streets of the district, the day that closes with the impressive funeral procession of "Silence"; at three in the afternoon of Good Friday, the human gathering in the Campo del Príncipe to recall the nones, the death of Christ, is quite impressive, under a silence only broken by the bells of Saint Cecilio that ring funereal tones, and finally, "Saint Mary of the Alhambra" must not be missed in her passage round the gardens of the monument from where she gets her name.

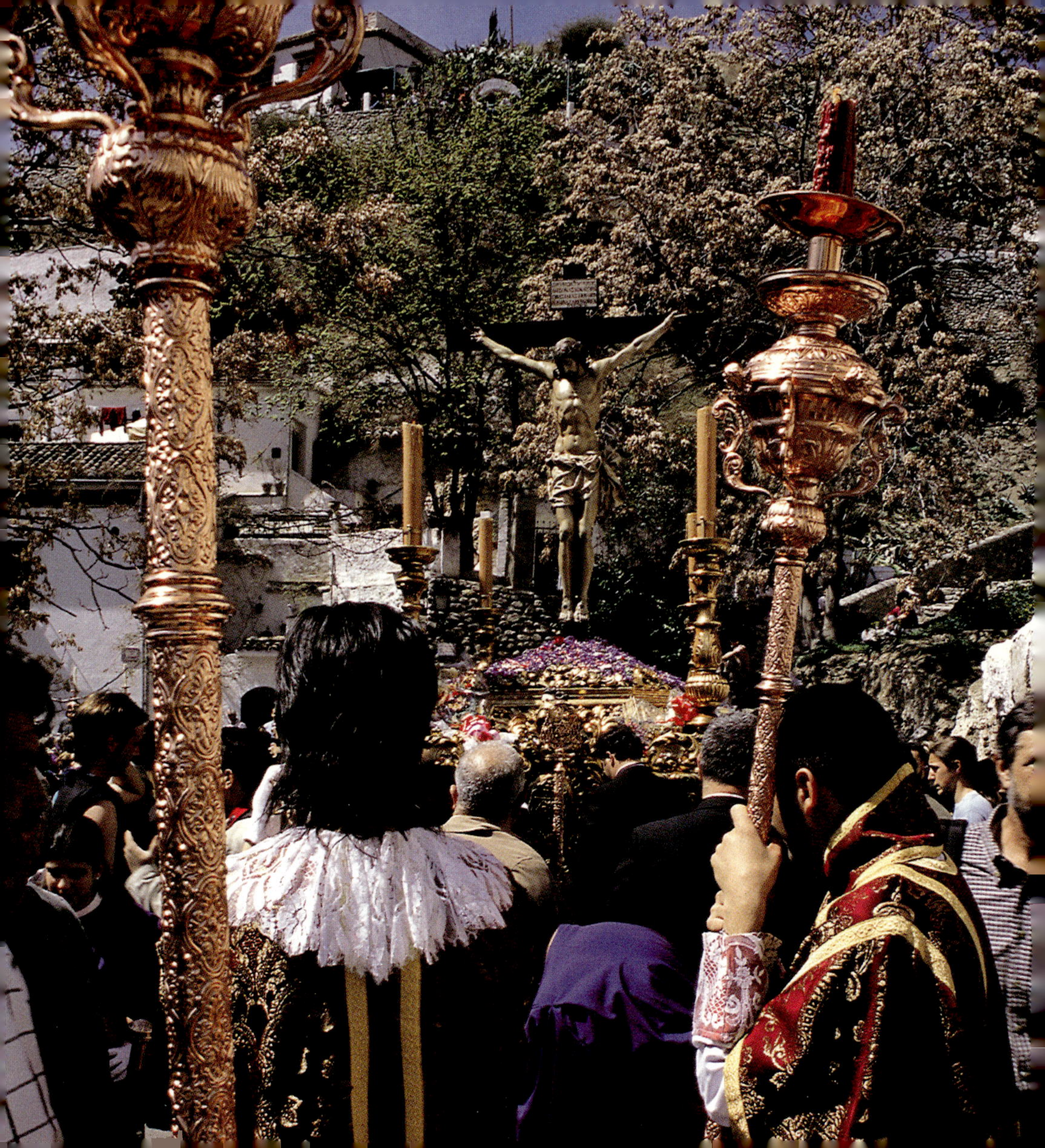

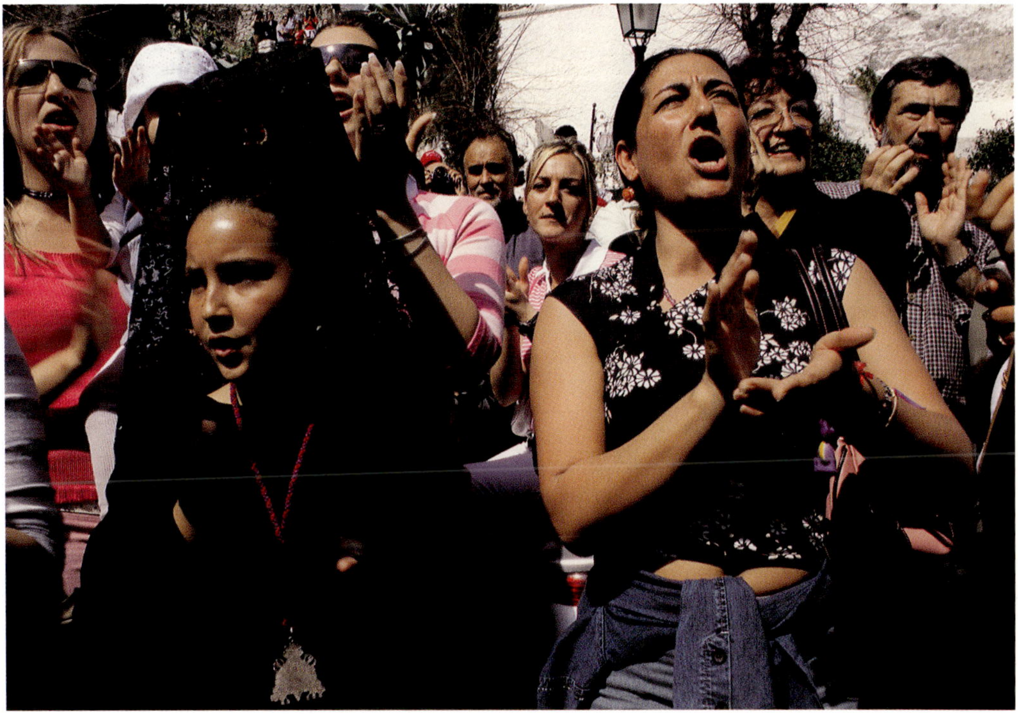

CHRIST OF THE GYPSIES
When it passes by
the gypsies sing to
it with all their heart.

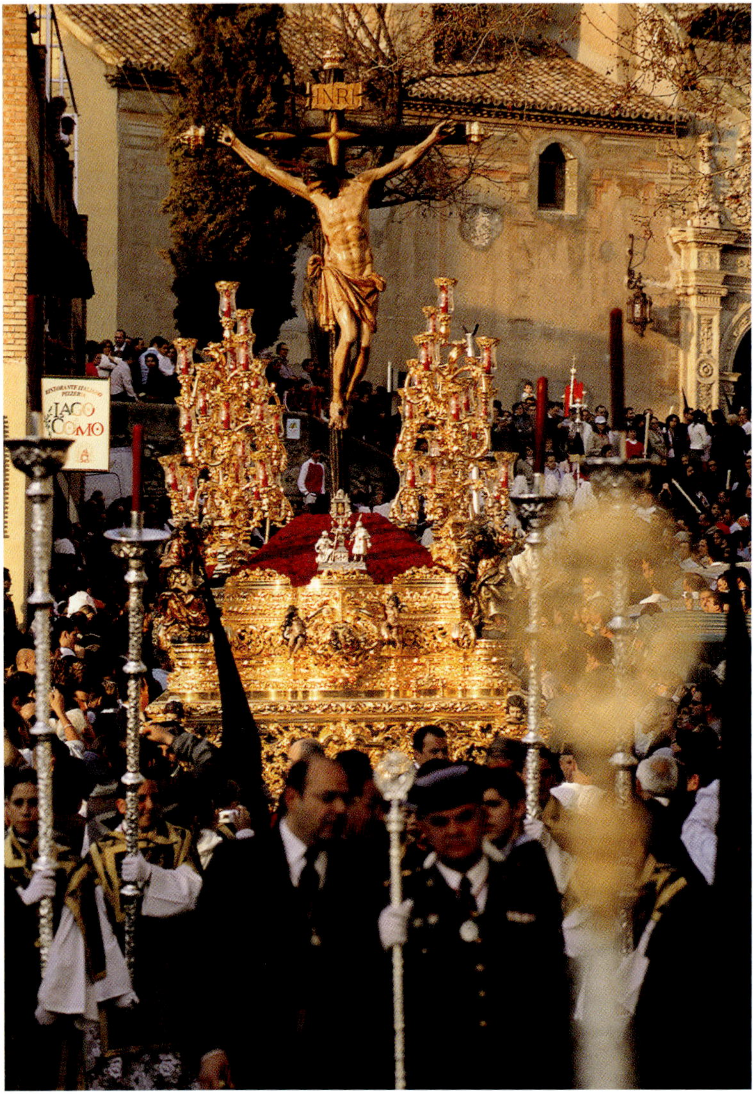

CHRIST OF THE FAVOURS
In Campo del Príncipe.

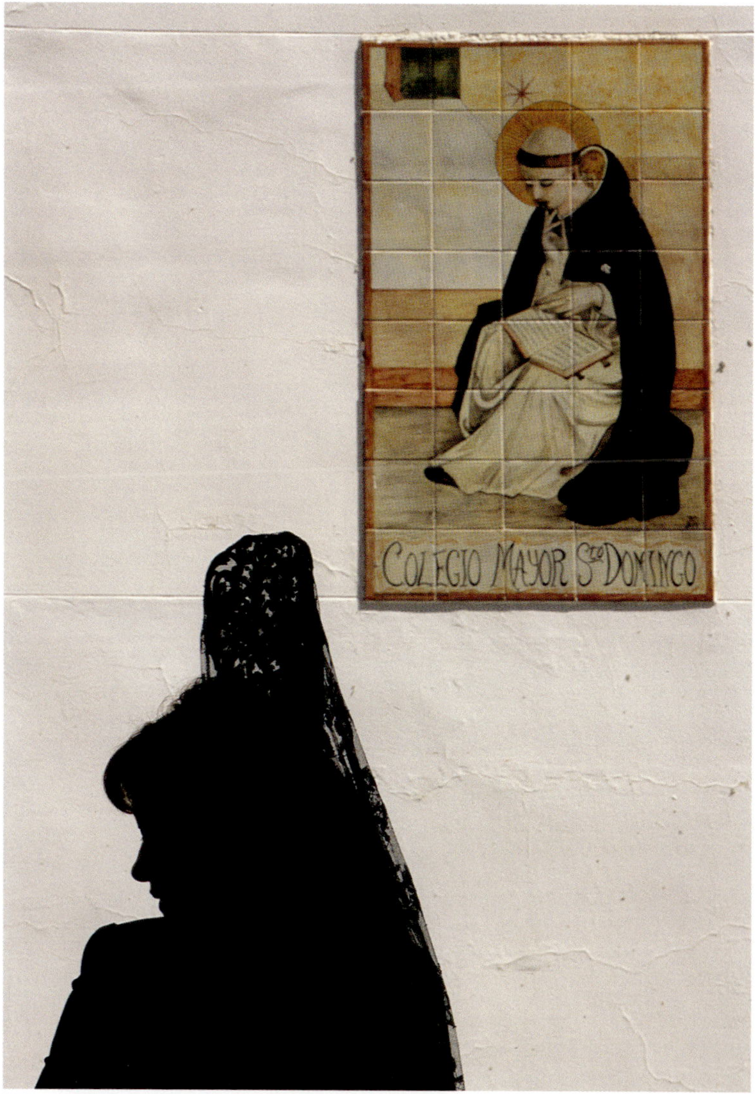

PENITENT WOMAN
Alongside the church of Santo Domingo.

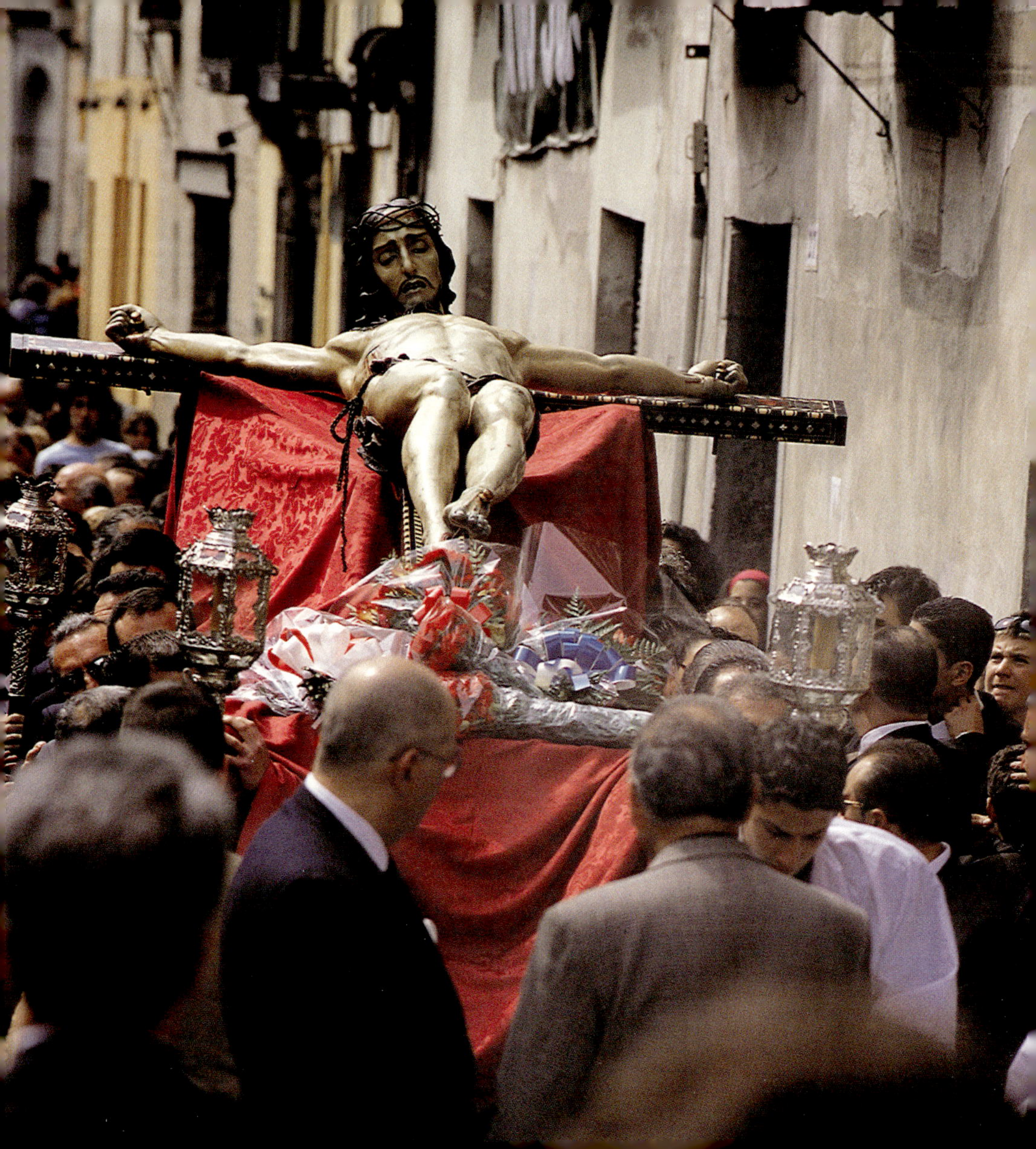

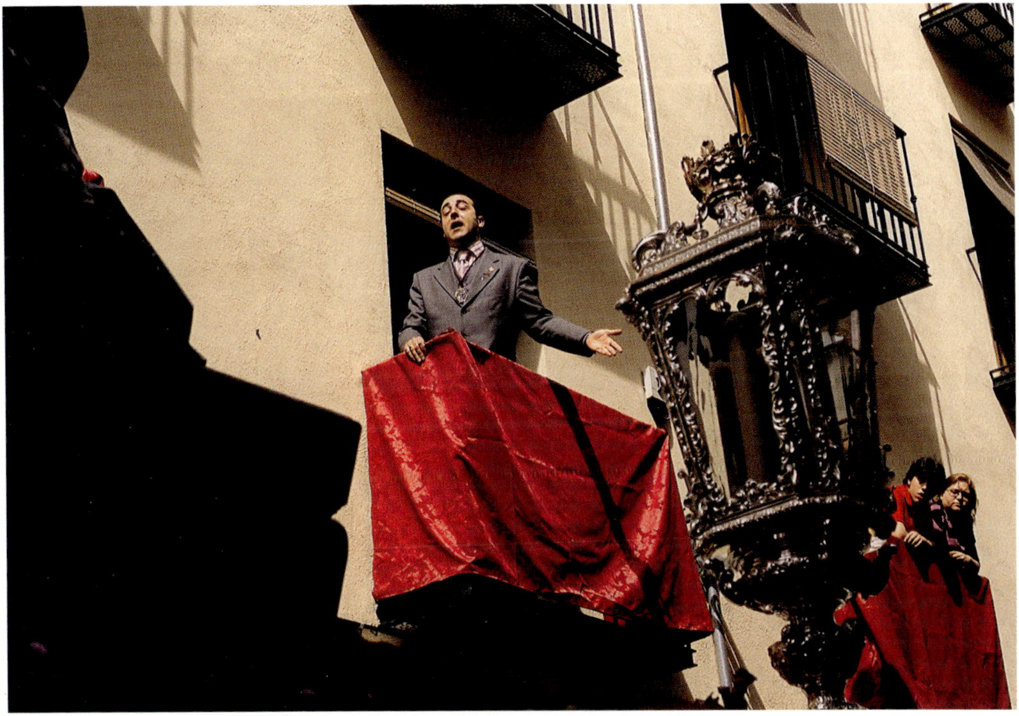

CHRIST OF THE SILENCE
In Carrera del Darro during a procession.

SACRED SONG FLAMENCO SINGER
Singing to the Virgin of the Soledad, in Calle Jarrería.

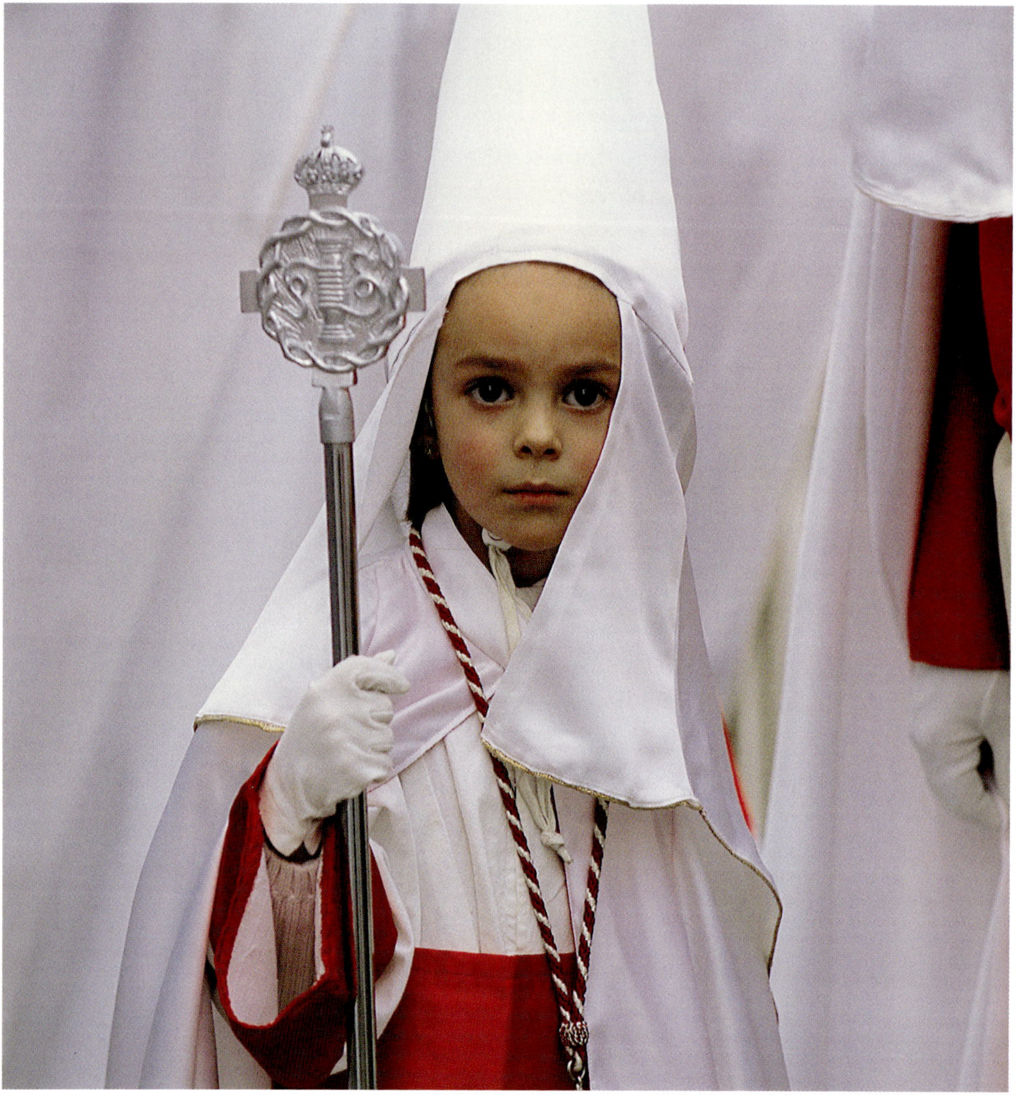

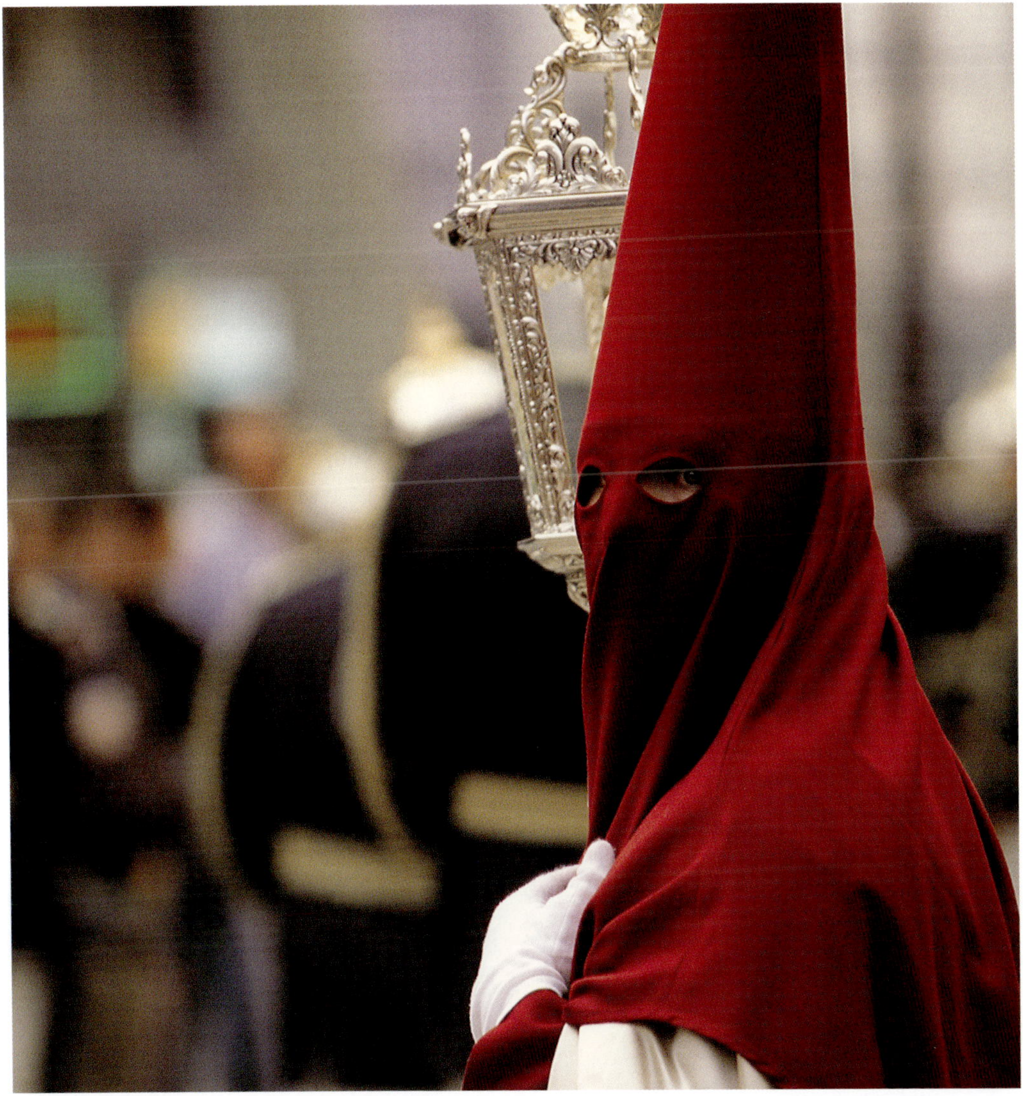

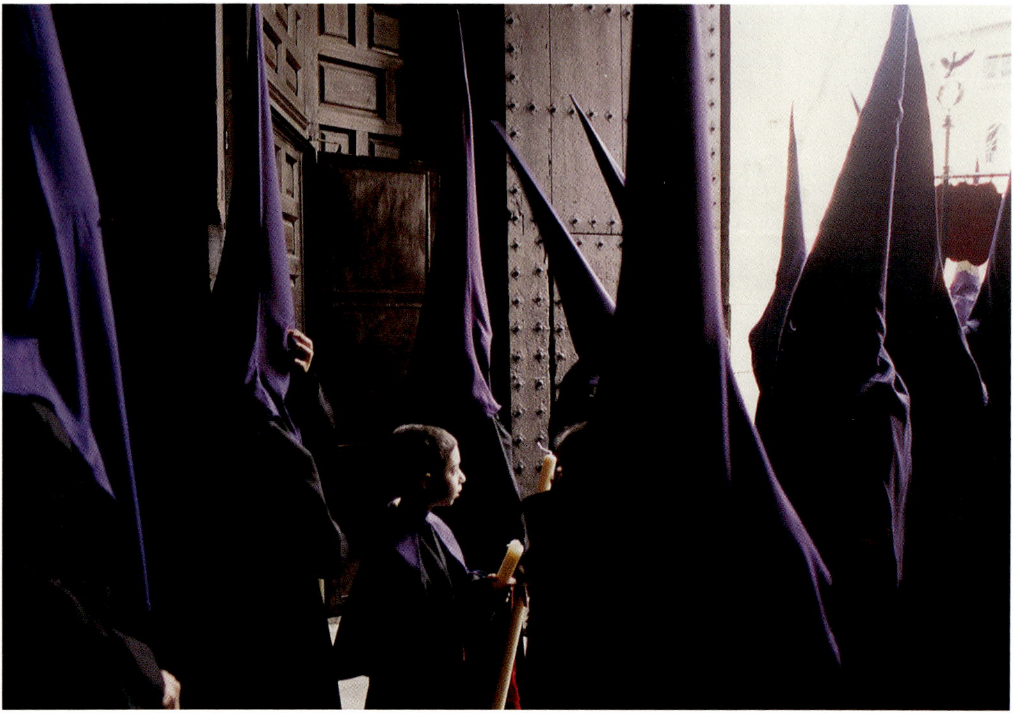

CHURCH OF SANTO DOMINGO
Penitents of the Soledad moments before staring the procession.

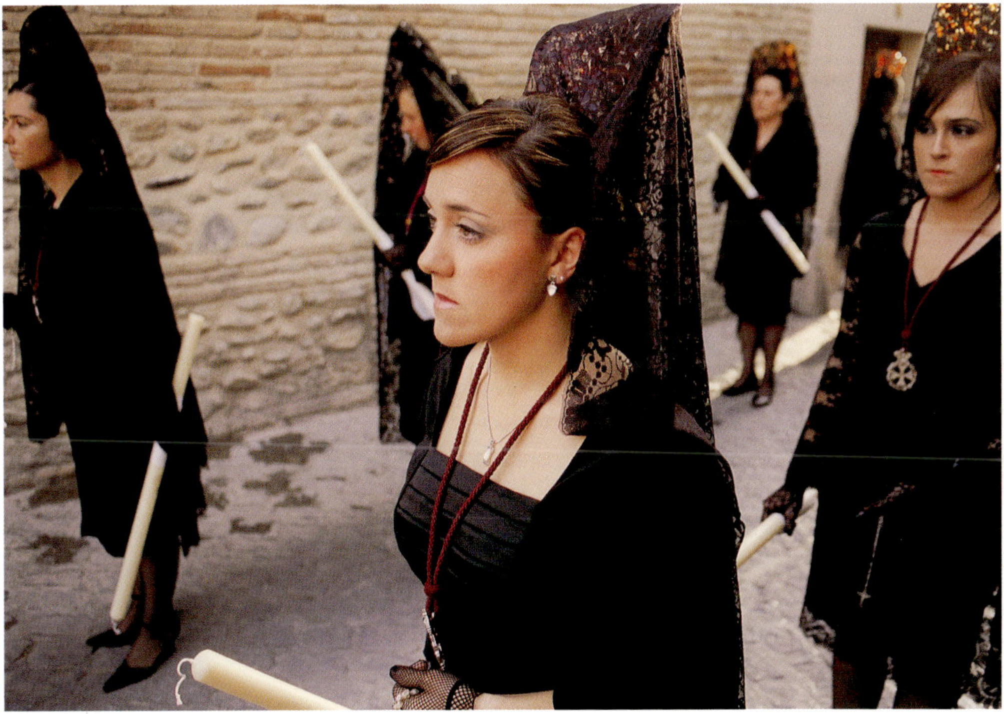

MAIDS
The mantillas fill the streets with respect.

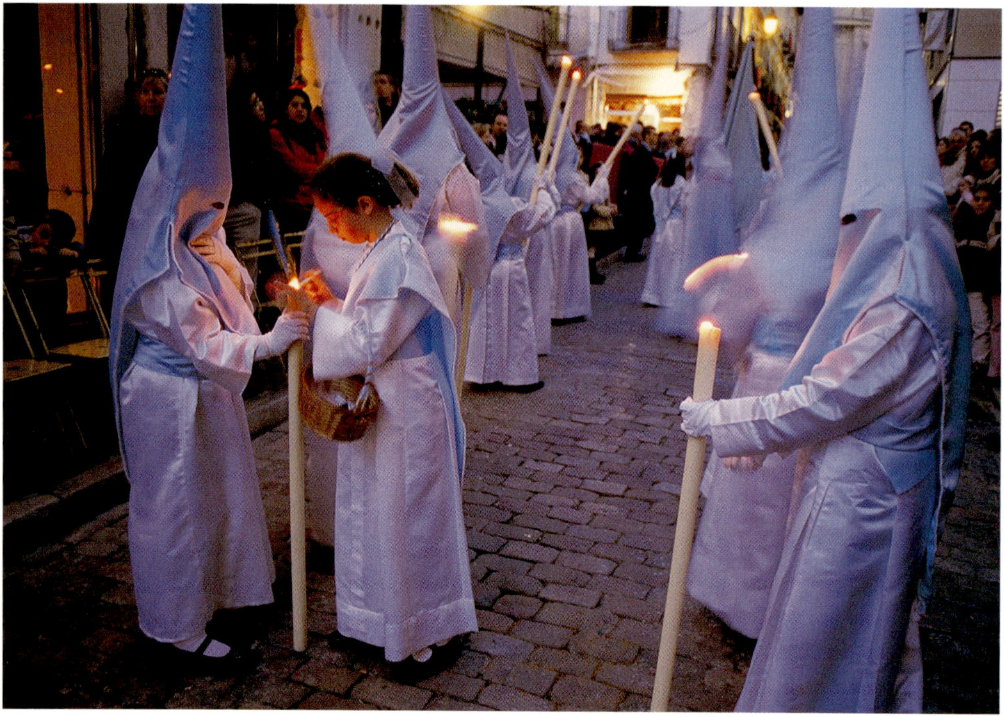

BROTHERHOOD OF THE RESURRECTION OF REGINA
Penitents.

BROTHERHOOD OF THE LAST SUPPER
Acolytes.

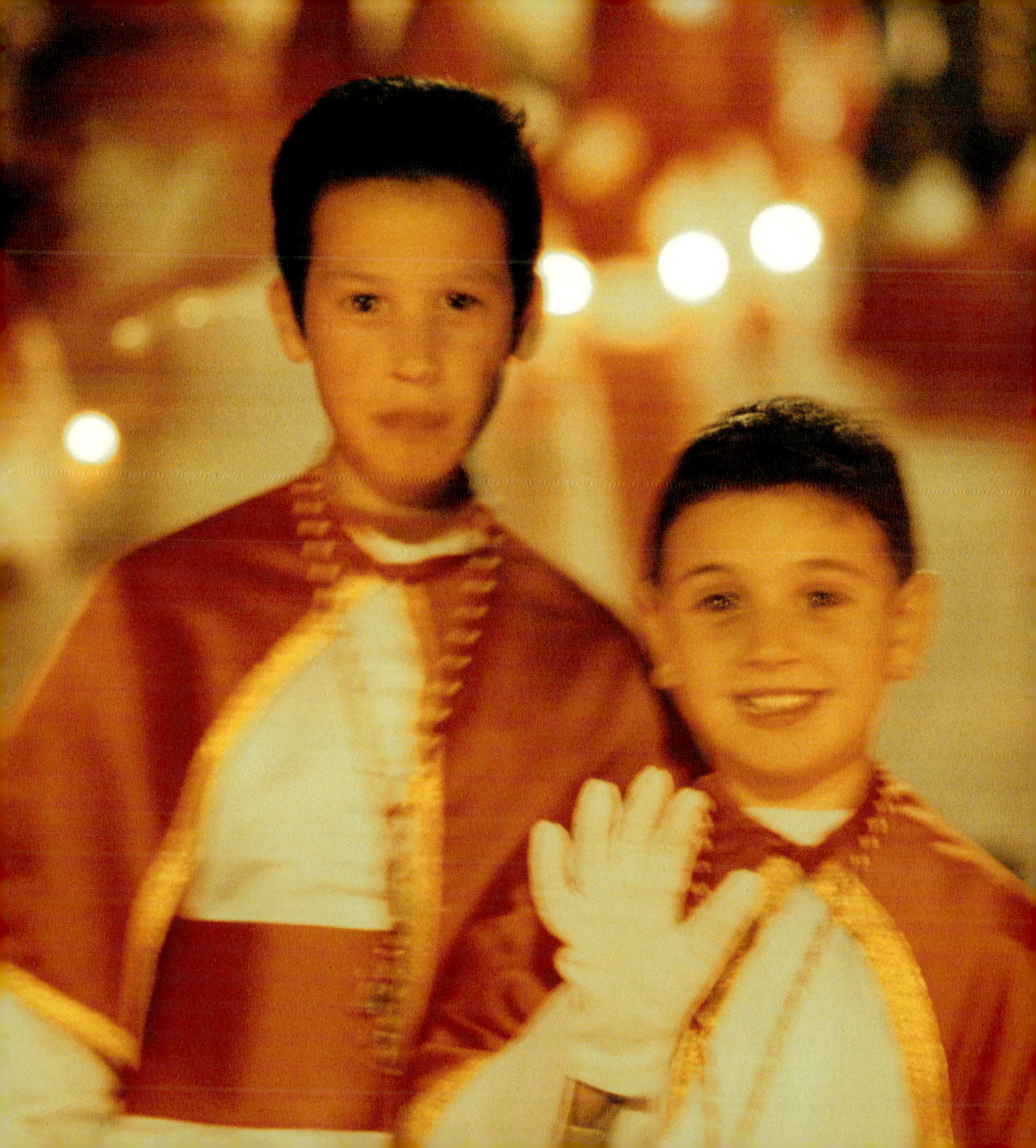

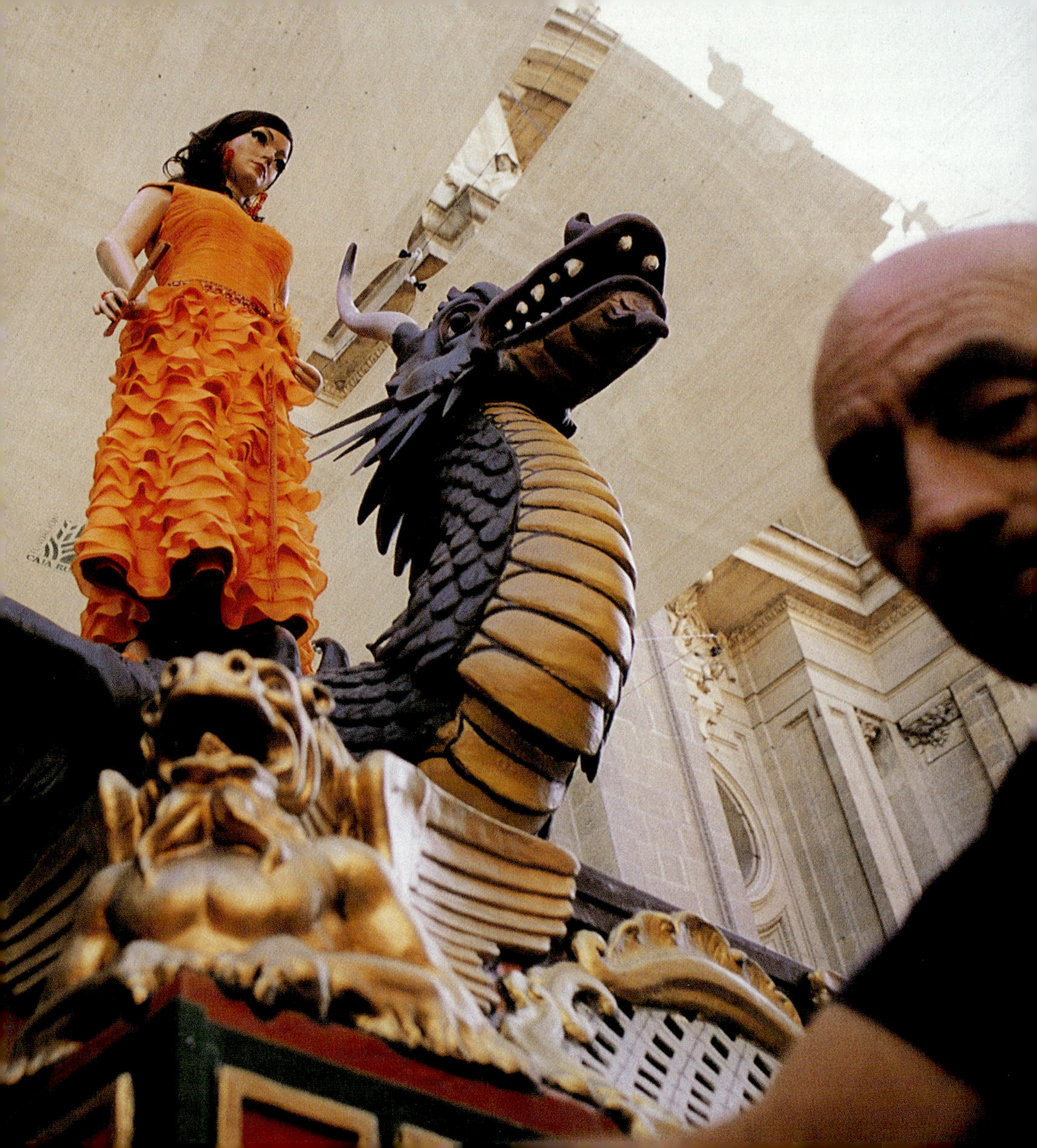

CORPUS CHRISTI

The festival of the Corpus Christi originated from the Council of Trent and was of special importance during the 17th and 18th centuries. On the Iberian Peninsula it became an established rite during the first half of the 14th century and cities such as Lleida, Valencia and Barcelona were the first to include it in their festival calendar. For the Catholic Monarchs the introduction of the celebration that honours the Eucharist was a tool, which along with the other festivals on the Christian calendar, formed part of a wider agenda to convert a whole people who had been under Islamic domination for eight centuries. Imposed by royal decree over more than five hundred years ago, the Granada Corpus Christi consists of a religious celebration around which a large programme of bullfighting festivals are held that feature the leading exponents of the day, and a big Fair where you can go horse-riding, have a go on the attractions of an amusement park, taste delicious local produce at the stands and dance through the night until the early hours. This is the Fiesta Grande of Granada: since long ago, the Corpus Christi, as well as its religious meaning, represents having fun, for young and old alike. "You must all appear to be crazy" is a sentence attributed to the Catholic Monarchs, with which they exhorted the population to enjoy themselves during the days that the festivities lasted. Of all the events held, the one that produces the biggest concentration of public is the traditional procession of the Corpus Christi, which fills the streets of the city with colour and crowds to see the passing of the Monstrance with the Holy Sacrament over a carpet of aromatic plants that stretch all along the route taken. This is followed by the Tarasca, a dragon-like beast, the Cabezudos or big-heads, and giants, which reproduce the passacaglia which a day before has passed by to announce the arrival of the most important days of the Corpus Christi.

THE DRAGON
Its appearance on the street is one of the most-awaited events of Corpus Christi.

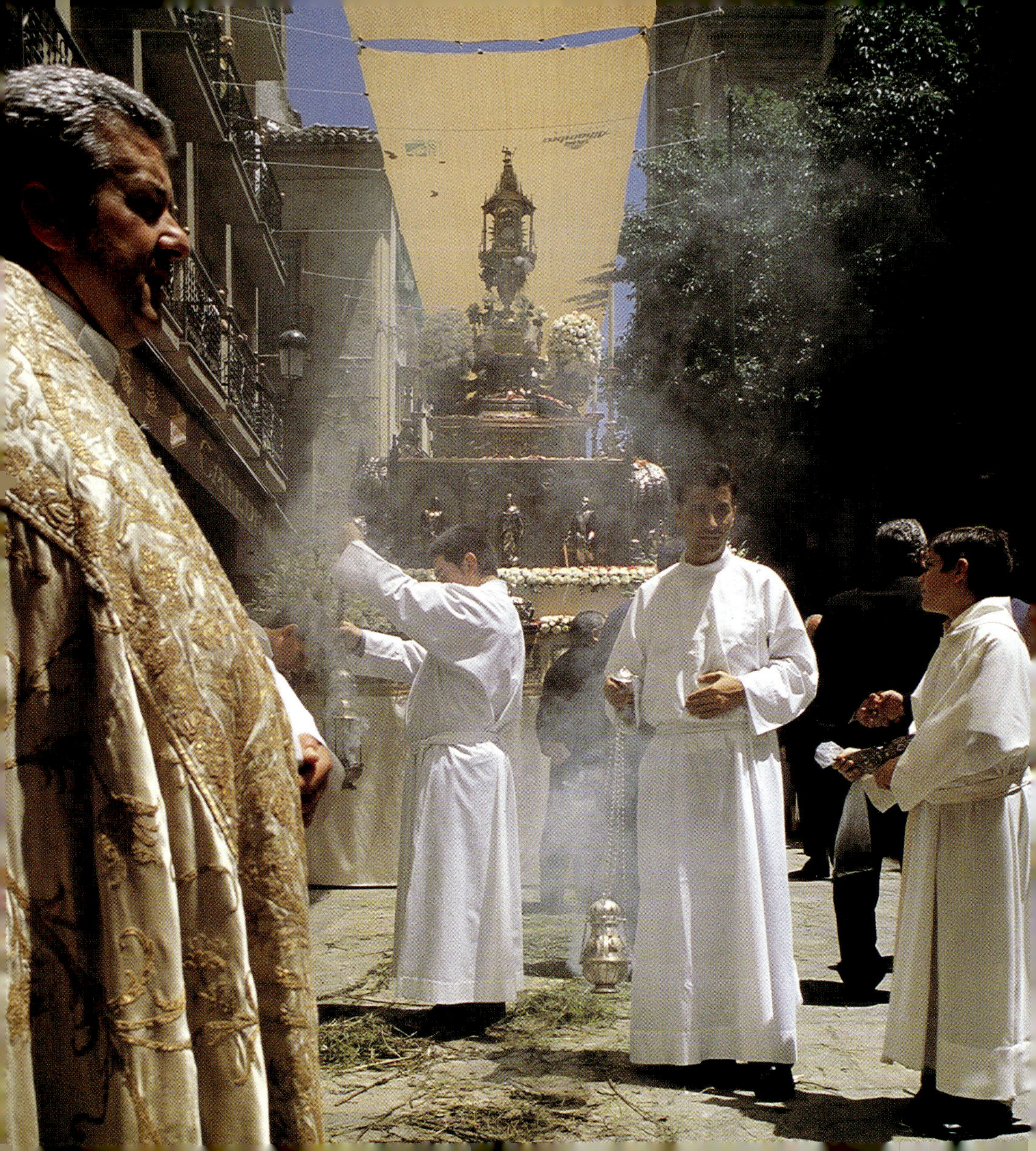

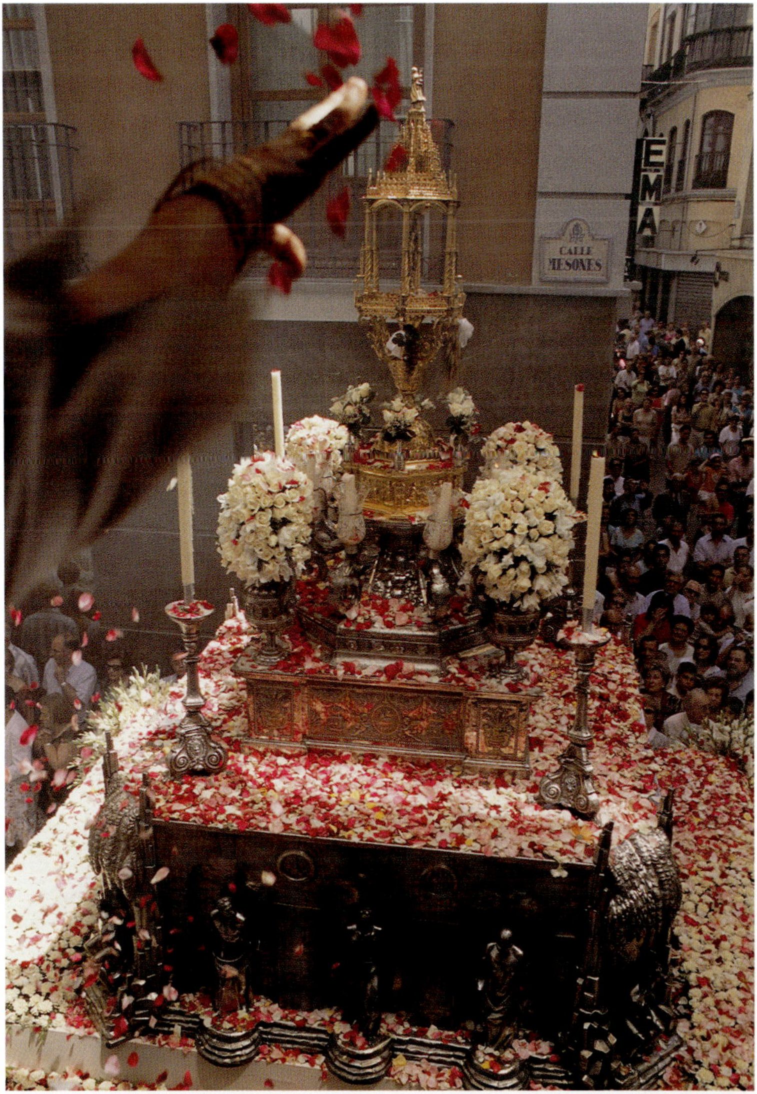

PROCESSION OF CORPUS CHRISTI
The Monstrance with the Holy Sacrament makes its way through the crowds, surrounded by columns of smoke smelling of incense and rose petals that are thrown down from windows and balconies.

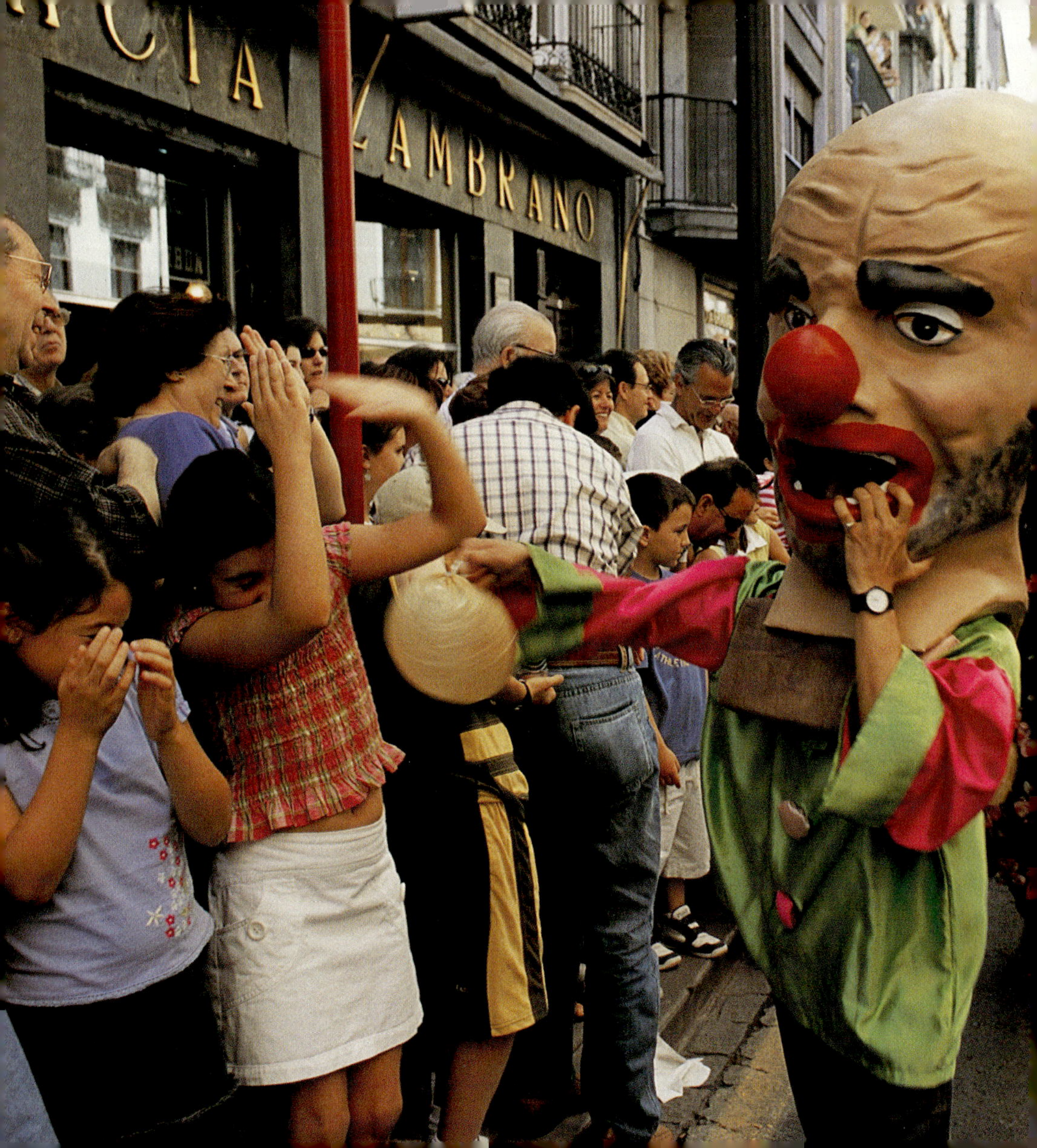
ZAMBRANO

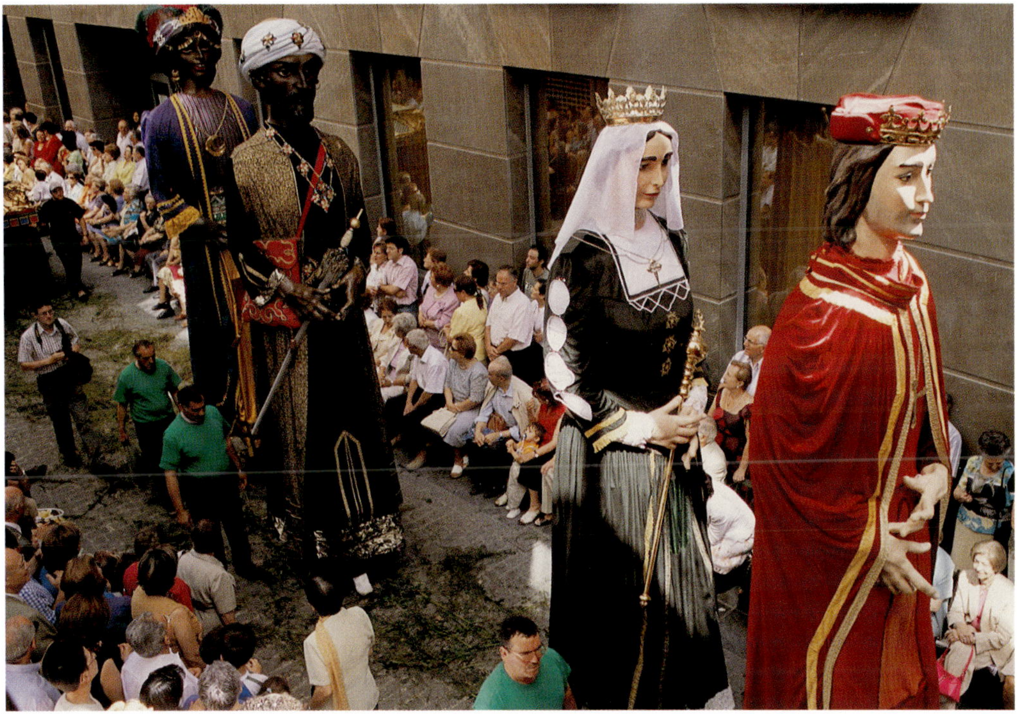

GIANTS AND BIGHEADS
They surprise and bring a smile to the faces of the youngsters and the not-so-young.

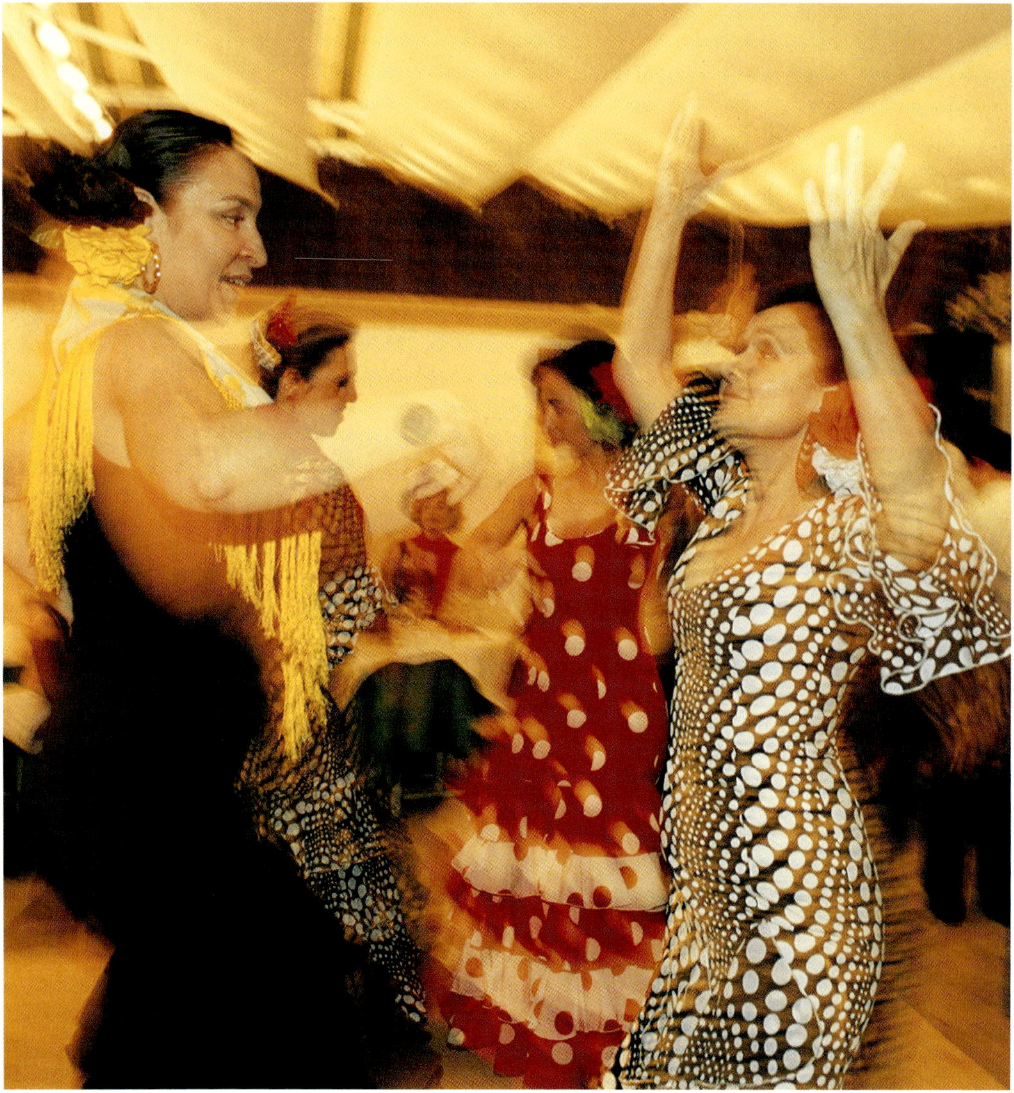

THE FAIR
When night falls dancing
is the main attraction
in the small venues.

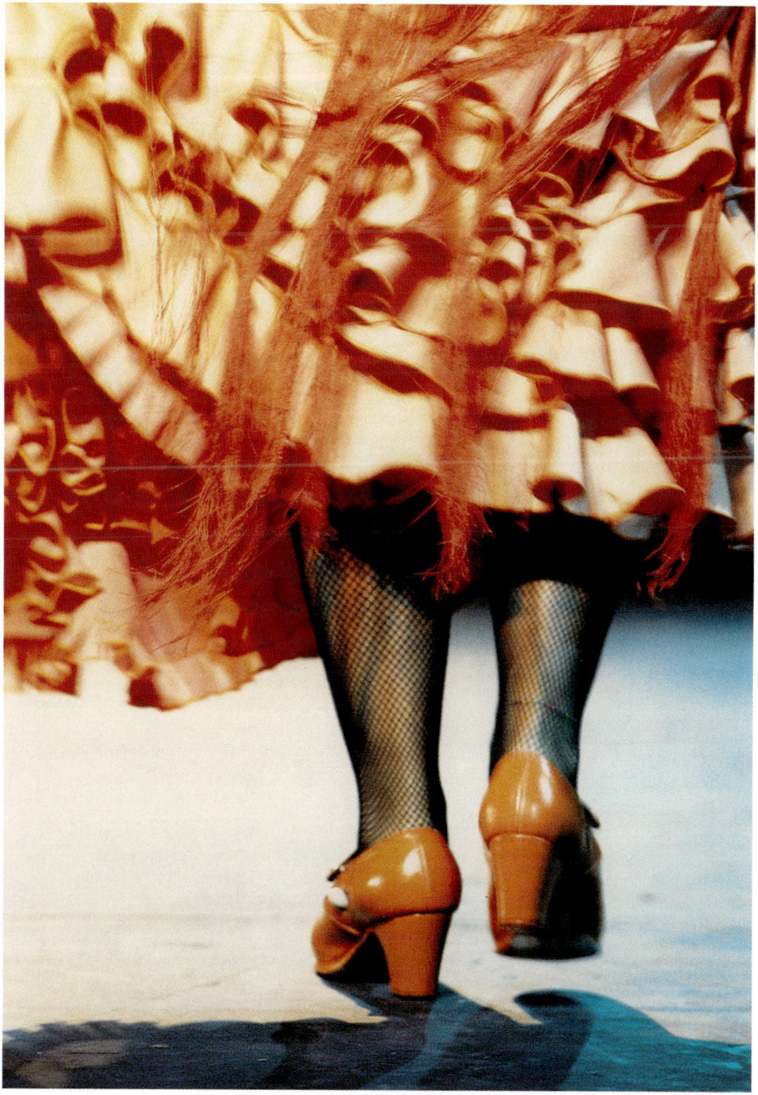

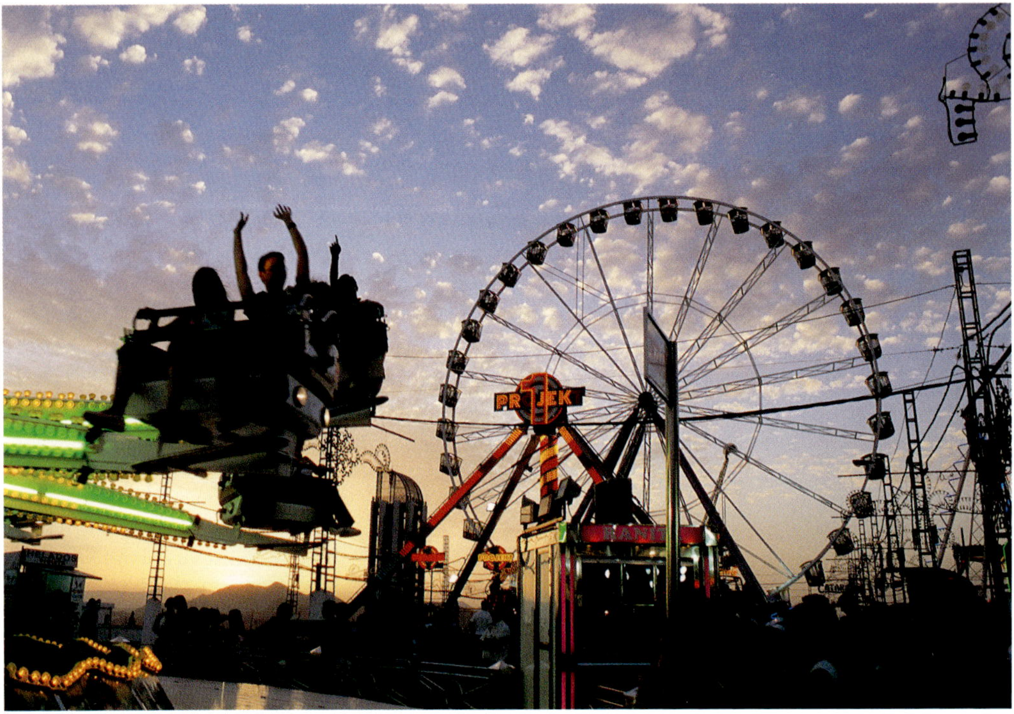

THE ATTRACTIONS
All the fun of the fair.

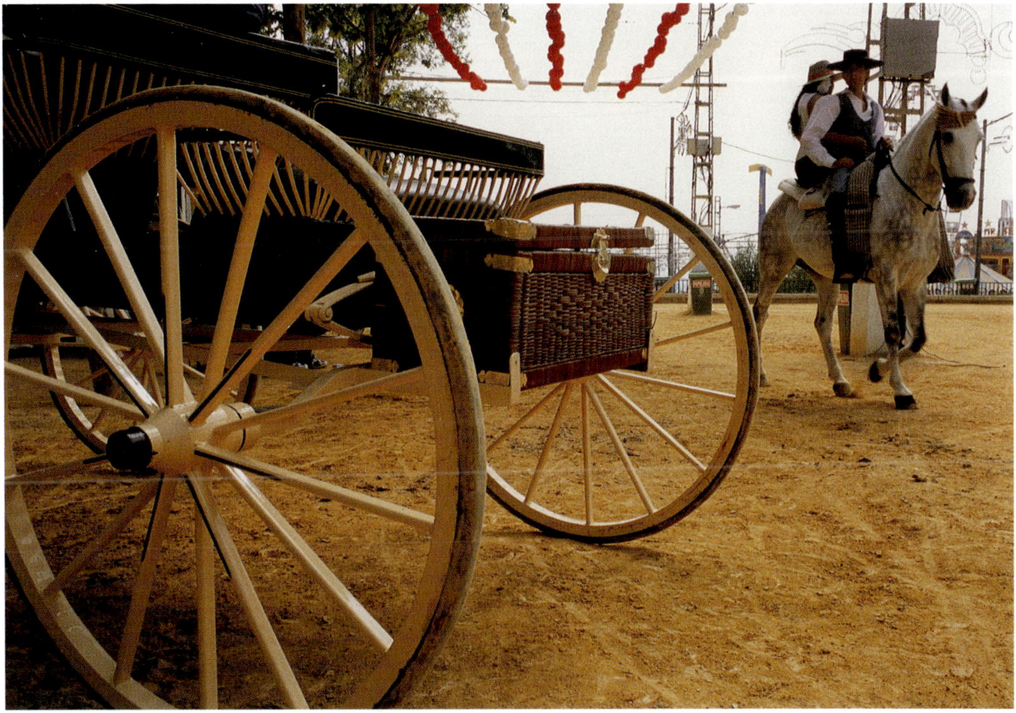

HORSES AND CARTS
An essential part of any fair worth its salt.

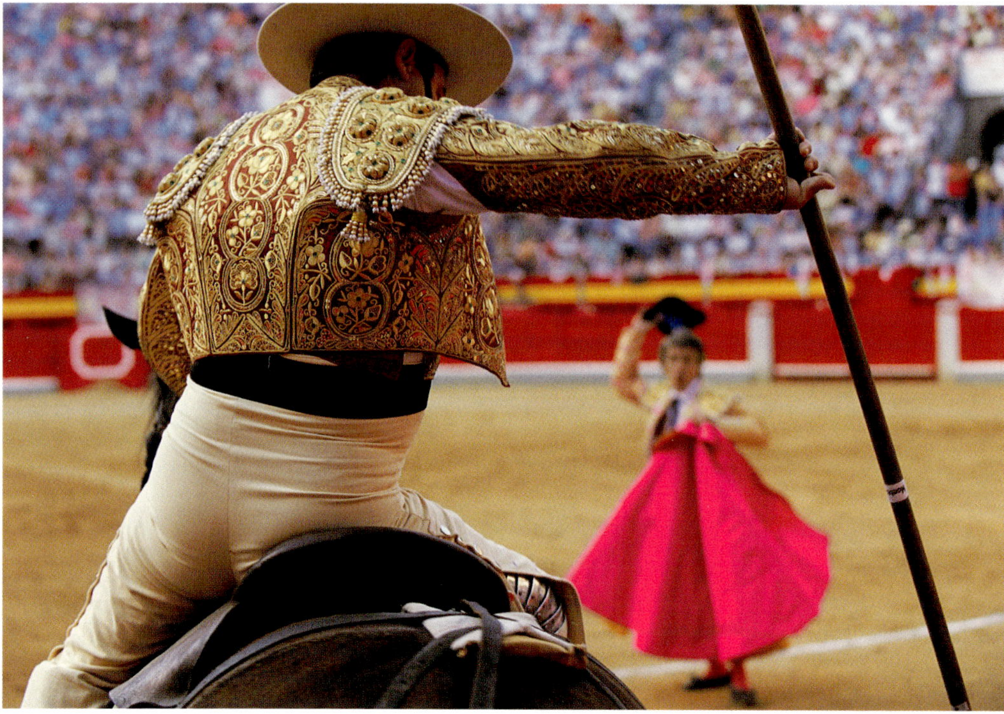

THE BULLFIGHTING EVENTS
They are one of the big activities of the Granada Corpus Christi.

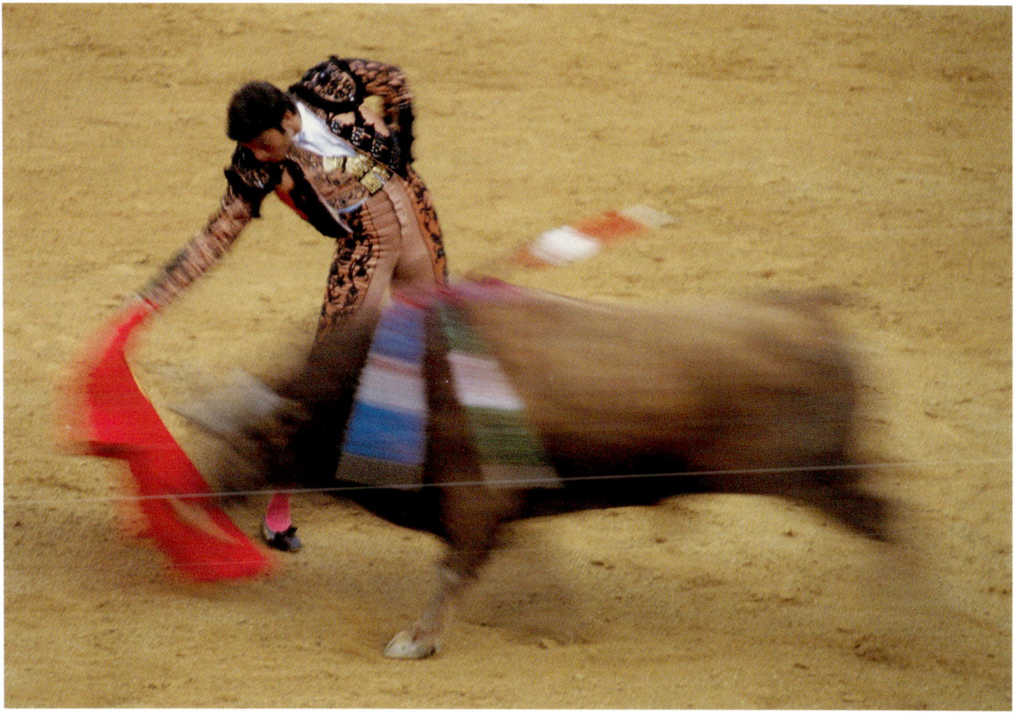

"MORANTE DE LA PUEBLA"
A natural.

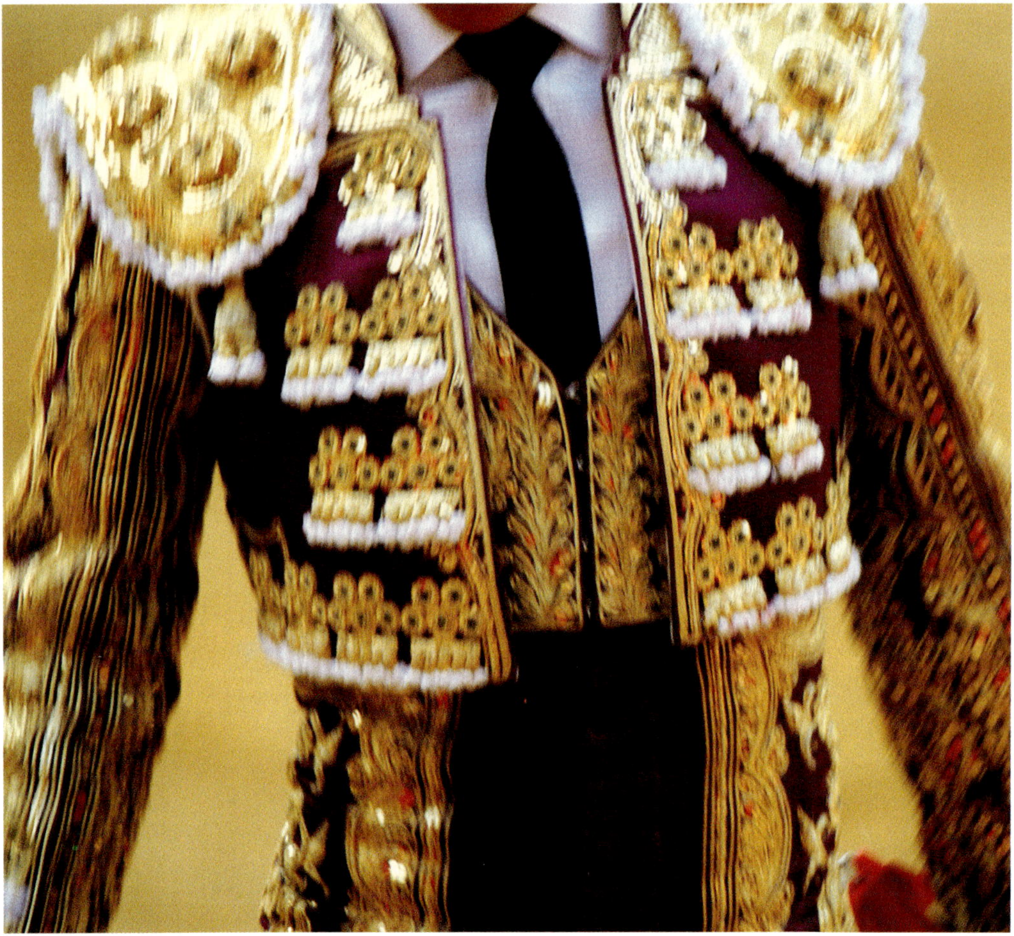

SUIT OF LIGHTS
It protects and distinguishes the figure of the bullfighter.

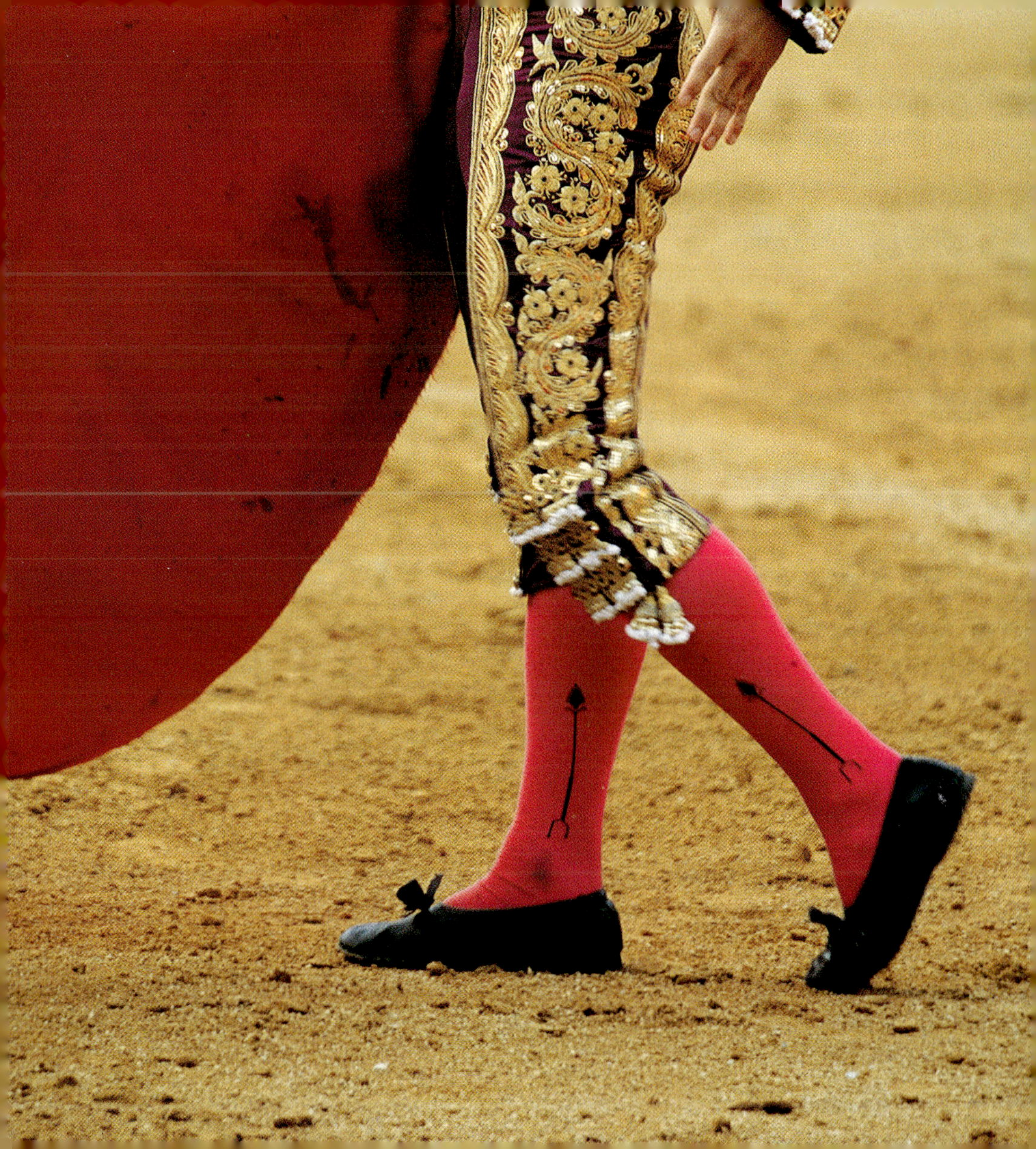

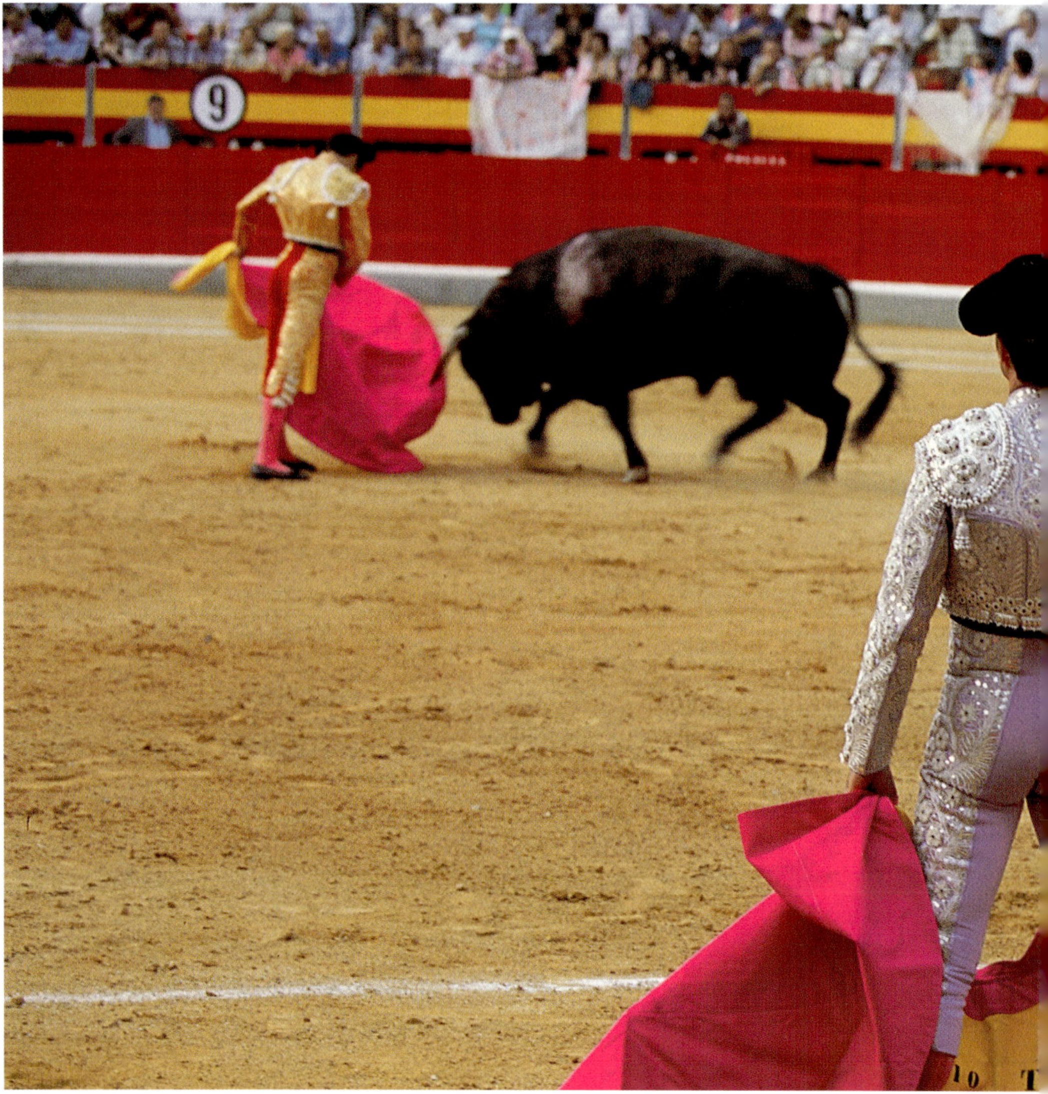

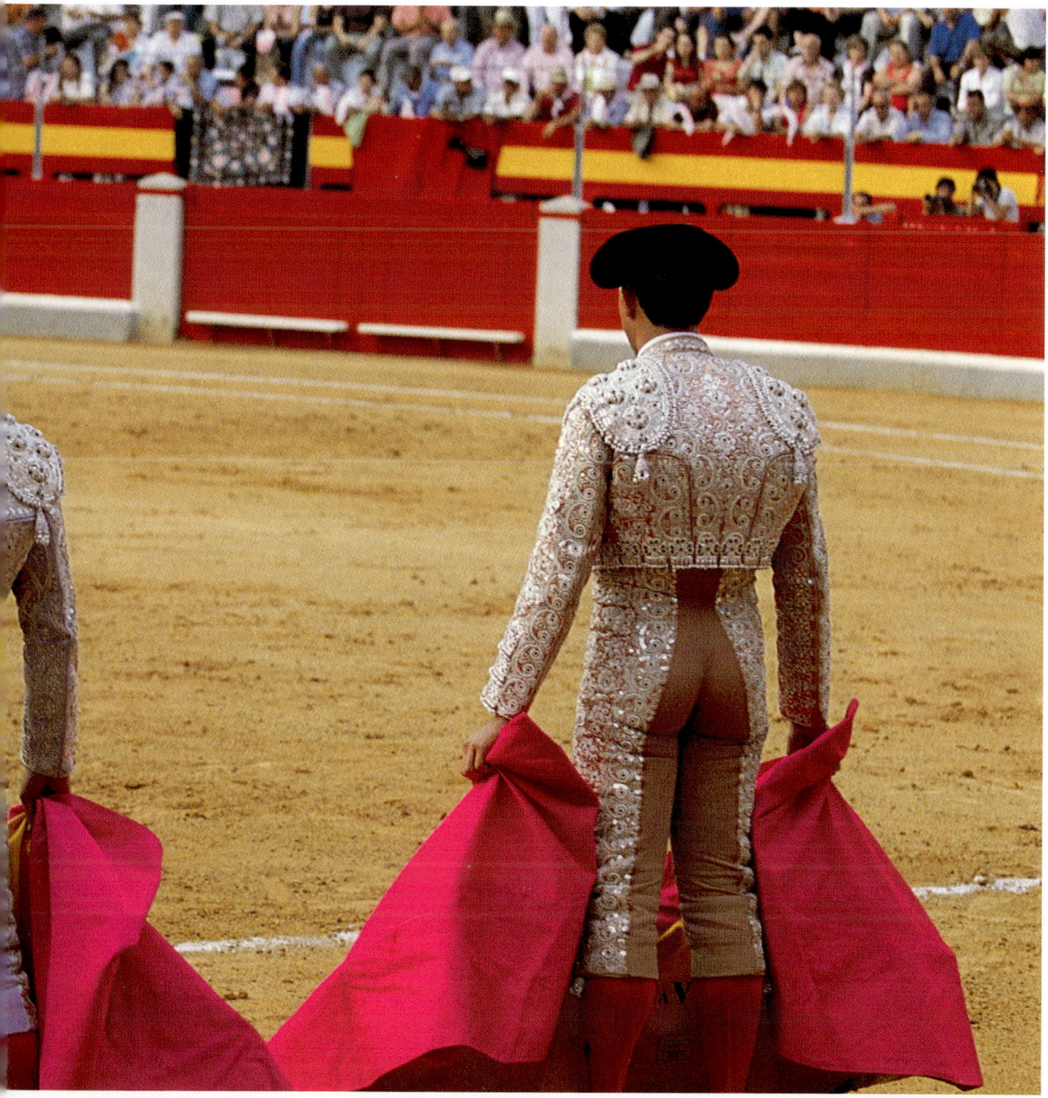

Published by
© **TRIANGLE POSTALS, SL**

Art Direction
JAUME SERRAT

Text and photography
© **LUCAS VALLECILLOS**

Graphic Design
JOAN COLOMER

Layout
GERMÁN CAMPOS
VADOR MINOBIS

Translation
STEVE CEDAR

Production
IMMA PLANES

Photomechanics
MOLAGRAF

Printed by
NG NIVELL GRÀFIC

Registration number
B: 33.343-2006

ISBN 84-8478-222-0

TRIANGLE POSTALS, SL
Sant Lluís, Menorca
Tel. +34 971 15 04 51
Fax +34 971 15 18 36
www.trianglepostals.com

TRIANGLE POSTALS